A MILITARY
HISTORY
OF CANADA

A MILITARY HISTORY OF CANADA

DESMOND MORTON

Fifth Edition

McCLELLAND & STEWART

Library and Archives Canada Cataloguing in Publication

Morton, Desmond, 1937–
   A military history of Canada / Desmond Morton. – 5th ed.

Includes index.
ISBN 978-0-7710-6481-4

   1. Canada – History, Military.   I. Title.

FC226.M68 2007   971   C2007-901297-3

We acknowledge the financial support of the Government of Canada through the Book Publishing Industry Development Program and that of the Government of Ontario through the Ontario Media Development Corporation's Ontario Book Initiative. We further acknowledge the support of the Canada Council for the Arts and the Ontario Arts Council for our publishing program.

Typeset in Garamond by M&S, Toronto
Printed and bound in Canada

This book is printed on acid-free paper that is 100% recycled, ancient-forest friendly (100% post-consumer recycled).

McClelland & Stewart Ltd.
75 Sherbourne Street
Toronto, Ontario
M5A 2P9
www.mcclelland.com

1 2 3 4 5   11 10 09 08 07

Contents

Acknowledgements

In writing this book, I recognize many debts: to mentors like Colonel Charles Stacey, to Alec Douglas, Norman Hillmer, and Jean Pariseau of the Directorate of History, National Defence Headquarters, to Joe Levitt of the University of Ottawa, and to Bruce White, a colleague at Erindale College, University of Toronto, and above all to a constant collaborator and friend, Barbara Wilson of the Public Archives of Canada. The maps were prepared by Brandon Besharah and the illustrations were collected with very particular help from Steve Jaunszems, Jocelyn Smyth, Ken Macpherson, and Norman Hillmer. As ever, I owe much to the sound practical advice of Dr. Paul Eisner. Clara Stewart typed and improved the manuscript with unfailing cheer and wit. Bill Fox designed the book with a patient regard for detail. Kathie Hill fended off callers with her unique tact and my wife Jan mixed encouragement and reassurance. I owe even more than my readers to my editor, Elizabeth Munroe, for she has made the text more readable for all of us but only I know the blunders I have been spared. Those that remain are purely my fault.Perhaps the most long-suffering helpers have been students in successive classes of "Canada and War," subjected to scores of contradictory theories, most of them disproved within the week. To them, in their successive scores, this book is dedicated.

Mississauga, March 17, 1985

Introduction

Since about 1815, Canadians have had to go abroad to fight. With trifling exceptions — the Fenian raids and the U-boats in the St. Lawrence during the Second World War are the most conspicuous — war has not come to Canada.

The distinction is enormously significant. Canadians remember wars fought in France, Italy, or Korea, not in the Richelieu Valley or along the Niagara Peninsula. Canadians by 2000 had come to see war as an aberration beyond their control and, fortunately, beyond their shores. Efforts by politicians, police, the media, the military, and even academics since 9/11 to make Canadians feel as endangered as Americans have had a contrived look. Were we more threatened by al Qaeda or by our trading partner closing our common border?

War has shaped Canadians more than most of them realize. Without European conquest, there would be no Canada. Without wars that stretched over seventy years, the bulk of North America might well have remained a French and Spanish possession. The separate existence of Canada was determined by the American Revolutionary War and confirmed by the War of 1812.

These wars not only made modern Canada possible; they helped shape the myths and memories of a divided national identity. A century and a half of struggle gave the *Canadiens* their sense of destiny, their determination to survive, and their own sense of separation from the mother country that had abandoned them. It took wars in 1775 and again in 1812 to convince English-speaking Canadians to pursue a separate destiny in North America. Both wars forged a grudging but inevitable partnership of French and English.

The wars of the twentieth century may have left Canada's own frontiers intact but there is little within the country that remained untouched. War compelled Canadians to choose between the Empire and independence and, in due course, it forced Canada into a new and more troubled dependence on the United States. War was the catalyst for an explosive industrial expansion and for much of Canada's system of social security. Indeed, it is hard to find an institution, from the family to trade unionism, whose history was not transformed by either or both world wars.

A people largely removed from the direct impact of war may be tempted to suffuse the experience in a warm, nostalgic glow. War exacted a greater price than most Canadians realize. The hundred thousand who died in the wars of this century and the hundred thousand more who returned permanently maimed in mind or body were among the finest of their generation. Who knows what they might have contributed to Canada and to humanity? Ernest Renan wrote that nations are formed by the remembrance of great deeds done together. Canadians at war did great deeds but they did not do them together, and war left a heritage of bitter differences, only lightly buried by the passage of time. Conscription crises divided French and English but others also have nourished grim memories, from the Métis defeated in 1885, to the Ukrainians and Japanese Canadians, interned because wars allowed old prejudices to be acted out.

Even the apparent achievements of war can be questioned in the light of hindsight. Canadians poured out lives and money in the conviction that the Great War would bring enduring peace; within a generation, their faith was mocked as an illusion. Even the great wartime industries, with their astonishing growth in output and sophistication, rarely led to enduring advances in productivity and innovation. On the contrary, we now suspect that that mushroom growth contributed to greater eventual dependence on foreign capital, management, and techniques.

More than most people, Canadians have distanced themselves from thoughts of war. On the whole, they have no affection for militarism or a military cast of mind. A persistent mythology has persuaded Canadians that an innate gift for war, whether demonstrated by the militia at Queenston Heights or by prairie-bred sailors escorting North Atlantic convoys, spares them the burdens of peacetime preparation.

Canada's attitude to war rests on more than innocent illusion; it is a product of historical experience. Unless this experience is understood, neither would-be defenders nor disarmers will ever understand the Canadian response to their respective programmes. How far have Canadian attitudes been shaped by our perennial role as dependent military allies? How could a coherent defence policy emerge in a century when Canada was simultaneously indefensible and invulnerable? Was it surprising that conscription for overseas service should provoke protest when fighting and even military service had so long been a matter of personal choice?

Most important of all these historical memories was Canada's status as a junior and often colonial ally. The key strategic decisions were made at Versailles, in Whitehall, and, latterly, in the Pentagon. As early as the native-born Marquis de Vaudreuil, governor at the conquest of Quebec, Canadians might argue different priorities but they could do so only as minor partners, even in their own defence. Without military support from the imperial protector, Canadians would have been almost helpless in their own defence. Yet the suspicion persists that the threats themselves increased because of the major partner's other commitments. Was New France lost because of the strategic needs of the Bourbon alliance? Could Canada have been pitched into a hopeless war with the United States in 1895 because of an Anglo-Venezuelan dispute over the border of British Guiana? Was she at war in 1914 and 1939 because of British policies in Europe?

The benefit of alliances is that they permit each partner to do less than might be necessary for nations on their own. This is also the greatest weakness of alliances. Self-interest remains the rule of nationhood. When, for example, in the Great War, Sir Robert Borden ignored that rule in his commitment to the higher cause of allied victory, the conscription crisis of 1917 was among the consequences. Borden's successors absorbed the lesson.

Canada has needed alliances because it was inconceivable that its population—whether the few hundred of New France in 1660 or the twenty-five million of the 1980s — could protect its vast geography. Not even Great Britain, at the height of her imperial power in the 1860s, could hope to defend her North American colonies from a determined American invasion. When British admirals and generals finally digested this disconcerting fact, the garrisons went home and Canada began her slow shift to the American orbit.

For most of the century after Confederation, Canada survived the paradox of being simultaneously indefensible and invulnerable. So long as the Royal Navy guarded the oceans, no invasion could come by sea. Until the first transpolar flights of the 1930s, it was unimaginable that a threat could come from the Arctic wastes. Peace with the United States demanded a prudent respect for American sensibilities and firm internal order. The presence of the red-coated North-West Mounted Police in Canada meant that American cavalry patrols had no reason to cross the border, as they often did into Mexico. In much of Canada, a small, ill-trained militia, recruited from volunteers, was sufficient to overawe Orange rioters, strikers, and farmers with a distaste for paying taxes.

In the circumstances, what possible basis could there be for a serious defence policy? Militia enthusiasts and occasional British officers might dream of war with the Americans but nothing reversed the real American predominance of the 1860s. Generals and colonels might fantasize but why should sensible politicians buy artillery or gunboats to support these illusions? Instead of being an insatiable consumer of alliance strength, as she had been until the 1860s, Canada instead became a modest and then a substantial supplier. The British Empire could no longer support Canada in North America but Canada could support the Empire — if she had the will to do so.

Mustering that will in a profoundly divided nation has been the predominant issue in Canadian political-military affairs, from the South African War in 1899 to the alliance systems of the Cold War. Why did Canada participate? The simplest answer is sentiment — the emotional allegiance a shrinking majority of Canadians felt for their ancestral homeland of Great Britain, seconded by a related feeling that the struggles were fundamentally just. Political leaders in 1899, 1914, and even in 1939 understood the power of that sentiment; the wisest of them also understood its limits.

Democracies find it difficult to wage limited, rational warfare. Only the emotions of a crusade can justify the inevitable sacrifices. Crusading demands volunteers; compulsion would sully the cause. Yet, by its essence, crusading is as intolerant of indifference as it is of opposition. A crusading majority easily forgot, in two world wars, that war sentiment was spread unevenly. Many Canadians felt no more than nominal allegiance to Britain. Few French Canadians felt instinctive kinship with the Empire or even with Europe. Their front lines began at Halifax or even at the Gaspé.

Canada's wars have exposed the fault lines which the Fathers of Confederation had hoped to bury and which successful politicians have always had to patch. Canada's armed forces have suffered from the suspicion that their allegiance is linked more to allies than to Canada. Canada's infant navy was almost destroyed at birth because, to some critics, it made Canada subservient to Britain. Army commanders were accused in both world wars of offering their men as cannon-fodder for British generals. Even the Royal Canadian Air Force never escaped the suspicion that it had sold its identity to the British in the Second

World War and to the Americans in the 1950s. By 1967, uniforms and traditions, naturalized after more than a century in Canada, seemed too British and too colonial for a country enmeshed in a different empire. Once converted to green, were the forces suddenly too American in allegiance as well as in equipment, doctrine, and appearance?

Yet, in important ways, Canada's armed forces and Canada's wars have fostered a sense of national identity and pride. The young Canadians who embarked for South Africa on October 31, 1899, may have responded to the call of the Empire. Within a month of arrival at Cape Town, they no longer wondered what it meant to be Canadian. The experience would be repeated in two world wars, in Korea, and in a host of minor peacekeeping excursions. Armed service has removed young Canadians from their home regions and exposed them to their whole country and the world.

These are themes of a book about Canadians and the ugly business of war. It is a book about peacetime as well as war because the two are intimately related. How far do peacetime illusions contribute to the inevitability and cruelty of war? Who, in time of war, does not yearn for peace? Who, in the current shadow of nuclear annihilation, can believe that old thoughts about peace and war can be tolerated?

I The *Ancien Régime*

Indian Warfare

Champlain squinted down the barrel of his arquebus, swivelled it slightly on its rest, and muttered a prayer. Then he fired. As the smoke cleared, his Algonquin and Huron allies roared with delight. Two of the Iroquois chiefs, identified by their plumes and wooden breastplates and shields, lay on the ground. One of them kicked convulsively. Another Frenchman fired. A third chief fell. The Iroquois line, stunned to silence, quivered and broke into flight.

Later, critics would blame Samuel de Champlain for making enemies of the Iroquois. A few would even blame him for introducing cruel European weapons to Indian warfare. Both notions are absurd. Joining the Algonquin, Montagnais, and Huron neighbours on a war party south to Lake Champlain seemed to the French leader to be the price of their friendship. That friendship was the vital prerequisite for his linked goals of trade and conversion. No doubt the old soldier in Champlain shaped his response to the Indian invitation but an Indian alliance was essential if the French were ever to make their way into the vast, mysterious continent.

Most aboriginal people seem to have had war as part of their culture and recurrent conflict was certainly part of the pattern of native life in north-eastern America. Ossuaries uncovered in Ontario bear mute testimony to battles of a thousand years ago. In the eleventh century, Vikings may have been the terror of Europe but they were driven from their North American settlements by fierce native warriors the Norsemen christened *skraelings*. In early contacts with Europeans, their Indian hosts boasted of their warlike prowess. In 1545, Donnacona proudly displayed to Cartier the scalps of enemies neatly stretched on a wooden frame.*

Native warfare seems to have owed little to territorial, trade, or dynastic aggrandisement. In studying the best known of the north-eastern Indian nations, George Hyndman concluded: ". . . the basic

---

*Some credulous historians and journalists have insisted, in the face of overwhelming evidence, that whites imposed the practice of scalping on Indians. This myth is demolished by James Axtell in *The European and the Indian* (New York, 1981).

reasons the Iroquois went to war were the desire for revenge and the necessity of replacing a deceased person in the maternal family." A subsidiary justification was to demonstrate the courage, endurance, and skill of warriors themselves. Like most aspects of native life, warfare was invested with careful ritual, from the first mustering of a war party to the ultimate torture and killing of captives. By their nature, blood feuds could never be resolved, since each act of vengeance demanded reprisal. Yet honour in each campaign seems to have been satisfied by a small handful of dead and prisoners. With a tiny population, Indians seem to have understood the danger of wars of extermination.

The native tactics encountered by Champlain in 1609 would have been recognizable to any European. The Iroquois had landed from their canoes and hurriedly built themselves a palisaded fort, emerging next day to fight in a massed formation. Warriors protected themselves with slatted wooden armour, proof against clubs and stone axes at close quarters and against flint-headed arrows at a distance. Sometimes, like the Greeks of classic times, opposing armies reduced bloodshed by allowing the outcome to be determined in a contest between rival champions.

The Iroquois whom Champlain helped defeat in 1609 were the heirs of people Jacques Cartier had met along the St. Lawrence in the 1540s. In the intervening years, they had retreated to the ancestral homeland in what is now upstate New York. Like most nomadic peoples, Champlain's Algonquin and Montagnais allies sneered at the stay-at-home Iroquois, with their longhouses clustered behind stockades, their clumsy dug-out canoes, and their cornfields. South of the lakes were few of the rich furs the European traders preferred.

Yet the Iroquois had advantages their enemies were slow to recognize. Like all Indians, the Iroquois men trained from youth as warriors and hunters, inuring themselves to hunger, pain, and fatigue. In a matrilineal society, women exercised significant influence through their responsibility for property and ritual but it was the women's work in the fields that gave Iroquois war parties an added advantage. Instead of subsisting from the hunt, Iroquois warriors carried *sagamite*, a coarse cornmeal porridge that fed them on the march. Their parties could travel silently and fast.

The Iroquois had also learned to work together. Whether the confederacy of the Five Nations followed white contact or immediately pre-dated it, the alliance could yield an army that was huge by Indian standards: two thousand men from a total native population in the North-East that has been estimated at only twenty-two thousand. United by kinship — the Iroquois called their confederacy "*Ganonsyoni*" or "Lodge Extended Lengthwise" — the ferocious and self-confident Mohawks in the Lake Champlain area kept the "East Door" with a strength of about three hundred warriors while the Seneca, most numerous at a thousand fighting men, kept the West. The Onondaga were the "Firekeepers" or central core of the confederacy while the Oneida and Cayuga were the junior partners.

If the white men did not introduce Indians to war, their introduction of firearms certainly transformed Indian fighting methods and, in the end, undermined most of the traditional bases of native warfare. At first sight, Champlain's arquebus was a poor alternative to the bow and arrow. Muskets were heavy, slow to load, highly inaccurate, and useless in wet weather. What they could do was kill, and even a wound from a lead musket-ball was likely to lead to fatal infection. At once, Indians wanted the new weapons and, when the French refused to sell firearms, Dutch traders on the Hudson River had no such scruples. Anyone who has ever tried to skin a rabbit with a stone knife or to boil water in a clay pot will understand why Indians would sacrifice a great deal for European goods and nothing commanded a higher price in raw pelts than a musket. Once acquired, the musket kept the Indian dependent on the trader for supplies of powder and shot and for repairs which could only be tackled by a well-trained blacksmith.

While firearms drove the Iroquois and other natives deeper into economic dependence on the European interlopers, their tactical response to the new weapons was ingenious, radical, and belatedly more influential than almost any other native impact on the whites. By the 1640s, Iroquois had abandoned mass tactics, wooden armour, and dependence on fortifications. When the French armed their Huron enemies, the Iroquois perfected concealment, dispersion, and ambush. The techniques of the hunt became the tactics of war. Instead of fighting in the open, the Iroquois learned to entice a better-armed enemy into dense woods where, suddenly, hundreds of hidden warriors would attack at short range. In battle, the Iroquois learned to spread out and seek to encircle an enemy. A war party on the move was widely dispersed to avoid ambush: "travelling calls" — simulated bird or animal sounds — controlled movement.

Through the seventeenth century, Indians adapted their way of fighting with surprising flexibility. Not until European armies had absorbed the terrible casualties of the 1914-18 War were their soldiers routinely trained to fight in ways Iroquois and other warriors had perfected three centuries earlier. Colonists in North America could not be so conservative. Periodically their armies marched into the wilderness, drums rolling, colours flying, sometimes to pay the terrible price of folly, sometimes merely to bemuse a hidden adversary. To survive, French and English colonists had to master the Indian way of war. Benjamin Church, among the ablest of New England soldiers and certainly the most principled, forced his men to disperse in the woods instead of remaining "all in a heap." Instead of firing volleys, which left musketeers helpless against assault at close range, frontier fighters learned to operate in pairs, so that half a force was always loaded to fire. Church boasted that his men had learned "to skulk" and to crawl on their bellies as close to an enemy as they could. To the proud professionals of the time, such tactics were intolerably degrading.

Colonists rapidly adopted the tools and equipment of Indian warfare. Moccasins became standard footgear for raiding parties and extra pairs were routinely carried for the benefit of any prisoners who might be brought home. In winter, Indian snowshoes and, in summer, Indian canoes allowed fighting men to move swiftly and quietly. Frontier soldiers adopted the *mitasses* or buckskin leggings as a sensible response to travelling through bush. The French went farther, often adopting the entire Indian costume from war paint to breech cloth. A few rivalled the incredible Indian skill with the tomahawk or throwing axe.

Most significant to Europeans was the seeming ruthlessness and terrorism of the Indian way of war. This was a paradox. European wars of religion had unleashed nauseating levels of savagery. Men, women, and children had been slaughtered in thousands and without mercy within living memory and sometimes within the personal experience of French and English colonists of the seventeenth century. Europeans grew up in conditions of brutal hardship, recurrent starvation, and casual cruelty. Most babies died in infancy. Forty represented old age. In France, minor criminals — men and women — were flogged or branded in public. Serious offenders were tied to a cart-wheel and clubbed to death. Torture was a routine judicial procedure. Religious heretics and witches could be burned at the stake and sometimes were.

Such customs easily crossed the Atlantic to New England or New France.

Yet, like most people, the European newcomers were prisoners of their own perceptions. Scalping, systematic torture of prisoners, and the refusal to distinguish sex or age in the victims of an Iroquois raid confirmed to the French that their enemies were savages. The Indian indifference to European taboos on cannibalism or the mutilation of corpses was especially shocking and it was too much to expect that newcomers would accept that such conduct grew out of native beliefs and principles. Yet, with no such religious justification, colonial soldiers on both sides came to emulate the ferocity and cruelty of their Indian allies and enemies. Both French and English knowingly launched Indian war parties to ravage frontier settlements and with them went militiamen or Rangers who boasted of their own ruthlessness and skill with the scalping knife. An observer of La Malgue's sack of Saratoga in 1745 watched French officers engage a captured British officer in courteous conversation while nearby ten captured redcoats hung by their heels, waiting for torture by Paul Marin's Christian Indians. An English visitor in 1780 recorded that British officers cheerfully exchanged a tobacco pouch made from Indian skin. If, as Europeans insisted, Indian war practices were barbarous, the influence was contagious.

The Indian example was far more pervasive than brutalizing. Among both French and American colonists, the experience of Indian warfare marked them off from their European roots and even from fellow subjects who visited the New World. The *milicien* in New France or the Ranger in the American colonies, dressed Indian-fashion in buckskin hunting shirt, became both the true defender and a proud alternative to the blundering professional soldiers from the homeland. The Indian style of warfare, with its dependence on individual courage and extraordinary skill, transformed both colonial and native societies. Among the Indians, it undermined the power of the sachems or hereditary peacetime leaders. As war became a way of life, Indians became increasingly dependent on their European allies for food and supplies as well as for the materials of war. Among Europeans, gradual mastery of forest warfare bred a self-confidence that helped bring Americans to a Declaration of Independence in 1775. Among the *Canadiens* of the St. Lawrence Valley, it bred a conviction that they could survive even after the last French soldiers and officials had dropped down the great river in October 1760.

Colonial Survival

War was not part of Champlain's grand design for New France and it was even more remote from the minds of his financial backers. Though their first building under the shadow of Cape Diamond was as fort-like as Champlain and his men could make it, their pious purpose was to convert the Indians to Christianity. To finance the enterprise, Champlain's backers had secured a royal monopoly of the fur trade. Devout colonists from France would feed the mission and, simultaneously, demonstrate to natives the joys of a settled Christian life.

Nor was war inevitable. The tiny Acadian settlements around the Bay of Fundy lived, for the most part, in peace with their Indian neighbours. Any fighting in the region was caused by their own quarrelsome and piratical proprietors, Isaac de Razilly and Charles de la Tour. In New France, the Iroquois were sufficiently distant and too fiercely engaged with their own Indian neighbours to spare more than an occasional war party for the St. Lawrence. Like most military alliances, the Iroquois did not lack enemies.

Even as Champlain struggled to establish his post at Quebec and to develop links with the Hurons, the Dutch entered the Hudson River. By 1614, they had established a post at Albany, close to the Mohawks. Shrewd and adaptable as ever, the Iroquois found a new destiny. Short of good furs in their own territory, they became middlemen, exchanging Dutch goods for pelts from the interior and taking a proper cut. As in most businesses, there was a single flaw: competition. Why should interior tribes deal through the Five Nations when they were used to paddling down the Ottawa and the St. Lawrence to trade with the French? The solution was as obvious to the Iroquois as to any well-educated European: force. Perhaps for the first time, Indian warfare acquired a strong tinge of collective self-interest.

New France's backers were soon ready to quit. In 1628, the Kirke brothers, English pirates, had seized a supply fleet, wrecked the little community at Quebec, and dumped Champlain and most of his followers in England. Four years later, the indomitable founder of New France had returned and painfully rebuilt the ruins, but his backers never quite recovered from bankruptcy. Since the enterprise was private, and the King was too preoccupied with foreign and civil war to help, the Company of New France itself had the costly burden of recruiting soldiers and colonists. It did little of either. The handful of

French drilled in their spare time, lived in fear, and waited for the annual convoy from France.

By now, the French had their own middlemen, the Hurons. Linked to the Iroquois in culture and agricultural pursuits, the Hurons were traditional rivals of the larger Five Nations Confederacy. The price of the French trading partnership was acceptance of Jesuit missionaries. The unintended consequence of the Mission to Huronia was an appalling smallpox epidemic that may have eliminated up to half the Huron population in a decade. Deliberate germ warfare could not have been more effective. Utterly demoralized by the terrible toll, its military power undermined, the Ontario-based tribe fell easy prey.

In the summer of 1648, with most Huron warriors escorting the annual fur shipment to Montreal, the Iroquois struck with swift ferocity. Men, women, children, missionaries included, were slaughtered; whole villages were destroyed with an annihilatory fervour designed to teach the Hurons a lesson. In the winter of 1649, a season when warfare was hitherto virtually unknown, the Iroquois struck again across Lake Ontario. At the Jesuit mission at Ste. Marie, watchers saw the smoke rising from distant villages. At St. Ignace, Jean de Brébeuf, Gabriel Lalemant, and dozens of nameless Indian martyrs died at the stake. Utterly demoralized, missionaries and Indians alike abandoned Huronia.

The Iroquois devastation of Huronia was a tactical triumph and a strategic nullity. Without the Hurons, the northern tribes could deal directly and even more profitably with the French. Long before, Champlain had sent adventurous young Frenchmen to winter with the Indians; they and their successors would keep business flowing. Since 1642, Paul de Chomédy, Sieur de Maisonneuve, had established a particularly devout little settlement on an island where the Ottawa and the St. Lawrence met. Whatever its value as a mission station, Montreal was ideally located for the new shape of the fur trade — if its few inhabitants could survive.

The odds favoured the Iroquois. By 1650, the French colony mustered only 675 souls. In 1652, after a tragic and foolhardy brush with the Mohawks, only ten of the original forty settlers of Trois-Rivières were still alive. Iroquois raiding parties reached as far downriver as Tadoussac, burning, killing, and hurrying male and female captives to their fate.

Bitter internal divisions added to the colony's misery. The Jesuits defied any governor who denied them pre-eminence. In 1651, they got their choice in Jean de Lauzon, an otherwise sordid character who extracted a raise in his own salary at the cost of disbanding a defence force that had provided the scattered riverside settlements with a mobile reserve. The bitter rivalry between Quebec and Montreal was renewed when Lauzon forbade Maisonneuve and soldiers he had recruited in France to go upriver until his own danger was past.

Iroquois attacks were intermittent; only fear was persistent. Colonists drilled as militia in their spare hours, fumbling with unmechanical fingers to master the complex routine of loading, priming, and firing their primitive muskets. At Montreal, strict orders commanded farm workers to take weapons to the field. Those who forgot died. In ones and twos, the Iroquois took their toll. Then, for a time, while the confederacy quarrelled, rested, or fought others in its circle of enemies, New France would be quiet. Occasionally captives, bearing the scars of their torture, would return. For a time in the 1650s, fifty Frenchmen lived among the Onondaga, supporting a peace-seeking sachem. Warned in the nick of time of a change of heart, the party organized a huge feast for their hosts and slipped away when the last gorged Iroquois had fallen asleep.

In 1660, the confederacy determined to strike a massive blow. On May 15, before he was burned at the stake at Quebec, an Iroquois prisoner announced that a huge army was on its way. At Montreal, a month earlier, a young officer of the garrison, Adam Dollard Des Ormeaux, proposed to collect some of the pelts the town's traders utterly lacked. He and sixteen companions would slip out, intercept Iroquois hunters on the Ottawa River as they returned from a winter's trapping, and restore Montreal's fortune and his own. The Iroquois had ambushed Huron canoes; now Dollard would do as much to the Iroquois — and with as little risk.

Joined by Algonquin and Hurons, Dollard set up his ambush near the Long Sault on the Ottawa. On May 2, he sprung the trap, killing thirteen Onondaga. No one told the Frenchmen that these were scouts for the army. Within hours, two hundred more Onondaga had appeared. Dollard and his men seized food and weapons and raced for a broken-down Algonquin palisade. For eight days, they stood the siege. Enticed by Hurons adopted by the Iroquois, thirty of Dollard's allies leaped over the wall and deserted. The rest fought on. Iroquois crept under the wall and set it alight. Dollard set a fuse to a barrel of gunpowder and tried to heave it over the wall. It caught on a branch and fell back. Injured and blinded by the smoke, the defenders were over-whelmed. In the melee, only five French and four Hurons became prisoners. All soon died. With eighty of their own dead, the confeder-acy army dissolved. Montreal was safe. A few days later, more than sixty canoes, laden with two hundred thousand pounds of furs, passed the Long Sault and reached Montreal. The town was not just safe; it was now rich.

Yet the war continued. In 1661, Pierre Boucher, the tough gover-nor of Trois-Rivières, took the message to France: surely it was shame-ful to the king that his subjects should be at the mercy of "les sauvages." The message was opportune. That year, the king's chief minister, the powerful Cardinal Mazarin, died. At the age of twenty-three, Louis XIV finally had come into his own. France was united, powerful, and at peace. In 1662, a first small contingent of royal troops landed in the colony. In 1663, the king and his new minister, Jean-Baptiste Colbert, reached a firm decision about New France: henceforth, the colony would be governed like a province of old France. Instead of being appointed by a commercial company, the governor would represent His Majesty. An intendant would mind the king's business, including the administration of his forces. As for fighting the Iroquois, it took until March 1665 for a formal decision: troops would be sent, Louis XIV proclaimed, "to carry the war to their doors, to exterminate them entirely."

All that summer, shiploads of soldiers landed at Quebec. Most wore the chestnut-brown uniforms of the Carignan-Salières Regiment, fresh from war with the Turks. From the West Indies came the Marquis de Tracy, a general sent to manage the campaign. Boatloads of troops headed upriver to Sorel, and by winter, four new forts barred the Mohawk route down the Richelieu River.

In January 1666, at the insistence of the new governor, Rémy de Courcelle, three hundred regulars and two hundred militia set out in mid-winter for Iroquois territory. Soldiers utterly unequipped for their first Canadian winter found it a harrowing experience. The guides got drunk, supplies gave out, and the exhausted, frost-bitten expedition would have faced disaster if it had not straggled into the little Dutch settlement of Schenectady. Iroquois dogged the long march back, slaughtering stragglers or hauling them off for a slower death *au petit feu*. More than a hundred men perished.

Courcelle and Tracy were undaunted. In September, twelve hun-

dred troops and militia and six hundred boats travelled up the Richelieu and onto Lake Champlain. With flags flying and drums rolling, the
army marched through Mohawk country, feeding itself from captured
corn. If the Iroquois had thought to burn their fields, the French might
have starved; instead the French burned the longhouses and left the
Indians to freeze or starve.

More than the other nations, the Mohawks had kept the confederacy
in the war. In 1668 they sued for peace; it lasted a full generation.

That year, the king summoned most of the Carignan-Salières home.
Several officers and almost four hundred men took their discharge,
encouraged by royal decree to become settlers. Most were located in
the Richelieu Valley, with their former officers acting as seigneurs. If
the Iroquois came that way again, they would find settlers able to use
their old army muskets, and officers who would be natural leaders.

The military influx of 1665 transformed the colony. To the religious
and the pious laity, the illusion of a quiet, conformist little Christian
community was gone. "Since they have come here," complained Father Etienne de Carheil, "we have seen only universal corruption which
they have spread by their scandalous conduct." Indian converts,
claimed the missionaries, had been disillusioned by the behaviour of
supposedly Christian troops and even more by the failure of the clergy
to influence the newcomers.

War had transformed Champlain's dream out of recognition.

Frontenac's Wars

In February 1666, when the French reached Schenectady, they learned
for the first time that the Dutch colony was now English. Not for the
first time, the outcome of a European war switched the ownership
of North American real estate. New Amsterdam was renamed for the
English king's sailor-brother, the Duke of York.

To the French, the news came as a mixed blessing. For the moment,
England's Charles II, a secret Catholic, was His Most Christian Majesty's ally, but for how long? Since 1066, England and France had been
hereditary enemies. Trade, dynastic ambition, and religion had all played
their part. Now, as France emerged as Europe's strongest military and
industrial power, England would help form a series of alliances to keep
Louis XIV in check. How far could Charles and his brother control
their Protestant subjects?

It was true that Europe had learned a bitter lesson from the terrible

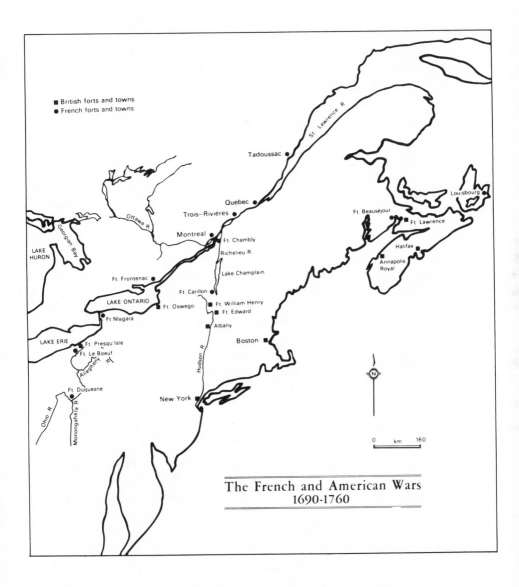

British forts and towns
French forts and towns

St. Lawrence R.

Tadoussac

Quebec

Trois-Rivières

Ottawa R.

Montreal

Ft. Chambly

Richelieu R.

LAKE
HURON

Georgian Bay

Lake Champlain

Ft. Frontenac

Ft. Carillon

LAKE ONTARIO

Ft. Oswego

Ft. William Henry

Ft. Edward

Ft Niagara

Albany

LAKE ERIE

Ft. Presqu'Isle

Ft. Le Boeuf

Allegheny R.

Hudson R.

Boston

Ft. Duquesne

Ohio R.

Monongahela R.

New York

Ft. Beauséjour

Ft. Lawrence

Louisbourg

Halifax

Annapolis
Royal

N

0   km   160

The French and American Wars
1690-1760

wars of religion. The carnage had destroyed states and toppled dynasties; future wars would be limited. The new professional armies might be recruited from the dregs of society but trained soldiers were too scarce and costly to be wasted. To control losses, campaigning stopped in winter. Prisoners were exchanged. Instead of plundering the countryside and deserting, soldiers would be kept under tight discipline and fed, so far as possible, by carefully organized commissariats. France was a pioneer of such professionalism: the tough, though conventionally minded, soldiers of the Carignan-Salières were part of the result.

In their long rivalry, the French and English had fought with different weapons. As an island power, England depended on her Royal Navy, corruptly managed to be sure, but officered by hardened veterans who had learned their trade at sea. The army was small, equally corrupt, and led too often by amateurs. Unlike the navy, it was burdened by suspicions inherited from Cromwell's military dictatorship. Thanks to Colbert, France's fleet had grown in size and efficiency but France's safety depended on the best army in Europe. Yet what could even the finest army do to help a remote colony if the Royal Navy controlled the oceans and even the narrow seas between England and the continent?

News of a European war could take months to reach the New World and each colony would react differently. Collectively, the English colonies far outweighed New France and Acadia but collective action never happened. Even within the colonies, long-settled tidewater residents paid little attention to anguished appeals from the frontier. Pennsylvania Quakers preferred to pay hostile Indians to pass through the colony to attack their neighbours. In Massachusetts, war was a signal for Boston merchants to fit out privateers to prey on enemy shipping. In any Anglo-French war, New York would bear the brunt of most attacks from New France.

As a royal colony, New France could hardly pretend to ignore Louis XIV's wars. On the whole, geography and alliances kept her reasonably safe. Vast barren lands separated her from Hudson Bay, where the English had begun trading in 1670. To the east, mountains and fierce Indian allies, the Micmac and Abenaki, provided a barrier against New England. For half the year, the St. Lawrence was barred by ice; for the other half, shoals and fog discouraged unwary invaders. Only to the south, where the Iroquois lived, did New France lack natural barriers or man-made defences.

To Jean Talon, the king's first intendant in New France, the answer was population. The king should send more ex-soldiers; what they lacked in farming experience they would make up as fighting men. On the whole, Talon wanted a prosperous, self-contained colony, with agriculture productive enough to feed France's slave colonies in the West Indies. Such a compact little colony would attract few enemies.

Yet even Talon understood that the only real wealth in New France came from the fur trade. At the same time that he compelled habitants to labour dutifully on their farms, Talon's own money was invested in the trade. As for the king's new governor, Louis de Buade, Count Frontenac, the fur trade was the means by which he planned to recoup a fortune squandered in good living at the royal court. Why else would the old soldier spend years in a country that was ice-bound half the year and fly-blown the other half? Canada was his chance to get rich quickly.

At Frontenac's insistence, agents again headed west, reaching deep into the continent to find new sources of fur and the Indians to trap and trade them. Louis Jolliet, Father Louis Hennepin, Daniel DuLhut, and Frontenac's favourite, Robert René de la Salle, reached as far as Lake Superior and south to the mouth of the Mississippi. If anyone objected to the cost or the risks, it was easy to insist that the expeditions spread the word of God or sought the great western ocean. And when Frontenac's letters, full of wit and judicious flattery, were distributed by his wife to influential courtiers, who could criticize the gallant governor?

Yet, as anyone could tell, Frontenac's venture could only renew the old Iroquois war. Somehow, the confederacy had rebuilt a trading economy, crushing more Indian neighbours, reaching westward, and delivering the fur shipments to Albany. Thomas Dongan, the New English governor, was an Irish Catholic who once had fought in the armies of Louis XIV but he bore the French no good will. If he did not urge the Iroquois to attack New France, he did nothing to hold them back.

When war came in 1683, Frontenac was gone. Not even his letters could conceal the endless wrangling with Talon's successor as intendant, Jacques Duchesneau, and with the austere and arrogant Bishop Laval. The new governor, Joseph Antoine de la Barre, was a naval officer with an unearned reputation for courage. La Barre closed La Salle's remote posts and handed over the furs at Fort Frontenac, established

on the future site of Kingston, to one of his own friends. Such crook-
edness disgusted the colonists; such weakness inspired the Iroquois.
In raids and ambushes, they set out to destroy the rest of the colony's
far-flung posts. La Barre pleaded for troops; the Minister of Marine and
Colonies scraped up a few hundred men recruited from dockyard slums
— the *troupes de la marine* — and despatched them in 1683. With
these unpromising soldiers, colonial militia, and Indian allies, La Barre
set out for Iroquois country.

Near the future site of Oswego, La Barre halted, made camp, and
waited for Iroquois emissaries. Hundreds of his men fell sick from dysentery. Supplies failed. So did La Barre's valour. Surrounded by rest-
less Iroquois, the French governor meekly consented to abandon the
west, including Fort Frontenac, and retreated to Montreal, delighted
to find his scalp in its natural place.

There was no such pleasure in the colony or in France. At once a
tough, pious cavalry officer, Jacques-René de Brisay, Marquis de
Denonville, was sent to replace La Barre. New France was galvanized.
Militia trained in earnest. A hundred men set off under the Sieur de
Troyes to make the near-impossible overland journey to Hudson Bay.
No matter that England and France were at peace; three English posts
and a rich stock of furs fell to De Troyes's weary men. As for New
York, Denonville urged the king to buy it or seize it. By 1687, he was
ready for the Iroquois. At the site of Fort Frontenac, backed by a
respectable force, Denonville met forty envoys from the Onondaga.
The issue struck the governor as simple: the Indians were common
criminals who had taken arms against Louis XIV. At his command, the
Onondaga were seized, chained, and shipped to France as galley slaves.
Then Denonville crossed Lake Ontario and ravaged the land of the
Seneca.

This time the Iroquois did not make peace. The treachery to leaders
of the most honoured nation of the confederacy and the devastation
of Seneca land were injuries beyond even the normal limits of a blood
feud. Since 1668, the habitants had lived free from fear; few were ready
for the terrible new onslaught. Farms scattered along the river banks
were utterly vulnerable to sudden attack. Denonville's few regulars
could do little beyond protecting the towns; his militia dissolved in a
rush to guard homes and families. Fort Niagara was abandoned; Fort
Frontenac was surrounded. Mohawks, pouring up the old Richelieu
River route, almost captured Fort Chambly. Everywhere came reports

of farmsteads destroyed, whole families slaughtered or dragged into captivity. Late on August 4, 1689, Montrealers saw flames break the darkness across the river. By dawn, fifty-six farms in the seigneury of Lachine were in smoking ruins. A hundred men, women, and children were dead or prisoners. No one in the terrified town even dared attempt a pursuit.

By then, the despairing Denonville had resigned. His plea to return the surviving Onondaga from the galleys had been heard. With them, older and more gouty, came Frontenac. That year, both sides of the Atlantic tried to digest a political revolution. In England, Protestants and the Dutch king, William of Orange, had toppled the former Duke of York, James II, from the throne. Allowed to escape, James found refuge in France. William's reward was a firm English alliance against Louis XIV and a share of the English throne. War followed at once.

Frontenac crossed the Atlantic in 1689 with enough ships and men to capture New York. Delays and contrary winds held up the French fleet and it headed, instead, for Quebec. It was October when the stout old governor landed. Instead of an amphibious assault, he ordered what the French already called *la petite guerre* (or what later eras would call *guerilla* or "little war"). In effect, it was the Indian style of war: small, swift-moving raiding parties, striking without warning and wreaking merciless havoc. No doubt the lively spirits of New France rejoiced. They were convinced that Governor Dongan had armed and inspired the Iroquois; the fact that he had been deposed and imprisoned after the Protestant revolution of 1688 made attack all the more tempting.

That winter, two hundred carefully chosen *Canadiens* and Indians tracked silently south on snowshoes. They fell on the sleeping village of Schenectady, repeating most of the horrors of Lachine. Another raiding party struck at Salmon Falls in New Hampshire. At Portland, the defenders managed to hold off an assault of Canadian militia and Abenakis. The attackers rolled a barrel of burning tar against the wooden stockade and the town promptly surrendered. All winter, New France welcomed triumphant raiders with their loads of booty and trail of bedraggled prisoners. Behind them, in the English colonies, helpless terror turned into a burning urge for vengeance.

Massachusetts had its own way of fighting back. In 1689, a former ship's carpenter named William Phips had fitted out ships at his own expense, raided defenceless Acadian settlements, seized Port Royal, and returned to Boston loaded with plunder. Knighted for his exploits, Phips was the logical man to lead a bigger, bolder expedition against Quebec. Through the summer of 1690, Boston merchants collected ships and men. Late in August, with thirty-four ships and two thousand raw militia, Phips set sail. It was October 15 when he finally reached the basin before Quebec and cold autumn winds warned of the imminent freeze-up. Many of his men were sick; hundreds died. There was no time to batter Quebec into submission. On October 18, Major John Walley led thirteen hundred of his Americans in a landing on the Beauport shore. Only a few hundred militia and Indians were on hand to stop the invasion but in the dense undergrowth, they managed to stop Walley's demoralized, sickly troops. Cold, frightened, and ravaged by smallpox, the Americans withdrew on the night of October 21-22. In panic, Walley's men fought for places in the boats and abandoned all but one of their guns. On October 25, Phips weighed anchor and sailed home to Boston.

Phips never knew how close he had been to victory. All summer, most of New France's defenders were at Montreal, waiting for a New York invasion that never got organized. Quebec's fortifications had been notoriously neglected, yet Frontenac left only a few hundred men to stop a landing on the only obvious beach. Still, to the victor belongs the interpretation of history. While grateful Quebeckers erected a new church dedicated to Notre Dame de la Victoire, the old governor set to work with a nimble pen to underline his courage and genius. To Phips's emissary, Frontenac had replied: "I will answer your general only with the mouths of my cannon and the shots of my muskets that he may learn that a man like me is not to be summoned in this fashion." Of such bravado are legends made.

On both sides, the war again degenerated into small raids and sudden slaughter. Unable to organize a serious attack, New York left the fighting to the Iroquois, a division of the risks which the Indians were not slow to notice. The French at least sent some of their own men to share the hardships and dangers and to learn the techniques. In such warfare, the *Canadiens* developed their own heroes — and heroines. For two long days in 1690, Marie de Verchères, a Canadian-born woman, defended her home from Indian attack. Two years later, it was her daughter's turn. Madeleine de Verchères was only fourteen when a Mohawk war party swooped on her seigneury, seizing twenty settlers. She raced the Indians to the family fort, slammed the gate, and rallied the few terrified defenders for a day and a night until help came.

The most famous heroes of New France belonged to the Le Moyne family. The father, Charles, survived Iroquois torture to be adopted into a Mohawk clan. He emerged as interpreter, military leader, and seigneur of Longueuil, south of Montreal. His fortune in the fur trade supported fourteen children, twelve of them sons. Among them, the Sieur de Ste. Hélène led the expedition to Schenectady, managed Frontenac's guns at Quebec, and died fighting Major Walley's men. Another son, François de Bienville, caught fifty Oneida in a house near Repentigny. Having lost five men in a futile attempt to storm the house, Bienville set the place alight. As the Oneida chanted their death song, some called out to know the name of their enemy. To die by an unworthy hand would be a deep disgrace. Bienville showed himself and shouted his Indian name. At once, an Oneida shot him dead. At the funeral, the Iroquois sent ambassadors to comfort the young man's father. On both sides, honour was served.

Few could match the exploits of Le Moyne's third son, Pierre, Sieur d'Iberville. In 1686, he went with De Troyes to Hudson Bay, seized an English ship, and sailed her back to Quebec. In 1689, with a single ill-armed vessel, he captured three English ships. In 1696, he not only captured most of Newfoundland but also, late in the season, headed back to Hudson Bay in his little ship, the *Pélican*. In a memorable battle, he lost his ship, captured two larger British warships, and sank a third. In 1703, he became the first French governor of Louisiana and, when he died of yellow fever at Havana in 1706, the *Canadien* was one of France's greatest naval heroes.

Wars are not fought only by heroes or for them. By the 1690s, the Iroquois were tired of fighting English battles and wanted peace. Frontenac found war too profitable. While it continued, he could collect a personal cut of vast sums spent by the royal treasury on Indian allies and maintaining distant forts. The belated fortification of Quebec was necessary, costly — and profitable to the governor and his friends. In 1696, after strict orders from France, Frontenac ravaged the Oneida and Onondaga country south of Lake Ontario, but still there was no peace. Only in 1698, after Frontenac's death, was a treaty signed. Half the fighting men of the confederacy were gone. Only by avoiding the white man's wars could the Iroquois survive.

When those wars resumed, in 1702, the Iroquois did their best to stay neutral. A new French governor, Philippe de Rigaud de Vaudreuil, made a quiet truce with New York. French furs, blockaded by the Royal Navy, found their way to market via Albany and the Hudson River. Between Acadia and Massachusetts, there was no such truce. In 1703, Abenakis began raiding New England settlements and in 1704, a French and Indian force left sixty-five victims in the snow at Deerfield. In response, the New Englanders sent a force under Benjamin Church. He burned Grand Pré, knocked down the Acadians' dikes, but failed against Port Royal. Only in 1710 did the capital of the neglected colony fall to the English.

Queen Anne's War — better known as the War of the Spanish Succession — dragged on for eleven years. By North American standards, the war was fought on an enormous scale. At Blenheim in 1704, a hundred thousand soldiers met in battle; by nightfall, half were dead or dying. Under the Duke of Marlborough, allied armies finally defeated Louis XIV's veterans. Few on either side could worry about colonies.

In 1711, Marlborough's jealous rivals extracted enough of his British troops to launch a major thrust at Quebec. An easy victory in the New World would show that England had more than one military genius. Instead, bad luck and worse management dogged the expedition. Some of the ships were wrecked on Egg Island in the Gulf of St. Lawrence and the rest headed home. The first the *Canadiens* knew of their peril was when drowned British redcoats began drifting ashore.

When war ended in 1713, France was the net loser; her possessions in the New World were part of the price. Both Acadia and the little fortress at Placentia in Newfoundland were abandoned to Britain. So were the posts on Hudson Bay. Only Ile Royale, the mainland portion of Acadia (the future New Brunswick), Louisiana, and New France remained. The image of the Sun King, Louis XIV, was fatally dimmed and within a year of the humiliating Treaty of Utrecht, he was dead.

A Military Society

A century of war had shaped the people of New France, giving them heroes, institutions, and a common identity. Of ten thousand immigrants from France, over a third were soldiers. By common account such men made indifferent farmers or tradesmen but it was their military skills New France had needed. Talon's dream of diversified industries and of feeding the West Indies from the produce of New France had long since faded. Even self-sufficiency was all that any intendant sought. War also realigned the fur trade. Whatever profits it brought now seemed incidental to the need to foster Indian alliances and to control vast inland territories for future imperial needs.

The royal government that began in 1663 was well adapted to a colony at war. The governors of New France and of the three major towns were always army or navy officers. Among the first responsibilities of the intendant were military administration and the maintenance of a militia organization. In turn, the militia provided a basis for centralized administration: local militia captains or *capitaines de la côte* were chosen by the intendant and soon became his agents for such local chores as road-building or the periodic census. While England's colonies were left to their own devices to organize defences, France's treasury poured vast sums into the North American colonies. The habitants were unrepresented in democratic assemblies, but they also paid no taxes.

Certainly the habitants were compelled to serve in the militia, an obligation which became obsolete in France itself as the century progressed. From the 1650s, the Iroquois wars had left no alternative. When Frontenac arrived in 1672, he complained that militia organization had been utterly neglected; a year later he boasted that it was now complete. Both claims were exaggerated. In New France the militia was far more than a local defence force. Because the colony's young men, like their Indian counterparts, learned warlike skills from childhood, they became New France's front line. What soldier fresh from France could be trusted to manage a canoe in white water or to cover endless winter trails on snowshoes? Even when trained troops were fit for forest warfare, the militia organization provided the transport corps any major expedition required.

Colonial administrators had to remember the severe limits in using the militia. Even sending a few hundred men on a distant raid left fields untended and communities unprotected. From first to last, New France faced a desperate labour shortage. Because militia expected to be paid and equipped and even armed (for they invariably brought the oldest and most useless firearms to a muster), they were not cheap.

The obvious alternative was a garrison of regular troops but, after the Carignan-Salières returned to France, it was a long time before the colony saw the king's soldiers again.

It was not simply that the armies of eighteenth-century Europe would be out of place in North America. To perform effectively on battlefields such as Blenheim or Fontenoy, soldiers had to act like pipeclayed automata, marching in perfect alignment, absorbing heavy casualties at point-blank range, loading and firing their primitive muskets with robotic precision. Such armies might be recruited from the wretched of society and disciplined with brutal severity but long training made them too costly to waste. Moreover, the officers of that century's armies came almost exclusively from the nobility. Some inherited great wealth; others hoped to gain it from gallant service or from the innumerable bribes, rake-offs, and speculations with which society rewarded office-holders. Unless, like Frontenac, they were financially ruined, aristocratic officers had no wish to serve in a remote and barbarous colony and French kings respected their feelings.

To create colonial garrisons, the Ministry of Marine and Colonies evolved its own small army from soldiers employed to guard naval dockyards. The *troupes de la marine* wore the same off-white uniforms and carried much the same weapons as the king's *troupes de la terre* but the men were organized in companies, not regiments. Officers in the regular army purchased their commissions and subsequent promotions; Colbert insisted that his officers would be selected for ability and promoted by seniority. Even common soldiers could aspire to a commission though few of the scrawny youths collected from seaport slums harboured such ambition.

In some ways, the *troupes de la marine* were a disappointment. From the first expedition under La Barre in 1684, it was evident that they could hardly fight the Iroquois. Even fully drilled, their training had little relevance to wilderness warfare. Instead, an ingenious expedient emerged. Because New France had no barracks, the king commanded that the *troupes* would be billeted with the habitants. What in France would have been a heavy penalty became a blessing. An extra pair of hands to chop firewood, clear land, and bring in the harvest was well worth an extra plate of food, a place at the fireside, and a modest payment. The *troupes* did sentry duty, drilled, and sometimes joined major campaigns and raids but much of their time was spent as ill-paid workers, releasing the young men of the colony for more hazardous and adventurous service.

Since few noble officers wished to serve in the colony, Colbert accepted Denonville's advice to make commissions in the *troupes de la marine* available to sons of leading *Canadiens*. Since an officer's commission represented minor nobility, such appointments were soon eagerly coveted; how else could the sons of humble fur traders make the social leap from commoner to aristocrat? While few *Canadiens* were content to serve as common soldiers, even a chance at a commission led dozens of ambitious young colonists to serve as cadets, corporals, and even privates as they waited their turn for advancement. In turn, the "colonial regulars," as the *troupes* were soon termed, got the services of tough, ardent young men who knew as much as anyone about the techniques of Indian warfare. It was they who organized and led the flying columns of Indians and militia in *la petite guerre* on the English colonists.

Whatever their military limitations, the *troupes de la marine* became part of New France as the few ragged companies of redcoats Britain kept in her colonies never did. Canadian-born officers naturally identified with the colonies. Among them, enrolled illegally at the age of ten, was Governor Vaudreuil's son, Pierre. Even when the strength of the colonial garrison was cut drastically after the Treaty of Utrecht, the number of companies (and officer vacancies) was unchanged. The *Canadien* interest prevailed. As French influence and fur trading spread westward after 1714, officers of the colonial regulars commanded the new forts and their men provided the garrison. Only officers, insisted Governor Beauharnois in 1729, had the sense of honour and the military attributes needed for Indian relations.

Honour did not interfere with personal profit. In France, army officers scorned commerce and were forbidden to meddle in business. The New World had different rules. Paul Marin, Sieur de la Malgue, amassed 300,000 livres during the three years he commanded a post south of Lake Erie. His military pay was 3,000 livres. In 1717, three western posts cost the royal treasury 50,000 livres; by 1754, under military management, the annual cost was 183,427 livres. Coached by the officers on the spot, the governor insisted on the military benefits of drawing Indians away from rival English posts. Meanwhile, *Canadien* officers could make fortunes.

Indeed the whole colony prospered. Population spurted from 19,315 in 1714 to almost sixty thousand in 1755. The amount of cleared land more than tripled. Visitors marvelled at the affluence of habitants who could afford to keep horses merely to race each other. At the same time, they noted that farming methods were primitive and the industries dreamed up by intendants systematically failed or were sustained by subsidies. Even the fur trade was unprofitable. Yet, insisted the contemporary wisdom of the time, colonies were indispensable to France's prosperity.

For New France, part of the secret of affluence was massive military spending. War, W. J. Eccles has argued, was the real staple industry of New France. In 1712, in the midst of war, Louis XIV spent 150,000 livres from his hard-pressed treasury to administer New France, 25,000 on fortifications, and 150,000 on the *troupes de la marine*. By 1730, the annual cost reached 500,000 livres; by the 1740s, when the royal accounts fell into hopeless arrears, costs soared into the millions. Whatever the expense to France, the colony was the beneficiary. Exhausted and bankrupt she might be after the long, disastrous War of the Spanish Succession, but France poured more money than ever into securing her shrunken North American possessions.

At Quebec, Chaussegros de Léry spent a fortune on surprisingly futile efforts to improve the fortifications. His expertise also endowed Fort Niagara with elaborate stone defences, making it a costly but impressive French bastion in the west. Vastly more elaborate and expensive was France's attempt to transform the foggy tip of Cape Breton Island into the "Dunkirk of New France." Urged by Governor Vaudreuil, approved by the king, Louisbourg's fortifications would have done credit to a European city. Five great bastions, batteries for hundreds of guns, barracks, and an entire town were conceived by Jean-François de Verville in faithful deference to the teachings of the great French fortress designer, Vauban. Construction was another matter. Swiss and French soldiers, drafted as both garrison and labour, showed no enthusiasm for their work. Crooked French contractors sold carefully quarried stone and bricks in New England and substituted inferior materials. Even honest workers could not make cement harden in the foggy, rainy weather of Cape Breton nor could they keep water from working into cracks, splitting stonework when it froze. The first governor of Louisbourg, Jean-Baptiste DuQuesnel, was a drunk; his successor, Louis Dupont DuChambon, was no improvement.

The reputation of Louisbourg exceeded its strength. As a base for a powerful French fleet, the fortress threatened the real protector of Britain's American colonies, an all-powerful Royal Navy. Yet few people also recognized Louisbourg's great weakness. It was not the walls. Any fortress can be captured, even if DuChambon's six hundred regulars and thirteen hundred militia had enjoyed higher morale. The problem was French naval weakness. After his fleet was defeated at La Hogue in 1692, Louis XIV lost interest in his navy. The army came first. French shipbuilders continued to produce the finest warships in the world but there were too few of them. Britain's crudely built ships ranged the oceans; French naval vessels spent too much time in harbour. When they emerged, lack of experience took a heavy toll. Without a strong fleet, Louisbourg's power to protect French fishing vessels or the approaches to Quebec extended no farther than the range of her cannon.

Many other features of New France's military society suggested strength but concealed weakness. In Europe or the American colonies, a prudent merchant made wealthy by trade or a government contract might invest in a new industry or improved farming. In New France, military values were reflected in a desire for a fine appearance, lavish hospitality, and a retinue of servants. Officers hoped that a few years in a remote post would earn them enough to retire to France and perhaps even to cut a figure at court. If habitants seemed like spendthrifts, they only imitated the colony's leaders.

New France might have survived as a small, well-guarded colony in the valley of the St. Lawrence. Instead, at Louisbourg and in the west, military policies made her dangerous to her neighbours. With their twenty-to-one dominance in population and resources, the anxiety of the English colonies would become fatal to New France.

Clash of Empires

Like empires, the fur trade was inherently expansive. Better pelts were always available beyond the horizon. Hudson's Bay Company factors could rest beside their half-frozen sea only because they had no competitors in their vast hinterland. The French and Americans had no such option. American traders had already penetrated the rich green valleys beyond the Appalachian mountain chain. In 1727, the New Yorkers burst through to Lake Ontario, building a well-fortified post at Oswego.

On the whole, the French won the economic competition in North America and around the world. Whatever the Industrial Revolution might later achieve for Britain, France's industries in the eighteenth century were cheaper and more productive. In the long peace after 1714, French ships and products began squeezing the British from traditional markets. Though the governor of New France first proposed to uproot Oswego by force, he soon concluded that the New Yorkers posed no real threat to French markets.

A quarter-century of relative peace ended in 1739 when Britain declared war on Spain. The formal justification was trivial: a Spanish coast guard had slashed the ear off an English sea-captain. In Parliament, the young William Pitt roared that free-born English seamen were chained in Spanish prisons. In fact, British merchants believed that a brisk little war would restore their trade. They were soon disabused. A respectable little naval victory in the Caribbean was forgotten when an ensuing British military expedition foundered because of yellow fever and mismanagement. By 1744, when France finally joined the war against Britain, she backed the winning side.

A swift French sailing ship brought news of war to Louisbourg. At once, privateers and raiding parties swooped on Acadia. The main British post, Annapolis Royal, would have fallen had the French commander been a trifle more determined. As it was, morale in the French stronghold soared with the influx of plunder and captured ships.

This was precisely what New Englanders had feared. Long before the war, Governor William Shirley of Massachusetts had matured his plans. Spies and deserters reported every detail of Louisbourg. Lacking siege guns, Shirley ordered shells cast in the calibre of French cannon. William Pepperell, a merchant and militia officer, invested his fortune in organizing a military force. Commodore Peter Warren, whose own rising wealth was invested in the American colonies, promised full support from his North Atlantic squadron. Mutual self-interest spawned a rare feat of naval-military co-operation. Planning paid off. While Warren's ships blockaded the harbour and intercepted reinforcements, Pepperell's men swarmed ashore, seized the isolated Royal Battery, and turned its guns on the town. Guided by a tiny handful of skilled gunners, the Americans were soon hurling their Boston-made shells at the town. After a mere month and a half, Louisbourg's governor hauled down his flag and agreed that he, his soldiers, and the towns-people would be ferried home to France.

News of the disaster struck an otherwise victorious France like a thunderbolt. Elsewhere she had routed a British army at Fontenoy and almost toppled Britain's government by backing Bonnie Prince Charlie's Highland host on its march south to Derby. In New France,

La Malgue returned from a devastating raid on Saratoga, driving a hundred wretched prisoners before him. Louisbourg had to be avenged. In 1746, a powerful fleet under the Duc d'Anville left France, certain to perform the errand. Instead, by the time a storm-battered remnant of the fleet anchored in Chebucto Bay, Louisbourg was safe from recapture. The Duc d'Anville died, his successor committed suicide, and Admiral La Jonquière took the survivors home. A supporting expedition from New France, 680 militia under the Sieur de Ramezay, had to content itself with capturing Grand Pré in a driving snowstorm before making its weary way home.

Yet the Treaty of Aix La Chapelle in 1748 did what d'Anville's fleet had failed to do. To win back Louisbourg, France sacrificed her wartime gains in the Netherlands and India. Boston, swollen with justified pride at its military feat, erupted in fury. In France, too, many questioned the bargain. In Europe, peace was welcomed as a chance to salvage battered economies; in North America, the treaty marked only a truce. France's exhausted treasury somehow found the funds to rebuild Louisbourg and erect a new fort, Beauséjour, on the Isthmus of Chignecto. From there, the ferocious Abbé Jean Le Loutre could set his Micmac converts on the English. In 1749, the British offered a belated answer to Louisbourg. A fleet anchored in Chebucto Bay, thousands of soldiers and settlers rowed ashore, and the best harbour in North America was christened Halifax in honour of the British peer who had approved the venture. Once again, French-speaking Acadians were warned to swear an oath of allegiance to Britain. Having survived forty years without formally choosing sides, very few saw the need to do so.

While Le Loutre's Indians preyed on unwary Halifax settlers and soldiers, it was not in Acadia but in the west that tensions grew. The issue was Ohio — the land of the beautiful river.

Setting aside Indian claims — as Europeans almost invariably did — American trade unquestionably dominated the region. In the English colonies, only the eldest son could inherit the family farm; that guaranteed a tide of land-hungry younger sons. Providently, the Virginia legislature chartered the Ohio Company to divide up the trans-Appalachian land, to the profit of Governor Robert Dinwiddie and his affluent associates. At Quebec, it was agreed that La Salle had long ago claimed the Ohio country for France and the land would someday be needed for a link with Louisiana. To settle the matter, Céleron de

Blainville was sent in 1749 to inspect French trading posts and to bury a number of lead plates confirming French possession. Behind him, at a discreet distance, Ohio Company agents dug up the plates and reassured nervous Indians.

Did France need the Ohio country? Montreal merchants insisted the region produced few furs. Summers were hot and the land was swampy. No one then realized a connection between the clouds of mosquitoes and the fevers which killed many and affected almost everyone. La Jonquière, now governor of New France, ignored such practical details. If the English were not hemmed in behind their mountains, there would be no holding them. Besides, the land was French. In 1753, Pierre Marin, Sieur de La Malgue, the hero of the Saratoga raid and a man of brutal determination, set out with two thousand troops, Indians, and militia to build a fort where the Ohio and Allegheny rivers met. There was no easy route and La Malgue drove his men hard across swamps and along streams so shallow that they had to drag their heavily laden boats. His health ruined, La Malgue insisted he would "die like a soldier." His men had no choice. After months of labour on starvation rations, four hundred had died; only eight hundred could still stand. A horrified governor marvelled that the walking skeletons had not been slaughtered by Indians. Blame inevitably fell on the latest intendant, transferred from Louisbourg in 1746. As usual, François Bigot deflected the criticism with cynical brilliance and some justification. In their massive swindles, Bigot and his associates seem to have concentrated on the royal treasury. Habitants and soldiers were plundered only incidentally.

La Malgue's effort was not in vain. By 1754, Fort Duquesne (named for the latest governor) occupied the future site of Pittsburg. A French force captured the leading pro-British chief, La Demoiselle, and handed him to their Indian allies to be eaten. Local natives digested the lesson and switched sides.

The Ohio Company was upset. In 1753, Dinwiddie sent a young protégé, George Washington, to command the French to leave. After a courteous but firm rebuff, Washington promptly returned a second time to build his own fort. This time he and his men were escorted to the frontier. Once again Dinwiddie despatched his trusted emissary, this time with a force of raw Virginia militia. Washington's frightened men murdered a French emissary and withdrew to an ominously named Fort Necessity. After a nine-hour siege, enlivened when the

Virginians broke into the liquor supply, Washington gave up. Once again he and his men were bundled back over the mountain, abandoning supplies, equipment, and evidence of the Ohio Company's plans to colonize the land. Such documents cemented the French-Indian alliance.

Officially, Britain and France were still at peace; in America they were now at war. For once, Virginia's appeal for aid was answered. In October 1754, Lieutenant-General Edward Braddock was appointed commander-in-chief in North America. Two regiments from the Irish establishment were ordered to America; three more were recruited on the spot. For the first time, it was apparent that Britain was determined to eradicate French power from North America. In Braddock's plan, Beauséjour would be taken. An army of New Yorkers would advance on Montreal by the Lake Champlain route; a smaller force would take Fort Niagara. Braddock himself and his regulars would see to Fort Duquesne.

Braddock was no nincompoop. It was a measure of his competence that he got an army of 2,200 men and a vast waggon train through the Appalachians to Ohio. He was also no frontier fighter. At Duquesne, the French felt doomed but Daniel de Beaujeu led 108 colonial regulars, 146 militia, and 637 Indians out to give battle. Late on June 9, as the British struggled across the Monongahela River and up the steep trail, the two forces met. Instead of racing forward to attack, as military convention dictated, Braddock's advance guard fell back, creating utter confusion. Indians and *Canadiens* spread out, took cover, and picked off officers and drummers. Sweating redcoats tried to form line and failed. Panic spread. Braddock fell, mortally wounded. Soldiers and militia broke for safety. Barely a third, including George Washington, got away. The British lost 977 men; the French 23, among them Captain Beaujeu. Among the trophies were Braddock's plans for the entire campaign.

No sooner had Britain despatched regulars to North America than France followed suit. Reluctantly, King Louis xv gave his approval. Six new battalions, three thousand men in all, were formed from veteran regiments of the *troupes de terre*. They sailed in April 1755. At once a Royal Navy squadron sailed in hot pursuit, capturing three of the transports. In London, British ministers assured the French ambassador of their profound desire for peace.

Among the passengers to reach Quebec that year was New France's native son and new governor. Pierre de Rigaud, Marquis de Vaudreuil, had seen very little military service since he became an officer in the colonial regulars at the age of ten, but his increasing ranks had kept pace with his rise in colonial administration. Vaudreuil's widowed mother kept watch over her family's affairs at court. A general, an admiral, and now a governor among her sons were some evidence of her influence. Another passenger, Baron Dieskau, commanded the king's troops but he was ordered to take his orders from Governor Vaudreuil.

After the capture of Braddock's plans, Vaudreuil's orders were plain enough. Little could be done for Beauséjour. Commanded by one of Bigot's creatures, Louis DuChambon, Sieur de Vergors, it surrendered easily. Thanks to sickness, desertion, and colonial rivalries, the planned British expedition to Niagara never got started. It was the Lake Champlain thrust that was dangerous. In William Johnson, Commodore Warren's estate agent and nephew as well as superintendent to the Iroquois, New York had a promising commander but, as usual, the colonies dragged their feet about sending him troops. Advancing from the north, Dieskau easily outmanoeuvred William Johnson, his amateur opponent, but in the ensuing confused battle, both sides could claim victory. The best evidence for the Americans was that they discovered poor Dieskau, slightly wounded, sitting on a stump and took him prisoner. Courtesy prevailed and he was soon on his way to France.

With civility or not, the war had now begun in earnest. Among its saddest victims were the Acadians. Some had been found among the defenders of Beauséjour. Neutral or not, Acadians posed a threat to nervous British commanders, already contemplating a reinforced Louisbourg. New Englanders clamoured for Acadian lands. In the summer of 1755, the decision was made. British soldiers routed thousands of Acadians out of their homes, loaded them and the few possessions they could carry into ships, and scattered them along the Atlantic seaboard. Many others hid in the woods or fled to Louisbourg or Quebec. Everywhere the refugees carried their terrible warning of what a British conquest would mean.

France furiously denounced the unofficial war in the New World but even when England finally declared war in May 1756, the French took a month to reply. Secretly, French strategists had hoped to tie down Britain's army and fleet in the remote American theatre. A small investment of *troupes de la terre* was well worth it. Conveniently, the

British agreed: the experience of Fontenoy had taught them the cost and futility of heavy continental commitments. History had unrolled as both sides wished. Yet Braddock's fate and the ensuing carnage along the frontiers, as Indian war parties ranged deep into settled areas, warned that North America promised few easy victories.

At Quebec, the Canadian-born Vaudreuil understood *la petite guerre* and remained convinced that no other strategy could tie down more British troops. Such a strategy would also protect the vast fur-trading hinterland from which so many *Canadiens*—officers and merchants alike — drew their fortunes. Dieskau, the conventional European general, had insisted on a more narrowly defensive strategy for New France. Now that accident—or his own misjudgement—had removed the general, Vaudreuil saw no need for a successor. At Versailles, this was considered out of the question. The king's soldiers were entitled to a proper general.

Louis-Joseph de Montcalm-Gozon de St. Véran, like Vaudreuil, had his roots in the proud, impoverished nobility of southern France. If the Vaudreuils prospered in the colonies, the Montcalms had served as soldiers, and few were braver or more experienced than the forty-four-year-old Marquis. Still, it was a bitter wrench to leave a lovely young wife to serve in a remote, obscure colony. The reward, for an ambitious man, was promotion to major-general. Even hesitation had earned him a stern warning from his aged mother: the Montcalm family did not ignore the king's wishes!

An awkward arrangement could have been workable if both the governor and the general were determined to co-operate. Almost from the first meeting, though, they detested each other. Both were stubborn, arrogant men. Montcalm had a sharp wit and a brilliant tongue; no one ever called Vaudreuil clever. Except to his family, Vaudreuil was a cold, reserved man; the general, on the other hand, was plump, lively, and immensely popular with almost all his officers.

French regular officers had already found much in New France to condemn. Prices were high, conditions crude, and habitants showed little of the servility the nobility expected from the peasantry. It was easy to blame Vaudreuil for the sordid embezzlements of Bigot and his common-born associates: Michel Péan, whose pretty wife served as Bigot's concubine; Joseph Cadet, the butcher's son whose ration contracts made him a multi-millionaire; or François LeMercier, the ex-private who organized the colony's artillery—for a profit. Vaudreuil was not in fact responsible for Bigot and he had suffered in an earlier governorship by quarrelling with his intendant. The governor's task was to defend New France and for that he had to depend on Bigot's brilliance in finding resources for the military effort.

The real issue between governor and general was not popularity, but how best to save the colony from a mounting Anglo-American assault. Vaudreuil wanted to fight on the frontiers, sending his *Canadiens* and Indian allies to do their worst. Frantic appeals from English settlers would compel the British to waste their army in scores of tiny forts. Montcalm disagreed. Like Dieskau, he was a conventional soldier. The cruelty of *la petite guerre* and the indiscipline of the men who fought it disgusted him. The *Canadiens* would make excellent troops, but only when they had been transformed into well-drilled regulars.

The new general arrived as formal war between Britain and France began. He brought two extra battalions, giving New France 4,000 *troupes de la terre*, 2,000 colonial regulars, and a potential 10,000 militia. At Louisbourg there were 1,050 of the king's troops, 900 *troupes de la marine*, and 1,400 in the town militia. It was little enough to face a million and a half American colonists or the 44,000 regulars that Britain would eventually deploy in North America.

Even before Montcalm landed, Vaudreuil had made his plans for 1756. By June, militia and Indians had isolated Oswego. On August 10, grumbling at the diversion, Montcalm arrived to take charge of the siege. Within a few days, Rigaud, the governor's brother, had seized a key blockhouse, one of LeMercier's gunners had killed the British commander with a lucky shot, and Indians had intercepted messages warning the garrison to expect no relief. That message, politely delivered by a French officer, led to prompt capitulation: 1,600 prisoners, 121 guns, and a wealth of ships, furs, and supplies were taken. The entire British campaign plan for the year collapsed. In New France, the victors quarrelled bitterly over who deserved credit for the triumph while habitants contemplated the worst harvest in years. Prisoners from Oswego, added to French soldiers and Acadian refugees, only increased the number of hungry mouths to be fed.

By 1757, a new British commander, Lord Loudoun, and thousands of reinforcements had arrived. Once again, the British promised that a powerful army would sweep up the Lake Champlain-Richelieu route. Once again, the American colonies dickered and dithered over their contributions. Even more troops gathered at Halifax for an assault on Louisbourg. Detecting a divided enemy, Vaudreuil sent Montcalm and eight thousand regulars, militia, and Indians down Lake Champlain in a pre-emptive strike. While the *Canadiens* and Indians sealed off the British advanced base, Fort William Henry, Montcalm's regulars laid formal siege. After six days, twenty-four hundred men, most of them British regulars, surrendered in return for conditions familiar in European warfare — safe passage out of the battle and no further service in the war. Montcalm was delighted; his Indian allies were outraged. Such decorous procedures were no part of their tradition. As the redcoats marched away, Indians and some *Canadiens* rushed in for the slaughter. A white-faced, furious Montcalm hurled himself into the melee. So did some of his officers. Fifty British soldiers lay dead; another five hundred were rescued or ransomed. A further hundred British were not heard of again.

The disaster at Fort William Henry traumatized New York and caused fresh quarrels at Quebec. Montcalm might well have seized the main British base, Fort Edward. His militiamen, he argued, were needed for the harvest. His Indian allies were satisfied with their booty — or dissatisfied with their commander — and went home. Montcalm had no means to supply his remaining three thousand men and it would have been rash to risk his army. To eighteenth-century soldiers, rashness was the unforgivable sin.

The British now feared that, by provoking war, they had committed that precise sin. From around the world came news of failure and defeat. A powerful French fleet at Louisbourg had kept Loudoun's army at Halifax. In London, defeatists predicted an early peace. Instead, Britain got a new prime minister. For a generation, William Pitt had been Parliament's perennial carping critic, helping to drive Britain to war in 1739 and then condemning every disaster that ensued. Yet Pitt was also a man of steel will, yearning for soldiers and sailors who would fight, not make excuses. Pitt's plans for North America hardly differed from Braddock's; what he added was determination.

Of course, the French and British strategies meshed. If Pitt saw New France as the Carthage that must be destroyed, to Versailles, she was a cat's paw, to attract British troops and, if need be, suffer for it. When the French ships reached Quebec in the spring of 1758, they brought a mere handful of reinforcements and horrifying news. The fleet that had saved Louisbourg had brought raging typhus back to France. In the dockyard towns, ten thousand had died. The French fleet was crippled. Across the Atlantic, colonists and soldiers, reduced to half-rations and the hated horsemeat, would fight on. The Vaudreuil-Montcalm feud would persist, unchecked and unabated.

With renewed grumbling, Montcalm carried out the governor's plan for 1758. Half the army, under his able and discreet second-in-command, the Chevalier Lévis, would attack from Oswego. The rest, thirty-three hundred regulars, colonials, and militia, would face the British from a strong point at Carillon at the head of Lake Champlain. In fact, the promised fort turned out to be little more than a palisade.

Lord Loudoun was an obvious casualty of Pitt's search for resolute commanders. A junior colonel, Jeffrey Amherst, was promoted to major-general, given thirteen thousand regulars and a powerful fleet, and sent off to Louisbourg. By June 1, when the British arrived, a little French squadron of thirteen ships had been scraped together to help save the fortress, but foul weather was Amherst's worst problem. Not until June 7 could he try a landing. His junior brigadier, a sickly redhead named James Wolfe, watched as boats filled with redcoats shattered on the rocky foreshore. A single lucky craft steered into a protected inlet. Wolfe followed at once, led his cheering soldiers ashore, and seized a key French battery.

Once ashore, the British virtually repeated Pepperell's tactics of 1745. They captured the Royal Battery, turned the guns on the town, and hammered the French warships to pieces. A single frigate, commanded by a resourceful Acadian, Robert Vauquelin, got away. For seven weeks, the British battered Louisbourg until its courageous governor, Augustin de Drucourt, agreed to surrender. Fire-eaters like Wolfe yearned to press on to Quebec (as Pitt had intended). Instead, Amherst was shaken by bad news from Lake Champlain. It was there that his efforts were needed.

On much of the frontier, the British and settlers had reason to rejoice that summer. General John Forbes retraced Braddock's path over the mountains, avoided an ambush, and would have taken Duquesne if the defenders had not blown it up. Forbes rebuilt it as Fort Pitt. Another British-American column under Colonel John Bradstreet crossed Lake Ontario, seized Fort Frontenac, and returned laden with plunder. Local Indians revised their alliances or, like the Iroquois, leaned their neutrality in a more British direction.

Yet everything depended on the Lake Champlain front. James

Abercromby, Loudoun's successor, was a gouty old veteran but Pitt had heard that he would fight. He certainly had the means — fifteen thousand men, six thousand of them regulars. Far to the west, Lévis abandoned his expedition and raced to Montcalm's aid. Faced with this threat to his flank, a cautious general might have withdrawn; a clever one would have manoeuvred Montcalm out of his position. Abercromby simply decided to push ahead, trusting his disciplined redcoats to batter their way through. It had happened before.

On a steaming July 7, it almost happened again. While Montcalm's white-coated regulars held their ground, sweating British "lobsters" dressed ranks and advanced, only to be driven back by French volleys. Again and again they tried. A shirt-sleeved Montcalm spotted symptoms of panic on one of his flanks. At once, he threw his tiny reserve behind the shaky battalion, restoring morale. As dusk approached, it was the British who gave way. That night, the French counted 600 dead redcoats; their own loss was 362.

Later myth-makers would claim Carillon as a victory for the *Canadiens*. In fact, it was a triumph for the regulars and a demonstration of disciplined firepower that even impressed Indian allies. Carillon, or Ticonderoga as the British called it, was the first European-style battle in North America.* The outnumbered French had earned their praise. There was no such compensation for the Englishmen and Scots whose lives were forfeit to Abercromby's stupidity. Pitt needed more than fighters; he needed brains.

Crisis and Fall

Carillon was triumph enough for Montcalm; for New France it was soon a faded memory in the worst winter of the war. In the west, French power had collapsed. The fall of Louisbourg could only mean that Quebec would follow. The last ships down the St. Lawrence in 1758 carried urgent if contradictory appeals from Vaudreuil and Montcalm, with agents to lend them passion. Then those in the colony not fortunate enough to feast at Intendant Bigot's table faced the long, hungry winter. Montcalm's officers in particular, driven to bankruptcy by high prices and low pay, pleaded for leave to return to France. Out

---

*Quebec's fleur de lys flag, adopted in 1946, was supposedly *le drapeau du Carillon.*

in the villages and farms, the ordinary soldiers quartered with habitants fared better, but only the richest and most powerful escaped the pinch.

In France, ministers and officials listened to the emissaries from New France, set their problems in the context of a war that was now going very badly for France, and hardened their hearts. "Sir, when the house is on fire one does not worry about the stables," a minister told Montcalm's *aide-de-camp*, Louis-Antoine de Bougainville. "No one," replied the already famous savant, "will accuse you of talking like a horse." A delighted Madame de Pompadour, the king's mistress, insisted that the witty Bougainville be made a colonel. That changed nothing. For 1759, insisted Louix XV's new minister, the Duc de Choiseul, France would concentrate her fleet and armies to invade Britain. Beyond bags of despatches, a few hundred ill-favoured recruits, and some medals, there was not much for New France.

At least there was luck. Convoyed by Captain Vauquelin, a large supply convoy beat the British blockade and reached Quebec in early May. Bougainville was among the first to land. In recognition of his victory, Montcalm would be a lieutenant-general — equal in rank to Vaudreuil. To Vaudreuil came secret instructions to "defer" to the general. For a time, ministers had toyed with recalling Montcalm; the fear of royal displeasure deterred them. The very least Versailles could have done for New France — clarify the authority of two quarrelsome men — was left undone. In Quebec, Montcalm simply took charge, detaching small forces to protect Montreal, abandoning western garrisons to their fate, and mustering all the troops and militia he could at Quebec. Somehow, Versailles had insisted, Montcalm must preserve a foothold as a basis for bargaining when an eventual peace treaty was negotiated.

In England, Pitt had no intention of allowing such a possibility. A French invasion, he scorned. The "somewhat elephantine" Amherst could be commander-in-chief in America; to take Quebec Pitt sought someone still more aggressive. Why not James Wolfe? At thirty-two, he had spent half his life at war or training a series of battalions to perfection. He was a calculating, friendless man with a brutal streak made apparent in Scotland in suppressing the rebellion of 1745. To Pitt, ruthlessness was welcome.

Once chosen, that young general could have little complaint about his troops or colleagues. Though he collected only two-thirds of a promised twelve thousand men, his battalions were the pick of the army. Two of his brigadiers, Robert Monckton and James Murray, were Wolfe's choices; only the third, George Townshend, a godson of the king, was appointed by court favour. The accompanying fleet, under Admiral Charles Saunders, was the strongest the Royal Navy could assemble. Three years of fighting had swept away the cobwebs and most of the incompetents.

The supply ships had brought Montcalm ample warning of Wolfe's approach. The French general enjoyed his new authority. As he had long desired, the best of the *Canadien* militia filled out the depleted ranks of his regulars. They would learn discipline by example. One of his aides organized New France's first cavalry squadron. Vaudreuil scoffed. The English, he insisted, would never even get up the river. He had not bothered to post a battery at the traverse below Quebec because no ships could pass it without French pilots. By June 26, Saunders's fleet was riding at anchor off Quebec. Between them, the future Pacific explorer, James Cook, and a renegade Canadian mariner, Denis Vitré, had managed the passage. That afternoon, Wolfe's army set up camp on the Ile d'Orléans. By June 28, the fleet had survived a summer storm and fireship attack. On June 30, Monckton's men seized the heights of Lévis, opposite Quebec. Within two weeks, despite militia and Indian attacks, Monckton's guns began pounding the besieged city.

That much was easy. The rest seemed impossible. As Phips had learned seventy years earlier, Quebec posed an awesome challenge. Frontal attack was impossible. Miles of steep cliffs guarded one flank; the Beauport shore, where Montcalm's army waited patiently, protected the other. Desperately, Wolfe weighed and abandoned schemes. He took out his frustration on brigadiers and troops alike. He sent Townsend ashore below Montmorency Falls and was no farther ahead. Disease and ever-present Indians took a demoralizing, daily toll.

On July 31, he ordered an attack at the Montmorency end of the Beauport shore. Shallow water kept Saunders's ships from giving close support but Wolfe's men stormed ashore, crossed the beach, and desperately struggled up a steep slope. From the French trenches they were an easy, helpless target. Suddenly a blinding downpour soaked firearms on both sides and sent the British survivors rolling down the slope for lack of a foothold. As the storm cleared, the French looked down on the tangle of dead and wounded bodies and stood silent in horror. A few even tried to drive off the Indians and militia who came out to finish the slaughter. "Ye that love fighting will soon have enough," Ned Botwood had written the night before, "Wolfe commands us, my boys, we shall give them Hot Stuff." He was among the dead.

Wolfe's despair was now complete. He blamed soldiers, brigadiers, even the faithful Saunders, for his failure. Sick in mind and body, he took to his bed. A year before, he had condemned "these hell-hounds of Canadians" for their barbarity. Now he unleashed his American Rangers — "the dirtiest, most contemptible cowardly dogs" Wolfe had called them until they saved his men from the Indians — on a defenceless countryside. They and British troops burned fourteen hundred farm-steads, killing and scalping when they met resistance. "*M. Wolfe est cruel*," observed Bigot.

Other officers tried to save the expedition. Saunders boldly slipped warships upstream, past Quebec's powerful batteries. Murray's brigade began raiding Montcalm's supply lines. More and more French troops, under Bougainville, had to march wearily up and down the shore, watching for a British landing. Still, Montcalm knew, such ventures could not take Quebec. Time was on his side. British deserters let him know that Saunders already was worried about being trapped by St. Lawrence ice.

On August 31, Wolfe had recovered enough to consult his brigadiers about yet another assault on the Beauport shore. Unanimously they opposed him. Instead they urged that all available men — barely six thousand were now fit for service — should be brought upriver and landed behind Quebec. A gloomy Wolfe agreed. Then, on September 8, he spotted the Anse au Foulon, a little cove barely three kilometres from the city walls. Instead of landing at Pointe aux Trembles, it was at the Anse that the army would go ashore. After collecting his men and exhausting Bougainville's force with endless counter-marching, on the night of September 12-13, Wolfe was ready. Soldiers filed into boats, dropped downriver, and almost magically found the cove in the dark. At once they clambered safely to the top. A feeble guard, commanded by Captain Vergors, the luckless ex-commander of Beauséjour, was dispersed or captured. As the dawn mist rose over Quebec on September 13, a long red line of soldiers faced the city's weakest front.

There the British might well have stayed. Quebec's landward walls were weak but Wolfe had only two cannon. Positioned between the city and the superior numbers of Montcalm and Bougainville, the British would have been hopelessly trapped. Wolfe's great luck lay not in getting up to the Plains of Abraham but in Montcalm's furious reaction.

Exhausted from a summer of sleepless nights, enraged that Wolfe had apparently outsmarted him, Montcalm's emotional temperament got the better of his professional caution. Would the French fight? Of course. For two hours, regulars, militia, and Indians poured over the St. Charles River bridge and up the slope to form line outside Quebec's wall. Guns were hurriedly mounted on the few available carriages and rolled through the city gates.

At 10 A.M., Montcalm ordered an advance. The thin British line rose from where it had been lying to avoid French bombardment and dressed ranks. Coming down the Buttes au Neveu, the French line moved faster. Militiamen with the regular battalions reverted to habit, and threw themselves down and fired. Sergeants tried to force them to their feet. The line was broken. Through the smoke of battle, the French saw the British raise their muskets. A devastating blast tore through their ranks. A second British rank advanced through the smoke cloud, stopped, aimed, and fired. It was too much. The king's troops broke. White-coated regulars and militia fled. Montcalm, his side torn by a cannon shot, was helped through the city wall. Behind him, the army dissolved. Only militia and Indian sharpshooters covered the retreat, causing most of the British losses of sixty-eight dead and six hundred wounded. New world warfare saved an old world army. French losses, less carefully counted, were about six hundred.

Back on the Plains, Wolfe was dying from his third wound. Monckton was hard hit. When Bougainville appeared, two hours too late, it was George Townshend who mustered a couple of weary battalions to chase him away. He had no energy or talent for pursuit. Instead, it was Vaudreuil who collected the defeated army, consulted surviving officers about a counter-attack, and accepted their advice to escape by a round-about route to Montreal. On the way, he met Lévis, hurrying from the south. The army turned and marched north. The little cavalry unit raced toward Quebec, laden with supplies for the starving city. They were hours too late. True to Vaudreuil's instructions, the Sieur de Ramezay had just surrendered the city. He was too much a gentleman to reverse his word.

Quebec was captured. New France survived. To the south, Fort Niagara had fallen but Amherst's army was no closer than the Ile aux

Noix. At Quebec, James Murray remained for the winter with most of Wolfe's army. Townshend and Saunders went home to England. Late in the season, a few French ships slipped past Quebec. In separate despatches, Vaudreuil blamed Montcalm for the colony's ruin while Lévis confidently insisted that massive help could restore Quebec. He could not know that most of France's fleet had been destroyed in two disastrous naval battles at Lagos and Quiberon Bay.

Through the winter Murray drove his shivering, scurvy-ridden men to improve Quebec's defences. A cultured, bilingual soldier, Murray wooed the remaining colonists and shared his army's rations with the homeless victims of the summer depredations. Yet none of his new *Canadien* friends warned Murray that Lévis was coming. Late in April, as the ice broke up, the French commander brought his entire army north — 3,889 regulars, 3,021 militia. Only a half-frozen French artilleryman, clinging to an ice floe after his boat sank, gave Murray notice. With hours to spare, the British general went out and collected his outposts. Next day, April 28, he mustered his gaunt, ailing survivors outside the walls and prepared for battle.

It was an odd repetition of the September fight. This time, the French defended along a line of woods and buildings at Ste. Foy while the British wearily plodded through mud and snow to attack. After fighting that was far more bloody and desperate than the previous year, the French prevailed. Barely two-thirds of Murray's army struggled back to the city; 1,104 lay dead or wounded. Lévis lost 833. True to his stubborn character, Murray fought on. Behind Quebec's frail walls, now pierced for British cannon, Murray's men waited. So did Lévis's army. The fate of New France depended on whose flag appeared down the long expanse of the St. Lawrence.

On May 9, both sides spotted the first sail. Both armies cheered. Then the French fell silent, as they saw the faint red of a British ensign. The frigate HMS *Lowestoft* had returned. Newspapers, reporting French disasters, were kindly delivered to Lévis's headquarters. Soon, more British warships appeared. On May 16, the French abandoned their camp and marched south.

That summer, British columns advanced on Montreal from three directions. A tiny French fleet, with a mere nine hundred reinforcements, was intercepted, chased, and destroyed in the mouth of the Restigouche River. Torn between British threats to burn their homes and Lévis's promise to unleash the Indians on deserters, the *Canadien* militia dissolved. The Iroquois long since had made their peace through Sir William Johnson and his Indian Department.

By September 6, Amherst had reached the outskirts of Montreal. With understandable anguish, Vaudreuil prepared the surrender terms. For his part, Lévis insisted on the honour of his regulars. The king would forgive no insult: his regiments must keep their arms and colours. Amherst was unimpressed. The colonists would be secure in their property and religion but there could be no honours for an army guilty of "setting on the Indians to commit the most shocking cruelties." Without respect, Lévis insisted, his men had no choice but to fight to the death. At last Vaudreuil asserted himself. Such insanity would destroy Montreal and ruin his fellow *Canadiens*. He would accept personal responsibility for the terms and brave the king's wrath. Defiantly the French regulars withdrew to Ile Ste. Hélène, burned their regimental colours, and surrendered. On September 9, 1760, New France was no more.

It could still have been revived. In 1763, New France was still one of the counters French negotiators might have demanded from a victorious but weary Britain. By then, Pitt was driven from office and lesser men prevailed. Instead, the French bargained for fishing rights off Newfoundland, the tiny islands of St. Pierre and Miquelon, and, above all, for the rich sugar islands of the Caribbean.

The reasons were complex and sad. Belatedly, the greed of Bigot, Cadet, and their accomplices had underlined how little France gained from those *"quelques arpents de neige"* and how much they cost. Faced, from 1755, with evident British determination to crush New France, the French had used that determination as a ploy to divert British military and naval resources. They had sacrificed their colony to a more central national need.

There was also an element of cunning in French policy. No minister had done more, through strategic folly, to lose New France, but the Duc de Choiseul was a prophet in 1763 when he explained that France's presence in America had held Britain and her colonies together. Robbed of that danger, Britons and Americans would fall on each other's throats. Within twelve years, he was proved right.

The tragedy of New France was played out to the end. Its memory survived. The sacrifice of the colony to France's interests persuaded *Canadiens* to look to themselves for survival. The long ordeal of the Iroquois wars would endow them, as it did New Englanders, with the conviction that they were a chosen people. From the later phases of the struggle, the *Canadiens* would inherit a sense of frustration and betrayal. English-speaking Canadians might portray Wolfe and Montcalm as equal heroes in the climactic battle on the Plains of Abraham. To *Canadiens*, for all his faults, Vaudreuil would remain the native-born leader whose alternative strategy might somehow have prevented capitulation.

On such dreams and memories does nationhood depend.

II The British Empire

American Revolution

Historians often confuse wisdom with prophetic skill. In 1760, no one knew that the Duc de Choiseul would live to see an American republic. No one believed that New France's destiny was settled for a century. The clergy, a few seigneurs, and the habitants remained; the colony's leaders and the soldiers departed with Vaudreuil. Some, unable to find roots in France, would later return. Until war's end, New France would be governed, like any other occupied territory, by military representatives of the conqueror, exercising martial law but content to let people solve their problems in ways "agreeable to their own laws and customs." Murray at Quebec, Colonel Ralph Burton at Trois-Rivières, and Major-General Thomas Gage at Montreal found the *capitaines de la côte* especially useful. A society managed by militia captains appealed to military minds.

The war dragged on. In the spring of 1762, a French fleet landed seven hundred men and captured St. John's, Newfoundland, to the delight of the Irish half of the island population. In September, however, a British force landed at Torbay, fought the French at Quidi Vidi, and chased them to Signal Hill. Abandoned by their fleet, the remnant surrendered on September 20. Inland, fighting ended with the capitulation. With frigid formality but no bloodshed, British garrisons displaced the French at Detroit and a dozen tiny posts in the west.

The newcomers had much to learn. Not all Indians were ready to abandon their French allies without a fight. Under the British, the era of lavish presents, generous prices, and charity in hard times ended. Sir Jeffery Amherst took a dim view of providing funds from the Crown for erstwhile enemies of the king. A host of anxieties and grievances became fuel for the oratory of Pontiac, a war-chief of the Ottawa. With encouragement from some French traders (though none from French posts in Louisiana), Pontiac managed a brilliant series of operations in the summer of 1763. By pure cunning, Indians seized eight British posts, killing or capturing the tiny garrisons. Only at Fort Pitt and Detroit did commanders see through the Indian stratagems. Both were tightly besieged while Indian war parties ravaged the frontier.

Using some of the Indians' own tactics, British columns finally rescued both Pitt and Detroit. Part of Colonel Bradstreet's expedition to Detroit was a battalion of three hundred *Canadiens*, commanded by an ex-officer of the *troupes de la marine*, the Sieur de Rigauville. Raised as volunteers, the men returned from a bloodless expedition well-satisfied with their pay and eager to serve again. Without the French aid Pontiac had promised, the rebellion faded and the Indian leader was reviled by disillusioned allies and ultimately murdered by them.

Peace with France and Pontiac's defeat should have brought contentment to Britain and her American colonies. The reverse was true. The Seven Years War had ended in triumph for the British but it was not the war to end all wars. France and Spain would seek revenge. Each victory only added to the cost of defending distant territory but Britain felt itself on the edge of financial ruin. A government that had never collected more than £15.5 million in taxes in a single year faced a national debt of £130 million. To raise taxes would ruin British merchants and delight their competitors. Pontiac's rebellion only underlined the proper solution: surely Americans could help pay for a garrison provided for their protection! Americans disagreed. The two thousand white settlers and four hundred soldiers who had died because of Pontiac did not greatly trouble the consciences of American leaders. As for the costly struggle to take New France, it was, Benjamin Franklin explained, "really a British war." The argument turned nasty. Taxation resistance led to coercion. Troops sent to protect the American colonies were redeployed to repress them. The First British Empire was well on the road to Lexington Green and revolution.

In 1766, Guy Carleton, Wolfe's former quartermaster-general, replaced Murray as Lieutenant-Governor of the newly named province of Quebec. Carleton disliked Murray but he inherited the Scottish general's fondness for the *Canadiens* and he soon shared Murray's distaste for the English and American merchants who had followed the army of occupation in hope of fast profits. To a member of the Irish Protestant ascendancy, there was much to admire in Quebec, from the patient, hard-working habitants to the remnant of elegant seigneurs. Even a Protestant could approve of an ultramontane Catholic hierarchy eager to render to a British Caesar all it had ever given to a French Catholic king. In contrast to the troublesome American colonies, Carleton's Quebec could be a bastion of conservative values if properly managed. Moreover, it could master up to eighteen thousand militia, "of which Number," Carleton reported with some historical license, "above one-half have already served with as much Valor, with more zeal, and more military knowledge for America than the regular Troops of France, that were joined with them."

To ensure that Britain's government and Parliament shared his view of Quebec, Carleton spent four years of his governorship in England. He returned in the fall of 1774 with a Quebec Act that fulfilled his expectations of all that clergy and seigneurs could wish in return for delivering an army of loyal habitants. By giving Quebec the old hinterland of New France, the Act even compensated the English-speaking merchants for the return of French civil law and the lack of an assembly.

Carleton, of course, had utterly misunderstood the *Ancien Régime*. That Americans would add the Quebec Act to their grievances might be predictable; that habitants detested a now-legally-enforceable tithe and that they felt no loyalty to their seigneurs was beyond his comprehension. Carleton's misjudgement would have serious consequences.

By rights, Nova Scotia should have been the fourteenth colony in revolt. Half its people were New Englanders; if there were grievances in British North America, Nova Scotians shared them. Geography and the Royal Navy set different rules. Except for the eighty men Jonathan Eddy gathered to attack Fort Cumberland in 1776, only to be chased back to Maine, Nova Scotians kept rebellious thoughts to themselves and prayed to escape both American privateers and the Royal Navy's press gangs. In return, Halifax prospered as mightily as ever from the war and enough of the bounty spread to the outports to make loyalty agreeable.

Quebec was a very different matter. Within a month of the skirmishes at Lexington and Concord, Ethan Allen and Benedict Arnold had seized the old fortresses of Ticonderoga and Crown Point and occupied St. Jean. Despite a *mandement* from Bishop Briand proclaiming "the unavoidable duty of defending your country and your King with all the strength you possess," Carleton's summons to the militia brought superficial compliance in the Quebec region and angry resistance around Montreal. At least one loyal seigneur was beaten and another driven from his village. Only a handful of *Canadiens* followed the Sieur de Belestre to St. Jean though they were enough to drive back the Americans.

The Continental Congress was determined to take Quebec. Not only would it pre-empt a British strike from the north; there would be symbolic satisfaction in rescuing oppressed victims of the Quebec Act. At

Boston, George Washington besieged General Gage and the main British army; at Albany, a smaller army mobilized against Quebec. Richard Montgomery, an able ex-British officer, took command. Carleton, now desperate, allowed three-quarters of his tiny garrison to become besieged in the run-down little fort at St. Jean. From September 4 to November 3, Major Charles Preston held Montgomery's army but Carleton failed utterly to mobilize a relieving force. Once St. Jean fell, the Americans raced to Sorel, cut river communications, and took Montreal. Carleton escaped down the St. Lawrence in a tiny open boat.

Carleton reached Quebec on November 20. On the way he slipped past another American army, which was too weary to fight. As his contribution, Washington had sent Benedict Arnold with twelve hundred Virginians and New Englanders up the Kennebec River, across swamps and icy wastes, and down the treacherous Chaudière. Barely six hundred exhausted, half-starved men were with Arnold when he reached the St. Lawrence. Stragglers and Montgomery's army gave the Americans two thousand soldiers to take Quebec. Carleton found eighteen hundred men, most of them militia, bolstered by ninety regulars and five hundred sailors and marines from warships in harbour. In the circumstances, he wisely waited behind his walls and refused even the customary parleys with the American generals. Montgomery and Arnold had problems too: no siege artillery, a surly population that demanded cash for its supplies, and an army whose term of enlistment expired on December 31. That alone settled the plan: a direct assault at each end of Quebec's Lower Town. If sympathizers in the city did not turn on the British, merchants would compel Carleton to surrender to save their warehouses.

At 4 A.M. on December 31, in a howling snowstorm, two separate attacks began. Under the shadow of Cape Diamond, *Canadien* gunners opened fire on shadowy figures. Grapeshot burst among the Americans. Montgomery and some others fell dead; the rest fled. On the opposite side of the city, Arnold led the way into the St. Roch district, got lost among the warehouses, and was wounded. A Virginian, Daniel Morgan, took command, stormed the first barricade and was facing the second when a British counter-attack rushed in behind him. The Americans surrendered. By dawn, Carleton's men had collected four hundred prisoners and counted a hundred Americans lying dead in the snow. Paper streamers printed "Liberty or Death" fluttered from their caps.

The siege continued. Congress sent three more regiments to replace time-expired men and, in April, six more. A new general, John Thomas, arrived on May 1. On May 5, British warships broke over the horizon. Within minutes, the Americans had retreated south so quickly that a British patrol captured General Thomas's dinner.

The ships brought Carleton a promotion, seven battalions of infantry, four batteries of artillery, and a dashing young second-in-command, Major-General John Burgoyne, eager to make his reputation. He would not make it under Carleton. The British took two weeks to reach Trois-Rivières. A new American general, John Sullivan, crossed the river to attack, landed in the wrong spot, launched a brave but hopeless assault on a British position, and might well have been captured. Carleton let him escape. Beset with smallpox, desertion, and deepening habitant hostility, Sullivan took his bedraggled army home to Albany, praising God for his escape. Burgoyne would have given the credit to Carleton. By October 14, the British were no farther south than Crown Point. The British general called off campaigning, distributed his soldiers among the habitants, and warned, through the seigneurs, that quartering troops was part of the penalty for disloyalty the previous year.

Because of Carleton's lack-lustre performance, it was Burgoyne who led a reinforced army of British regulars, German mercenaries, and even a few *Canadien* militia south toward Albany in 1777. On both sides, Indians were at last involved. After two years of awkward neutrality, the Iroquois confederacy had finally split. The influence of Sir John Johnson, Sir William's son, and the leadership of Joseph Brant brought first the Mohawk, and then the Seneca and Cayuga to the British side. The Oneida were as committed to the American side. The other nations split or waited.

While Burgoyne took Ticonderoga and then lumbered slowly south with all the paraphernalia of European-style campaigning, Colonel Barry St. Leger mustered a few regulars, more Loyalist troops, and all the Indians he could persuade or bribe for a diversionary raid on Fort Stanwix and the Mohawk Valley. At Oriskany, the Iroquois annihilated a small American army but St. Leger had no guns that could even dent Fort Stanwix, and the expedition ended in utter disarray. The Americans and their Indian allies were free to head east to join the forces enveloping Burgoyne's struggling columns. At Saratoga on October 17, Burgoyne surrendered the remnant of his battered, hungry army, and headed home to resume his career as a dramatist. His soldiers remained to suffer and die in American prison camps.

Saratoga was decisive. Burgoyne's defeat persuaded France and Spain to seek the vengeance Britain had awaited since 1763. With her army trapped in an unpopular war and her navy over-stretched, Britain faced disaster. Minorca fell; Gibraltar was besieged. A powerful French fleet under the Comte d'Estaing headed for North America. At Quebec, Major-General Frederick Haldimand had replaced Carleton in 1778. A French-speaking Swiss, Haldimand was a shrewd choice but knowing the language would not keep *Canadien* loyalty if the fleur de lys appeared on the St. Lawrence. "Provided the French would send a fleet into the river," he warned, "they would to a man take up arms in favour of the rebels." Unaware of the jealous bickering that frustrated each Franco-American scheme to recover Quebec, Haldimand could only stand on the defensive, sending what little help he could spare to Loyalists and Iroquois who kept up the fight south of Lake Ontario.

The western frontier of New York was remote from the southern states where the war had moved after Saratoga. If it had a pretext, the campaign denied Washington's armies the rich food supplies from the Mohawk Valley. That, at least, was the reason Washington sent General John Sullivan in 1779, with an army of five thousand men, to devastate Seneca and Cayuga villages and destroy the "nest of Tory banditti" at Fort Niagara. The devastation was complete — and so time-consuming that Sullivan had to turn back with the approach of winter and his army nearly starved amidst its own depredations. At Fort Niagara, the British found themselves besieged by hungry, homeless Indians who had lost everything in the white men's quarrel.

The quarrel was, of course, more complex. It was a cruel civil war between Loyalist and Patriot, Mohawk and Oneida, in a crude frontier tradition. Brant and the New York Loyalist leader, John Butler, organized and led raids that reached south to Pennsylvania and east as far as Albany, where Butler's Rangers openly recruited in 1781. An American historian, Barbara Graymont, has carefully demolished most of the legend of savage atrocities attributed to the Rangers and the Iroquois and confirmed Joseph Brant's own reputation as a generally humane and forebearing commander. It was the legend that mattered, of course, because it added a sordid and despicable aspect to a war that most in Britain now wished to end. Since such people rarely admitted that Indians had a real claim to land, it was assumed that they fought only as auxiliaries, bribed by rum and blankets. The truth — that the Iroquois were fighting for their land — would be admitted two centuries too late.

Half a continent away, the fight was being settled. In the boldest British venture of the war, Lord Cornwallis had led his small army through the Carolinas only to be trapped at Yorktown between an overwhelming French and American army and a victorious French fleet. On October 19, as a band played "The World Turned Upside Down," the Cornwallis army surrendered.

For the British, it was the end of any will to fight. Only peace could break the fatal alliance of France, Spain, and the Americans. Peace might restore trade and even good will. In the circumstances, British negotiators bargained from weakness and, not for the last time, from ignorance. For a time, they were even tempted by Ben Franklin's suggestion that they throw in Quebec and Nova Scotia, retaining only territory north of Lake Nipissing. The French, anxious to keep the Anglo-American rivalry alive, persuaded the British to maintain their presence.

As it was, the vast western hinterland of New France below the Great Lakes was passed to the Americans. The Maine-Nova Scotia boundary on the St. Croix River left no safe or usable overland route from the Atlantic to the interior. Choosing the 45th parallel as the southern limit to Quebec left Crown Point and Ticonderoga in American hands. Indeed the entire boundary, vaguely sketched on dubious maps, would take sixty more years to confirm.

As for the Loyalists, white and Indian, they had become an embarrassment to the peacemakers. The Congress, said the treaty, would urge the states to restore property and civil rights to those who had not borne arms; the others would have one year to settle their affairs — if the respective states agreed. As for the western Indians, whose lands had been transferred to the new United States, there was no mention and little thought. Their enemies and their allies agreed to make peace without even consulting them.

Loyalist Colonies

At Paris in 1783 Britain accepted the independence of most of her American colonies while, more implicitly, the Americans agreed to a separate destiny for the northern half of their continent. Neither side considered the arrangement final: eighteenth-century treaties rarely were. For the Americans, when time made the United States stronger, the map could be redrawn; for the British, defeat was easier to accept if they believed that it could someday be reversed. Meanwhile, both sides acted as though the peace might only be a truce.

For the British, the most urgent peacetime problem was coping with seventy thousand Loyalist refugees. The first of them had fled Boston in 1776; others trickled north after Burgoyne's defeat in 1777. Like most refugees they were unwelcome; their presence, their losses, and their grievances only reminded the British army of its failures. Neither *Canadiens* nor Nova Scotians felt any obligation to make room for them. At the war's end, the last British commander, Sir Guy Carleton, held the Americans at bay as thousands of frightened Loyalists crammed into ships in New York Harbour. Most headed for Nova Scotia, some for Great Britain or the Caribbean. Other Loyalists filtered north to Lake Ontario or followed Butler's Rangers across the Niagara River.

Only the British garrison had the means to feed the hungry and often penniless refugees. Only the army had surveyors competent to lay out new settlements. In Nova Scotia, the governor, Colonel John Parr, was hardly displeased when settlements of once-prosperous Loyalists failed at Annapolis Royal and Shelburne. By expelling a few Acadians from the St. John River Valley, he could distance himself from the problem and create a vast military colony for thirteen disbanded Loyalist regiments. By the end of 1783, ten thousand unhappy people had been deposited at Parrtown to find their way upriver or along the Fundy shore. A year later both Parr and the Loyalists were content that Nova Scotia had been severed at the Missiquash River, that New Brunswick and a separate colony of Cape Breton Island were created, and that Parrtown could be renamed Saint John. Colonel Thomas Carleton, Sir Guy's brother, arrived as lieutenant-governor. Carleton established his new capital at Fredericton, too far up the river for an American raid and somewhat removed from the grumbling of his disillusioned people.

At Quebec, Major-General Haldimand was hardly more welcoming than Parr. Carleton's Quebec Act had been designed for a population that would forever be Catholic and French; the Loyalists were unquestionably English and largely Protestant. Loyalist leaders like Sir John Johnson made it clear that they expected law and custom to be changed to suit the newcomers. As for Loyalist claims to have borne the heat of battle, Haldimand refused even to speak to Colonel Butler because of his alleged barbarities. Such episodes had helped wreck the British cause. The vacant Eastern Townships seemed the logical place for Loyalist settlement; Haldimand disagreed: the Townships were needed, in his view, for French Canadians. Instead, to Loyalist dismay, the surveyor-general, Major Samuel Holland, laid out sixteen townships in the wilderness west of the seigneury of Longueuil, along the St. Lawrence and Lake Ontario. The settlements of German and Loyalist veterans would not only be remote from the *Canadiens*; they might also improve the defences of western Quebec.

Military minds favour military solutions. Not only were the Loyalists located by regiments but officers were granted far more land than their men. A major or colonel received a thousand acres, a captain seven hundred, a private a hundred. When the senior officers of one regiment insisted that they had been promised five thousand acres, Haldimand quintupled the grants for all ranks. Land, after all, seemed limitless and its purchase from Mississauga—the Indians who had gradually replaced the Hurons during the previous century—cost very little. Favouring officers reflected a proper military view of social hierarchy. Besides, it went without saying that Loyalist officers must have sacrificed more than their men. Indeed, Haldimand even apologized for ignoring rank when location tickets were issued by lot; the officers had assumed they were also entitled to pick the best land.

Among the Loyalist settlers were the Iroquois. Bitter in their sense of betrayal, the Six Nations followers of Joseph Brant accepted defeat and a new but narrower territory on the watershed of the Grand River or near the Bay of Quinte. Farther west, the Indian allies whom Britain had abandoned in 1783 refused to make peace with the Americans. Indeed, it seemed all too likely that their rage would extend to the British. Haldimand's solution was to keep the Union Jack flying from the western posts in hopes that somehow the Indians might negotiate a neutral state south of Lake Erie. A pretext was easy to find: the Americans had done nothing for the Loyalists — and of course they never would.

In its first years, the new British North America was very much a military society. Army officers distributed land, tools, seed, and the military rations that sustained settlers for the first three years. Army surgeons provided at least a few outposts with professional medical care. Governors and many of their officials were chosen from the ranks of half-pay British officers; their political and social theories, inevitably, reflected the ideology of an officers' mess. Loyalists came from every social class but colonels and captains proliferated in their ranks.

Yet the military image was superficial and transitional. Nothing in

British or colonial tradition placed great stock in the perspicacity of colonels. Neither civilian officials in London nor settlers in the New World deferred instinctively to the wisdom of Parr, Carleton, or Colonel John Graves Simcoe, Upper Canada's hyperactive lieutenant-governor from 1792 to 1796. The military dream of turning officers into landed gentry collapsed under the high price of labour. Five thousand acres could not make a colonel into a squire if he could not pay men to clear them or find tenants willing to rent farms. Privates fared better than captains in the humble, back-breaking life of frontier farming. In the "starving years" of 1788-89, in Upper Canada, and somewhat earlier in the New Brunswick settlements, the brutal truths of pioneer life prevailed. One casualty was the notion that the Loyalists formed an "army-in-waiting." In New Brunswick, Carleton found that most of them had sold their muskets for the bare necessities of food and seed.

In 1786, Sir Guy Carleton, now Lord Dorchester, returned to Quebec as Captain-General and Governor-in-Chief of British North America. It proved to be a frustrating conclusion to his career. Five years later the Constitutional Act, which separated Upper and Lower Canada and gave both of them representative institutions, showed how few of his ideas had prevailed. Soldiers would still be governors in British North America but henceforth it was their professional, not their political wisdom that was more needed. Section 46 of the Constitutional Act reiterated a section of the Declaratory Act of 1778: never again would Britain's Parliament tax a colony. While colonies were expected to keep up a militia, their defence would be financed by British taxpayers. By obvious corollary, British governments would be judges of what defence was necessary.

For at least a century after 1783, the military problem of British North America was clear enough: how could scattered, underpopulated, and ill-developed colonies be defended in any war with the United States? It was a problem rendered deceptively easy by the tiny strength of the American regular army, the lack of an effective United States Navy, and the chronic preference of Congress for a dubious but cheap "minuteman" tradition. British officers who had shared professional humiliation in the Revolutionary War were not deceived; given time, the Americans could create a powerful army. Given her worldwide commitments, it was by no means certain that Britain could respond.

Though Dorchester and his successors as governor-in-chief were responsible for all of British North America, there was little relationship between the defence of Canada and the security of Nova Scotia "and her dependencies." Each region held roughly half of the British regular garrison and faced its problems separately.

So long as the fortress-dockyard of Halifax was safe, the Royal Navy could safeguard Nova Scotia, Cape Breton, Prince Edward Island, and Newfoundland from all but an occasional raider. Local militia could do the rest. New Brunswick, with its unsettled border, caused more concern. The assumption that Loyalist settlers would provide a stout line of resistance faded with the demoralization of the St. John River settlements and the discovery that most of the Loyalist veterans had long since sold their muskets. Still, any serious invasion could be harassed from the sea.

At Halifax, successive garrison commanders complained of rotting blockhouses, a ramshackle citadel, and steady desertion from their understrength battalions. In 1794, George III's fourth son, Prince Edward of Kent, took command. An ardent soldier as well as something of a libertine, the royal prince summoned engineers, called out the militia, and put them to work lopping fifteen feet off Citadel Hill. He then erected some of the present massive structure, added an offshore fort and some Martello towers, and left Halifax stronger than Louisbourg had been and rather more useful.

The Canadas had no such fortune. A few thousand British troops were scattered from Quebec to Michilimackinac. Carleton's engineer, Captain Gother Mann, reported in 1788 that the frontier forts, without exception, were in a state of decay. The reason was simple. Their walls had been built with log cribs, filled with earth. They could take plenty of pounding by artillery but in a few seasons in the Canadian climate they had cracked and rotted. Understandably, Britain would spend nothing on posts it would have to hand to the United States. More puzzling was the neglect of Quebec. Every plan for the defence of Canada repeated the scenario of 1759 and 1775—the remnants of a British garrison surviving a winter siege to welcome a rescuing British fleet in the spring. Yet Quebec's landward defences remained as Murray had left them in 1760. As for Ile aux Noix, St. Jean, and Chambly, the frontier forts that had resisted invasion in 1759 and 1775, they were soon in ruins while Montreal's walls were demolished in 1801 because they had become a public hazard.

At least there were precedents for the defence of Lower Canada;

Upper Canada's plight seemed hopeless. Most probably it would be cut off by the now-traditional invasion up the Lake Champlain-Richelieu route. Certainly its scattered settlers and tiny garrisons could not resist a serious American assault. By the 1800s, Loyalists and their descendants numbered eighteen thousand but they had long since been outnumbered by so-called "late Loyalists" and Americans who promised no more than a mumbled allegiance in return for free land. Colonel Simcoe's patriotic illusions that British institutions would make monarchists of the immigrants had saddled Upper Canada with a population of questionable loyalty.

Yet even Upper Canada was not really hopeless. By attracting immigrants, Simcoe had done much to open up and develop his province while settlement south of the Great Lakes languished. The Revolutionary War had shown the enormous importance of controlling the lakes. Since Carleton Island was on the American side of the border, the British had to rebuild a naval base at Kingston. The Provincial Marine kept busy supplying the distant posts. Its officers might be superannuated and sometimes incompetent and the ships might fall far short of Royal Navy standards, but the Provincial Marine was the only armed fleet of consequence on the Great Lakes and the advantage was incalculable.

Upper Canada was the link to Britain's most worrisome problem, the western Indians. Without the arms and ammunition and gifts supplied by the Indian Department, could the Shawnee, Miami, and other native peoples have defended their territories and slaughtered the ill-disciplined American militia armies sent against them in 1790 and 1791? Or, from an American viewpoint, were the British responsible for inspiring the Indians and for providing the means for savage massacres? In 1794, two issues were settled. At the battle of Fallen Timbers, Anthony Wayne's well-disciplined troops destroyed Indian resistance and Chief Justice John Jay won British agreement to abandon the western posts. The most serious reason for Anglo-American conflict vanished. So did the British hope of an Indian buffer state. The Indians did not stop resisting, even after the Treaty of Greenville in 1795 forced them out of the Ohio country. In the handsome, eloquent Tecumseh and his scrawny mystical brother, Lolawauchika, the Indians found fresh leaders and renewed determination.

Jay's Treaty reflected European, not American, concerns. By 1793, Britain had been swept into a coalition of European monarchies bent on crushing the young French Revolution before it destroyed them. With barely a year's interval, Britain's war with the Republic, Directory, and Empire would last a generation, until 1814. As Americans debated whether their alliance with the old French monarchy extended to the new Republic, Britain sacrificed the western posts to avoid adding another enemy to her list.

The long war with France brought many dangers. In Quebec, seigneurs and Catholic clergy deplored the Revolution and Bonapartism and renounced their last, residual loyalty to France; how far did their attitude extend to habitants or to an emerging class of educated *Canadien* professionals? How better to cement the loyalty of leading *Canadiens* to Britain than by commissioning their sons as British officers in conscious imitation of the old *troupes de la marine?* Charles de Salaberry was among the first. The long war also called for stronger colonial garrisons than Britain could provide. The solution was a form of "colonial regular"—provincial corps like the Royal Nova Scotia Regiment, the King's New Brunswick Regiment, or in Upper Canada, Simcoe's special pride, the Queen's Rangers. Its members soldiered for two days a week, built roads or forts for two more days, and spent the rest of their time as pioneers. Such corps had limited military value. The two battalions of Royal Canadian Volunteers, recruited in Lower Canada, barely reached half-strength and inspecting officers complained that the ranks were filled by old and feeble men. In the wake of the Treaty of Amiens, the provincial corps were disbanded in 1802, only to be revived when war resumed. Regiments were formed of "fencibles," recruited in Newfoundland, Nova Scotia, New Brunswick, and Lower Canada, who agreed to serve only in North America though they were paid, trained, and wore the uniforms of British regulars. The New Brunswickers, in 1811, agreed to serve anywhere and became the 104th Regiment of Foot. The corps remained, like its fellow regiments, desperately short of men. A private's shilling a day (before "stoppages") was a poor wage in North America.

After the battle of Trafalgar in 1805, any serious naval threat from Napoleonic France vanished, but Britain remained almost alone in a struggle that pitted most of conquered Europe against her. Desperate circumstances justified desperate remedies. A Royal Navy blockade was backed by orders-in-council virtually banning neutral ships from European harbours. Americans, having acquired most of the shipping business of Europe, were most affected. In Washington, President Jefferson's response was an embargo on all trade with Europe, one of the most unpopular laws in American history and the cause of both disaffection and massive smuggling along the Canadian border. In 1807, a British frigate battered the American warship *Chesapeake* into surrender simply to remove four alleged deserters. This folly provoked instant war fever across the United States. In the crisis, a mere colonel, Isaac Brock, found himself in command in Canada. Responding to imminent war, Brock called out a fifth of Lower Canada's militia but not a man in Upper Canada. He dared not, as he confessed, reveal the fact that not a single musket was available to arm Upper Canada's defenders, even if they had been willing to serve.

Britain's response was a new governor, Lieutenant-General Sir James Craig, a battalion of aged veterans, and a shipment of arms for Upper Canada. Craig's appointment was unfortunate. As a soldier he did his best, reorganizing the militia, building Martello towers to strengthen Quebec, and developing the plans his successor would use in the coming war. As a governor, he was a tool of francophobe advisors like Chief Justice Jonathan Sewell. When *Canadiens* protested the steady influx of Americans as settlers in the Eastern Townships, Craig backed Sewell's view that it was "indispensably necessary to overwhelm and sink the Canadian population by English Protestants." When a popular editor, Pierre Bédard, tested the limits of British free speech, Craig threw him in jail. The *Canadiens*, complained Craig, boasted of their military prowess, "but they have not the most distant idea of being Soldiers or the slightest desire of becoming such. . . ." It was fortunate for Canada that by 1811, weary and close to death, Craig asked for relief. His successor, Sir George Prevost, had been lieutenant-governor of Nova Scotia since 1808. A veteran of the Revolutionary War, French-speaking and congenial, Prevost restored *Canadien* morale and allegiance within months. Bédard was released and made a judge. A new French-Canadian regiment, the Voltigeurs, was formed and De Salaberry was given command.

In Upper Canada, Isaac Brock not only commanded the troops but had replaced an absent governor. His military problems were more intractable than Prevost's. Of eleven thousand militia, he confessed, barely four thousand could be trusted to fight. His solution was ingenious. Even an assembly dominated by recent American arrivals let him train two thousand men who might either volunteer or be chosen by ballot. As "flank companies" of militia regiments, they would serve while the bulk of the colony's manpower remained safely and productively at work. The loyal wheat would be separated from the indifferent or hostile chaff. It was all Brock could do and it was little enough.

That spring, all along the American frontier the atmosphere crackled with the expectation of war. The official grievances might lie on the sea but it was the border states that wanted war. "Agrarian cupidity, not maritime rights," sneered John Randolph, "directs the war." His War Hawk enemies, sent to Congress in 1810, implicitly agreed. Seizing Canada would avenge British-inspired Indian wars and provide rich rewards in fertile real estate. Goodness knows, it would be easy. On June 18, President James Madison submitted to their pressure. War was declared.

War for Survival

The War of 1812 was not a struggle of equals. Seven and a half million Americans were at war with half a million neighbours. Americans might be deeply divided about the war but the United States had only one war to fight. To Britain, North America was an exasperating distraction from the mortal struggle against Napoleon. Lord Wellington's army in Spain had a higher priority for reinforcements. If the Royal Navy had had enough ships and men to fight the United States, would her frigates have been so undermanned and battered? In the Canadas, Prevost counted only fifty-two hundred regulars and fencibles, twelve hundred of them with Brock in Upper Canada. His strategy, inherited from Craig and Carleton, was as predictable as the American invasion plan. Surely the Americans would concentrate on Lower Canada. If they took Quebec before the ice left the St. Lawrence in 1813, no British army could ever reverse the loss of Canada.

Prevost was right about the American plans, wrong about their capacity to carry them out. Having demanded war, Congress promptly slashed the Treasury's estimates. Half of the twelve thousand men of the U.S. regular army were still raw recruits. Some of their officers were superb; many were political hacks. In western states, militia thronged to enlist for the few months needed for victory. For all the talk of maritime rights, New England states adamantly opposed the war. Within weeks, Sir John Coape Sherbrooke of Nova Scotia had established a *de facto* truce with them. New Brunswick promptly followed suit. Both provinces could now spare troops for the Canadas. Madison's military advisors were superannuated Revolutionary War generals, hurriedly recalled from political jobs. Major General Henry Dearborn promised that his Northern Department would simultaneously attack Niagara, Kingston, and Montreal. Brigadier-General William Hull had collected two thousand militia for his triumphal advance from Detroit. On July 12, he crossed into Canada, chased a few local militia away, and issued a bombastic proclamation: "The United States offers you peace, liberty and security. Your choice lies between these and war, slavery and destruction."

Thanks to North West Company agents in New York, Prevost had word of the war by June 24. It flashed west so swiftly that a Provincial Marine warship captured Hull's despatches before he or his army knew for certain that hostilities had begun. Prevost's small professional army deployed in front of Montreal while Dearborn was haranguing his first few drafts of militia. Two regiments, the 41st and 49th, remained in Canada with the battalions that came to replace them. Prevost sent both back to Brock in Upper Canada.*

He needed them. Hull's bravado was well-founded. Across Upper Canada, local officials curried favour with American sympathisers. Iroquois on the Grand River Reserve, disillusioned by their allies, proclaimed neutrality. Instead of leading a campaign, Brock was compelled, as administrator of the province, to summon the legislative assembly and waste vital weeks while a majority solemnly refused him any of the powers or resources he needed. On August 3, when the politicians finally went home, Brock promptly proclaimed martial law on the authority of his king's commission and set off for war.

He had some good news. On July 17, Captain Charles Roberts at Fort St. Joseph took his tiny garrison, and some Nor'westers and Indians and terrified the Americans at Michilimackinac into surrender. The victory brought Brock, 50 regulars and 250 militia to Amherstburg. There he found Britain's most valuable ally of the war. On the whole, western Indians wanted British victory because Americans represented the juggernaut of settlement, but it was not their war. Not even the costly generosity of the Indian Department could always buy their

---

*British battalions had ten companies; a grenadier company of the tallest men took the right of the line; a light infantry company of the most active men took the left. These were the elite units of the battalion. Sometimes they were removed to form special battalions.

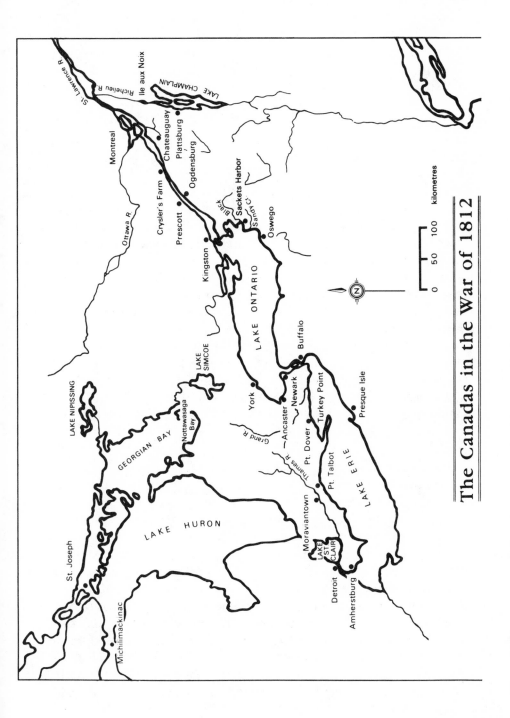

The Canadas in the War of 1812

St. Lawrence R.

Richelieu R.

Ile aux Noix

LAKE CHAMPLAIN

Montreal

Chateauguay

Plattsburg

Ogdensburg

Ottawa R.

Crysler's Farm

Prescott

Black

Sackets Harbor

Sandy Cr.

Oswego

Kingston

LAKE ONTARIO

LAKE NIPISSING

LAKE SIMCOE

Buffalo

York

Newark

Nottawasaga Bay

GEORGIAN BAY

Ancaster

Grand R.

Pt. Dover

Turkey Point

Presque Isle

Pt. Talbot

Thames R.

LAKE ERIE

St. Joseph

Moraviantown

LAKE HURON

LAKE ST. CLAIR

Detroit

Amherstburg

Michilimackinac

kilometres

0   50   100

services. Tecumseh felt differently. A year before, Governor William Henry Harrison had led his militia into Indian territory. At Tippecanoe he had enticed Tecumseh's brother into a disastrous battle. Then Harrison had scornfully invited Tecumseh to take his grievances to Washington. Instead, Tecumseh went to Amherstburg. From the outset of war, he and a few hundred followers had harassed Hull's supply columns and isolated Detroit. At once Brock and Tecumseh found a bond. Though Brock's war experience was slight, both men were instinctive, aggressive fighters.

In a week, both proved it. By now, Hull had forgotten bravado and clustered his army behind the walls of Detroit. Indians intercepted most of his appeals for help. On August 16, Brock laid siege to the town but it was Tecumseh's five hundred warriors who terrified Hull into surrender. More than two thousand American troops gratefully trusted their lives to Brock's few regulars. American weapons armed the militia of Upper Canada. The luckless Hull was traded back, court-martialed, and sentenced to be shot. Only his service in the revolution thirty years earlier saved him.

News of Detroit swept Upper Canada. Brock felt the change at the Grand River. The Mohawks were now ready to fight. Local magistrates remembered their allegiance. Militia began appearing for service. Incorporated battalions, created from flank companies, after a summer's training began to look like soldiers. They were needed. Playing for time, Prevost had accepted Dearborn's offer of a ceasefire on August 9. The respite allowed another battalion to head for Upper Canada but, when Madison cancelled the agreement on September 4, Prevost was clear: there would be no more help. It was better to abandon Detroit than weaken Lower Canada.

Niagara was now the crucial frontier. All summer, General Stephen Van Rensselaer had dithered and delayed as his army grew to sixty-three hundred. At last, on the night of October 13, Americans stormed ashore at the village of Queenston. Woken by the firing, Brock galloped to the scene, rallied defenders, and led them up the hill to recapture a vital battery. A musket-ball killed him instantly. The troops reeled. More troops arrived, among them a company of black militia. Resistance stiffened. Major-General Roger Sheaffe, Brock's American-born deputy, sent reinforcements to the right, to shoot down the invaders from the top of the escarpment. Suddenly, the battle ended. A thousand exhausted U.S. regulars gave up. Across the river, three thousand

New York militia had refused to move. No law, they told Van Rensselaer, could make them fight outside their state.

Van Rensselaer made two more bungled attempts to cross the river and gave up. On November 23, Dearborn finally advanced on Montreal only to find that his New Yorkers also refused to cross the border. Instead of easy conquest of Canada, the United States had lost Michigan. Only a handful of brilliant victories over British frigates by the despised U.S. Navy gave Americans any cause to rejoice. Madison fired his war secretary and gave Governor Harrison command in the west, but better generals were hard to find.

The British also needed time and leadership. No one had really expected the war to last a second year. Brock's victories made it inconceivable to abandon Upper Canada. Perhaps he would have known what to do but his successors, General Sheaffe as administrator and commander and, in the west, a mercurial Welshman, Colonel Henry Procter, were distinctly lesser men.

Not even genius would have been able to solve the problems of waging war in a remote, roadless province. It was a quartermaster's nightmare. Upper Canada produced almost nothing for its own defence. Everything, from bullets to boots, had to be lugged along a supply line strung perilously from Great Britain to Amherstburg. Most of the food supply came from the United States, smuggled by New England and New York farmers who preferred British gold to penniless patriotism. Everything else had to cross the Atlantic and come up a lake and river system that was frozen for six months and open to American attack for the rest of the year. Six companies of the 104th Regiment marched overland from Fredericton to Quebec but the experiment was not repeated. A hundred miles of the St. Lawrence was shared with the United States. Fortunately, local New Yorkers took an attack by Glengarry Fencibles on Ogdensburg in February in a friendly spirit. The American troops departed and both smuggling and river traffic resumed without serious interruption during the rest of the war.

The Great Lakes posed a more serious problem. Brock's success in 1812 owed much to the Provincial Marine, the much-maligned service that nonetheless dominated both lower lakes and delivered troops and supplies with fair fidelity. By the year's end, the situation had changed. At Sackets Harbor, Commodore Isaac Chauncey presided over a furious building race. With most American ports tightly blockaded, he had his choice of seamen, shipwrights, and stores. On Lake

Erie, a gallant American boarding party burned the brig *Detroit*, seized an armed schooner, and ended the Provincial Marine monopoly. On November 10, Chauncey was strong enough with seven little ships to chase the Provincial Marine's pride, the *Royal George*, into Kingston Harbour. It did not stir for the rest of the season.

The Admiralty brusquely took charge, dismissed the colonial officers, and sent Captain Sir James Yeo and five hundred officers and seamen to regain command of the lakes. The difficulties were incredible. Every item in a ship of war, from a binnacle to a bowsprit, had to be wheedled from a British dockyard, shipped across the Atlantic, and conveyed bodily up five hundred miles of river and rapids or hauled over hopeless roads. What little Yeo could spare was forwarded to the one-armed Lieutenant Robert Barclay at Amherstburg.

The significance of commanding Lake Ontario was soon apparent. On April 26, Chauncey's squadron bypassed Kingston and headed for York. Seventeen hundred American troops poured ashore, and the local garrison, under Sheaffe's command, had barely time to burn Chauncey's true target, a nearly finished ship, before it was scattered. In revenge for losing General Zebulon Pike and a hundred men when a powder magazine exploded, the Americans burned the assembly buildings, ransacked churches, and departed with such trophies as the Speaker's wig and the parliamentary mace. Sheaffe, who led the surviving troops to Kingston, was made the scapegoat for the humiliation. On the next occasion that Chauncey left port, Prevost joined Yeo for a sudden attack on Sackets Harbor. A sudden offshore wind foiled the plan and by the time troops landed, a tough New York militia general, Jacob "Smuggler" Brown, drove them off with losses.

Meanwhile, Chauncey's squadron was off Fort George on the British side of the Niagara River on May 25, helping American soldiers force their way ashore. Henry Dearborn was the nominal commander but the arrangements were controlled by a skilled young American professional who had survived the battle at Queenston. Like most officers, Winfield Scott had quickly been exchanged. Fort George was his revenge. It was not complete. With half the defenders dead or wounded, Brigadier-General Henry Vincent pulled out the survivors, abandoned the peninsula, and regrouped his army at Burlington Heights. It made no sense to stay and be captured. The wisdom was soon evident. Two of Dearborn's brigades, after a week's rest, started in pursuit. On June 5, the weary marchers pitched camp at Stoney

Creek. Suddenly, in a pell-mell chaotic night attack, the British were on them. By dawn, both American brigadiers were prisoners and the shaken remnant marched gloomily back to Fort George. Vincent cautiously followed behind a screen of Mohawks, Caughnawagas, and a few western Indians. He could not have done so if Yeo's squadron had not appeared, bringing supplies and persuading the cautious Chauncey to keep his distance.

After Stoney Creek, the Niagara Peninsula had a quiet summer. One modest episode has become a Canadian legend. On June 24, an American regiment, sent on a raid from Fort George, ran into an ambush of Caughnawagas and Mohawks and a single company of the 49th Regiment commanded by an Irish ex-ranker, Lieutenant James Fitzgibbon. To him they gratefully surrendered. Fitzgibbon's own modest account fits the facts: ". . . the only share I claim is taking advantage of a favourable moment to offer them protection from the tomahawk and the scalping knife." The terror of Indians, Brock's most powerful ally in the West, had spread east. Legend and her own claims insisted that word of the raid had reached Fitzgibbon when a militiaman's valiant wife, Laura Secord, slipped past American sentries. It may well have happened, though the cow Secord supposedly drove along her route is apocryphal and Iroquois scouts had their own excellent warning systems.

Good news from Niagara was not matched from the west. Procter did his best. By January, Governor Harrison had collected sixty-three hundred regulars and frontier militia and headed for Detroit. Procter gathered regulars, militia, and Indians, crossed the river, and wiped out the American advance guard of nine hundred men at Rivière Raisin. It was frontier war at its cruelest, with atrocity stories enough to disgust the British, terrify American soldiers, and enrage American opinion. Procter kept trying to imitate Brock's style but he was now both dependent on the Indians and unable to supply them. The 1812 harvest had been a failure. A dry summer left water-powered flour mills immobilized. Rations for his ravenous allies ran out. Instead of attacking Harrison's supply depot at Sandusky, Indians insisted on a long and futile expedition to take Fort Meigs on the Maumee. Another murderous victory over an American relief expedition was no compensation for the expedition's lack of success. An attack on Fort Stephenson was a complete failure.

Procter was at the end of his tether, pleading vainly for regulars, utterly disgusted with his allies, and helpless from lack of supplies. His frustration found a target in Barclay. At Put-in Bay, across the lake, Commander Oliver Perry was producing a fleet. If Barclay had any courage, Procter declared he would forget his excuses and sink the enemy. A major-general was a powerful critic for a mere naval lieutenant. After arming his rebuilt *Detroit* with a mixture of guns from Fort Malden, and adding soldiers and militia to his handful of trained seamen, poor Barclay set out to fight Perry. A favourable wind took him to Put-in Bay. Unexpectedly, it then shifted. Perry now controlled the action and his heavier guns could batter Barclay's improvised warships. By dusk on September 10, every British ship had surrendered. Barclay, his remaining arm shattered, was a helpless prisoner.

Procter had left himself in a trap. To Tecumseh's dismay, the British abandoned Detroit and Fort Malden. The militia disbanded but Tecumseh had no choice but to follow Procter's 877 remaining soldiers. Harrison, with 3,500 men mounted and on foot, pursued. Near Moraviantown, on October 5, he caught the British rearguard. The weary and demoralized redcoats, mostly of the 41st Regiment, turned to fight. Harrison's Kentucky horsemen, barely visible, charged through the trees. For once, the British line dissolved. Hundreds of redcoats died or surrendered. On the flank, Tecumseh and a few followers fought and died. Procter and his family had hardly stopped. They and about 240 survivors eventually straggled into the camp at Burlington Heights.

At Kingston, Sheaffe's successor, Major-General George de Rottenberg, now feared that Upper Canada must be abandoned. Worse still, on October 17, an American army of eight thousand men had finally sealed the St. Lawrence while five thousand more were moving north on Montreal. The battle for Canada's survival was nearly over.

Struggle for a Stalemate

To the defenders of Upper Canada, October 1813 was the time of despair they might well have experienced a year before. Loss of Lake Erie imperilled the entire west. Only by a painful overland journey from York to the mouth of the Nottawasaga River could Michilimackinac be sustained, but for how long? On September 28, Chauncey's heavier guns drove Yeo's squadron to shelter in Burlington Bay. A week later, the Americans snapped up six of seven schooners carrying troops and casualties to York. Meanwhile, a powerful American army had gathered at Sackets Harbor and another waited at Plattsburg on Lake Champlain, ready for the stroke British strategists had long been dreading: the coordinated attack on Montreal.

From Washington, of course, the war looked very different. The worst news came from Europe. A year before, in the summer of 1812, Napoleon had been at the height of his power. Seizing a British colony looked easy enough when Britain herself was wrestling with a world conqueror. The intervening year had seen Napoleon invade Russia and return with only the ghostly wreckage of his *Grande Armée*. Suddenly, most of Europe was in arms against him. In Spain, Wellington's army had suffered bitter set-backs in 1812; now it was poised to invade France itself. The unthinkable had happened. Napoleon would be beaten. The United States might face Britain's naval and military might alone.

Moreover, American commanders continued to frustrate the president and his secretary of war, John Armstrong. Far from occupying western Canada, General Harrison sent his militiamen home to Kentucky with their grisly trophies and came east to bask in glory. Instead of attacking Kingston, the one stroke that would have ended British resistance in Upper Canada, Dearborn and Chauncey had ignored Armstrong's views and wasted the summer by raiding York and skirmishing on the Niagara Peninsula. At last Dearborn received a long-overdue dismissal but his successor in command of the 9th Military District was Major-General James Wilkinson, a veteran with a reputation as a nimble scoundrel and a record, as history would show, as a traitor. True to form, the aging Wilkinson took most of the summer to report to Sackets Harbor, and then wasted a further couple of months being sick and visiting Niagara. Next, he twisted Armstrong's orders into a mandate to advance on Montreal instead of Kingston. By typical coincidence, the commander at Plattsburg, Major General Wade Hampton, was a sworn personal and political foe of Wilkinson.

The result was predictable. After one tentative advance (halted because a long drought had left no water for his horses), Hampton switched fronts to advance up the Châteauguay River. By now, with a meagre harvest collected, Prevost called out eight thousand *Canadien* militia. Some of them, with Voltigeurs and other fencibles commanded by Colonel de Salaberry, met Hampton's army of four thousand on October 25. Next day, after an American flank attack had floundered all night in dense bush, a sharp little action was enough to persuade Hampton to go home. The usual "council of war" gave him authority.

Wilkinson set out more bravely, with fourteen regiments of infantry, two of dragoons and three of artillery, loaded into a massive flotilla of barges and flatboats. Pausing for a week because of storms, the eight thousand Americans continued down the St. Lawrence, pursued by a tiny force of nine hundred British regulars under Colonel John Morrison of the 89th Regiment. On November 11, Wilkinson sent a brigade of American regulars to rid himself of the British. At Crysler's Farm, Morrison's little force held off a piecemeal American attack and then chased the dazed survivors away. That was enough for Wilkinson. He abandoned the campaign, crossed the river to New York state, and went into winter quarters.

Collecting his army had denuded the Niagara frontier of all but New York militia. In early December, most of them wound up their enlistment and went home, not waiting for their replacements. The wretched American commander at Fort George wisely abandoned his post on December 10; less wisely he accepted an offer from the Canadian renegade, Joseph Willcocks, to burn the town of Newark (now Niagara-on-the-Lake) and most of Queenston. The misery of civilians, left homeless on a bitter, snowy night, was soon avenged. The latest administrator of Upper Canada, Lieutenant-General Gordon Drummond, was forty-one, Quebec-born, with most of Brock's dash though not all his luck. On December 16, he was on the scene. Three nights later, British troops crossed the river, burst into Fort Niagara, and bayoneted some of the American defenders in their beds. The nearby village of Lewiston was burned. On December 29, regulars and militia put the torch to Black Rock and Buffalo at the other end of the Niagara River. This was the "prompt and signal vengeance" that Drummond vowed "for every fresh departure by the Enemy, from that system of warfare which ought alone to subsist between enlightened and civilized nations."

The little string of victories restored morale among Canadians and generals. At Kingston, winter allowed shipwrights to hurry completion of two powerful new frigates, the *Prince Regent* and *Princess Charlotte*, that would surely give Yeo renewed dominance on Lake Ontario. A few more regiments and 216 badly needed sailors and marines came overland from New Brunswick that winter and more than 1,600 Royal Marines reached Quebec just before freeze-up. They were all the more desperately needed because too many of Prevost's 15,000 regulars and fencibles were weary and demoralized after two years of long marches, short rations, and heavy casualties. Few had any enthusiasm for Canadian conditions. Many suffered from the chronic swamp fever that a later generation would diagnose as malaria. Prevost's troops had performed incredible feats against a brave but ill-led enemy; commanders and the public were starting to take the incredible for granted.

The Americans had absorbed some painful lessons of warfare. The age of obese, elderly amateurs was ending; a tough new breed of generals like Winfield Scott and Jacob Brown had emerged. Their model was their most formidable enemy; the disciplined British redcoat. Save that they wore grey, American regular infantry, in their tall shakos and white crossbelts, were becoming indistinguishable from the British in appearance and, more important, in drill and firepower on the battlefield. As for their fleet, no one could make Chauncey bold, but his builders were the best an ingenious nation could produce. Yeo's frigates might be first in the water but the USS *Superior* would give the Americans a 62-gun warship that could blast anything else out of the lake. All winter, guns, spars, even a huge anchor cable were collected at Oswego to be shifted to Sackets Harbor when the lake was open.

Yeo knew the danger. That winter he pleaded with Prevost for a combined attack on Sackets Harbor. Ever cautious, even timid as he sensed the advantage swinging to the British side, Prevost refused. To collect enough troops would weaken Niagara and Kingston. Perhaps Prevost remembered his own failure the year before. Instead, Drummond and Yeo had to be satisfied with an attack on Oswego. On May 6, British troops landed, chased off the garrison, and loaded badly needed naval stores for Kingston. If they had known, they might easily have pushed a few miles inland to capture the 32-pounder guns intended for the *Superior*. Instead, Yeo moved off to blockade Sackets Harbor, hoping to intercept them.

Two hundred New York farmers hoisted the *Superior*'s anchor cable on their shoulders and lugged it overland. Next, one of Chauncey's able assistants loaded the guns on bateaux, assembled a powerful escort of troops and Oneida Indians, and set off down the lake shore. At Sandy Creek, he took shelter. American prisoners betrayed the secret and a force of British sailors and marines was sent in hot pursuit. In true Royal Navy style, Commander Stephen Popham boldly led his men into the creek only to be trapped in an ambush. After a quarter of his men were killed or wounded, Popham surrendered. It was a disaster Yeo could not afford. The guns reached Chauncey and Popham's skilled seamen could not be replaced. On June 6, Yeo sadly returned to Kingston to preserve his fleet and watch over the building of the biggest ship ever, the *St. Lawrence*, whose bulk and 112 guns would make her bigger than Nelson's *Victory*. Completing her, of course, would strain British supply lines and naval stores to breaking point.

In Europe, that spring, France had collapsed. On March 31, allied armies entered Paris. At Toulouse on April 10, Wellington won his last battle on French soil; a day later, Napoleon abdicated. Already the Duke had turned his mind to North America, a continent he had never seen but whose military hazards he recognized: "In such countries as America," he had written to Lord Bathurst, the Secretary for War and Colonies, "very extensive, thinly peopled, and producing but little food in proportion to their extent, military operations by large bodies are impracticable, unless the party carrying them on has the uninterrupted use of a navigable river, or very extensive means of land transport, which such a country can rarely supply." By June 3, Bathurst sent new directions to Prevost, though it was mid-July before they arrived.

As early as December 30, 1813, partly to keep the Russian Tsar from insisting on being arbitrator, the British government had invited President Madison to discuss peace. The worried president persuaded Congress to agree and the American delegation, including Henry Clay, had been approved. Prevost would even have negotiated a truce and a full exchange of prisoners but this time it was Whitehall that refused. Bathurst's instructions confirmed the new British optimism. Canada, of course, must be safeguarded and its frontier, if possible, made more secure by occupying Fort Niagara, Detroit, the Michigan territory, and anything else available. Yet the dread memory of Saratoga persisted. Prevost might go south to Lake Champlain, "always, however, taking care not to expose His Majesty's Forces to being cut off by too extended a line of advance." To help, fifteen thousand of Wellington's troops and four of his best brigade commanders were already on their way.

That was no help to Drummond. Suddenly the Americans were on the move, seemingly unimpressed by European events. With Yeo preserving his fleet in Kingston, American ships safely moved Wilkinson's army, now commanded by "Smuggler" Brown, back to Niagara. Command of Lake Erie let American militia, dragoons, and Canadian renegades roam the Canadian side, pillaging, burning, and creating deep hatreds but only rarely being intercepted and driven off by local militia or patrols of British cavalry and troops. More important for the campaign, American ships could embark Brown's army, land it opposite Fort Erie, and catch Drummond and his local commander, Major-General Phineas Riall, between two fires.

The British were not alarmed; they had met this kind of threat before. With fifteen hundred regulars, two hundred militia, and three hundred Indians, Riall headed south and, on July 5, met Winfield Scott's brigade at Chippewa. Though he was almost caught drinking coffee at a farmhouse, Scott got away on foot, formed his troops, and waited silently as Riall sent his men forward in a precipitate attack. The British got a devastating surprise. Far from fleeing, Scott's men opened fire and manoeuvred like the professionals they had become. Out of 1500 men, Riall lost over 500 dead and wounded; Scott, with a slightly smaller force, lost 270. Riall withdrew and Brown advanced to besiege both Fort George and Fort Niagara, confident that Chauncey would soon join him. In fact, the American fleet did not appear but Drummond did, with all the British troops he could collect. Brown withdrew and then, worried about his supplies, marched back again. Late on the afternoon of July 25, the two armies clashed at Lundy's Lane, south of Queenston.

It was a soldiers' battle, fought hand to hand late into the night. The British battalions held their ground; brigade after brigade of Americans pushed forward, hidden by dense smoke and then twilight. On both sides, guns were pushed into the front line until they were muzzle to muzzle. British battalions gave ground; Drummond drove them back. Riall was wounded and then captured when his stretcher-bearers blundered into American lines. Brown and all but one of his generals were wounded. So was Drummond. Finally, the Americans had no more reserves. A single British regiment, arriving late, was thrown into the fight. At midnight, the exhausted Americans fell back. Drummond forced his men to advance a mile and there the worn-out survivors slept. Next day, the exhausted Americans withdrew to Fort Erie.

If he had pursued the Americans, Drummond might have done fatal damage to the best American army. It was utterly beyond his strength or that of his men. By August 3, when the British reached Fort Erie, it had been rebuilt and garrisoned. By now, American dominance of Lake Ontario left Drummond with an acute supply shortage. Steady driving rain turned roads into quagmires and converted the land around Fort Erie into a dreary malarial swamp. British morale plummeted. An attack on August 15 was an utter failure. One veteran regiment, De

Watteville's, refused to fight. Others were little better. More than nine hundred British, including some of the ablest of Drummond's officers, were killed, wounded, or captured. Finally, Drummond withdrew to Chippewa but the Americans, too, were demoralized. By late October, they had abandoned Fort Erie. Completed at last, the *St. Lawrence* made a single voyage escorting supplies and reinforcements to Niagara. It was now Chauncey's turn to take shelter and to wait for his own answer — two monstrous battleships, each bigger than Yeo's new flagship. Surely that was a challenge the British could never match.

Very few of Wellington's veterans had come to Upper Canada. Prevost had sent some of his own troops on a weary march around Lake Ontario and it was the newly arrived veterans who would move south to fulfil one of Bathurst's orders: destruction of the American naval establishment on Lake Champlain. So far, the U.S. ships had done little damage: a single raid on Ile aux Noix had ended, thanks to alert *Canadien* militia, in the capture of two American schooners. The American naval commander, Thomas MacDonough, had mustered four ships; the British had three, with a fourth racing to completion. Prevost, impatient for once, refused to wait. On August 31, he set out with 10,351 men, most of them resentful at being switched to the wilderness of North America and all of them dubious about Prevost and the colonials on his staff. Captain George Downie, freshly arrived to command the British squadron, had a fine fighting record but Prevost repeated Procter's folly by alternately bullying and shaming a junior officer into battle. On September 11, with carpenters still trying to finish his only real warship, Downie sailed into action only to be killed as his little fleet was battered into submission. MacDonough earned his victory; Downie had not deserved defeat. Ashore, Prevost's men could have pushed into Plattsburg and won at least a symbolic victory. Instead, Prevost called them back and the humiliated veterans plodded back to Canada through days of driving rain. "I had to determine," Prevost explained, "whether I should consider my own Fame by gratifying the Ardour of the Troops in persevering in the attack, or consult the more substantial interests of my Country by withdrawing the Army which was yet uncrippled for the security of these Provinces." Very few of his resentful subordinates agreed with his choice.

News of Plattsburg was all the more depressing because of victories everywhere else. From the far west came word that Nor'Westers and a few troops had taken Prairie du Chien on the Mississippi in remote

Wisconsin. On August 4, the little garrison of Michilimackinac sallied out and drove off a powerful American attack from Detroit. The Americans had brief revenge when they drove ashore and sank the schooner *Nancy* at Nottawasaga, but the enterprising crew borrowed canoes and captured first one and then a second American armed schooner. For what it was worth, the Royal Navy now commanded Lake Huron.

Far more dramatic events were occurring along the Atlantic seaboard. A new, more aggressive naval commander, Sir Alexander Cochrane, promptly cancelled trading licences with Americans: "I have it much at heart to give them a complete drubbing before peace is made," he reported to Lord Bathurst. Sir John Sherbrooke also ended Nova Scotia's truce. On July 11, British troops occupied Eastport, Maine, and in early August, a British squadron destroyed an American gunboat flotilla and entered Chesapeake Bay. On August 19, Major-General Robert Ross landed four thousand British troops and set off for Washington. His opponent, Brigadier-General William Winder, was one of the Americans captured at Stoney Creek. At Blandensburg, the British won an easy victory over Winder's five thousand militia and a tougher fight with a contingent of seamen. To loud international disapproval, the British burned or ransacked Washington's public buildings and headed back to their ships. Belatedly, the British explained that it was retribution for the sack of York in 1813. Whatever the world thought, such Canadian patriots as Archdeacon John Strachan entirely approved. The British met more formidable resistance at Baltimore. General Ross was killed and American shore batteries kept British warships at a distance as well as providing enough fireworks to inspire Francis Scott Key's patriotic poem and eventual national anthem.

From Baltimore, the British expedition sailed north to Halifax to learn that Sherbrooke had managed a virtually bloodless invasion of Maine. From the Passamaquoddy to the Penobscot rivers, the British had achieved absolute control at a cost of one man dead. Both a military governor and a customs collector were appointed at Castine and the latter's revenues from the vigorous resumption of trade would later help to endow Dalhousie University in Halifax.

Throughout the late summer and fall, peace negotiations had proceeded at the Belgian city of Ghent. Five extremely able American commissioners faced three admittedly mediocre British representatives. That might hardly have mattered if only events in North America had been considered. They were not. Britain was now utterly weary of war. Merchants were indignant that their ships still fell victim to American privateers when, from their perception, the real war had ended with the fall of Napoleon. Worst of all, Europe itself seemed to be drifting back to war as allies quarrelled and Bonapartists surfaced in France. The British government turned, as it would again, to the Duke of Wellington. His advice was conclusive. The war had gone better in North America than anyone had a right to expect. Without controlling all the lakes, including Erie, no real gains could be made. The only sensible basis of settlement, British ministers concluded, was a *status quo ante*. On Christmas Eve, the delegations assembled at Ghent, abandoned their ambitions, and signed the treaty.

It was just as well. Three weeks later, a major British raid on New Orleans was driven off with the loss of a quarter of the eight thousand British and black troops involved. Both sides had had enough.

British Garrisons

Most Canadians thought a *status quo* peace was a poor return for three years of invasion, destruction, and death. Prevost, recalled in disgrace for the unfortunate Plattsburg campaign, also became a scapegoat for Canadian frustrations. The War of 1812 was reshaped to suit local mythology, with Châteauguay and Queenston reflecting the French-English duality and the American-born Laura Secord symbolizing heroic Canadian womanhood. In Upper Canada, those who had supported Brock in 1812, from York's Archdeacon John Strachan to the autocratic Thomas Talbot of the Lake Erie settlements, felt entitled to monopolize provincial leadership to the exclusion of both older "American" settlers and untried newcomers. Throughout British North America, the war made it easier to label critics as disloyal.

In fact, Prevost's caution had served Canada well and the war had been good to most British North Americans. Even in Upper Canada, traces of destruction were hard to find within months of the peace. Maimed veterans, surviving on meagre pensions and charity from the Patriotic Fund, were easily forgotten. Farmers and merchants soon mourned the years when British agents bought anything they could provide and paid in army bills faithfully redeemed at par. Members of disbanded regiments, located where strategy, not agricultural science, dictated, found pioneering hard. In 1820, Robert Gourlay reported that not one in fifty of the soldiers settled in Lanark County had remained. The fault lay less with character, as the scornful Gourlay alleged, than with rocky soil. Excluded from Upper Canada by new alien laws and wartime memories, American settlers flooded into Ohio and northern New York. Travellers contrasted the vigour and prosperity of the post-war United States with the relative poverty and stagnation of the Canadas. Resentment at the contrast fed the angry political controversies that would burst into rebellion in 1837.

In the meantime, both sides rapidly disarmed. A shrunken American army returned to the Indian wars. At Sackets Harbor, workmen roofed over the hulks of Chauncey's unfinished battleships; at Kingston, the Royal Navy also built a storehouse or "stone frigate" to hold material salvaged from its rotting warships. The British garrison in North America fell by 1819 to under seven thousand troops. Elaborate plans to reform the militia were forgotten. A force of thousands of men, with scores of battalions, was formidable only on paper, though it did allow hosts of eminent but unmilitary citizens to bear the title of colonel or captain. The annual muster on the king's birthday provided communities with a welcome festival, complete with political speeches, scraps of old uniforms, and barrels of bad whiskey.

Yet, for half a century, war with the United States was a regular and recurrent possibility. Defence of the Canadas in such a war was the most intractable military problem in the British Empire. Canadians might believe that the war was halted on the verge of easy triumphs; British soldiers and sailors knew otherwise. If Chauncey's huge battleships had been launched, they would have controlled Lake Ontario. At Chippewa and Lundy's Lane, Winfield Scott had shown that American soldiers could match British redcoats. Even if the British had held on to all of the land it had in Maine or Michigan, Americans would not have rested until the territory was regained. No sober planner could count again on the stunning ineptitude with which Americans had managed the war and, with each year of peace, the United States grew stronger.

Faced with peacetime retrenchment, the Royal Navy made some tough choices. "It is certainly a fine country," Rear Admiral Sir David Milne wrote of Upper Canada, "but too distant for us to defend against so powerful a neighbour." Disasters on Lake Erie and Lake Champlain and the losing struggle to sustain Yeo's squadron were memories the Royal Navy was content to exercise. In the spring of 1817, Sir Charles Bagot and Richard Rush of the U.S. State Department initialled an agreement limiting each side to a single ship (with a single gun) on Lake

Champlain and the lower lakes and two on the upper lakes. By 1830, the British abandoned any pretence of maintaining their rotting warships; in 1834 the Kingston dockyard was closed. The Rush-Bagot Agreement might later be glorified as a symbol of peace; in practice, it conceded American control of the lakes in any future war.

Could Canada be defended without controlling the lakes? The Duke of Wellington insisted that adequate fortifications and a vast network of canals based on Upper Canada's rivers and lakes could make a defensive victory possible, at an estimated cost of £1,646,218 (about a fifteenth of Britain's annual public revenue). The Duke's prestige and the real possibility of war persuaded the British government to accept much of the programme. In the 1820s, the enormous citadels which still dominate Halifax and Quebec were finally begun. In Ile aux Noix, Fort Lennox replaced a rotting structure. While a small government subsidy for the Lachine Canal and an even tinier one for the Welland Canal persuaded commercial promoters to improve navigation, military efforts were reserved for improvements on the Ottawa River and the 200 kilometre Rideau Canal, linking Ottawa with Kingston. In 1832, construction began on the first of six huge forts* designed to make Kingston impregnable.

Disillusionment began with dramatic cost overruns. Fort Lennox, promised "for the trifling sum" of £19,000, cost £57,688. Quebec defences, estimated at £70,000, had devoured £236,000 by their completion in 1831. On the Rideau, Lieutenant-Colonel John By overcame incredible difficulties, including the death of five hundred workers from malaria in a single summer, but a canal system that was expected to cost £169,000 was delivered for £1,134,000. By's career was ruined and the prestige of the Board of Ordnance never recovered. Kingston's defences stopped with a single redoubt, Fort Henry. The Duke's scheme to link the Ottawa with Georgian Bay, Lake Simcoe, and the Bay of Quinte survived in the corridors of Whitehall only as a ghostly reminder of the stupendous extravagance of Canadian defence. Wellington, of course, never crossed the Atlantic.

As commander-in-chief, the Duke of Wellington contrived to hide most of Britain's peacetime army in India and the colonies. The North

---

*Fort Henry, one of Kingston's modern tourist attractions, was only one of six "casemated redoubts" intended to provide all-round defence. If all had been built, tourist guides might not preserve the myth that the fort faces the wrong way.

American garrison roughly matched the strength of the U.S. regular army. Scattered from Halifax to Fort Malden, British army officers found a North American posting healthy but dull. Hunting and amateur theatricals were a thin substitute for the military opportunities of India or the Cape Colony. Flirting could lead an officer into an imprudent marriage. A few talented soldiers recorded the landscape in watercolours or reflected a fascination with natural science. Others escaped boredom through alcohol or long periods of leave. Men in the ranks served out a twenty-one-year enlistment in conditions that attracted only the desperate or the dissolute. Marriage, for example, was permitted only a tiny quota of men. Desertion was the main attraction of a North American posting: the United States was rarely far away.

Desertion was one perennial problem for British garrisons; the amount of aid to the civil power that they were expected to give was another. Why pay police or firemen when any two local magistrates could call out the troops? Once handed a signed requisition, an officer had little recourse. He and his men might face furious Orange and Catholic rioters, striking navvies on a canal site, or a hired election mob, recruited to overawe timid voters. Whatever happened, the troops took the abuse. When blood was spilled in an 1832 election riot in Montreal, British officers were jailed on the charge of murder. *Patriote* orators improved the occasion with suggestions that the bloodthirsty redcoats had deliberately slaughtered innocent *Canadiens*.

In both Canadas, neither British garrisons nor the militia escaped the tensions which led to armed rebellion in 1837. When historians study the pre-1837 records of the sedentary militia battalions, they will find one of the best sources for the study of local struggles between Reformers and Tories, *Patriotes* and *bureaucrates*. One of the preliminaries of the struggle was the systematic stripping of militia commissions from allegedly "disloyal" political opponents.

In turn, both the followers of William Lyon Mackenzie in Upper Canada and the *Patriote* supporters of Louis-Joseph Papineau urged an American-style republic which could easily lead to annexation by the United States. One demand was election of militia officers. Opponents of the rebellions, from Catholic bishops to recent British immigrants, feared that Papineau and Mackenzie would reverse the outcome of the War of 1812.

In Lower Canada, the *Patriotes* faced a tough opponent. Sir John Colborne, former lieutenant-governor of Upper Canada and one of

Wellington's colonels, commanded only eight weak battalions in a situation where virtually every *Canadien* responded emotionally to Papineau's nationalist arguments. From November 16, when civil authorities finally issued warrants for the arrest of Papineau and his associates, it took Colborne less than a month to crush resistance in the Richelieu Valley and in the Deux Montagnes region of Montreal. It was not painless for either side. Years of peacetime routine had allowed British regulars to forget the need for planning and administrative competence. The defeat of Colonel Charles Gore's half-frozen, exhausted soldiers at St. Denis (at the hands of *Canadiens* led by war-seasoned veterans like Wolfred Nelson and Charles Jalbert) could have been a signal for province-wide revolt. Euphoria vanished when an equally ill-equipped British column captured St. Charles two days later. British regulars crushed the last *Patriote* stronghold, St. Eustache, on December 14 but undisciplined loyalist volunteers from Montreal earned Colborne his name of "Vieux Brûlot" by burning St. Benoit and pillaging farms on the triumphal march home.

In Upper Canada, the bravado of Sir Francis Bond Head in sending the single British battalion to Montreal encouraged Mackenzie to summon followers to seize unguarded arms at Toronto. Word of St. Denis brought hundreds more of the ill-armed volunteers to Mackenzie's side. While Bond Head dithered between over-confidence and panic, resistance was organized by the aging veteran of Beaver Dams, Colonel James Fitzgibbon. He and the much younger Colonel Allan MacNab mustered and armed a ragtag army and, on December 7, led it north to an almost bloodless encounter. The rebels fled.

So far, Upper Canada's rebellion had been *opéra bouffe*; the comedy was now over. Contrasting sharply with Lower Canada, where the harshest judicial penalties were short-lived exile in Bermuda, two of Mackenzie's lieutenants were hanged, another died in jail, and many more were sent to Australian penal colonies. Both Mackenzie and the *Patriote* leaders continued their rebellion from the safety of the United States. Public support rallied massively to the Canadian exiles and their claim that a little American help would throw off the yoke of oppression was easily believed. Hunters' Lodges sprang up in border communities to mobilize young Americans. Within days, Mackenzie and Rensselaer Van Rensselaer, the dissolute son of the former New York general, had occupied Navy Island above Niagara Falls. To relieve the boredom of his loyal militia, Allan MacNab sent a few boatloads of

Canadians to capture Mackenzie's supply ship, the *Caroline*. Ignoring the technicality that the steamer was moored to the United States shore, the Canadians cut her loose, killed an American who happened to be aboard, and sent the *Caroline* crashing over Niagara Falls.

Needless to say, it was an act of war. So was official American indifference, as "Hunters" plundered state armouries of cannon and muskets, collected money, and prepared to invade the Canadas. British reinforcements poured overland from New Brunswick, helping to revive Maine's claim to most of the neighbouring province's interior. News of the rebellion coincided in Britain with an outburst of romantic loyalty to a new young queen, Victoria. The rebellions were interpreted as an insult, aggravated by insolent Americans. By spring, thousands of British troops, including two cavalry regiments and two battalions from the Brigade of Guards, waited to disembark at Quebec.

Once again, the border was aflame with rumours, fears, and occasional violence. Thousands of militia, delighted to be embodied and paid after a year of bad harvests and business depression, watched every beach and forest trail. Indians volunteered to relive ancestral exploits. At Amherstburg, militia seized a schooner carrying arms stolen from a Michigan armoury and destined for rebels. In March, regulars, militia, and Indians crossed the ice to attack a rebel force on Pelee Island. On May 29, American river pirates embarrassed the rebel cause by burning the steamer *Sir Robert Peel*. "Remember the *Caroline*," they shouted as they robbed the passengers. The *Patriotes* dismissed Papineau in favour of firebrand leaders, collected arms, and despatched secret emissaries to create an elaborate secret society of "*Chasseurs*" throughout Lower Canada.

Through the summer of 1838, while the new Governor General, Lord Durham, pursued his official mission of information-gathering and reconciliation, Colborne deployed his troops, rebuilt the militia, and spread a network of trusted bilingual officers to collect the information the civil authorities had failed to provide in 1837. On the day that Durham left, recalled prematurely at the behest of his British enemies, the second Lower Canadian rebellion broke out. On November 3, Robert Nelson crossed the border with a few men, $20,000, and a tiny cannon. At Napierville, the *Chasseurs* network collected three thousand *Canadiens*; more gathered at Beauharnois and Chateauguay. Within hours, Colborne's men were on the march. So were a thousand volunteers from Glengarry in Upper Canada. English-speaking farmers turned out along the border as planned. Desperate rebels, abandoned by their leaders, decided to fight their way back to the United States. At Odelltown on December 9, militia and rebels met in a bitter fight. By the end, the *Patriotes* were broken. Watchers from Montreal could see pillars of smoke behind the advancing columns of British, volunteers, and Indians. Cartloads of miserable, mud-spattered prisoners rumbled into Montreal. Passers-by jeered and spat their contempt. Now the harsh example of Upper Canada could be followed since Colborne's courts martial administered the law. In all, 108 rebels were tried, 12 were hanged; most terrible of all in *Canadien* eyes was the fate of the 57 sentenced to the distant penal colonies of Australia.

In all of British North America, the rebellions left bitter memories. The lower provinces of Nova Scotia and New Brunswick would never quite trust the loyalty of the Canadians. In each of the Canadas, rebellion had been a form of civil war, splitting communities and even families, sending hundreds and perhaps thousands into exile. The internal conflict had become an undeclared war along the border. On November 12, 1838, as Colborne's men crushed the last embers in Lower Canada, hundreds of American "Hunters" poured ashore near Prescott in a mad invasion attempt led by a romantic Polish exile, Nils von Schoultz. By the time British artillery had shattered the stone windmill where the invaders took refuge, 80 regulars and militia had been killed or wounded. The Hunters lost 50 dead and wounded and 160 prisoners marched into the cells of Fort Henry. Neither the admiration of his captors nor the arguments of his lawyer, John A. Macdonald, saved Von Schoultz from the gallows.

As part of his mission, Durham had earlier opened negotiations with President Martin Van Buren. He also did his best, in a flying visit to Niagara, to lend his patronage to Anglo-American good feeling. Belatedly, Van Buren sent General Winfield Scott and a handful of troops to enforce neutrality in 1837-38, but his efforts were less significant in dampening American enthusiasm for war than palpable rebel failures. The danger of war remained, heightened by military efforts on both sides. By the spring of 1839, Colborne commanded 10,500 British troops while 4,500 militia and volunteers watched the border for both rebel activity and army deserters. Along the Maine border, encroachments by American lumbermen led to the undeclared "Aroostook war," though rival forces of British regulars and Maine militia left any fighting to sheriffs' deputies and town constables. On the Great Lakes, the

Royal Navy returned. In January 1839, Captain William Sandom had reopened the Kingston dockyard and armed four gunboats. All the risks of an incipient building race were obvious when, in 1840, Sandom launched HMS *Minos* on Lake Erie, followed by two more paddle-gunboats on Lake Ontario. The Americans answered with the USS *Michigan*, an iron side-wheeler launched at Erie in 1843. Both sides agreed, to their mutual surprise, that the Rush-Bagot Agreement never really had referred to steamers.

Throughout the 1840s, Britain and the United States verged on war. Resolution of each crisis brought another. The Webster-Ashburton Agreement of 1842 ended the Maine border dispute only to be followed by a sharp conflict over the pro-British Moskito Indians of Central America. British dreams of seizing a Pacific port, perhaps San Francisco, turned into a real Pacific crisis when the tide of American immigration expelled a feeble Hudson's Bay Company from Oregon. Americans appeared bent on showing that their God-given "manifest destiny" was to govern all of North America. Only accident kept Americans in 1846 from seizing all the Pacific coast as far north as Alaska. Mexico, instead, was the victim of the expansionist mood.

For two generations, the British had considered the costs and risks of defending their North American colonies. The problems had grown worse with time; the benefits had grown no greater. It was time for new, radical, and even dangerous ideas to be considered.

Imperial Doubts

For generations almost no one questioned why Great Britain must defend her North American colonies or why the cost must fall on British taxpayers. The answers were too obvious. Colonies were the only safe source of resources, the only secure markets. A ruling class raised on the classics understood the significance of *coloniae* nor was it tolerable that British territory should fall to the "bumptious Jonathan," as the English disdainfully referred to Americans. Private doubts the officers might have had about facing the rising strength of the United States could not efface the memories of victory in the War of 1812. Among the conservative institutions of a Whig and Tory Britain, few were as bound by victorious traditions as the army. What had suited Wellington would last forever.

Yet ideas unthinkable to one age become the orthodoxy of the next.

For half a century, the hard logic of Adam Smith and Jeremy Bentham gnawed away at old principles of a protected colonial empire. Manufacturers, eager to buy in the cheapest market and sell in the dearest, gained new power in British politics with the Reform Act of 1832. Among the new heroes was Lord Durham—"Radical Jack" to his admirers. Uninhibited by local knowledge, Durham had swiftly analyzed the grievances of 1837 and found solutions: uniting the two Canadas would soon drown the *Canadiens* in the progressive English spirit. A separation of local and imperial concerns would allow the assembly to function like a real parliament. Other reformers went farther. Even as Canadians and their British governors struggled through the 1840s toward Durham's vision of "responsible government," the doctrine of free trade triumphed in Britain. Durham had foreseen no more than colonial autonomy within the empire; others insisted that true logic led to the dissolution of a needless, costly empire. Colonies, like adolescents, must if necessary be forced to full independence.

Sentiment aside, the facts were impressive. In 1844, on the eve of abolition of the Corn Laws, Britain exported as much to the United States as to all her colonies—£8 million worth—but the latter cost £4 million to administer while an embassy and a few consulates in the United States cost a mere £15,000. And three-quarters of the cost of colonies was their defence. Would the Canadian oligarchies have driven people to rebellion, demanded Durham's aides, if their arrogance was not backed by a British garrison? Did even sentiment count when so-called "loyalists" stoned Lord Elgin's carriage in 1849 and demanded annexation to the United States, merely because the British had destroyed their protected businesses by adopting free trade?

Whatever Durham may have believed, to his brother-in-law, Lord Grey, as colonial secretary a decade later, "responsible government" included an obligation for Canadians to pay the full costs "including military protection." Canadians, of course, had no such notion. Like their American neighbours, few took the slightest interest in military matters in peacetime. Even the recurrent war scares produced only momentary excitement and a durable conviction that the causes lay in American politics or British arrogance. In the booming 1840s, Canadians simply had too much to do to waste time or money on military matters. Indeed even the annual musters and the elaborate paper structure of the sedentary militia began to fade in all the North American colonies. Diplomats and soldiers might worry about border conflicts and imminent war with the United States; Canadians were too busy clearing land, digging canals, planning the new-fangled railways, and, above all, making money.

Through the 1840s, British garrisons remained twice as large as they had been in 1837. To cope with desertion, British taxpayers paid three troops of Canadian cavalry and a company of black Canadians to watch the border. In 1840, older and married soldiers were drafted into a new regiment, the Royal Canadian Rifles. Families and the hope of a pension would distract them from the glittering attraction of the United States. Certainly British garrisons would be a permanent feature of the Canadian landscape whatever London radicals and Manchester mill-owners might say.

Yet change occurred. In the 1850s, the garrison began to shrink. The urging came from Lord Elgin in Canada, the orders from London; "If you wait til Doomsday," the Governor General had warned, "you will never get a military man here to agree to such a course." The provincial troops were disbanded; gunboats were paid off; Kingston was closed as a naval base in 1843. Concentrating the remaining troops at Halifax, Kingston, and Quebec made military sense; it also cut down the tiresome, tricky calls for aid to the civil power. The outbreak of the Crimean War might well have completed the process, as virtually the whole of the British garrison departed for the campaign. Lord Elgin's concluding triumph, the Reciprocity Agreement of 1854, created such a flood of good feeling along the border that almost no one missed the troops.

Indeed the tide of military enthusiasm that swept the colonies during the Crimean War suggested that Britain might well be able to shed its entire North American defence burden. Nova Scotia and New Brunswick poured out their imperial devotion in stirring resolutions. From a remote Vancouver Island, Governor James Douglas promised to lead Indians against Russian trading posts if only the order came. In the Canadas, the provincial government hired British pensioners to guard abandoned forts and, as a shrewd exchange for the British ordnance lands — real estate retained by the British for military purposes — promised to reform its militia system. The resulting volunteer militia had recruited most of its five thousand men by the end of 1855 and enthusiasm forced the provincial parliament to double the force in 1856.

Yet there were critics. "The whole thing," complained the Reform leader, George Brown, "was unnecessary." It was also a dreadful precedent to assume even the slightest share of a British responsibility. By 1858, when legislation creating the volunteer militia had to be renewed, Canadians were satiated with military excitement and preoccupied by a sharp economic depression. Stirred by yet another threat of war with the Americans, the British restored their garrison to its pre-1854 strength. On the Pacific coast, British gunboats pursued disaffected and piratical Coast Indians, while a company of Royal Engineers reached the Cariboo in 1858, officially to build roads and in practice to remind American gold-miners that they were standing on British soil. A year later, Royal Marines and American soldiers confronted each other over the sovereignty of San Juan Island in Puget Sound. What else was new?

A good deal. The chaos in the Crimea had discredited the myth of Wellington's invincible army, exposed colonels and generals as blunderers, and given civilians a fresh self-esteem as military experts. Who had done more to expose military incompetence than Mr. William Russell of the *Times* or Miss Nightingale at the Scutari hospital? The new civilian expertise began to shape military policy. In 1860, newspapers warned that France's new armoured battleship, *La Gloire*, could sink the British fleet and spearhead an invasion. The prime minister, Lord Palmerston, ever-responsive to England's jingo moods, proclaimed that "steam had bridged the Channel" and commanded his colleagues to find £10 million for fortifications. A hundred thousand fellow subjects created the Volunteer movement, an army of artisans and shop-keepers that drilled nightly against the imaginary threat.

In the circumstances, it was now intolerable that most of Britain's army was still hidden in remote colonies or that the few regiments at home consisted of recruits waiting to go abroad. As for North America, civilians could now ask questions soldiers instinctively suppressed. Americans, Palmerston complained, might be "the most disagreeable fellows to have to do with" but they were on the spot, powerful, and utterly unscrupulous, while Britain was remote, weak, and unlikely to defy her own powerful cotton interests by risking war. Moreover, by the 1860s, there was both a bright and an alarming feature to American relations. The election of Abraham Lincoln in 1860 spurred hopes among most of Britain's ruling class that his entirely unpleasant country might dissolve, leaving the gentlemanly and cotton-rich South as a survivor. The alternative, allegedly fostered by Lincoln's secretary of state, William Seward, was that the United States might find belated unity in a war with Britain. Even if the southern states seceded, Canada would be a convenient consolation prize.

Certainly, as British politicians and their military advisors contemplated the North American problem in the summer of 1861, Canada was defenceless. As ever, the lower provinces could depend on a British fleet and the local militia had been revived a year before to add martial splendour to a ceremonial visit by the Prince of Wales. In the upper provinces, the militia had also recovered slightly but the twenty-two hundred British regulars were barely a third of Prevost's army in 1812. Schemes to widen canals and to prefabricate iron gunboats for the lakes remained on paper. Surely, a British parliamentary committee had urged, the time had come to distinguish between imperial fortresses, which served British interests, and local defences, which must depend on the colonists themselves. Such logic was too harsh—for the moment—and a few thousand soldiers were despatched on the huge steamer, *Great Eastern*. But not more. Canadians must be forced to face their responsibility.

Suddenly, calm reason disintegrated. On April 12, 1861, firing on Fort Sumter opened the American Civil War. On November 8, an American warship stopped the British steamer *Trent*. American sailors bundled two Confederate representatives over the side. "I don't know whether you are going to stand for them," Palmerston shouted as he hurled his hat on the Cabinet table, "but I'll be damned if I do." On both sides of the Atlantic, war fever surged. Canada would be the battlefield. The caution of the summer guaranteed that it would be lost. How could it possibly be reinforced so late in the year? In a frantic mobilization, made possible only by post-Crimea reforms, the British army somehow collected 10,500 troops, hired ships, and sent them across the Atlantic. In Washington, Seward made a grudging apology for the *Trent* affair and ostentatiously invited the British troops to land at Portland, Maine, to take the British-owned Grand Trunk Railway to Canada. The British, equally stubborn, insisted on despatching over seven thousand men by the winter trail through New Brunswick. Fussing staff officers, terrified of a Crimean-style disaster, spared no expense. In London, the formidable Florence Nightingale was consulted daily about the comfort of the troops. Far more worrying for British generals was the limited ability of the Nova Scotia-born hero, Sir Fenwick Williams, who would have had to command the defending armies. A strong staff, including the self-assertive Colonel Garnet Wolseley, was some compensation.

There was no war. Thanks to Lincoln and Prince Albert, Queen

Victoria's dying husband, both sides drew back from the brink. The Confederate commissioners were released and the American Civil War continued its long, bloody course. Yet the *Trent* affair was decisive. It set in train a series of events that guaranteed that, within a decade, Britain would have abandoned the land defence of its North American colonies and those colonies would have been pressed into a single Confederation stretching from the Atlantic to the Pacific.

For a start, the crisis forced competent British officers to consider the defence of Canada and how hopeless the assumptions of 1812 had become. For fifteen hundred miles, the border was defenceless or indefensible. Fort Lennox was now a boys' reformatory; Fort Malden a lunatic asylum. Command of the lakes was inconceivable. Arrogant assumptions about the American army rapidly dissolved after visiting officers returned with reports of its wealth of equipment and growing competence. Surely the only way to fight the United States was on the Atlantic seaboard with a superior fleet, not by sacrificing a few thousand regulars in the heart of the continent.

Such a strategy abandoned the United Canadas. Was that now unthinkable? For once the colonials had surely done their best. The United Provinces ordered a hundred thousand rifles; thirty-eight thousand militia were called out to train, and a new commission urged a militia of a hundred thousand men. Perhaps it was worth the £1 million Britain had spent in the wake of the *Trent* affair. Then came stunning news: on May 20, 1862, the Canadian Parliament had rejected the militia bill and thrown out the government that proposed it. British politicians and editors vied with each other in their outrage. The lesson was too clear: "Canada," explained the *Times*, "has learned to trust others for the performance of services for which weaker and less wealthy populations are wont to rely exclusively on themselves." Each British soldier, explained Robert Lowe to a parliamentary committee, prevented a hundred colonists from drilling. Garrisons were "an opiate to put the Colony to sleep."

British officers met in committees, formulated plans, and devised schemes for fortification. Perhaps, they estimated, 150,000 men and £2 million in defence works might make Canada safe. The mood of Britain's parliament made their plans irrelevant. Since even the most costly plans foresaw the abandonment of Upper Canada (the older terms remained in military usage), they could not be accepted by any Canadian government, even if it had been willing to share the burdens. Yet the risk of war grew. In July 1863, the fall of Vicksburg and the North's victory at Gettysburg guaranteed that the Confederacy would fall. Then, surely, the Americans would turn their vast army northward to avenge the conspicuous British favouritism to the South. "War," claimed the Irish-Canadian leader, Thomas D'Arcy McGee, "is an appetite that grows with feeding."

A succession of Confederate-inspired pinpricks along the border, culminating in 1864 in the St. Alban's raid and the release by a Canadian court of the raiders, added to the tensions. In turn, the tensions propelled Canadian politicians to Charlottetown to promote the dream of North American union. A host of reasons backed the idea: deadlock in the Canadas, dreams of western expansion, personal ambition, even the problems of gaining a credit rating for railway expansion. Yet every problem was linked to the fear of war and invasion. Only a British North American Confederation could make possible an Atlantic rail link for Canada. Only union would give endangered colonies a chance to borrow on London financial markets. And, from a British perspective, only Canadian Confederation would allow a dignified military withdrawal.

How necessary that withdrawal had become was underlined by Lieutenant-Colonel W. F. D. Jervois, an engineer officer who had compiled the latest and most realistic of analyses of the British North American defence problem. As befitted an engineer, Jervois's report called for massive fortifications and the abandonment of hopeless outworks. In the tradition of Carleton, Prevost, and Carmichael Smyth, Jervois appealed for earthwork defences at Montreal, but it was Quebec, the ultimate citadel for a British army, that needed the most massive works. Whatever its military realism, Jervois's analysis destroyed any basis for Confederation. It demanded too much from Britain, already more preoccupied with Prussia than with the United States. It offered no reason for the Maritime colonies to get involved.

That autumn, delegates from most of British North America met at Quebec. Balls, receptions, and banquets punctuated the secret bargaining sessions. Among the waiting officials, discreet in side-whiskers and morning coat, was Colonel Jervois, a fresh report in hand. With reasonable precautions — perhaps $2 million in fortifications — Canada could indeed be made secure. Quebec, Montreal, and some place to the west — wisely unspecified — could be fortified and defended. The militia and the British could do the rest. Misgivings and doubts were far from silenced. Maritimers wondered at the incubus they were acquiring; Canadians complained that the lower provinces added no more strength than extra sections of a fishing rod. The fact remained that the critics were amateurs; Jervois was the professional. (So much was he the professional that Jervois had a further generation of service to imperial defence before he retired as Inspector-General of Fortifications.)

One further assurance was necessary. After the Canadian Parliament had endorsed the Quebec resolutions, it voted next to seek $2 million in loans for fortifications — subject to British guarantee. Most astonishing, it also passed militia estimates totalling $1 million. Then the leading members of the Confederation coalition — John A. Macdonald, George-Etienne Cartier, John Galt, and George Brown set off for London. By the time they arrived, the Civil War had ended at Appomattox.

Eighty years later, C. P. Stacey would denounce "those elements in English society which had been outspokenly scornful of and hostile to the Northern cause now sinking into what can only be described as a blue funk at the apparent prospect of the war which their own attitude had done so much to provoke. . . ." British North America seemed a cheap offering to placate a victorious and vengeful North. In such an atmosphere, the Canadian willingness to do all that had been asked of them was by no means welcome. Yet, without friendly gestures, Confederation might not occur and the British scheme for extricating itself might fail. It was a time for words. The colonial politicians must solemnly be reassured. On June 17, 1865, the colonial secretary, Edward Cardwell, could report the judgement of Her Majesty's ministers to the Governor General, Lord Monck, in Ottawa:

> It seemed sufficient that Her Majesty's Government should accept the assurances given by the Canadian Ministers on the part of Canada that the Province is ready to devote all her resources both in men and money to the maintenance of her connexion with the Mother Country, and should assure them in return that the Imperial Government fully acknowledged the reciprocal obligation of defending every portion of the Empire with all the resources at its command.

That statement would be the basis of a new imperial relationship. Like it or not, Cardwell and the Canadians had cautiously begun to turn a colonial dependency into an alliance of equals.

III   The Young Dominion

A Canadian Responsibility

Within a decade, British politicians, Tory and Whig, had rid themselves of two linked problems. Defending Canada was militarily hopeless; it was also contrary to a growing anti-colonial mood. With the sense of triumphant righteousness that prevails in most imperial capitals, the British government determined that it would be best for everyone if Canadians took on their own defence. Britain, of course, would still be there but, as Edward Cardwell grandly proclaimed, Canada's security "would ever principally depend upon the spirit, the energy and the courage of her own people."

Like a proper Victorian parent, Britain must first prod her offspring into maturity in military matters. Certainly, long years of dependence had bred some infantile notions of war. The prevalent Canadian militia myth left the impression that soldiers were created, not trained. In recurrent crises, arms, equipment, and fortifications simply appeared without costly Canadian effort. Now the colonials would learn. Of course indifference to military preparedness had its own logic. On both sides of the American border, capital and labour were too scarce to be wasted on military show. Roads, canals, and the Grand Trunk Railway, the longest line in the world, served military as well as civil needs. More to the point, British North Americans had contributed little to the incessant conflicts of Whitehall and Washington. Canadians did not care if Americans bombarded Moskito Indians in Nicaragua and they had not let the Confederate cruiser *Alabama* escape from Liverpool to prey on American shipping. To tell the truth, few Nova Scotians would have cared if the mountains and pine swamps of British Columbia had been lost to the American faith in their "manifest destiny." The British expected Canadians to defend themselves from dangers the British themselves had helped create.

Certainly the colonists had had defence on the cheap. The formidable paper strength of the sedentary militia cost almost nothing. By 1840, the militia rolls of the United Canadas boasted 426 battalions, 235,000 men. During the Oregon crisis of 1845, New Brunswick reported 27,532 men in its militia and Nova Scotia 40,997. Prince Edward Island, too nervous to muster its disgruntled tenant farmers, merely estimated the strength at 8,000. Yet in all the provinces, the militia was unarmed, untrained, and by the 1840s, unorganized. The historic principle of compulsory service was fading fast. In the wake of the 1837 risings, companies formed for service were filled by volunteers. In 1846, a new Militia Act for the Canadas formally recognized the volunteer principle, provided there was no cost to the taxpayer. The Montreal Fire Brigade enrolled as a battalion; the York Troop of Cavalry (forerunner of the Governor General's Horse Guards) did not bother.

War in the Crimea sent a gust of military enthusiasm across the colonies. New Brunswick and Nova Scotia passed patriotic addresses to the Queen. In the Canadas, Sir Allan MacNab sponsored a commission charged with recommending militia reform and an "efficient and economical system of Public defence." The members found inspiration in New York, Connecticut, and Massachusetts, where an equally defunct militia system had been supplanted by gaily uniformed volunteer regiments. The commission recommendations, embodied in a Militia Act of 1855, permitted an "Active Militia" of five thousand men, armed, equipped, and paid five shillings a day for ten days' training a year. Over objections from *Rouges* and Reformers, the alarming precedent was approved by fifty-eight votes to thirty-four for a three-year trial.

The minister responsible, Colonel E. P. Taché, could boast of immediate success. Within weeks, the first unit — a French-speaking artillery battery at Quebec — was complete. Others soon followed. Units doubled as social clubs, electing officers, buying their own uniforms, and expelling "undesirables." At least five new companies insisted on Highland dress; others were "principally, if not entirely Irish." The clamour to join forced the Government to double the strength in 1856 — though the extra units were unpaid. War fervour even persuaded the British to raise a regular regiment in the colony, the 100th Royal Canadians. Within three months, 1,027 men had enlisted. Well-connected young Canadians became officers.

Enthusiasm wanes as well as waxes. By 1858, Canadians were too preoccupied by economic depression even to renew the 1855 Act. Most of the volunteer units collapsed. Recruiting for the 100th Regiment ended when it was sent to garrison Gibraltar. Military spirit revived only in 1860 with the visit of the Prince of Wales. A chance to parade before Queen Victoria's son, and especially the opportunity to meet him, spurred prosperous Nova Scotians and New Brunswickers as well as Canadians to launch their own volunteer units. More than ever, social distinctions marked the force. Like other corps, Halifax's Chebucto Greys chose a splendid uniform too costly for mere labourers to afford. William Otter, later a general and the reputed "father of the force," was blackballed by an elegant Toronto company because his membership in the local fire brigade marked him as vulgar. The fact that Otter's grandfather had been Lord Bishop of Chichester helped save his militia career. Some of the oldest regiments of the Canadian Armed Forces, the Canadian Grenadier Guards of Montreal, Toronto's Queen's Own Rifles, and the Halifax Rifles in Nova Scotia, trace their official origin to 1860.*

The Trent affair of 1861-62 added substantially to the volunteer force in the Canadas; Nova Scotia reverted to the traditional compulsory system, enrolling 59,379 men and training and arming 45,600 of them. Threat of war persuaded Canada's aging and unpopular government to do more. As Minister of Militia Affairs, John A. Macdonald called on the province to raise an active force of 50,000, with both volunteers and balloted men paid to train for fourteen to twenty-eight days a year. By the time the legislation was debated, the crisis was well past. The *Trent* crisis was forgotten, the Americans were trapped in their civil war, and the *Rouge*-Reform coalition had an issue. A. A. Dorion warned *Canadiens* that their sons would be torn from the farm to fight in British wars; the Reformer, George Brown, insisted that the existing volunteers would defeat the Americans in the event of war, and the volunteers naturally agreed. Macdonald retreated to the bottle, *Canadien* politicians defected, and on May 20, defeat on the Militia Bill toppled the government.

Most Canadians never quite understood the British outrage at the defeat of the 1862 Militia bill. An unpopular government had merely come to an overdue end. The new regime allowed ten thousand volunteers to drill for twelve days and, when tensions rose along the border, increased the total. If the British raged at Canadian negligence, George Brown's *Globe* had a characteristic response: "We cannot agree to the dogma that Canada should provide entirely for her defence when

---

*The Halifax Rifles could only be part of a Canadian Militia from Confederation in 1867. On the other hand, some militia units with political influence have been allowed to concoct fictional lineages extending back to the War of 1812, or even the Revolutionary War. Military history, like most human activity, has its comic side.

she is not the author of the quarrels against the consequences of which she is called to stand upon her guard." Scintillating brevity was not Brown's style, but his message had a certain logic.

Britain's ruling class openly sympathized with the secessionist South in the American Civil War. So did a small minority of Canadians, among them Toronto's Colonel George T. Denison, the colony's self-proclaimed military thinker. After July 1863, when defeat at Vicksburg and Gettysburg sealed the Confederacy's fate, such southern sympathies became acutely dangerous to Canada. Fire-eaters like Denison had an answer for the timid: if 3.5 million southerners had almost beaten the North, what could 3.5 million British North Americans achieve when backed by Britain's might? Few knowledgeable officers or thoughtful citizens shared such sanguine illusions. Fear of being trapped in so one-sided a contest was a powerful anti-Confederate argument in the lower provinces. The fear grew fast after October 19, 1864, when a band of Confederate raiders slipped over the Canadian border to ransack St. Albans, Vermont. Two months later, when a foolish Montreal magistrate freed the raiders, the American Senate indignantly ended the Reciprocity Agreement and President Lincoln imposed passports on the Canadian border for the first time in history. Linked with the depredations of the *Alabama* on the high seas, the St. Albans affair seemed deliberately to provoke the United States to send its huge armies north. The worried Canadian coalition voted $1 million for the militia, renewed a tired promise to fortify Montreal, and sent its leading members to London to seek reassurance from Edward Cardwell.

The Canadian visit coincided with the South's surrender. After Appomattox, American hostility to Britain continued; the vast Northern armies did not. Within weeks, thousands of men headed home. The huge improvised fleet dissolved. Within a couple of years, American military power was a memory — or a future possibility.

A real threat remained. Since the 1840s, the United States had become home to hundreds of thousands of Irish refugees. The Fenian Brotherhood, a secret society committed to violence, had concocted a plan: a vast army, recruited from Irish veterans, would hold Britain's American colonies as hostages for Ireland. Colonists, groaning under the British yoke, would receive the Fenians as liberators. American politicians, eager for Irish votes, would cast a blind eye on filibustering for freedom.

The plot was no secret. The Fenians openly collected arms and money. Most Canadians were furious and alarmed. *Canadiens* had no love for the Irish; Protestants bristled at a possible Catholic invasion; even many Irish-Canadians cursed the Fenian folly. The British garrisons, cut in 1863-64, were promptly reinforced. Canadian spies permeated the Fenian ranks but their "secret" plans were in any case usually shared with the press. Repeatedly in 1865 and 1866, thousands of militia turned out to face an imminent invasion. For St. Patrick's Day, 1866, more than fourteen thousand Canadians volunteered for duty. Two and a half months later, on the night of May 31, the attack finally came. Instead of the promised thousands, "General" John O'Neill led a mere six hundred Fenians across from Buffalo to Fort Erie. At dawn on June 2, near Ridgeway, the Fenians ran into two thirsty, sweaty battalions of militia, marching across country to join a British column. The Canadians turned, advanced like regulars, and on the verge of victory, were tumbled into confusion by contradictory orders. Moments later, a flood of panic-stricken volunteers poured down the sunken road to Ridgeway. The shaken Fenians soon retraced their steps to Fort Erie. After scattering a few militia who had arrived in their absence, most of O'Neill's men crossed to Buffalo to be interned. The Canadians tried their few prisoners and sent most of them to the penitentiary.

Historically, the Fenians were probably a blessing to Canada. They united the country as nothing else could. A comic-opera attempt to invade Campobello Island helped persuade New Brunswick voters that they needed the new Canadian Confederation. For another couple of generations, Fenians became the handiest bogey for any Canadian politician faced with unrest or disaffection. For the militia, the raids provided an incentive for training and a stiff but relatively cheap lesson in the value of discipline. When Fenians returned in 1870, Canadian militia along the Quebec border had no difficulty in driving them from Eccles Hill and Trout River. The Fenians also provided an unanswerable argument for the British military presence. Since Canada was only an innocent proxy for Irish hatred of England, the British had an obligation to defend her borders. Indeed they did. By the summer of 1866, the British had raised their Canadian garrison to 11,741 men and held 4,969 troops in the Nova Scotia command. The Royal Navy reopened Kingston as a base and maintained fifteen gunboats on the lakes. British officers trained the militia and organized a memorable camp at Laprairie for over a thousand volunteer officers. On the rumour that the Fenians would be equipped with modern weapons, Britain even rearmed the Canadians with new Snider-Enfield breech-loading rifles. Throughout, Canadian officials complained, criticized, and haggled over the costs.

Confederation changed little. The New Dominion was as much a colony as the old provinces; technically, Ottawa's responsibility for "militia and defence" represented an allocation of power to the new central government, not a reduced British control. Sir George-Etienne Cartier, the aging senior partner in the Confederation coalition, underlined the importance and political sensitivity of the portfolio when he agreed to become Minister of Militia and Defence in Sir John A. Macdonald's new government, but Cartier's description of the militia as keystone to the arch of a new nationality was hyperbole, not reality. The first Militia Act, adopted in 1868, merely extended the provincial system of the United Canadas to the whole Dominion. An Active Militia of forty thousand might be enrolled by ballot but clearly it would be based on volunteering. Nine military districts — four in Ontario, two French-speaking and an English-speaking district in Quebec, and one each for New Brunswick and Nova Scotia — created a basis for recruiting new units of cavalry, artillery, and infantry and for mustering the "Reserve Militia." By February 1869, Cartier reported 37,170 volunteers and 618,896 men in reserve. Political patronage helped fill out a militia staff of half-pay British officers and impecunious militia veterans.

Whatever proud Canadians might believe, the militia remained an auxiliary to the British garrison. No more than in 1866, when volunteers had lacked tents, blankets, and rations, was the force equipped for the field. In active operations, the British would have to provide every necessity, from generals to field hospitals. Yet, even as Cartier defended his new Militia Act, its governing assumptions crumbled. The British took the next step. They had insisted that Canada take a dominant part in her own defence; by the end of 1868 they were determined that Canada accept the whole burden.

In hindsight, it was predictable: the pattern was set when the British committee had insisted in 1861 on distinguishing "imperial fortresses" like Halifax from mere colonial defence. Staff officers like Colonel Jervois had merely put on paper the inarticulate fears of British generals that Canada presented a hopeless strategic problem. With their assumption that British taxpayers would remain an uncomplaining milch cow, ready to provide military funds at any time, Canadian politicians had aggravated the difficulties. "An army maintained in a country which does not even permit us to govern it," complained the Tory chancellor of the exchequer, Benjamin Disraeli, "What an anomaly!" His Liberal counterpart, Willam Ewart Gladstone, had opposed every single military contribution to Canada: "The more Canada and the British Colonies are detached as to their defensive not less than their administrative responsibilities, from England," Gladstone argued, "the more likely the Union will be to study friendly relations with them."

Through most of the 1860s, Gladstone and Disraeli were mere leaders-in-waiting, grumbling as £300,000 were poured into Quebec defences and as regiments poured across the Atlantic at each expression of Yankee "sauciness." When Cartier and his colleague, William McDougall, arrived in London in December 1868, they had no intimation of change. They expected to haggle over the usual militia accounts and seek British help in bullying the Hudson's Bay Company out of Rupert's Land and the little Fort Garry colony. Indeed, they may never have realized that they were witnesses to an imperial revolution.

That month, the British Liberals won their first clear majority in decades. For the first time, William Gladstone was unquestioned prime minister, with enough of a majority to make his will prevail. A deft and agile politician, Gladstone knew his middle-class constituents. They wanted retrenchment. They were worried about the power of Prussia. They were ashamed that Britain was impotent in Europe. Edward Cardwell, the new secretary of state for war, would satisfy them with the boldest army reforms in a century. Regiments, called home from the Empire, would create a field army. Abolition of purchase would open officers' commissions to ability. Keeping half the army in England would make it possible to recruit soldiers for less than a lifetime. It would also save money.

The protests from colonial politicians were expected and ignored. If Cardwell eliminated New Zealand's garrison in the midst of a Maori war, what hope did Canada have of concessions? Only Halifax, as the Royal Navy's North Atlantic base, was spared. Quebec might have shared its status; a secret revelation that its new fortifications would be useless against modern weapons sealed its fate. Politicians, editors, even Fenians, could not alter new British policy.

Certainly there were backward glances. British generals pleaded for Ottawa to pay for the nucleus of a Canadian army. Elderly soldiers in the Royal Canadian Rifles prayed that Canadian pay might supplement their meagre pensions. Fenian raids in the spring of 1870 led General James Lindsay to beg Cartier to respond. Ottawa was silent: to answer would merely legitimate the British action. In fact, such stubbornness merely reinforced Whitehall's resolve. When the Canadians ignored offers to buy surplus arms and stores, Whitehall ordered them returned to England. Unwanted army blankets were shipped to victims of the great Chicago fire.

As one lonely concession, the British reluctantly accepted a share of restoring authority in the remote Red River colony, sold to Canada as part of a $1.5 million deal with the Hudson's Bay Company. Ignored in the transaction, ten thousand inhabitants were by no means certain they preferred Canadian sovereignty to the frail government exercised by the company. When William McDougall foolishly asserted his non-existent authority as the Dominion's lieutenant-governor for the territory, Métis buffalo hunters bundled him over the border and their ambitious young spokesman, Louis Riel, proclaimed a provisional government. After two attempts by local Canadians to unseat him, Riel singled out his most truculent prisoner, Thomas Scott, and had him killed.

This cruel folly almost destroyed the possibility of any solution. While the joint representative of Canada and the company, Donald Smith, patiently manoeuvred Riel and the Métis into a settlement, the fury of Ontario transformed a military display of sovereignty into a punitive expedition. Cartier's scheme to send equal contingents from Ontario and Quebec with four hundred men of the British 60th Rifles foundered when only Ontarians enlisted. After innumerable delays, some from Cartier's fears of his Québécois constituents, some from American hostility at the Sault, and some from simple inexperience, Colonel Garnet Wolseley took his 1,044 men across Lake Superior and along the rugged canoe route to Fort Garry in the summer of 1870 without losing a man. A nervous Riel did not wait to meet the expedition. Denied a fight, the flamboyant Wolseley left his Canadians behind as an army of occupation and set off, as ordered, for the East. The well-publicized conclusion to a useful career in Canada helped launch his career as the "very essence of a modern major-general" in late-Victorian England. "All Sir Garnet" meant a job well done. In fact, ill-disciplined Canadians compounded the Scott tragedy with killings of their own.

That winter, the 60th Rifles found themselves alone at Quebec's

Citadel, the last British regiment in central Canada. They remained only because, as a second concession, they might reassure Canadians during the painful negotiations of the Treaty of Washington. On November 11, 1871, a British troop-ship arrived to take them home. Local militia battalions, the 8th Royal Rifles and the 9th Voltigeurs, formed guards of honour as the 60th Rifles — the old Royal Americans — marched down the narrow streets from the Citadel for a final time. Canadian gunners fired a salute. At last, or too early, Canadians must defend themselves.

Militia and Defence

After 1871, the Canadian frontier really did become the longest undefended border in the world. Hastily embodied artillery batteries at Quebec and Kingston, stiffened by retired British officers and sergeants, doubled as guards, caretakers, and instructors for other militia gunners. At Fort Garry, a few hundred temporary soldiers idly waited release and a chance to farm Manitoba's rich black soil. Only at Halifax, rebuilt and rearmed in the 1860s, did two British battalions garrison a real fortress.

Without debate or deep analysis, the young Dominion evolved its national security policy. The first principle was to avoid conflict with its only dangerous neighbour, the United States. British negotiators had administered the lesson in preparing the Treaty of Washington in the winter of 1871. As a helpless Macdonald watched, the British traded Canadian claims for American and went home content. Never again would Britain risk war in North America. Canadians could profit from the example: they, too, could cultivate their gardens or their fortunes.

Canada's second line of defence was Cardwell's commitment of 1865. The million dollars a year voted after the St. Albans crisis became, after 1867, an annual insurance premium against the day when Canada might seek from Britain "all the resources at its command." From time to time, it was necessary to show the British that money was spent to good purpose. Appointing a more senior British officer as general officer commanding the militia in 1874 would appear to strengthen discipline and military efficiency. Opening Canada's Royal Military College in 1876 at the old Kingston dockyard did little good to the militia but passing British visitors never failed to praise the little institution. After 1880, its best graduates could secure British army commissions. In 1878, a Liberal minister of militia and defence confessed that he "always felt that the amount we paid annually for military purposes was more to show the Horse Guards our willingness as far as possible to take upon ourselves a fair share of our own defences than for any other purpose."

Such an atmosphere did not foster energetic or efficient military institutions. The final repulse of the Fenians in 1870 allowed public interest to languish. Even at the height of the excitement, employers had fired workers for attending military drill; by the early 1870s, volunteer units reported difficulty in filling their ranks. In 1872, many militia officers opposed the government because Cartier refused to invoke compulsory features of the 1868 Militia Act. For lack of men, the senior French-speaking battalion, the 4th Chasseurs Canadiens, collapsed. Soon the depression of the 1870s overshadowed manpower problems. Between 1871 and 1876, defence spending fell by two-thirds to only $650,000. Gradually, the annual total struggled back to the target of $1 million a year, but the effects on the volunteers were permanent.

In the face of financial constraints, British generals urged the government to cut the number of units and volunteers to a level that could be properly trained and equipped. For eminently political and practical reasons, the government preferred an oversized, badly equipped, and ill-trained military organization. A large force with a purported forty thousand members looked impressive on paper. More regiments meant more officers and more small communities where favours could be granted. Of course a militia with too many officers, too little training, and worn-out equipment had little fighting value. No professional soldier believed that the sham battle or ceremonial review that climaxed a twelve-day summer camp was a preparation for war. Instead, such spectacles pandered to the conceit of politicians and militiamen and the pleasure of tax-paying spectators.

The post-Confederation militia was a social and political institution. With no enemy or war to fight, the force found other purposes for existence. A common function for a battalion was to mobilize its members at the polls. In the first seven parliaments after Confederation, between a quarter and a sixth of the members were militia officers. The annual debate on the militia estimates was known as "Colonels' Day." Non-military MPs stayed away. Through political connections, officers could lobby for fresh issues of uniform, an extra turn at camp, or the transfer of an unpopular staff officer. On the eve of the 1891 election, the colonel of the 10th Royal Grenadiers sought two extra companies after claiming: "you can always rely on the Grenadiers being a good Conservative Regiment." Once Toronto had proved its Tory loyalty, the city was also granted a brand new regiment, the 48th Highlanders. In the circumstances, there was much to be said for tight limits on defence spending. When Sir John A. Macdonald died in 1891, the British commander of the militia, Major-General Ivor Herbert, noted:

> He looked upon money voted for militia purposes only as a means of gaining political ends, but he was honest enough to keep that use of it within strict limits, and consequently cut down the militia estimates to the lowest possible figure. He knew that at any time he could obtain an increased vote but he also knew that any money so voted would not yield any corresponding efficiency, but merely add to the party claims that would have to be satisfied from that source.

Going to a militia camp was a common Canadian experience. Between 1875 and 1896, about twenty thousand men attended each summer; thereafter the numbers rose sharply. Militiamen enlisted for three years but rural battalions until 1896 attended only in alternate years and a majority of volunteers probably only attended once. The attractions were small; pay was fifty cents a day for a twelve-day camp. The uniform was second-hand and, in the absence of dry-cleaning, very much as the previous wearer had left it. The honour of representing the county at Sussex, Laprairie, or Niagara-on-the-Lake seems modest. Perhaps the boredom of rural life and a chance to pass some of the familiar tests of young manhood were impetus enough to attend.

A battalion might muster on a warm June morning to travel by train, steamer, and sometimes on foot to Lévis, Barriefield, Sussex, or wherever civic or party pressure dictated. A few colonels detoured through Montreal or Toronto to fill out their ranks with the unemployed. At camp, militiamen slept in long lines of bell tents, each under his own greatcoat and a couple of the notoriously thin, moth-eaten militia blankets. Men were issued the traditional pound of beef and pound of bread, supplemented by a few ounces of tea, sugar, salt, vegetables, and whatever the colonel had had the wealth and generosity to purchase. No wonder camp canteens were popular and profitable. Training was simple and repetitive. Battalions drilled their men, mounted guards,

marched to the ranges to fire thirty rounds from the well-worn Snider-
Enfields, and occasionally indulged in a sham battle. Afterwards, volunteers were free to visit the local town and test the patience of local
fathers and temperance enthusiasts. On the last day, tents were struck,
camp equipment was returned to store, and battalions wended their
way home. Captains collected rifles, equipment, and uniforms, certain that in a couple of years their men would be "in Manitoba, the
States or otherwise occupied." The city battalions and a very few rural
units drilled annually in ugly shed-like armouries, prided themselves
on smart uniforms and vigorous social and athletic activities, and despised the rough and ready rural corps.

Almost everything depended on the officers. In a society acutely
conscious of social status, a militia commission became a badge of
respectability. Compelling would-be officers to spend three months
at a military school barred access to men without means. Elaborate
mess etiquette was a key feature of the training. City regiments demanded an entry fee and required officers to buy elaborate uniforms
from British military tailors. Militia rank might not be a perfect test of
respectability but it was the best available. Lord Minto, as Governor
General, announced that officers who might not otherwise be socially
acceptable at Government House would be received in uniform. In
Canada, noted a Montreal newspaper with helpful clarity, "an officer
is useful to his regiment because he has the means to spend and the
will to spend it; the regiment is useful to him because the paths
toward social distinction are smoothed for the militia officer."

Critics of the Americanization of Canadian manners and morals
might take comfort from the militia. Ottawa found little money to
modernize arms and equipment inherited from the 1860s but private
benefactors and even county councils paid for kilts, busbies, helmets,
feather bonnets, regimental badges, and any available British military
dress. Though Ottawa economized by buying obsolete uniforms from
British suppliers, minute changes in British drill books were instantly
adopted. Such influences could be harmless and even beneficial. The
British regimental tradition proved a valuable heritage. Militia officers
who reiterated British doctrines on the subordination of the military
to civil authority and the separation of the army from partisan influences would learn the dangers of a double standard. Yet the British-
ness of the militia had less charm for *Canadiens*. Fewer French than
English Canadians had wealth or the will to lavish it on a militia bat-

talion. Without private means, the force was feeble. Only at Quebec, where rank and uniforms *"faisaient la pluie et le beau temps"* in the social season, were there social rewards for military-minded *Canadiens*.

The consequences were more serious than anyone knew. In 1868, Cartier had been conscious that his new institution must appeal to both French and English, yet it was he who appointed a surplus politician, ignorant of drill, to one of two key French-speaking positions. French-speaking ministers dominated the Militia Department from 1868 to 1892 but too often their Quebec appointments were political hacks. Cartier had identified a critical military problem for Canada but neither he nor his successors worked very hard for a solution. Half the Canadian officers in the Red River expedition of 1870 spoke French but almost all the men in the ranks were English-speaking. In 1879, attempts to revive the Chasseurs Canadiens foundered when organizers adopted the uniform of the Papal Zouaves, the young *Canadiens* who had volunteered to serve the Pope in 1868. Officials rejected "foreign fancy dress." No one, then or later, questioned the suitability of Highland kilts.*

Whatever its limitations, Canada's militia was equal to its only real responsibility, aid to the civil power. From 1855, when the brand new volunteers were summoned to separate warring Catholics and Orangemen in Guelph, the militia served in scores of episodes, major and minor. Volunteers guarded a hanging, broke up illegal boxing matches, defended innumerable strike-breakers, and compelled farmers to pay taxes. In 1875, cavalry, infantry, and artillery escorted the body of Joseph Guibord past sullen crowds to final burial in Montreal, after his widow had won a court action to have her excommunicated husband's body buried on consecrated ground. At Quebec, gunners from the permanent battery separated Irish and French workers battling for jobs. In Toronto, Montreal, Saint John, and Charlottetown, volunteers turned out in the 1870s to keep Orangemen and Catholics from mayhem. Instead of making the duty attractive to the volunteers, the Militia Act allowed a couple of magistrates to call out troops but left it to the commanding officers to collect their pay from a frequently recalcitrant municipality. Far from supporting the fabric of social or-

---

*In 1880, the 5th Battalion, the Royal Scots, was allowed to wear kilts, the first militia regiment so distinguished. The Montreal unit survives as the Royal Highlanders of Canada.

der, employers often fired workers absent on strike duty. Even the federal government docked the pay of civil servants who did duty during an 1891 episode in Ottawa; those who held senior posts were ordered to resign their militia commissions. In the circumstances it may be surprising that militia turned out so cheerfully. One reason was the middle-class membership of city battalions like the Queen's Own Rifles or Montreal's 5th Royal Scots (now the Black Watch). Another factor was the prospect of excitement in otherwise drab lives.

Maintaining internal order was an aspect of national security. The periodic American invasions of Mexico and Caribbean countries were a reminder of how domestic disorder could attract foreign intervention. In the unsettled Canadian West, that prospect was more than theoretical. Ottawa believed that Americans would use any pretext to disrupt Canada's destiny as a nation *a mari usque ad mare*. Macdonald's original plans for the Canadian takeover in the Northwest had included a 250-man police force. "It seems to me," he wrote, "that the best Force would be Mounted Riflemen, trained to act as cavalry, but also instructed in the Rifle exercises. They should also be instructed, as certain of the Line are, in the use of artillery." The polymathic police force was temporarily forgotten after the decision to send Wolseley's expedition. By making Manitoba a province, Ottawa lost the right to have its own local police. Instead, after 1870 a small permanent military garrison showed the flag, and provided dependable backing to local officials and an armed escort for officials negotiating treaties with the native people. The 300-man Manitoba Force absorbed money the government might have spent on a territorial police.

News of the Cypress Hills massacre in 1873 forced Ottawa to revise its plans. The murder of Indians by American wolf-hunters could have sparked retaliation, which would draw U.S. cavalry across the border. A first contingent of the new North West Mounted Police, 150 men, spent the winter of 1873-74 under training by the Manitoba Force. Another 150 men went west in 1874 with grudging approval from the new Liberal government of Alexander Mackenzie. The Governor General argued Mackenzie out of arranging a joint expedition with the Americans. Instead, the raw force headed west in the summer and fall of 1874, narrowly escaped disaster, and with ample help from Indians and Métis, learned from its mistake. The NWMP became a versatile, inexpensive means of maintaining both the law and Canadian sovereignty. It also provided a badly needed national legend.

The United States was not quite the only threat to Canadian security. At Aurora in 1874, the quirky and intellectual Liberal, Edward Blake, reminded his listeners that "Tomorrow, by the policy of England, in which you have no voice or control, the country might be plunged into the horrors of war." Those horrors came very close in 1878 when a British government intervened dramatically to save the ailing Turkish Empire from Russia. For their part, the Russians chartered a freighter, the *Cimbria*, loaded her with men and guns, and sent her to Eastport, Maine, to fit out privateers in event of war. Canadian politicians belatedly remembered that a "dominion from sea to sea" included two defenceless coasts, several vulnerable ports, and a very large merchant and fishing fleet. Demands that the British send fast cruisers went unanswered. An inspection of Canada's coast artillery found only ancient smooth-bore cannon, abandoned by the British and useless against armoured ships. A Montreal firm agreed to cut rifling into the barrels of the old guns, a cheap expedient abandoned when the firm fortunately went bankrupt.

Canada's response was characteristically unadventurous. A single officer visited a defenceless British Columbia, borrowed guns from a reluctant Royal Navy, and built a lonely earthwork battery at Victoria. British officers demanded that Canada spend $250,000 to defend Saint John and Sydney. It would be cheaper, Canadian politicians responded, to let the Russians blaze away. The Liberals voted a mere $10,000 for defences. Happily, the crisis passed, but it had consequences. From the short-lived Russian war scare would grow new concepts of defence for the British Empire and new responsibilities for Canada.

Canada's First War

Crises are easier to foretell in retrospect. By the early 1880s, most Canadians could contrast their restored prosperity with the dreary, depression-ridden 1870s. In 1879, Sir John A. Macdonald's re-elected government had delivered its "National Policy." Within two years the NP's protective tariff seemed to be delivering jobs, profits, and expansion. A Pacific Railway was under construction. When the west filled with people, and wealth poured back and forth across the country, Canada's destiny would surely be complete.

Easy re-election in 1882 gave the government money and courage to create long-promised permanent schools for the militia. Liberals repeated old constitutional shibboleths about a "standing army" but Tories welcomed Adolphe Caron's assurance that the new units would provide jobs for "some good young fellows." A troop of cavalry at Quebec, small infantry companies at Fredericton, St. Jean, and Toronto, plus the two existing artillery batteries created new patronage opportunities without exceeding the sacred budget maximum of $1 million. Besides, the new schools might even improve the force.

Canadians felt confident, by 1882, that the West was theirs, though the new railway and a resulting flood of settlement would make it certain. The programme of treaty-making, land surrenders, and annuities had been accelerated by the unexpected extinction of the great buffalo herds. In 1878, fear that hungry Indians would become dangerous persuaded Ottawa to authorize militia in the tiny prairie settlements but the crisis passed and nothing was done. Instead, the NWMP was left with the thankless task of helping compel nomadic hunters to become passive agriculturalists within a single generation. Bitter experience, unaltered by the Sioux victory over the 7th U.S. Cavalry at Little Bighorn in 1876, convinced Indian elders in Canada that resistance was impossible. Younger men responded with a growing frustration and bitterness. The prestige and self-confidence of the mounted police rapidly dissolved. By 1883, arresting a native required a small military operation. The Métis, who had welcomed the force with polite resignation, grew as resentful as the Indians when Ottawa, besieged with conflicting advice, postponed settlement of their land claims along the South Saskatchewan. The police became the local scapegoats. Morale and discipline suffered.

Even white settlers developed bitter grievances. When the Canadian Pacific Railway reached Winnipeg in 1883, prices did not fall as expected. When the railway chose a southern route across the prairies, speculators who had bought land along an expected northern route were ruined. Almost without local military resources since the Manitoba Force was disbanded in 1877, Ottawa hurriedly authorized a new militia battalion in Winnipeg, the 90th Rifles (now the Royal Winnipeg Rifles). The NWMP was expanded to 550 men. In June 1884, white settlers and Métis persuaded Louis Riel to return from his Montana exile to lend his political experience to their cause. A bitter and unstable man, with deep personal grievances, Riel not only prepared a petition but dreamed of uniting Indians and Métis in a theocratic state of his own conception. By repeating the tactics of 1870, Riel hoped to compel the acquiescence of Ottawa. The government of Sir John A. Macdonald would not oblige him.

On March 18, 1885, Riel proclaimed his new government, appointed his *exovedate* or council, and summoned two leading Cree chiefs, Poundmaker and Big Bear, to join him. The rebellion had begun. It became an operation in aid of the civil power only a week later when Riel and his military lieutenant, Gabriel Dumont, defeated a force of a hundred mounted police and special constables at Duck Lake near Batoche. Procedures, established in 1878, allowed Edgar Lewdney, lieutenant governor of the North-West Territories, to apply for aid to Military District No. 10, which covered the West. Major-General Fred Middleton, the relatively elderly British officer commanding the militia, had been sent from Ottawa a week before Duck Lake, because the local militia staff officer was reputed to be a drunken incompetent. Middleton reached Winnipeg on the day of the battle; by nightfall a special train carried him and all the available Winnipeg militia west to Qu'Appelle.

The crisis united the Dominion. English Canadians remembered Thomas Scott and 1870; French Canadians were appalled by Riel's anti-Catholic apostasy and by the murder at Frog Lake, on April 2, of two Catholic missionaries. Within hours, Toronto's Queen's Own Rifles and 10th Royal Grenadiers had each mustered 250 men for service and many more had to be turned away. Militia colonels across Ontario deluged Ottawa with offers of service. Warned in advance, the two permanent batteries had loaded field guns on railway flatcars and were the first to depart. In his own province, Adolphe Caron called on the 9th Voltigeurs de Québec and the 65th Carabiniers Mont-Royal. Officials of the unfinished Canadian Pacific Railway insisted that they could carry troops across the gaps; a government, desperate to prove the value of its huge investment, welcomed the news and despatched the first of thirty-five hundred eastern Canadian militia on what proved for many to be the most arduous experience of the campaign. Battalions of clerks, students, and factory workers struggled through snow, bitter cold, and freezing rain to reach the Lakehead and Winnipeg. Another thirty-five hundred volunteers were recruited in the west as mounted scouts, home guards, and infantry.

At the outset, Riel had the initiative. Terror of the Indians sent panic-striken settlers fleeing to police forts. An NWMP detachment at Fort Pitt abandoned its post. At Battleford, more than five hundred whites crowded into the mounted police stockade. Crees from Poundmaker's reserve formed a warrior lodge and ransacked the town. At Prince Albert, two hundred police, under Commissioner A. G. Irvine, waited passively for orders that never came. Yet Riel did nothing with his opportunity but consult his voices and pray. Instead of the foolish MacDougall, Canada's leader on the scene was a stout white-whiskered veteran who mixed common sense and pomposity in equal measure. General Middleton had a simple plan: Riel's *exovedate* at Batoche was the centre of resistance: capture it and rebellion would cease. Since Canada (and her foreign creditors) would not tolerate a long, costly campaign, Middleton must move fast.

Two difficulties dogged Middleton's plan. Save for a few permanent troops, the militia from Winnipeg and the east was almost wholly untrained. Many had never even fired their rifles; Indians and Métis, he was told, were crack shots and the kind of fighters who had destroyed the U.S. cavalry in 1876. A greater problem was moving horses, waggons, and men across the prairie. By marching overland to Clark's Crossing on the South Saskatchewan River, Middleton reached the maximum range of his land transport; thereafter river steamers would have to solve his logistical problem. Inexperience he could handle only by personal vigilance, great caution in operations, and training on the march.

On April 6, Middleton and a few hundred Winnipeggers set off. Other troops from the east joined them along the trail. More were sent to Swift Current to travel by river steamer. On April 10, urgent orders from Ottawa compelled Middleton to divert Colonel William Otter at Swift Current northwards to rescue Battleford. At Calgary the retired General T. B. Strange led a column of Winnipeggers and Montrealers north to Edmonton and then east to pursue Big Bear and the Crees involved in the Frog Lake killings. The public and politicians had affected Middleton's plans but its main thrust remained: concentrate on Riel at Batoche and leave the Indians for later.

For weeks, Riel refused to respond. A night attack might easily have panicked Middleton's raw soldiers. "It would be too barbarous," Riel told Dumont. It was also not in the Métis tradition: they had out-fought the Sioux by staying on the defensive, and Fish Creek was the boundary of their chosen territory. Only on April 23 was Dumont allowed to fight. At once he rode south with two hundred Indians and Métis and set up an ambush, at Fish Creek, designed to slaughter the Canadians

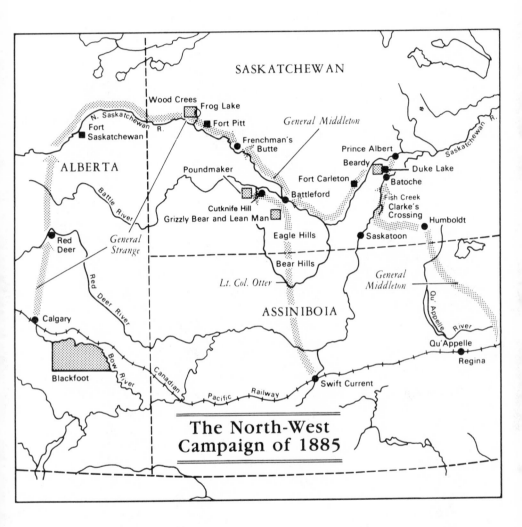

SASKATCHEWAN

Wood Crees
Frog Lake

N. Saskatchewan R.

Fort Pitt

General Middleton

Fort Saskatchewan

Frenchman's Butte

Prince Albert

ALBERTA

Beardy

Duke Lake

Poundmaker

Fort Carleton

Battle River

Batoche

Battleford

Cutknife Hill
Grizzly Bear and Lean Man

Fish Creek
Clarke's Crossing

Humboldt

General Strange

Eagle Hills

Saskatoon

Red Deer

Red Deer River

Bear Hills

General Middleton

Lt. Col. Otter

ASSINIBOIA

Qu'Appelle River

Calgary

Bow River

Qu'Appelle

Canadian

Regina

Blackfoot

Pacific   Railway

Swift Current

The North-West Campaign of 1885

like buffalo when they marched into the coulee. Middleton was no buffalo. He and his scouts exposed the ambush but his soldiers, easy targets on the skyline, could not drive Dumont's men from the creek bottom. As a heavy rainstorm darkened the afternoon sky, the Canadians withdrew to camp to reflect on their fifty-five dead and wounded. Long after most of his men, Dumont went back to Batoche.

Canadian newspapers called Fish Creek a victory but it was easy to read between the lines that the British general had stumbled. In delightful contrast, the Canadian-led column had marched 160 miles in six days to rescue Battleford on the same day, April 24. Colonel Otter was an instant hero. Local citizens demanded revenge and, on May 1, despite Middleton's clear instructions, Otter set out to punish the Crees. At dawn next day the Canadian column climbed Cutknife Hill and paused for breakfast. In the Indian village below, men grabbed their weapons, raced through familiar coulees and poplar bluffs, and soon surrounded the 350 Canadians. Both of Otter's cannons collapsed on their rotten carriages. A Gatling machine-gun, loaned by its American manufacturer, blazed away without effect. At noon, Otter chose to retreat. Poundmaker forbade his warriors to follow. "When my people and the whites met in battle," he said later, "I saved the Queen's men." It was the truth. Journalists, however, insisted that Cutknife was a victory and Otter a Canadian hero.

Middleton was exasperated by Otter's folly and frustrated by his own immobility. Hudson's Bay Company officials had exaggerated the potential of river navigation; their steamer, the *Northcote*, was delayed until May 5. As their courage recovered, militiamen grumbled at "Old Fred's" timidity. At Batoche, spies kept Dumont well-informed. Once it arrived, Middleton fortified the *Northcote* and sent her downriver as a diversion: The Métis commander hauled the Batoche ferry cable out of the water to catch and capsize the little steamer like a toy boat in a brook. Other Métis and Indians dug rifle pits while Riel prayed, recorded his visions, and passed fresh laws through his *exovedate*.

Early on May 9, the *Northcote* appeared, scraped under the ferry cable at the cost of mast and funnels, and disappeared downriver in a wild blaze of rifle shots. Its American master refused to risk any more in a foreign quarrel. Next, from the banks above Batoche came the booming of cannon. Middleton had arrived. Métis and Indians swarmed up the slope and again caught the militia on the skyline. Once again, Middleton saw incipient panic spreading. Retreat would turn into a disaster. Instead, he summoned his waggons, formed a makeshift fort, and made camp. His chief staff officer, Lord Melgund, rode south that night, ostensibly to rejoin his pregnant young wife, but also to guide an avenging British army if Middleton and his men were wiped out.

Next morning, the Canadians were still alive. Middleton began looking for a better plan. On May 11, he found it. Leading his mounted scouts around Batoche, he saw that Dumont's outnumbered men had to race across the prairie to occupy alternative positions. On the morning of May 12, Middleton repeated his movement. When the Métis had shifted, he would fire a cannon and his infantry would attack. Nothing happened. The furious general was told that the troops back at camp had not heard the gun go off. That afternoon, Middleton sent militia battalions out to their old positions. On the right, a unit of rural Ontarians, commanded by Lieutenant Colonel Arthur Williams, a Tory MP, bridled at the General's rebuke. Once in place, the Ontarians kept going. Other battalions — the 10th Royals and the 90th Rifles — followed. Cheering and shouting, the Canadians poured down the hill. Many of the Métis facing them had long since been reduced to firing pebbles and bits of metal. The old men stayed and died; others fell back, killing and wounding thirty Canadians. Dumont pleaded with Riel to flee. In the confusion, they were separated. Three days later, the Métis leader surrendered.

From Batoche, Middleton led his victorious troops north to Prince Albert, pouring his scorn on the unhappy NWMP commander and his "gophers."* Steamers carried the Canadian troops up the North Saskatchewan. Near Battleford, Poundmaker brought his band to surrender. Far to the west, Strange's column of militia, cowboys, and police, barely two hundred men and a gun, met Big Bear on May 28 at Frenchman's Butte. Lost and confused in dense poplars and swamp, the militia drew back. The Indians too, alarmed by the artillery shells, fled but then returned, collected prisoners and possessions, and headed deep into the bush. For most of June, columns of militia and troops combed the woods and muskeg in vain. It was the Indians who released their prisoners and scattered. On July 2, when Big Bear and a young companion surrendered, the rebellion was over.

---

*Commissioner Irvine soon retired to be warden of Stony Mountain prison in Manitoba. Gophers are small unloved prairie rodents with a zest for burrowing.

To many Canadians, the 1885 campaign took on epic proportions. Newspaper coverage was intense. The young Robert Borden, a Nova Scotia anti-confederate, discovered his first stirring Canadianism as he watched fellow Haligonians entrain for the North-West. Victory far sooner than realists had expected was a dangerous reinforcement to the militia myth; volunteers returned in triumph, grumbling only that their British general had been too slow and cautious.

The truth was that the Canadians had been lucky in their commander and their enemy. The militia's losses — 26 dead, 103 wounded — could have been much heavier. The price — $4.4 million with a further $3 million in civil claims — provided ammunition for the Liberal opposition, but the bill was much lower than the government had expected. Riel had discouraged Gabriel Dumont with his indecision and his visions; Dumont's own passive tactics had been no match for those of an experienced and able professional like Middleton. Big Bear and Poundmaker, portrayed in the eastern press as bloodthirsty savages, were anxious and humane moderates, holding back their followers and, in the circumstances of war, impeding their effectiveness. Middleton's planning was not impeccable but he had acted boldly when experts in the east and west had counselled caution. For a man of sixty-five, his energy was astonishing and his pomposity might be forgiven. Four years later, the government allowed him to be hounded from the country on the charge that he had stolen furs during the campaign. Queen Victoria dealt appropriately with the charge by making her old general the Keeper of the Crown Jewels.

Few critics, then or since, understood Middleton's logistical problems. The solution was provided by the Hudson's Bay Company. Its network of posts and transportation systems gave Middleton a ready-made supply system though, of course, at a respectable mark-up. The CPR, on the other hand, was by no means as indispensable as it has been portrayed. The Americans allowed supplies, ammunition, and any militia permitted to make the trip to pass through the United States. The misery, delay, and cost of the CPR route around Lake Superior had good political justification, but it was not a military necessity.

The 1885 campaign was the Dominion's first real war. It foreshadowed much that would happen in future wars. A brief experience convinced the raw Canadian officers that they did not need the fussy tutelage of British generals like Middleton. The initial good feeling between French and English eroded rapidly. The two French-speaking battalions were diverted to Alberta on legitimate grounds that they should not have to fight French-speaking Métis. Alarmist telegrams from the two politicians commanding the battalions got wide and contemptuous publicity in English-speaking Canada; there was no comparable recognition of the dogged good spirits and valiant service of the *Canadiens* in Strange's column nor of the largely French-speaking permanent artillery from Quebec.

In the 1885 crisis, the militia machinery, creaky and flawed, had worked. Canada had not had to turn to the United States for medical aid, as one militia doctor demanded. Troops had been supplied, maintained, and cared for in the field. A lot of the credit belonged to Adolphe Caron. A lightweight in the cabinet, a notorious patronage-monger in Quebec politics, Caron in the crisis proved energetic, inventive, and efficient. He galvanized the officials in his sleepy department and, on the whole, he supported his commander in the field. That did not make Caron a reformer. Despite its obvious defects, the Dominion's armed force had passed its first test: reform and improvement hardly seemed necessary.

A few drew different conclusions. Otter, defeated at Cutknife Hill, was one of them. Whatever the press alleged, he understood that the Cree chief had saved him and his column. As at Ridgeway, nineteen years earlier, Otter had watched raw troops and inexperienced officers throw away the chance of an easy victory. The answer was discipline, training, and professionalism. Otter was unusual. More typical was Colonel George Denison, the former Confederate sympathiser and self-taught cavalry expert whose ego had been battered by the disdain of British officers. In 1866, Denison had also seen the Fenians, but in retreat. In 1885, he and his Toronto cavalry squadron fretted in idleness at Humboldt while Middleton depended on western settlers and their rough prairie ponies to do his scouting. What might appear as common sense struck Denison as an affront. Canadians, in his view, no longer needed British military leadership or example.

Already 1871 seemed a long time ago.

Imperial Defence

No sooner had Gladstone's government called home the imperial garrisons than Britain's imperial pessimism began to lift. In 1874, the man who had called colonies "millstones around our neck" took his

Conservatives back to power by appealing to imperial sentiment. In fact Disraeli and Gladstone had more common ground than might appear: the Liberal believed Britain was too weak for worldwide burdens; the Conservative looked to the colonies to strengthen Britain's military and economic power. Certainly from Britain's viewpoint, Prussia's 1870 triumph over France and the emergence of a new German empire shifted the European balance. German might was based on industrial and scientific resources that rivalled and would soon surpass those of Britain, the self-proclaimed "workshop of the world." Britain's greatest safeguard was her fleet but revolutionary changes in propulsion, armour, and gunnery imposed a heavy financial strain if the Royal Navy was to remain modern. A steam-powered navy depended on dry docks and coaling stations as the sail-powered fleet of Nelson's day never had. Having left her colonies to their own devices, Britain needed them again. The 1878 Russian crisis only underlined the lack of defended overseas bases and their importance if Britain's merchant marine was to plough the oceans in safety. In the wake of the crisis, a Royal Commission began collecting data and considering policies which would rationalize British defence policy in time of war. The return of Gladstone in 1880 short-circuited the commission but its work continued in obscure interdepartmental committees.

While the navy's concerns were paramount in British defence thinking, no analysis could ignore the British army's manpower problems. Cardwell's reforms had only transformed the difficulties without curing them. Low pay and dependence on volunteers forced the British to recruit only the poorest, but slum-bred soldiers took years to become fit for active service. Short service left little time for mature soldiers to be used. No sooner had regiments come home than fresh crises in India, South Africa, and Egypt sent them out again. Officers with Canadian experience looked to the Dominion for help. At the height of the 1878 crisis, Sir Edward Selby Smyth, the British officer commanding the Canadian militia, talked of raising a division of ten thousand men. Others were more eager for peacetime recruiting. Sir John A. Macdonald offered no encouragement. Certainly, he agreed, the British had every right to recruit in a colony but even the worst-paid Canadian labourer would scorn the shilling a day of a British soldier and no Canadian government would welcome the export of able-bodied men from a labour-hungry country. Canada's manpower contribution remained the four graduates a year from its Royal Military College and occasional officers eager for active service. When a British army occupied Egypt in 1881, Major P. O. J. Hébert from the Canadian permanent force accompanied the expedition. He died of fever in Cairo.

The distinction between British and Canadian responsibilities was illustrated by the 1884-85 crisis when Major-General Charles Gordon was besieged at Khartoum. To help his army navigate the Nile, Lord Wolseley asked for the Canadian *voyageurs* who had helped him in 1870. With Ottawa's consent but wholly under British auspices, 386 Canadian boatmen were recruited and sent to Egypt. The excitement of the Sudan campaign and a simultaneous Russian threat to Afghanistan produced war hysteria in Britain and a flurry of volunteering by Canadian officers. A cavalry contingent from New South Wales spent months at Suakin, broiling under the Red Sea sun. Colleagues pressed Macdonald to show the same imperial patriotism. With blunt common sense, Macdonald refused:

> Why should we waste money and men in this wretched business? England is not at war but merely helping the Khedive to put down an insurrection. . . . Our men and money would therefore be sacrificed to get Gladstone & Co., out of the hole they have plunged themselves into by their own imbecillity (*sic*).

In fact, Macdonald took no further interest in imperial defence matters. Attempts to prod the Canadian government failed. In 1887, after Canadian representatives at the first Colonial Conference had parried criticism of Canada's military efforts, Caron launched an elaborate "Commission on the Defences." It met once, adjourned to await its terms of reference, and never reconvened. British interest was languid too: it took several years before Whitehall noticed that the Canadian committee had never functioned.

The mood changed in the 1890s. General Middleton's successor was a very different officer. Colonel Ivor Herbert was young, energetic, and full of ideas. He was also a Catholic and fluently bilingual. By publishing official unit establishments, he revealed the absurd ratio of officers, non-commissioned officers, and bandsmen to privates — 1 to 2.24 in 1894. He created the post of quartermaster general and filled it with Major Percy Lake, a brilliant British officer with Canadian connections. In Quebec, Herbert involved the Catholic hierarchy in summer camps, made French a language of instruction, and outraged Ontario Orangemen by praising the Papal Zouaves of 1868. Herbert's main focus of reform was the permanent force. Ten years after its formation, the force was demoralized, ill-disciplined, and rife with desertion. Infantry schools at London, Toronto, St. Jean, and Fredericton now became companies of a new Royal Canadian Regiment of Infantry (RCRI). The two artillery batteries at Kingston and Quebec had been joined by a third at Esquimalt in 1887. Herbert found the West Coast battery in the final stages of collapse, convinced the Canadian authorities to pay for a small British garrison, and restructured the artillery in separate field and garrison divisions. The cavalry school and a mounted infantry school, started at Winnipeg by Middleton in 1885, became squadrons of the new Royal Canadian Dragoons.

Herbert's reforms made the permanent force more useful to the militia. What volunteers needed, as much as training, was a model of professional efficiency. A more covert purpose was to create a tiny Canadian regular army which might some day be interchangeable with British units. Either role offended most militia officers. After all, it was their regiments that were supposed to form the front line of Canada's defence; the school corps were their servants. Resentment found a focus in 1894 when Herbert and Lake concluded a deal to purchase a new rifle for the force. "We can't have both camps and rifles," the minister of militia told Parliament. Militia outrage at being deprived of the annual outing was doubled when Herbert used some of the surplus funds to assemble the entire permanent force infantry to train at Lévis.

Herbert's achievements owed much to the turmoil after Macdonald's death. The last of three ministers, J. C. Patterson, was, Herbert confessed, "the laziest man I ever knew." That made him easy to handle but no protection in a crisis. After Patterson, at Herbert's urging, foolishly offered the RCRI as a garrison for Hong Kong, both minister and general soon departed. A new minister firmly put the permanent force in its place, cancelled the order for new rifles, and made peace with the militia lobby.

Militia politics made less sense at the end of 1895 when Canada found itself involved in the worst Anglo-American war scare since 1861. The issue was an obscure border dispute between Venezuela and British Guiana but anti-British speeches were popular on the eve of an American election. At the climax of the crisis, the newest British general, W. J. Gascoigne, found himself without a staff, a plan and, thanks to a fierce but unrelated Canadian political crisis, a minister of militia. Like some of his predecessors, Gascoigne was appalled by Canadian insouciance in the face of imminent war. There was no way Canadians could have known that a collapse of the New York stock exchange and dire warnings from American generals and admirals would persuade President Cleveland to accept a compromise. Britain, too, recalled its old resolution not to tangle with the United States in the New World. Both countries accepted a settlement and found new enemies: Spain and the Transvaal.

In Canadian military history, 1896 was a decisive year. In the aftermath of the Venezuela crisis, both the British and the Canadians did some overdue thinking. Reflecting on the possible war, the British army decided that its plan would have been to land troops at Boston or New York "and make a vigorous offensive gesture." Certainly no army would be sent to Canada. As for the Royal Navy, it had no intention of convoying troops anywhere until the growing U.S. Navy was defeated. Though it took a long time before the two services actually met, both the army and navy gloomily concluded that such a war was unthinkable. This conclusion was not transmitted to Canada. Instead, Canadians paid for a new defence review, headed by Major-General E. P. Leach of the Royal Engineers. Completed in 1898, two parts of his report offered a defence plan and a list of the costly reforms necessary to make the plan succeed. A third, secret, report went straight to Britain. Unless and until Canadians had completed the reforms, Leach warned, the British army should not get involved in Canadian defence.

For Canadians, the main event of 1896 was the victory of Sir Wilfrid Laurier's Liberals. For most of the ensuing century, Canada would be ruled by Liberals. One reason was that economic gloom began to lift in most of the world. "I do respectfully urge you," a worried General Gascoigne wrote to the new prime minister, "to send me a Minister who will take a real broad interest in the Militia and, above all, one who is likely to stay." Laurier's choice was a Nova Scotia country doctor, militia surgeon, and businessman, Frederick Borden. A *bon vivant*, capable of playing the fiddle and step-dancing at mess dinners, Borden was also no fool. A conscious reformer, he understood that support from cabinet and caucus depended on observing the rules of patronage. Borden lasted until the defeat of the Laurier government in 1911. He was probably the most important peacetime defence minister in Canadian history.

Borden's mettle was soon tested. The Conservatives had approved regulations limiting the term of command of militia regiments; Borden enforced them. One fellow Liberal, Colonel James Domville, threatened physical violence. Borden wrestled money from reluctant colleagues to rebuild rifle ranges rendered dangerous by high-velocity bullets from Lee-Enfield rifles purchased at the height of the Venezuela crisis. Beginning with a medical service, Borden slowly added supply, transport, signalling, ordnance, and intelligence corps to the militia organization.

In 1898, the dutiful but uninspired Gascoigne was succeeded by Colonel Edward Hutton. The choice seemed ideal. Able, energetic, with a keen sense of publicity, Hutton had recent experience in a similar job in New South Wales. In a whirlwind of speeches, receptions, and inspections, Hutton surveyed his new command and proclaimed as his slogan, a "National Army" for Canada. This had two meanings: a balanced army, complete in every department and ready to take the field; it also meant an army immune from political influences. "A good army, a national army," Hutton told a Toronto audience, "must be one which is apart from party, and which sinks all individual views, be . they political or religious, in the general welfare of the country."

In principle, who could disagree? When Hutton, in his first report, published a fierce indictment of Canada's defences, Borden became anxious. Most of the faults of the force dated from Tory times but, after three years in office, the Liberals would begin to get the blame. Hutton's hostility to political patronage extended to civilian management of the militia's pay, stores, and engineering departments. Borden could hardly quarrel with most of Hutton's reforms. Improving the artillery and switching the emphasis from drill to field training at summer camps made sense. A sharp directive to militia staff officers and instructors to learn French produced predictable grumbling and a warm glow of appreciation from *Canadien* officers. Yet Borden would not have been a politician if he had not wondered what damage Hutton's speeches were doing to Liberal fortunes. Separating the militia from politics meant, in practice, that a British general, not a Canadian minister, would be the main defence authority. That, in plain language, was unconstitutional.

Unlike Herbert, Hutton's priority was to improve Canadian defences against any future Venezuela crisis, not to help in meeting imperial manpower needs. The permanent force no longer exchanged units with the British garrisons at Halifax or Esquimalt. Hutton spoke and wrote of a Swiss system of militia, with the "school corps" playing an important but subsidiary role. The only distraction came in the summer of 1898 when two hundred men were rushed to the Yukon to assert Canadian sovereignty and back the hard-pressed Northwest Mounted Police during the Klondike Gold Rush. Yet, for the British and Canadians alike, a major preoccupation was the approaching war in South Africa.

The Jameson Raid had helped divert attention from the "Christmas crisis" over Venezuela in 1895 but it was only one step in the worsening relations between the self-governing colonies of the Cape and Natal and the neighbouring Boer republics of the Transvaal and Orange Free State. The issues were complex and, to most Canadians, remote, but they could not escape involvement. As one way to bring pressure on the Boers, the British persuaded Laurier to seek a unanimous vote of Parliament to support the British cause. On July 3, 1899, the Canadian House of Commons obliged. Would Canadians do more? Lord Minto (the former Lord Melgund and a close personal friend of Hutton), now Governor General of Canada, understood the Colonial Office's wishes. By early July, he and Hutton had drafted a plan for a small Canadian contingent of twelve hundred men. Lieutenant Colonel William Otter, commanding Ontario's Military District No. 2, was pencilled in as commander. Lieutenant Colonel Sam Hughes, a Tory MP and vigorous imperialist, would be one of Otter's subordinates. The scheme remained secret until September when Hutton finally shared it with his political superior, an enthusiastic Dr. Borden.

As the crisis in South Africa deepened, Britain's expectations from its colonies clarified. The War Office felt no need of colonial military might: experience of the Australians at Suakin showed how long it would take to train colonials to British standards. As colonial secretary, Joseph Chamberlain had a simpler demand. By offering soldiers spontaneously and enthusiastically, the colonies would demonstrate to a sceptical and hostile Europe the British Empire's reserve strength.

Would Canada go along? Some Canadians would not. In Toronto Goldwin Smith, the venerable English scholar who wrote so trenchantly of his adopted country, had already denounced the Americans' "splendid little war" on Spain. South Africa, he felt, was no better. Scattered idealists and pacifists insisted that Canada was a refuge from brutal imperialism. French Canada, in particular, had no ears for the calls of Empire, yet Laurier's own views might have been written by Sir John A. Macdonald:

We have a great deal to do in this country to develop it to its legitimate expansion. Military expenditure is of such a character that you never know where it will end. I am not disposed to favour it. We have done more in favour of Imperial defence in building the Intercolonial and the Canadian Pacific than if we maintained an army in the field in those last twenty years.

Laurier was a politician on the eve of an election year. Torontonians, English Montrealers, and perhaps most Canadians read the struggle in South Africa as an issue of British right and Boer wrong. Colonel Sam Hughes announced that he would, if necessary, lead a private contingent to the war: thousands of offers, he claimed, poured in. Both Hutton and Minto were appalled. A privately raised contingent was precisely what Chamberlain did not want but it might give Laurier the excuse to do nothing. When Hutton tried to muzzle the Tory colonel with military regulations, Hughes exploded at the assault on his freedom. As the crisis reached its climax, two like-minded but out-sized egos collided.

On October 3, as Britain went to war, Ottawa received a Colonial Office circular thanking it for its patriotic offer of a contingent and accepting four 250-man units to be embarked for Cape Town by October 31. Simultaneously, the October issue of the *Canadian Military Gazette* appeared with full details of Hutton's 1200-man contingent. When the government then announced that it had no plans for a contingent, a partially pre-planned uproar burst about its head. On October 9, when Laurier returned from a short visit to Chicago, a private note from the editor of the pro-Liberal Toronto *Globe* warned that he must "either send troops or get out of office."

Rarely in a crisis has a Canadian cabinet been more divided. Most Ontario ministers clamoured for a contingent; the elderly Irishman, Richard Scott, was as fervently opposed. Quebec's J. Israel Tarte, architect of Laurier's 1896 victory, insisted that Canada had no business sending soldiers when she had no voice in imperial decisions. Behind Tarte was a brilliant young back-bencher, Henri Bourassa, and behind both of them, as Laurier knew, was a powerful if inchoate feeling in French Canada that the Dominion had no business risking lives in England's colonial wars. Somehow Laurier found a compromise: the government would organize, equip, and despatch a contingent of volunteers but, once in South Africa, Britain would pay. Parliament need not be summoned for so modest a purpose. On October 14, the painfully chosen words of the compromise were published as an order-in-council:

> The Prime Minister, in view of the well-known desire of a great many Canadians who are ready to take service under such conditions, is of opinion that the moderate expenditure which would thus be involved in the equipment and transportation of such volunteers may readily be undertaken by the Government of Canada without summoning Parliament, especially as such expenditure under such circumstances cannot be regarded as a departure from the well-known principles of constitutional government and colonial practice nor construed as a precedent.

Of course, it was a precedent. Parliament was not summoned because the Liberal caucus might well have torn itself apart. Despite reluctance even to take on the burdens of defending their own country, the crisis made an apparent majority of Canadians insist on involvement in a distant imperial conflict. It would happen again.

South Africa and After

By October 14, Canada had only nineteen days to meet Chamberlain's deadline. The contingent was ready in eighteen. Instead of four small units, Lord Minto insisted that no less than a full infantry battalion would befit the Dominion's dignity. Laurier glumly agreed. From Vancouver to Halifax improvised recruiting stations collected men. Choosing a commander was easy: Lieutenant-Colonel William Otter was native-born, experienced, and a disciplinarian, if luckless in battle. The rest of his officers were announced only after two weeks of frantic political lobbying. Meanwhile, summer uniforms were manufactured, arms and equipment collected, and the entire battalion assembled at Quebec City.

On October 30, 1,061 volunteers, including four nurses, four reporters, and twenty-three surplus officers crowded aboard the ss *Sardinian*. Among them was Colonel Sam Hughes. Hutton's objections to the abusive, insubordinate militia officer had been overborne by Laurier, Minto, and Hughes's own tears of contrition. Once aboard, Hughes proclaimed his independence of all military authority. That was the least of Otter's problems. Though every man of the 2nd

(Special Service) Battalion, Royal Canadian Regiment, was supposed to be a trained militiaman, few knew anything of military routine and many had no knowledge of drill. The month-long voyage to Cape Town on the cramped little ship (re-christened "The Sardine") and two more months at Belmont in South Africa were Otter's only chance to transform raw volunteers into a fair replica of a British line regiment. The experience was unpleasant and few of the Canadians gained any affection for their harsh, elderly colonel. Once the battalion was brigaded with British regiments and set out on the gruelling march to Pretoria, some of them began to understand Otter's reasons.

In the week-long battle at Paardeberg, February 18-27, the Canadians performed well under fire. On their first day, the battalion lost eighty-two casualties, most of them because an over-strained British colonel insisted on leading his men and the Canadians in a hopeless charge. A night attack on February 26 collapsed in confusion, with most Canadians racing back to their trenches, but a handful held their ground and at dawn they overlooked the Boer positions. By coincidence it was the very moment which Piet Cronje had already chosen to surrender. Journalists gave the Canadians the credit. On both sides, February 27 was remembered as Majuba Day, the anniversary of a Boer victory over the British in 1880. The notion that gallant colonials had avenged Britain's humiliation was irresistible to Imperial orators.

Back in Canada, Laurier's cabinet warmed to the approval in English Canada, noted only mild hostility in Quebec, and agreed to offer a second contingent. After a string of British defeats, the offer was accepted. Through December and January the Militia Department collected men and equipment for two small battalions of mounted rifles and three field artillery batteries. They sailed from Halifax 1,320 strong. As a final gesture the government agreed to replace British troops at Halifax and Esquimalt with a 3rd Battalion of the Royal Canadian Regiment. Other Canadian contingents were recruited in ways Laurier would certainly have preferred in 1899. Lord Strathcona, the former Donald Smith, spent part of his vast fortune recruiting a mounted rifle regiment in Western Canada. After both of Canada's official contingents had returned at the end of 1900, twelve squadrons of South African Police, four more regiments of mounted rifles, and a field hospital were recruited at British expense. Most of them arrived only at the end of the war in 1902.

The South African War did much to encourage a naive military enthusiasm in Canada. Newspapers boasted of Canadian exploits, and suppressed most criticism of Canadian defects. Readers thrilled to the courage of the four young men from Pincher Creek who held off fifty Boers until all were dead or wounded. At Liliefontein on November 7, 1900, three Canadians won the coveted Victoria Cross for saving a gun from capture. While Otter's footsore infantry kept up with the best British infantry, the feats of the Royal Canadian Dragoons, Canadian Mounted Rifles, and Strathcona's Horse seemed more in keeping with the adventurous colonial spirit. The war was also comparatively cheap. Of 8,300 Canadians enlisted, only 3,499 served at Canadian expense and, once in South Africa, the British paid most of the bills, including pensions. The 242 Canadian war dead touched only a minority of homes. Among the dead was Fred Borden's only son. A knighthood for the minister was meagre compensation for the two bereaved parents.

Enthusiasm for the war was not, of course, universal. Though the government provided a French-speaking company for Otter's regiment and French-speaking officers for one of the three artillery batteries and chose Lieutenant-Colonel F. L. Lessard to command one of the mounted rifle battalions, few *Canadiens* volunteered. Even in English Canada, the company from western Ontario needed reinforcements from Toronto. On the whole, English-speaking critics of the war learned to curb their tongues; French Canadians felt no such constraint. When Parliament met in 1900, Henri Bourassa denounced the sophistry of Laurier's order-in-council and claimed that British machinations had compelled Canada to offer troops. Nine Quebec MPs joined him in opposition to Laurier.

What Bourassa and most *Canadiens* did not grasp was how far participation in the war had fostered English Canadian nationalism. Active service gave Canadian soldiers fresh confidence in their competence. Sam Hughes's prophecy that Boers "on their old plugs of horses" would ride rings around the British proved true. Troops who departed as "soldiers of the Queen" returned as self-conscious Canadians. Sir Fred Borden, convinced that his son deserved a posthumous Victoria Cross, found common cause with Sam Hughes in resenting British arrogance. Perhaps Canadians were now good enough to emerge from their traditional military tutelage.

Not all Canadians ignored their own shortcomings. "We are a great nation of carpet knights," complained Otter when he read Hughes's boastful reports of his achievements. He had had other trials. Much

Canadian-made equipment was bad. The canvas uniforms chafed painfully and rotted quickly. Canadian-made greatcoats were too thin and the water-bottles were too small. The heavy western saddles wore out horses. British complaints that Canadian officers were not worthy of their men had some substance. If Otter was too strict, the colonel of the Canadian Mounted Rifles was described by a subordinate as not having "a great deal of iron in his make-up." A predecessor suffered a nervous breakdown. Other officers expected political influence to make them immune from discipline. Sometimes it did.

Service in South Africa was a precedent for Canada's role in two world wars and Korea. Providing an overseas contingent joined and even supplanted the older militia roles of home defence and aid to the civil power. South African experience dictated that Canadians in future would serve together under their own officers. Canadian commanders would carry a dual responsibility: to the government in Ottawa as well as to British superiors in the field. They would wrestle with politically influential subordinates and with the limitations of Canadian-made arms and equipment.

Military self-confidence took many forms. An early victim was General Hutton. The government never quite escaped the suspicion that he had helped orchestrate the newspaper agitation in 1899; they had growing evidence that Hutton was eager to repeat his fancied achievement in New South Wales of defeating a colonial government. At Borden's insistence, the government risked opposition criticism by dismissing the general. Minto's intervention and orders for Hutton to report to South Africa prevented an open scandal.

Another manifestation of military nationalism — and of the close alliance of the minister and Hughes, the new Tory militia critic — was the Ross rifle. Borden had failed to persuade the British to manufacture their Lee-Enfield rifle in Canada. Opportunely, Sir Charles Ross, a Scottish sportsman and promoter, promised Canada a superior rifle and a new arms industry. Colonel Hughes was an easy convert to Ross's charms. The more the British criticized the Ross rifle, the more fervent was Hughes's support. Unfortunately, criticism was justified: the Ross was long, delicate, heavy, and easily jammed by dirt and rapid firing. Only as a target rifle did the Ross have strong claims. As a keen marksman, Hughes was satisfied. Critics of the weapon faced formidable bipartisan defenders in Borden and Hughes.

One symptom of post-war self-confidence was Canada's defiant reaction to President Theodore Roosevelt's threats of what would happen if the United States' claims on the Alaska boundary were not satisfied. Americans, at the height of their own imperial expansion, were in a bullying mood; the British remembered past resolutions about North America and prudently retreated. Canadians, who had hoped at least for a compromise, felt bitterly deceived but they turned their indignation on the British, not the Americans.

Some of that wrath fell on the latest British commander of the militia. Lord Dundonald was one of the few generals who had enhanced his reputation in South Africa. His idea of a "skeleton army" was shrewdly adapted to a country that wanted to defy its powerful neighbour. As Dundonald argued, a "skeleton" of well-trained officers and other ranks in the militia would be fleshed out in an emergency by thousands of men who had learned drill in school and who had become crack shots through a network of rifle clubs. Somewhere between the Swiss and the Boer models, such an army would provide security from the Americans for a mere $5 million a year and a one-time expenditure of $12 million for arms and fortifications. Dundonald's scheme and his other ideas for reforming camps, pay, instruction, and the supporting arms and services of the militia found no opposition from Borden. What the Minister did resent was the new general's determination to lecture the government through speeches, press interviews, and leaked official reports. On the whole, Dundonald's reforms were adopted; the general himself felt utterly frustrated. Personalities were part of the explanation; Borden saw Dundonald as another Hutton.

Yet surely the system of command itself was faulty. Of eight British generals sent to command the militia, only the first had completed his term. Of the rest, some had disappointed the War Office; most had angered their Canadian employer. In 1873, it was possible to argue that Canadians wanted a British officer to keep their military efforts up to the mark; never in practice had such intervention been tolerable. For good or ill, Canadian governments had insisted on controlling defence policy. Generals who protested at neglect, corruption, or favouritism fared poorly at the hands of ministers, the militia, and the public.

A new Militia Act in 1904 symbolized new realities. In an early draft, Borden announced that command of the militia would henceforth be open to Canadians. Canadian officers would no longer automatically rank behind British officers. Royal authority over the force would no longer be delegated to the Governor General: Borden was tired of Lord Minto's meddling. In response to pleas from Minto and Dundonald, the British government did its best to deflect the Canadian minister. In 1904, Borden was invited to London to attend the new Committee of Imperial Defence and to be subjected to eloquent flattery. He also found reforms in progress which replaced the historic British post of commander-in-chief with an Army Council of senior civil and military officials. At once, Borden borrowed the idea. A Militia Council would allow him to get advice from a variety of sources. Dundonald could fill a new job as inspector general.

Instead, Dundonald disposed of himself. On June 3, 1904, he chose a banquet of militia officers at Montreal to denounce the minister of agriculture for meddling in the choice of officers for a new regiment. On June 10, Dundonald was dismissed. His plans for a political career in Canada were scotched by a sharp message from the War Office. "Men of Canada, keep both hands on the Union Jack," he told huge crowds in Ottawa; in Montreal, drenching rain dispersed crowds and Dundonald was soon gone. In an election year, the Dundonald affair might be damaging. Sam Hughes echoed the general's charge that the Militia Department was a "Military Tammany." Other Tories claimed that Borden was creating a huge staff. Fears for the British connection were softened when Borden announced that Colonel Percy Lake, the former quartermaster general, would return to fill the senior military position, as chief of the general staff. Although Brigadier-General William Otter took over the post in 1904, Lake was promoted to inspector general and British officers continued to hold the senior posts in the Canadian militia until fifteen more years and a great war had passed.

There was no precedent for the pace of military reform and militia expansion between 1900 and 1914: ability, British or Canadian, was at a premium. Under Borden, the Militia Council met often, produced serious political-military consultation, and recorded decisions with a formality new members (and historians) must have welcomed. In the west, a region which had provided a disproportionate number of Canadians for the Boer War, military organization began to develop in pace with the fastest growing region of the country. In the east, military districts were grouped as commands and later as divisions to allow decentralization, better staff work, and easier mobilization. From 1903, the Laurier government committed $1.3 million a year for new arms and equipment. If British manufacturers had met their delivery deadlines, the Canadian active militia would have been fairly well armed by 1914.

Not the least of Borden's reforms was a dramatic improvement in the militia's medical organization. Backed by his deputy minister, Dr. Eugène Fiset, who had been medical officer with Otter's battalion in South Africa, Borden attracted many of the country's leading doctors to the new medical corps. Fiset's experience with the disastrous typhoid epidemic during the South African campaign made him a passionate proponent of camp hygiene. When nurses were incorporated in the militia in 1906, Borden insisted that they be given full officer status, an example the British did not follow. Other corps and services gradually were added to the militia, often transforming civilian to military administration and eliminating at least some of the political patronage traditionally associated with the Department of Militia and Defence.

Perhaps the greatest contribution to Canadian military reform was the take-over of the British fortresses at Halifax and Esquimalt. German power and British concentration on home waters rendered both garrisons irrelevant. No sooner had the Committee of Imperial Defence decided to abandon its Canadian fortresses than it discovered through Borden that the Laurier government had every intention of taking them over. Not only was it a logical next step in Canadian nationalism, it would also be a less controversial use of Canadian manpower than in future imperial contingents.

On July 1, 1905, the two fortresses passed into Canadian hands though some British troops remained until Canadians could be recruited and trained. Militarily, some of the assets were questionable. Esquimalt had been judged indefensible and Ottawa did nothing to repair the weaknesses. Parts of new guns, abandoned by the British, littered an Esquimalt roadside for some years until they were shipped to Halifax. Experience of providing garrison troops in 1900 was a warning of the difficulty of enlisting Canadians for forty or fifty cents a day. Yet Halifax provided Canadian officers with challenging technical and professional problems. A garrison of a thousand men handling modern artillery and military engineering equipment forced a level of proficiency which the tiny, scattered military schools never exacted. Even women gained a foothold in the permanent force when nursing sisters were recruited for the military hospital.

Take-over of the fortresses completed the process begun in 1871.

Whatever some Canadians and most *Canadiens* might have wished, Canada did not opt out of imperial defence. Halifax and Esquimalt remained imperial fortresses. Their annual defence plans were submitted for British criticism. Imperial conferences in 1907 and 1909 committed Canada to standardize training and organization on British models. Canadian permanent force officers passed British promotion examinations — and prepared themselves by studying tactics suitable for Europe or the North-West Frontier of India. After 1909, a few Canadian officers attended the British Army's staff college at Camberley and many more participated in shorter courses at other schools.

Canada's official national enemy remained the United States. The expanding array of cavalry and infantry regiments and artillery brigades could only be justified by some future replay of the War of 1812. Sam Hughes, kept on strength as a militia staff officer, amused himself by planning an invasion of the New England states. Visiting British inspectors general drafted their reports as though the test of Canadian preparedness was an American invasion.

In reality, the Canadian militia was being prepared for a role in a great European war which, by 1909, seemed almost inevitable.

Militarism, Navalism, and War

Not all Canadians were appalled by the prospect of war. In the years after the Boer War, militarist thinking in Canada asserted itself with unexpected vigour. The poet Charles Mair spoke for a number of intellectuals when he claimed that war had rescued Britain from "the gangrene of wealth and luxury." Charles Darwin was invoked by Dr. J. T. Fotheringham to claim that "the condition of human progress most constantly in evidence, more far-reaching, most ineluctable, is rivalry, competition, the pitting of the strong against the strong." Fotheringham and W. H. Merritt helped create the Canadian Defence League at Toronto in 1909. Its call for universal military training was backed by businessmen, militia officers, clergy, and university professors. Among the financial backers were J. C. Eaton of the merchandising family and Sir Edmund Walker of the Bank of Commerce.

Proponents of patriotism, discipline, subordination, and order found a convenient vehicle in cadet training. Drill for the young was not new. Since the 1870s, J. L. Hughes, Toronto's superintendent of schools, had urged it as one of many educational reforms. By the 1890s,

Toronto's entire schoolboy population paraded for an annual military review. Hughes, an ardent feminist, would have extended the training to girls if public opinion had permitted. Cadet training was one military institution which also appealed to *Canadiens*. The Militia Department's first cadet regulations met a demand from Quebec and the first official corps after Confederation were sponsored by the province's classical colleges. Armand Lavergne, Henri Bourassa's military-minded lieutenant, assured an English-speaking audience in 1910 that "[t]here is no doubt that compulsory cadet service in the schools or educational houses of our country is most beneficial as it teaches the young men the lesson of patriotism and citizenship and teaches them to have a sane mind in a sound body."

Naturally the cadet movement waxed or waned with the general level of enthusiasm for war. It took Lord Dundonald's "skeleton army" scheme to give cadet training a place in the country's defence arrangements while Sir Frederick Borden embarked on a personal tour to implement the system across Canada. In September 1908, he finally completed an agreement with his native province of Nova Scotia: henceforth every teacher in the province would have to qualify in drill and physical training while male teachers must have military training as well. The Militia Department provided instructors, arms, books, examinations, and a bonus for the qualified. The catalyst was provided by Lord Strathcona: a gift eventually totalling $500,000 would be widely distributed as prizes for cadet efficiency. By 1911, six of the nine provinces and both the Catholic and Protestant education committees of Quebec had joined the federal scheme. In 1908, nine thousand boys had enrolled in cadet corps; by 1913, the total exceeded forty thousand, three times the number of Boy Scouts. Dr. Andrew Macphail, editor of the *University Quarterly*, rejoiced: "The school-mistress with her book and spectacles, has had her day in the training of boys; the sensible parents are longing for the drill-sergeant carrying in his hand a good cleaning rod or a leather belt with a steel buckle at the end. That is the sovereign remedy for the hooliganism of the town and the loutishness of the country."

Militarism drew a strong and indignant response. Farm organizations deplored the waste of time and money on the militia and the snobbishness of "gilded staff officers." A growing trade union movement noted the frequent use of the militia to break strikes and forbade members to join. In 1912, the Trades and Labour Congress pledged its support for the international call to meet any outbreak of war with a general strike.

Pacifism was an old and respected tradition in Canada, dating from the Dunkers and Mennonites whom Simcoe had welcomed as settlers and exempted from militia service. Later waves of immigration added to the list of religious conscientious objectors: it seemed a praiseworthy eccentricity in people who were unquestionably productive farmers. In the flood of settlers after 1896, many thousands chose Canada as a refuge from Tsarist or Hapsburg conscription. Native-born Canadians felt themselves immune from such European burdens. The *Farmers' Sun*, noting that three-quarters of the men in the permanent force were British-born, boasted: "The fact is a tribute to the common sense of our people." Far from improving character, as the militarists insisted, most Canadians believed that soldiering produced work-shy wastrels or worse. "I would as soon think of teaching my child to drink whiskey or steal as to be a soldier," insisted the venerable Grit, Malcolm Cameron, in an early debate on cadet training.

Militarists insisted that Darwin had showed the importance of struggle; their critics pointed to the progress of humanitarian reform, the Hague conference of 1899 and 1907, and the spread of arbitration. William Lyon Mackenzie King, an able mediator in industrial disputes and Minister of Labour after the 1908 election, won international recognition by urging mediation in all human conflict. Who was better fitted to represent Canada in planning the 1915 centenary of peace with the United States? It was King's leader, Sir Wilfrid Laurier, who provided the definitive statement of Canada's attitude to war and warlike preparations:

> There is a school abroad, there is a school in England and in Canada, a school which is perhaps represented on the floor of parliament, a school which wants to bring Canada into the vortex of militarism which is the curse and blight of Europe. I am not prepared to endorse any such policy.

Yet the final act of Laurier's government in the summer of 1911 was to assign a staff officer, Colonel Willoughby Gwatkin, to prepare a mobilization plan for one infantry division and a cavalry brigade to serve in "a civilized country." The European vortex was sucking Canada closer.

It was partly to escape that vortex that the Liberals had agreed to garrison Halifax and Esquimalt in 1905 and to establish a Canadian navy. Despite her coasts, her fishing fleets, and one of the largest merchant marines in the world, Canada had been content to rely on the Royal Navy. An ill-fated attempt to acquire a training ship ended in 1882 when the aged *Charybdis* was returned to Halifax. The Royal Navy was content: its doctrine decreed that the Empire's navy should be as indivisible as the seas themselves. Yet, by the early 1900s, as the naval building race with Germany gained momentum, both the navy and the British taxpayer wanted help. In 1909, when the British government proposed to build four huge new battleships, the navy demanded six and the public, inspired by sensational news reports and the Tory opposition, demanded eight. British Liberals, simultaneously building the first stages of a welfare state, looked to the colonies for financial help.

New Zealand, ever loyal, agreed. Australia already had a navy and, preoccupied with the "Yellow Peril" of Asia, wanted more. What of Canada? Laurier firmly opposed financial contributions. The Admiralty alternative — that Canada build a "fleet unit" for the Pacific — was unacceptable. Canada, after all, faced on two major oceans: only a squadron on each coast would be politically acceptable. Though British admirals believed that such a navy might be of very little use, they now also conceded that some help was better than none.

In Canada support for a navy seemed unanimous and bipartisan. George E. Foster, a respected New Brunswick Tory, proposed the idea on March 22, 1909; days later a Liberal version of his resolution passed without dissent. Then unity vanished. In both parties, French Canadian members reacted against any navy as a concession to imperialism. For their part, imperialists denounced a "tin-pot navy"* as a diversion from Britain's urgent need. The Conservative leader, Robert L. Borden, found common ground between the extremes of his party by opposing Laurier's Naval Service Bill when it appeared on January 12, 1910. Only party discipline kept the Liberals in line. By May 4, 1910, despite the furious debate, a Canadian navy had apparently been launched. Tenders were issued for four light cruisers and six destroyers. At Halifax a Royal Canadian Naval College was opened and two surplus British cruisers, the *Niobe* at Halifax and the *Rainbow* at Esquimalt, began service as

---

*The phrase seems to have derived from Stephen Leacock, Canada's best-known political economist, a Tory and, in the future, a popular humorist.

training ships. Rear-Admiral Charles Kingsmill, a Canadian who had made his career in the Royal Navy, agreed to become the service's first director. The government's Fishery Protection Service and sailors borrowed from the Royal Navy provided a nucleus of personnel.

The curse of the *Charybdis* pursued the new navy. The sneers of the Tories and the hostility of French Canadian nationalists continued unabated. While Tory imperialists raged that Laurier had turned his back on Britain in her moment of need, Henri Bourassa used his new paper, *Le Devoir*, to claim that the new fleet bound Canada to participate in any imperial war. Laurier insisted that only Parliament could hand over the ships to British command; Bourassa responded that their white ensigns made them objects of attack as much as any Royal Navy ship. A by-election in Laurier's old riding of Drummond-Arthabaska at the end of 1910 became the battleground for the navy issue. While the Conservatives financed *Le Devoir* and the *nationaliste* campaign, Bourassa and his lieutenants stumped the rural constituency, warning parents that their sons might soon be conscripted for the imperial fleet. The outcome was a Liberal defeat.

Ten months later, when Laurier called an early general election, voters could choose among the usual host of issues. Outside Quebec, the naval question ranked far behind the reciprocity issue. In French Canada, however, the Conservative-*nationaliste* alliance scored heavily in rural counties by exploiting suspicion of the navy and its vague association with conscription. Laurier entered the campaign with fifty of Quebec's sixty-five seats. On September 21, 1911, he retained only thirty-seven. Across Canada, the Tory crusade against closer economic links with the United States triumphed. Even without Bourassa's *nationalistes*, Robert Borden could become prime minister.

The ironies continued. Having helped defeat Laurier for his naval policy, Bourassa had to watch the new Conservative government propose a contribution to Britain of $35 million as the price of three new dreadnought battleships. To force his policy through Liberal obstruction, Borden applied closure for the first time in Canadian parliamentary history. A Liberal majority in the Senate promptly defeated the naval aid bill and defied the Conservatives to call a general election. The Conservatives halted recruiting for "Laurier's navy" and allowed the force to waste away. When war came, anti-oriental British Columbians had the awkward pleasure of seeing their coastline defended by cruisers of the Imperial Japanese Navy.

Canada's militia experienced no such eclipse under the new government. Personally defeated in 1911, Sir Frederick interceded with his cousin on behalf of Sam Hughes. The new prime minister had profound misgivings about his colleague; they were outweighed by Hughes's energy and knowledge and by his fidelity during the long years in opposition. Repentant and tearful, Hughes solemnly swore to mend his ways.

Thanks to Sir Frederick, the Tory militia critic had risen to be senior colonel in the force. Now, as minister, he behaved as both political master and commander-in-chief. Never before or since has so devout a militarist held the defence portfolio. Dressed in full uniform, Hughes attended manoeuvres, camps, and ceremonial parades. He harangued officers and men like a drill sergeant. In his office he took off his jacket, hoisted his feet on the desk, and entertained journalists and old cronies. Visiting newsmen were delighted by anecdotes, philosophy, and occasional tasteless displays by the minister, humiliating frightened subordinates.

Under the Liberals, the budget of the militia department had risen from $1.6 million in 1898 to $7 million by 1911. Despite a severe financial depression, Hughes managed to raise the total to $11 million in 1914. In 1904, 25,000 men had been trained; in 1913, 55,000 volunteers went to camp. New regiments, especially in the west, brought militia strength to 74,213, while the permanent force stood at 3,110 officers and men of other ranks. Personnel had outstripped equipment: two hundred modern guns met the needs of only two of six infantry divisions, but getting more depended on slow-moving British factories. In 1905, the Liberals had established a huge training camp at Petawawa in the Ottawa Valley but in the summer of 1914, Hughes added Valcartier, near Quebec, and plans were afoot for a new camp on the sandy Angus Plains north of Toronto. It would be named Camp Borden in honour of his predecessor.

Hughes delighted militia officers and militarists alike. When he assembled senior officers at the end of 1911 for their first-ever conference, Hughes promised free army boots, more camps and drill halls, and the government's full moral backing for the force. Militiamen were pleased when Hughes scolded the permanent force and staff officers for pretending to supplant the volunteers as Canada's first line of defence. They rejoiced that the few economies Hughes intended would be at the expense of men he called "bar room loafers." The minister's preoccupation with temperance was, however, a sore point. Liquor, he insisted, must be banned from the camps. As on most points, Hughes was inflexible. Apart from his own dry convictions, he shared his brother James's enthusiasm for cadet training: no evil influences could be allowed to affect the youngsters entrusted to his charge.

Travelling incessantly in his private railway car, Hughes made sure that Canadians heard his views. They were in stark contrast to the apologetic tone normally considered appropriate for a peacetime Canadian defence minister. An audience at Napanee in 1913 heard a typical message:

> To make the youth of Canada self-controlled, erect, decent and patriotic through military and physical training, instead of growing up as under present conditions of no control, into young ruffians or young gadabouts; to ensure peace by national preparedness for war; to make the military camps and drill halls throughout Canada clean, wholesome, sober and attractive to boys and young men; to give that final touch to imperial unity, and crown the arch of responsible government by an inter-Imperial Parliament dealing only with Imperial affairs.

Such views, together with Hughes's energy and charm, captivated many militia officers. So did the minister's policy of retiring older staff officers like Otter. Keen militiamen like Colonel Ernest Cruikshank, an able amateur historian, and Colonel J. P. Landry, son of the new Conservative speaker of the Senate, were chosen for vacancies that professionals had once considered their monopoly. In 1913 Hughes promoted Armand Lavergne, Bourassa's ally, to command a Quebec militia regiment.

The minister also made enemies. When he forbade *Canadien* regiments from parading under arms in Quebec's traditional religious processions, critics blamed Hughes's notorious Orange connections. The worst depression in recent memory made more and more Canadians exasperated with the excesses of "Drill Hall Sam." A resurgent Liberal Party found that the Tory defence minister was one of their easiest targets. Hard-pressed Canadians were aroused by news that militia staff officers had each been provided with a Ford car or that Hughes had taken militia cronies, their wives, and his own female secretaries on a prolonged excursion to the British, French, and Swiss manoeuvres in 1913.

Everywhere militarism ebbed away. In 1912, Professor Maurice Hutton of the University of Toronto had assured educators that the Empire could easily have too little militarism; she could never have too much. Two years later, when a contingent of the new Canadian Officers Training Corps was proposed for his university, Hutton responded that students would have no time for such activities. By early 1914, the Canadian Defence League gave up the ghost. That spring, when the Conservatives suffered an unexpected by-election defeat, party officials warned that Sam Hughes had been their main liability.

In July 1914, when Sir Robert Borden departed for a badly needed vacation, one of the problems he took with him was the need for a less bellicose minister of militia.

IV The Great War

"Canada Is at War"

Like so many earlier war scares, the European crisis of 1914 boiled up with incredible speed. Few Canadians could have believed that a terrorist assassination in an obscure Bosnian city would involve them. Most believed that Britain's peace-minded Liberal government would find a way to stay neutral. Indeed the thought enraged Sam Hughes. "They're going to skunk it," he fumed after officials persuaded him not to haul down the Union Jack at militia headquarters. They did not. At midnight, August 4, 1914, the British ultimatum to Berlin expired.

"When Britain is at war, Canada is at war," Laurier had said in 1910, "There is no distinction." There was also no argument. Canada was visibly united. Cheering throngs in Montreal outnumbered crowds in Toronto. By August 7, Canada's offer to bear the full costs of a contingent of twenty-five thousand men had been accepted. On August 18, Sir Wilfrid Laurier seemed to speak for both Liberals and Conservatives: "When the call comes, our answer goes at once, and it goes in the classical language of the British answer to the call of duty, 'Ready, aye, ready'." W. F. O'Connor, one of Borden's legal advisors, set out to draft emergency legislation. "Make absolutely certain," a Liberal member insisted, "that you omit no power that the Government may need." O'Connor's War Measures Act met the test.

Taking no interest in military matters, most Canadians assumed that the country was utterly unready for war. In fact, formal precautions had begun on July 31. A War Book, completed earlier that year, gave each department its orders. At Halifax and Quebec, port defences and an examination service mobilized to prevent a surprise attack. At Esquimalt, HMCS *Rainbow*, half-manned and without proper ammunition, bravely went to sea. If she had met the nearby German cruiser, the *Leipzig*, the much-maligned navy would have given Canada her first war heroes.

Thanks to Major-General Gwatkin, the new militia chief of the general staff, mobilizing twenty-five thousand men should have been easy. Colonel Hughes scrapped the general's plan, ordered contractors to Valcartier to build the longest rifle range in the world, and summoned volunteers by sending out hundreds of telegrams to militia colonels.

Throughout September, a sweating, swearing, sublimely happy Hughes pulled some kind of order from the chaos he had created. Most Canadians marvelled at the minister. Confusion pursued the contingent to the Quebec docks where men, horses, and equipment were somehow loaded in ships, to be sorted out in England. "Men," the minister's farewell message proclaimed, "The world regards you as a marvel." On October 3, the armada sailed, pursued from New York by a frenetic Hughes.

"Canada's answer," as a cartoonist called it, was anything but ready. Most men were untrained. Too many officers were over-confident amateurs, convinced that war was a prolonged summer camp. With the Contingent went almost all of Canada's modern guns and equipment. Yet no belligerent, not even Germany, was really prepared for the Great War. Generals predicted quick victories, won by cavalry, light artillery, and fast-marching infantry. One man, Ivan Bloch, had warned in 1898 that modern war would be a merciless, interminable struggle, ending in mutual exhaustion. On the whole, Polish-Jewish bankers were not heeded as military thinkers. The war, insisted the experts, would be short: anything else would be suicidal.

In fact, Bloch was right. The mood and energy mobilized for a short war made long wars inevitable. In the atmosphere of a national crusade, compromise was impossible and defeat unthinkable. The machine-gun, heavy artillery, and huge conscript armies favoured defence while all generals had been taught to attack. Few people in 1914 foresaw the terrible extent of the war. Lord Kitchener, the taciturn veteran recalled to the War Office, shocked his cabinet colleagues by demanding a million soldiers: Britain eventually needed five million. In Canada, General Gwatkin foresaw a recruiting crisis by early 1915. Bourassa, initially favourably disposed to the war, also warned the government "to take exact account of what it can do and to ensure our own national security before starting or pursuing an effort that it will perhaps not be in a state to sustain until the end."

Such caution was unfashionable. Crusades are not launched in moderation. Some Canadians fought for the Empire; others, like J. W. Dafoe of the Manitoba *Free Press*, insisted it was Canada's own war against Prussian militarism. Conservative thinkers like Stephen Leacock and Dr. Andrew Macphail promised that war would drive out selfishness, materialism, and petty politics. Clergy, abandoning their pre-war pacifism, assured congregations that Canada would be purified when she had passed through the terrible fiery furnace. Meanwhile, in a phrase instantly adopted, most Canadians tried to "do their bit."

There was plenty to do. A Canadian Patriotic Fund, like predecessors during the Crimean and Boer Wars, mobilized a vast national charity to support soldiers' families. By the end of 1914, it had collected $6 million and by the end of the war $47 million. From mid-1915, a Military Hospitals Commission co-ordinated the work of caring for sick and wounded soldiers, helping to create nursing homes, hospitals, and sanatoria with aid from the IODE, the Red Cross, and Khaki Leagues. Plans to finance the work with a Disablement Fund were dropped to avoid competition with the Patriotic Fund. By 1917, the Commission had over six thousand beds and its own artificial limb factory.

Remote from the war, Canadian patriots found enemies close at hand. By policy as much as neglect, Ottawa at first let German and Austrian reservists cross to the United States. In October, only under public pressure, did it begin opening internment camps. Across Canada, German teachers, engineers, and professionals were harried from their jobs and often interned. Port Arthur and Fort William interned unemployed workers of Austro-Hungarian origin to save relief costs. In British Columbia, union miners struck until "enemy aliens" were removed from the pits and locked up. By mid-1915, the camps held six thousand men and a few families. The four hundred thousand Canadians of German ancestry were another target. Commercial pressure eventually forced their main community, Berlin, to rename itself Kitchener.

Fervour owed something to anxiety. The best reason to expect a short war, experts insisted, was that no nation could stand the financial strain and economic dislocation. Massey-Harris, the huge farm implement manufacturer, had distributed its European exports but had yet to be paid when war broke out. Everywhere, employers laid off workers and buyers cut orders. Unemployment as much as idealism sent men flocking to Valcartier. Many were recent British immigrants who had failed to find a place in a suffering economy.

Supplying those soldiers was a lonely bright spot in the economy. When Canadian troops showed off their new boots, uniforms, and waggons, British orders would surely follow. Instead, a few months on Salisbury Plain showed that much of the equipment and clothing of the First Contingent was shoddy or ill-designed. Shady promoters, even when armed with a colonel's commission and a letter from Hughes, were bad advertisements for Canadian business. A well-established exporter, like the William Davies Co., quadrupled its business in the first year of the war but a British contract for 2 million Canadian boots did nothing to enhance Canada's reputation for quality. The prime minister himself intervened in early 1915. "A very painful and even bitter feeling is being aroused throughout the Dominion," he warned the British, "Men are going without bread in Canada while those across the line are receiving good wages for work that could be done as efficiently and cheaply in this country." It seemed hard, indeed, that Americans prospered while Canadians starved.

As the war degenerated into a stalemate, the British found themselves desperately short of artillery ammunition. A small Dominion Arsenal, opened in 1883 to make rifle bullets, had graduated by the eve of war to producing a few shells for militia artillery. Hughes summoned business cronies, formed a Shell Committee, and demanded business. The British asked no questions. A country with ten sets of inspection gauges had orders by Christmas for 2 million shells and 1.9 million brass casings. By mid-summer, 1915, the Shell Committee had $170 million in orders; it had delivered $5.5 million worth in a climate of profiteering and ill-concealed scandal.

Unfettered free enterprise had failed. With Borden's full support, the new British Minister of Munitions, David Lloyd George, stopped all orders until a new Imperial Munitions Board (IMB) took charge of the Canadian industry. While Hughes raged and industrialists grumbled, a self-made Methodist millionaire, Joseph Flavelle, put together an effective management team, squeezed the more notorious profiteers, and kept patronage-seekers at bay.

The new Board was autocratic, increasingly efficient, and unloved. It spotted manufacturers filling pinholes with paint and boldly using counterfeit inspection stamps. The West complained that the IMB discriminated against it. Flavelle replied, with proof, that not even specially high prices could make western contractors produce on time. Unions demanded the fair-wages clauses required in both Canadian and British government contracts. Flavelle bluntly answered that, without IMB contracts, union members would be out of a job. When Hamilton machinists struck, he broke the strike and used wartime censorship to keep the news out of the papers.

By 1917, the Board was the biggest business in Canada, with six hundred factories, one hundred and fifty thousand workers (including forty thousand women), and a turnover of $2 million a day. By

1918, its "national factories" produced chemicals and high explosives. When German U-boats threatened the sea lanes, the IMB turned to ship-building. Since thousands of young Canadians yearned to join the new war in the air, Flavelle persuaded the British to open training schools in Canada. The IMB's Aviation Department built Canada's first military airfield at Camp Borden in 1917 and soon added half a dozen more satellite fields. Canadian Aeroplanes Ltd., an IMB company, turned out twenty-nine hundred trainers and thirty flying boats. By mid-1918, an IMB operation in British Columbia, employing twenty-four thousand men, supplied forty per cent of the timber used in British aircraft manufacturing.

In 1914, no one hoped for a short war more than Sir Thomas White and officials in the Finance Department. By October, the government was spending half a million dollars a day on the war. Later, White confessed that his department lost control of spending. When the auditor general dared to query Hughes, the minister of militia gave him a public scolding. Federal government expenditure rose from $184.9 million in 1913 to $337.9 million in 1915 and $573.9 million in 1917. White was a timid, unimaginative financier who naturally had the confidence of the business community. Raising taxes, he feared, would discourage post-war immigration—and upset investors. Duties and excises were raised a little. Rich and poor alike, he explained, should make sacrifices. So should future generations: "We are justified in placing upon posterity the greater portion of the financial burden of this war," he explained, "waged as it is in the interest of human freedom and their benefit."

Who would lend the money? Already London was struggling to finance Britain's war effort. New York proved incredibly expensive. No one had dreamed of asking Canadians themselves for money and White certainly did not want to be the first. By 1915, he had no choice. A $50 million bond issue was placed — and was over-subscribed a hundred percent. The same happened again in 1916 and 1917. It was expected that a Victory Bond, aimed at small savers and boosted by patriotic advertising, might bring in $150 million: it delivered $500 million. Two later series were almost as successful. So were War Savings Certificates and, for children, War Savings Stamps.

The truth was that the war made Canada prosperous. The pre-war depression was due to huge unused capacity: three transcontinental railways, a northern Ontario mining frontier, hundreds of shut-down factories. Some hard-times lessons should have been heeded. Drought and crop failures had persuaded some western farmers to diversify from King Wheat. Wartime demand cancelled that wisdom. Wheat acreages soared from 10.3 million in 1914 to 15.1 million in 1915, a year of the best yields in memory. Farm prices outpaced costs. When harsher weather and soil exhaustion cut yields after 1915, Ottawa rapidly stepped in. In 1916, when Britain, France, and Italy centralized wheat-buying, Canada answered with its own wheat export company. A year later, when expected shortages produced a run on the Winnipeg futures market and prices soared, the government set the market aside, appointed a Board of Grain Supervisors and managed the market for the rest of the war. The seeds of future rural disaster were planted by inflated wartime prices.

Between them, food and munitions helped pay for the war. The value of the IMB's production, a billion dollars, equalled two thirds of Canada's military expenditure. Yet Canada's most important contribution to the war was manpower. At Halifax, in December 1914, Borden declared: ". . . there has not been, there will not be, compulsion or conscription. Freely and voluntarily, the manhood of Canada stands ready to fight beyond the seas." Already a Second Contingent was scattered in armouries and drafty exhibition halls across Canada. It left in the spring. Twelve regiments of mounted rifles were organized to defend the Suez Canel from the Turks; they were diverted to England. By July 1915, the approved strength of the Canadian Expeditionary Force reached one hundred and fifty thousand. In October, after a dispiriting visit to England, Borden pushed the total to two hundred and fifty thousand. In his New Year's message for 1916, the prime minister declared that Canada would send half a million men to the war.

There were only eight million Canadians; perhaps a million and a half were men of military age. How many were fit? Would a third of them volunteer? To recruit soldiers, General Gwatkin turned to the pre-war militia regiments. Many of their best officers had already gone. Equipment was scarce. Men waited months even for uniforms. Still, in eleven months, the old units raised almost ninety thousand men. Ottawa paid nothing. Advertising, band instruments, even the new battalion cap badges were financed by regimental funds or local subscriptions. Between October 1914 and September 1915, seventy-one new CEF battalions were formed, together with scores of artillery batteries, machine-gun companies, bicycle units, and other organizations.

Patriots clamoured for more. Hughes agreed. After August 1915, any group or individual could apply to form a battalion. The minister revelled in the frenzy. Recruiting leagues blossomed. In Edmonton, three battalions competed for men in February 1916; in Winnipeg, there were six; in Toronto, ten. Orangemen, "Sportsmen," "Pals" claimed battalions. Many promised Highland dress; others were reserved for the Irish. One unit promised mothers that its men would never touch liquor. Two battalions were reserved for Americans; another took "Bantams," men too short for the CEF minimum height of five foot two. Enthusiastic colonels and good-natured doctors ignored youth, old age, and obvious disability to fill the ranks. Only later would such men demand pensions and compensation. Colonels drew the line at colour. Japanese Canadians were rarely welcomed; blacks were segregated in a construction unit. Canadian Indians, however, were eagerly sought; colonels boasted of their ferocity.

Patriotic recruiting seemed successful, adding 123,966 men to the CEF's infantry battalions. The truth was more complex. Of 170 battalions formed after October 1915, only 40 reached full strength. Almost 60 per cent of the men joined before the end of 1915. From July 1916 to October 1917, only 2,810 men volunteered and went overseas as infantry. At the moment Borden promised 500,000 men, voluntary recruiting petered out.

Thousands of Canadians bypassed the infantry to join the artillery, engineers, medical, and army service corps. Urgent British appeals diverted many more to forestry and railway units. By 1917, young Canadians could also join the Royal Flying Corps in Canada. As it was, almost 1 in 6 Canadians between 15 and 54, 232,968 men, volunteered for the infantry. Many more volunteered for other branches of the CEF, returned as reservists to the British and allied armies, joined the Royal Naval Air Service or the Royal Flying Corps or even enlisted in the Royal Navy. By 1917, though no one realized it, Borden's target was close to being reached.*

Those who did not go had their reasons. By the summer of 1915, two of the sharpest goads for enlistment had disappeared. Few people now believed that the war would be short and exciting and no one needed work. Factory owners, desperate for labour, even demanded

---

*This analysis reflects unpublished research by Prof. R. C. Brown, kindly shared with me.

that skilled workers be sent home from overseas. In rural areas, farmers raised wages and pleaded for harvest leave so that soldiers could help in the fields. By 1916, the labour shortage was so acute that most interned aliens were released.

Manpower shortage was only part of the problem. By 1916 it was also obvious that the Great War did not unite all Canadians and that probably it never had. Differences which had seemed almost irrelevant in peacetime emerged as frightening cracks in Canadian unity. The war was more than a test of economic strength and physical courage.

Apprentice Army

On October 15, 1914, ships carrying the Canadian contingent reached Plymouth. Disembarkation was as chaotic as the loading at Quebec. Soldiers discovered the potency of British beer. Officers wangled leave. Equipment, hopelessly jumbled in the ships' holds, was finally heaped along roadsides so units could claim their own. In warm sunshine, the Canadians pitched their tents on Salisbury Plain. It was a brief prelude to the wettest English winter in memory.

Hughes grudgingly accepted a British officer, Lieutenant General Edwin Alderson, to command the new 1st Canadian Division. Alderson had commanded Canadians in South Africa but nothing had prepared him to deal with the minister of militia. Hughes had equipped "his boys" with Ross rifles, Oliver equipment (already condemned in South Africa), boots that dissolved in the mud, and "shield shovels," borrowed from a Swiss idea, patented by his secretary, Ena McAdam, and cordially detested by the troops. Alderson abandoned the shovels and most of the hurriedly collected cars, trucks, and farm waggons Hughes had procured for the contingent and replaced them with the British standard pattern. The Ross, for all its defects, went to France. The British were too short of rifles to replace it.

By December, Princess Patricia's Canadian Light Infantry (PPCLI), a battalion formed by a wealthy Montrealer, Hamilton Gault, and manned by British reservists living in Canada, was in action with a British division. Two months later, on February 16, the first units of the Canadian division landed in France. Two permanent force regiments, the Royal Canadian Dragoons and Lord Strathcona's Horse (later joined by the Fort Garry Horse from Winnipeg), stayed behind to form the Canadian Cavalry Brigade. Several extra battalions and hundreds of surplus officers, most of them already found wanting by Alderson or his subordinates, waited in England to replace casualties.

The war was not at all as generals had expected or as war artists had portrayed it. The first few months had seen dramatic movement and huge victories and defeats. From Mons, in Belgium, a tiny British army had been hurled back by the German advance only to rebound, with its French allies, at the gates of Paris. At Ypres in October, the remnants of that army had been annihilated but the British had stopped the last chance of a real German breakthrough. By Christmas, an unbroken line of trenches stretched from the Swiss frontier to the English Channel. Ivan Bloch's prediction had come true.

Into this trench warfare, Canadians came as raw apprentices. A few tours in quiet sectors taught them the basic rules. Between the lines lay "no-man's land," pock-marked by shell holes, strewn with barbed wire, abandoned equipment, and fragments of humanity. Snipers watched for the unwary. Machine-guns swept the landscape with random bullets. Heavy artillery, in growing numbers, searched out opposing guns or casually blasted trenches and dug-outs. Soldiers lived like moles, underground and in darkness. At night, they set out on weary, dangerous patrols or struggled to repair trenches and barbed wire. Working parties plodded up and down communication trenches, dragging food, water, and ammunition to the front. An hour before dawn and dusk, every man stood guard, for those were the likely times for an enemy attack. In daylight, a few men might sleep.

Behind the lines, the infantry was supposed to rest but usually there were loads to carry, reserve trenches to dig, or boots and buttons to be polished for a general's inspection. An occasional bath and disinfected underwear did not deter the perennial body lice. Few men starved but a coarse, unvarying diet of corned beef, biscuit or bread, tea, and cheap jam left soldiers perpetually hungry. In rear areas men slipped away to an *estaminet* for a standard treat, fried eggs and chips, but there was little real contact with the tough, bitter French or Belgian civilians whose land had fallen victim to war. In the trenches, men lived in rain or snow and always in the glutinous Flanders mud. Huge rats gorged themselves on leftover food and unburied corpses. Life was always dangerous. In its first quiet tour, the Canadian division lost a hundred dead and wounded. In the germ-ridden mud, almost every wound became infected. Military medicine had made incredible strides from earlier wars, particularly in controlling and immunizing

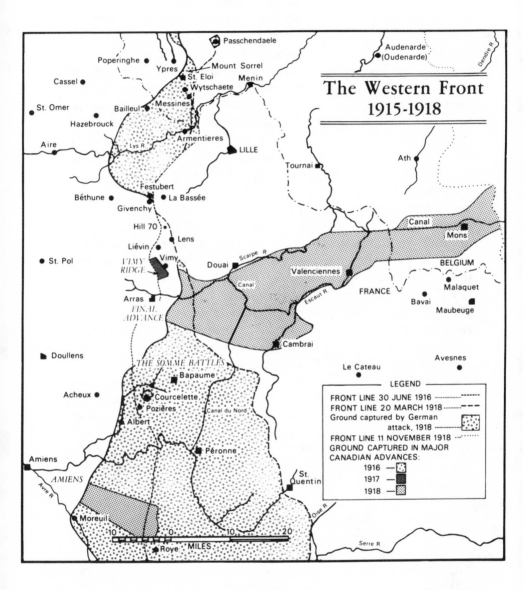

The Western Front
1915-1918

LEGEND

FRONT LINE 30 JUNE 1916 ············
FRONT LINE 20 MARCH 1918 - - - - - -
Ground captured by German
        attack, 1918
FRONT LINE 11 NOVEMBER 1918 ·········
GROUND CAPTURED IN MAJOR
CANADIAN ADVANCES:
        1916 —
        1917 —
        1918 —

Passchendaele
Audenarde
(Oudenarde)
Dendre R
Poperinghe
Ypres
Mount Sorrel
St. Eloi
Menin
Wytschaete
Cassel
Messines
Bailleul
St. Omer
Armentieres
Hazebrouck
LILLE
Aire
Lys R
Tournai
Ath
Festubert
La Bassée
Béthune
Givenchy
Canal
Mons
Hill 70
Lens
Liévin
Canal
BELGIUM
St. Pol
VIMY
RIDGE
Vimy
Scarpe R
Douai
Valenciennes
Malaquet
Arras
Canal
Escaut R
FRANCE
Bavai
FINAL
ADVANCE
Maubeuge
Doullens
Cambrai
Avesnes
THE SOMME BATTLES
Le Cateau
Bapaume
Acheux
Courcelette
Pozières
Canal du Nord
Albert
Péronne
Amiens
St.
Quentin
AMIENS
Avre R
Oise R
Moreuil
Serre R
10   0   10   20
Roye   MILES

against disease, but antibiotics were unknown and blood transfusion was a dubious experiment. Pneumonia and influenza were major killers, slaying more than three thousand young Canadian soldiers.

Trapped in a stalemate, generals dreamed and schemed of the great breakthrough. Mere passive defence was intolerable. Romantic literature persuaded them that raw courage could achieve anything. More scientific soldiers calculated the weight of artillery shells necessary to blast a way forward. Until 1916, only the Germans had such resources. Even then, armies could advance no faster than the couple of miles an hour an exhausted, over-burdened infantryman could manage. Behind him, roads would be clogged by marching battalions and endless columns of horses and waggons. In hours, an enemy could plug any gap with machine-guns, artillery, and counter-attacks.

For all their innate conservatism, generals welcomed new technologies. Only posterity can distinguish the geniuses from the crackpots. Ancient weapons of siege warfare — grenades, mortars, underground mines — reappeared. Greek Fire reappeared in the terrifying flamethrower. By 1916, soldiers resembled mediaeval pikemen in their steel helmets and goatskin jerkins. Horses still hauled most of an army's guns and supplies but thousands of trucks, buses, and staff cars bounced over the French *pavé* and huge tractors began pulling the heaviest guns. Colonel E. D. Swinton seized the idea of using caterpillar tracks to roll across the battlefield. At the Admiralty, Winston Churchill backed the idea of land battleships, armed with surplus small-calibre naval guns.

In 1914, eleven years after the first flight, airplanes were still fragile, dangerous toys. A single aircraft crossed with the Canadian contingent but Sam Hughes, like most people, had no faith in such contraptions. A year of war taught both sides that aviation was a major force. Only aircraft and balloons could allow generals to see beyond the enemy's lines. Bombing from German Zeppelins and later from heavy aircraft forced Britain to redeploy large, badly needed resources to protect her cities. German, French, and British engineers struggled to improve air frames and engines. Pilots learned to kill or be killed as they struggled to master a new environment. Until 1916, no one knew for sure what caused a spin or how to get out of it. One thing was certain. The air war was an escape from the grimy hopelessness of the trenches. In growing numbers, young Canadians headed for the British air arms. Perhaps because their accents and schooling were hard for the British to classify, they slipped through barriers erected to keep the lower classes from officer status and emerged as a growing share of the pilots of the Royal Flying Corps and the Royal Naval Air Service.

Most Canadians stayed on the ground. In mid-April 1915, Alderson's division took over the trenches at Ypres where British regulars had died stopping the last great attack of 1914. On April 22, a pleasant spring evening, the Germans released their latest surprise, 5,730 cylinders of chlorine gas. A rolling green cloud dissolved a French-Algerian division. Gasping and dying, terrified soldiers fled past the Canadian positions. That night, the Canadians struggled to close the gap; by dawn, they were driven out but the Germans did not follow. On April 24, the Germans turned on Brigadier-General Arthur Currie's brigade of westerners. Shells, chlorine gas, and waves of infantry broke over the Canadians. Men urinated on their handkerchiefs and held them to their noses to breath. The Ross rifles seized up from rapid firing or clogged in the mud. Two leading battalions were wiped out. Somehow the remnant fought on. Finally, British, Indian, and French troops took over.

The second battle of Ypres cost the Canadian division 6,035 men. Later, the PPCLI lost 678 men: only 150 survived. News of the battle brought a little of the war home to Canada. Self-congratulation and romantic images of soldierly courage overshadowed the mourning. Recruiting perceptibly picked up.

Men from the cavalry brigade helped fill the shattered battalions. Soon there was more fighting. At Festubert on May 18, the Germans pulled back slightly before a Canadian attack and then slaughtered Alderson's men on the barbed wire. The division lost 2,468 men and gained only experience. At Givenchy, a month later, a mine intended to devastate German trenches blasted Canadians as well. The assault failed. All three battles were part of a savage kind of education. At terrible cost, the 1st Division lost its misfits and learned its business. Some of the failures returned to England and Canada to be honoured and promoted.

In September, after a summer in England, the 2nd Division reached France. Canadians now formed a small army corps under Alderson; two of his brigadiers, Arthur Currie and Richard Turner, a Victoria Cross winner from South Africa, took over the 1st and 2nd Divisions respectively. Sir Sam Hughes (knighted and promoted for his own services) would have preferred to command the Corps himself. He blamed Alderson for the losses at Ypres and for daring to substitute the Lee-

Enfield for the Ross rifle in the 1st Division. "It is the general opinion," Hughes announced to Max Aitken, the millionaire publisher who represented him at British general headquarters, "that scores of our officers can teach the British officers for many moons to come."

In fact, Canadians still had much to learn. That winter, the Canadians faced Messines Ridge. From the high ground, the Germans could see all that happened in the Canadian lines; even their sewage flowed into Canadian trenches. The British had their own surprise: seven tunnels painfully bored under the ridge, each packed with explosives. On March 27, the mines exploded. A British division raced to the smoking craters and held them. On April 4, Turner's raw troops took over, ready for their first real battle. Two days later, German counter-attacks began. Sheathed in mist and rain, Canadians and Germans fought a desperate seesaw battle. By April 19, the Germans had won. Every crater was retaken. The Canadians had lost 1,373 men.

The disaster had to be explained. Air photos, taken in the few clear intervals, revealed that Canadian staff officers had mistaken craters 6 and 7 for craters 4 and 5. Artillery support had been utterly misdirected. Neither Turner nor his brigadiers had gone forward to check. British generals would have been dismissed. Aitken warned headquarters that if that happened, there would be an explosion. Sir Douglas Haig, the British commander-in-chief, took the hint: the scapegoat would be Alderson. His successor was a cheery cavalry officer, Lieutenant-General Sir Julian Byng. It was a good choice.

In March of 1916, despite distant warnings from Gwatkin in Ottawa that reinforcements might not be available, a third Canadian division was formed, largely with units in England and France like the PPCLI, the Royal Canadian Regiment (which had wasted a year guarding Bermuda) and the mounted rifles once intended for Egypt. On June 1, the 3rd Division had its own terrible introduction to battle. The division commander, Major-General M. S. Mercer, a Toronto lawyer, was in the front lines on Mont Sorrel when the entire hill shuddered under a deluge of German shells. Bodies, even whole trees, were hurled in the air. Mercer was killed; a brigadier was captured. Shell-shocked survivors could not hold the Germans. Mont Sorrel fell. Next day, a quick counter-attack by Currie's division failed. Currie demanded more time, more guns, and a chance to rehearse. On June 13, the Canadians took back Mont Sorrel. The battle cost eight thousand men but Byng and Currie had learned a lesson: patience and preparation won victories.

The British still believed in romantic courage. On July 1, 1916, they began the battle of the Somme. When the bombardment ceased, German machine-gunners scrambled from their deep dug-outs, dusted off their weapons, and slaughtered the flower of Kitchener's army. By nightfall, 21,000 British soldiers lay dead. Among them, at Beaumont Hamel, were 310 men of the Newfoundland Regiment. That did not end the struggle to break the German line. In three months, the British and French sacrificed 600,000 dead and wounded.

The Canadians were spared until September. There were advantages to being late. Instead of giving time to the Germans to recover, the artillery now conducted a "rolling barrage," creeping forward in front of the attackers. Swinton's secret weapon had emerged as "tanks," capable of crawling at a maximum of five kilometres an hour, proof against machine-gun bullets. They were a noisy amalgam of improvisation, hope, and mechanical defects. At Flers-Courcelette on September 15, tanks and guns got their chance. Frankly, the artillery worked better. All six of the tanks with Turner's division broke down but artillery fire pulverized the German lines. French Canadians of the 22nd Battalion and Nova Scotians of the 25th Battalion reached their objective and held it. "If hell is as bad as what I have seen at Courcelette," wrote Colonel Thomas Tremblay of the 22nd, "I would not wish my worst enemy to go there." Four days later, the 3rd Division took Fabeck-Graben but nothing the Canadians could do could get them to Regina Trench.

On October 10, the 4th Division joined the Corps. All summer its units had trained in England, under Sir Sam Hughes's eyes. The commander, Major-General David Watson, was a Quebec newspaper proprietor and the minister's choice. Conditions were appalling. Shells had pulverized the chalky sub-soil. Rain turned the dust to cement. Haig demanded a victory, however small. Regina Trench remained. Twice the 4th Division mustered its forces, tried, and failed. Each time, it learned. On November 11, experience paid off. The objective, "a mere depression in the chalk," was taken and held. The 4th Division, too, had passed from apprenticeship. The cost of the Somme for the entire Corps was 24,029 casualties.

The year had been a disaster for the allies. At Verdun and the Somme, the French and British armies suffered crippling losses. In the East, the Russian armies crumbled for lack of arms and leadership. The allies could supply neither. The only useful route to Russia, through the

Dardanelles, was lost when the Turks forced the British to abandon Gallipoli. At Kut-al-Amara and in the Sinai, the Turks, once held in contempt, had savaged British armies. Roumania entered the war as an ally to be beaten in a few weeks. At Caporetto, in early 1917, Italy would almost be driven from the war.

That winter, the coldest in twenty years, the Canadian Corps faced Vimy Ridge, a long whale-shaped hill that rose over the Douai Plain. The divisions were tougher now, though the shortage of good reinforcements was apparent. Divisional concert parties — the 3rd Division's "Dumbbells" were the best known—did their bit for morale. Leave was even more valuable but wounded men now knew that even a "Blighty" might not save them from return to the trenches. In 1916, the first few Canadians had been shot for desertion; in 1917, there would be more.

Vimy Ridge was more than an annoyance and a chance for Germans to see far across the allied lines; it was the corps objective. Byng knew how to prepare. A huge model of the ridge was built and Canadian soldiers walked over it until they knew its features by heart. Gunners practiced on captured German guns so they could make use of artillery taken in the assault. Their own guns could not be dragged forward in time. Huge bunkers and dug-outs were excavated and filled with supplies and ammunition. Miles of tunnel were dug. Colonel A. G. L. McNaughton, a former McGill chemistry professor, figured out how to locate German guns by sound and flash and then used Canadian heavy artillery to knock them out.

Early on Easter Monday, after days of artillery bombardment, the four Canadian infantry divisions advanced in line right behind a barrage of exploding shells. They found front-line Germans hiding in their dug-outs. Beyond them, fighting was fiercer. By 8 A.M. that morning, April 9, 1917, the 3rd Division pushed over the far side of the hill to see Germans streaming away in disorder. The 1st and 2nd Divisions took longer, but by evening their objectives were won. The 4th Division, on the crest of the ridge, had the hardest fighting. Germans, brilliantly sited around the Pimple, as the topmost point was christened, fought to the end. It was April 12 before Brigadier-General Edward Hilliam, a western rancher and ex-British ranker signalled: "I am King of the Pimple."

French and British divisions fought on the flanks but Vimy Ridge was the Canadian Corps's triumph. The apprenticeship was over; the master work was complete.

Nation at War

Nations, claimed the French philosopher, Ernest Renan, are built from the experience of doing great things together. For Canadians, Vimy Ridge was a nation-building experience. For some, then and later, it symbolized the fact that the Great War was also Canada's war of independence even if it was fought at Britain's side against a common enemy.

The government and most Canadians had no such concept in 1914. Pride swelled at the apparent solidarity of a world-wide empire. Britain's leadership was unquestioned. Men of the CEF were enrolled as "imperials" under Britain's Army Act. Officers carried temporary British commissions. George Perley, acting High Commissioner in London, assumed that the Contingent would be "entirely under the authority of the War Office and become part of the Imperial army in every sense of the word." No one presumed otherwise. When the Admiralty asked for every trained seaman and naval gun, Canada did her best to oblige. From strategy to finance, Britain's authority was supreme and unquestioned.

Yet even the most imperial-minded Canadians began to feel uneasy. Hughes, of course, was first. On the basis of early wild rumours, he sent Kitchener a sizzling critique of mismanagement at Ypres. Borden's concern began with a summer visit to England in 1915. Britain's governing class, complacent or querulous, shared none of his boring earnestness about the war. When finally he met Lloyd George, Borden was in a receptive mood for the Welshman's denunciation of officials "who could not have acted any differently if they had been traitors." Back in Canada, Borden's successive announcements that the CEF would be raised to a quarter and then half a million men were really bids for information and influence that the British clearly preferred to keep to themselves. Andrew Bonar Law, the Canadian-born Colonial Secretary, did not try to deny consultation "in a war in which Canada is playing so big a part," but how could secrets be shared across the ocean? If no scheme was practicable, Law concluded, "it is very undesirable that the question should be raised."

Law's answer, plus the severe pains of neuralgia, fired the taciturn Borden to uncharacteristic rage. "It can hardly be expected that we shall put 400,000 or 500,000 men in the field," he wrote Perley on January 4, 1916, "and willingly accept the position of having no more voice and receiving no more consideration than if we were toy automata." The anger passed and the letter was cancelled (though Borden was proud enough to print it in his memoirs). The truth was that neither he nor the British could devise effective consultation at a time when an ocean crossing took a week and when Ottawa notoriously leaked secrets like a gossip columnist.

Instead, the Canadian prime minister turned to the weary and necessary work of setting Canada's war machine to rights, holding a divided country together and, when time permitted, discreetly urging Americans to share in the struggle.

Certainly the Militia Department remained a central problem. Every possible fumbled function, from purchasing to the care of casualties, had been stripped away from Hughes to be handled by a separate board or commission. The presence of hundreds of CEF battalions and a hundred thousand recruits undergoing various approximations of training concealed the true extent of the recruiting crisis, even from the government. Yet one of the puzzles of the war is why Borden tolerated his Minister of Militia so long. Militia purchasing scandals in 1915 dissolved the party truce; the munitions scandals of 1916, which exposed Hughes's crony, J. Wesley Allison, gave the Liberals hope of early electoral victory. Critics might agree with Hughes himself who described the prime minister as "gentle hearted as a girl." Was Borden physically or morally cowed by a burly colleague with a genius for verbal abuse?

The truth was that Borden owed Hughes much from the opposition years. Was it disloyal to abandon a colleague under fire, whether in the trenches or in Parliament? Too often, Hughes's erratic judgements were right. Borden was shocked by Sir Sam's violent denunciations after Ypres but after his own summer visit, he wondered if Hughes had been justified. Hughes's intense nationalism, symbolized by the popular myth that he had dressed down Lord Kitchener for planning to disperse the Canadian contingent, reflected Borden's own growing sense of Canadianism. Hughes's perennial contempt for military professionals, shared with his overseas agent, Max Aitken, became an excuse for chaos and influence-peddling in militia administration. Surely Hughes was saving "his boys" from red tape and old-fashioned methods. How "his boys" felt only became apparent when Sam attended a hot dusty review at Camp Borden in July 1916. Toronto newspapers reported that the thirsty, fed-up recruits jeered their supposed hero.

Hughes's greatest influence was in England. When the British virtually washed their hands of the untidy clutter of units left behind by the 1st Division, some structure for training and reinforcements had to develop. Any base is regarded with contempt by fighting soldiers but the Canadian base was more contemptible than most. Some of the problems were due to surplus officers, scrambling for suitable positions. Their numbers grew as new CEF battalions poured overseas. Instead of finding volunteers for existing battalions, the Minister's policy of raising hundreds of battalions guaranteed that most of them had to be broken up. Subalterns and privates hurried off to France, leaving seniors with a burning sense of grievance and a desperate urge to find a dignified staff job.

A single authority might have created order; Hughes preferred to allow three senior officers to exercise a confused and overlapping authority so that every imaginable issue was referred to him. The nimblest of the three was Major-General John Wallace Carson, a Montreal mining promoter who manipulated a vague mandate to look after the soldiers' comfort into a position of power, largely by exploiting the fears and jealousies of permanent force officers and his own well-known friendship with Hughes. Meanwhile, a burgeoning, wasteful array of camps, offices, depots, hospitals, and commands spread across England. Thousands of Canadians, untrained or unfit for service, waited aimlessly while battalions in France pleaded for reinforcements. Twice Borden sent Hughes to England to sort out the mess. Instead, the Minister enjoyed his chance to inspect troops, instruct recruits in the rare art of bayonet fighting, and lecture British generals on how to win the war. Finally, in September 1916, without authority, he announced an "Acting Overseas Sub-Militia Council" with Carson as chairman and his own son-in-law as secretary.

Thanks to Perley, no friend of Hughes, Borden knew all about the mess. His patience snapped. When Hughes returned to Canada, he found that Perley would soon become Minister of the Overseas Military Forces of Canada, based in London. On November 9, after enduring rage, schemes, and threats of blackmail, Borden finally dismissed his troublesome minister.

In London, Perley faced a host of difficulties. Later, he confessed that he would never have taken the job if he had known the half of it. Every department, from chaplains to the veterinary service, needed overhaul. Worst was the medical service, bitterly divided by a report commissioned by Hughes and written by Colonel Herbert Bruce, a Toronto surgeon. Bruce condemned the permanent force officers who created the Canadian system and complained that Canadian wounded were treated in British hospitals and took too long to return to the front. The report, with its implications of gross incompetence and its hint that Canadians were cosseted by British nurses, outraged most CEF doctors and led the famous Sir William Osler to resign his position with the Canadian Army Medical Corps in protest. Perley's solution, in almost every case, was to bring back respected Canadian officers from France and give them a free hand. Major-General Richard Turner reluctantly left the 2nd Division to take command in England. A questionable field commander became a conscientious administrator. Perley disavowed the Bruce report (making himself a virulent enemy) and then quietly adopted many of Bruce's ideas. Next, Perley trimmed Canadian establishments in England and coerced the small army of surplus officers either to serve at a lower rank or to go home after a short "Cook's Tour" at the front.

Argyll House, the Canadian headquarters in London, soon became the symbol for all that fighting soldiers hated about staff officers living safely in the rear, but the era of humiliating Canadian inefficiency was over. Something else happened. A few words in the order creating the new Ministry redefined men of the CEF. Suddenly they were part of an overseas contingent of the Canadian militia. Canada had reached to England to take clear control; logically, Perley's authority must next extend to France. Only officials noted the change but the Canadianization of the Corps was almost complete. Observers noted the slow transformation of accents as the British-born "Old Originals" were promoted or became casualties, to be replaced by the Canadian-born recruits of 1915.

British tactics and practices continued. To the end of the war, key staff positions in the Corps and its divisions were held by British officers. They contributed much of the thorough, methodical approach to battle which the Canadian Corps considered its trademark. The Corps also depended on the skill and imagination of citizen-soldiers like Brigadier-General A. G. L. McNaughton, a chemistry professor who commanded the heavy artillery, or Major-General W. B. Lindsay, who rose to be Chief Engineer of the Corps. If there was a Canadian way of war, it depended on using the maximum weight of material to win objectives and save lives.

Symbolically, the Corps's Canadianization was complete on June 9, 1917, when Byng was promoted to command an army. Turner might have returned but the British, for obvious reasons, preferred Currie.

Perley recognized the merits of the plump ex-land speculator and Liberal from Victoria and Turner bravely accepted the decision. The complications in Currie's appointment came not from the British but from fellow Canadians. From Ottawa, Borden insisted that Sir Sam's son, Garnet, be given command of the 1st Division. Convinced that the ex-minister's son was unfit, Currie refused. The strain was all the greater because the new Corps commander simultaneously faced exposure for a serious pre-war financial offence, the misappropriation of a $10,000 government cheque. Thanks to help from wealthy brother officers, luck, and remarkable reticence on the part of Perley and the cabinet, Currie weathered the crisis.

How Currie and the Corps would fare was soon apparent. In August, he was given a major objective, the mining town of Lens. It was a bloody venture: hills surrounding the town v⁻ould dominate the advance. Why not capture one of them, Hill 70, and dare the Germans to take it back? Reluctantly, Haig agreed to the change of plan. On August 15, behind a smoke-screen of burning oil, two of Currie's divisions attacked. They broke through. Then, as Currie predicted, the Germans hurled 21 successive counter-attacks to drive the Canadians out. Each was shattered by concentrated Canadian artillery and machine-guns. The battle cost the Corps 9,198 men. The Germans lost 20,000. By the grim standards of war, it was a victory.

Both Lens and Vimy were diversionary attacks for a French offensive that failed miserably and for Haig's drive to Passchendaele. All summer and fall, British divisions poured into the Flanders battle. Shells created a bottomless mire; endless rains filled the quagmire. Men, supplies, even guns vanished in the mud. Wounded drowned. Safely hidden in concrete pillboxes on high ground, the Germans slaughtered the attackers. In four weeks, the Fifth Army lost sixty-eight thousand men. In October, Passchendaele was still German. Haig sent for Currie.

Currie knew the ground. It was the same Ypres front he had known in 1915. He protested. An attack would cost sixteen thousand men. Haig insisted. Currie made conditions: each missing gun must be replaced and secured on wooden platforms. Roads must be built; supplies stockpiled. Haig glumly agreed. Canadian troops, shivering under groundsheets, nauseated by traces of gas and the smell of decaying bodies, hardly noticed Currie's efforts.

On October 16, the 3rd and 4th Divisions attacked. They lost twenty-six hundred men. On October 30, they tried again, went one hundred yards, lost twenty-seven hundred men. Currie deliberately took a week to repair roads, bring up more guns, and switch to the 1st and 2nd Divisions. On November 6, the Canadians advanced, this time on drier land. Guns and infantry worked together. Somehow, Passchendaele was taken. The price was about what Currie had predicted, at 15,654 men. The victorious survivors marched south, pausing only to vote in a Canadian federal election.

The Corps came to symbolize Canada's wartime identity. Its maple leaf badges and the rectangular coloured patches of its divisional insignia gave its soldiers a common pride. Yet, at any time, it included only a third of the Canadians overseas. The Canadian Cavalry Brigade, commanded for much of the war by a former British politician, served in the Cavalry Corps. Canadian doctors and nurses cared for British troops in the Mediterranean. A contingent of river pilots and marine engineers provided water transport on the Tigris. Most of the light railways behind the British lines were built and serviced by Canadian railway troops. Companies of the Canadian Forestry Corps met wartime timber needs by felling forests in Scotland and the Jura region of France.

For all its incipient nationalism, the Borden government showed no enthusiasm for a Canadian air force. Thousands of young Canadians found their own way as pilots and, occasionally, as mechanics, to the two British flying services. On April 1, 1918, when the services amalgamated as the Royal Air Force, twenty-two thousand Canadians were in its ranks, doing every kind of duty, from spotting enemy submarines to flying heavy bombers over Germany.

The stars of the new arm were fighter pilots. Nowhere did men's lives depend more on technology. The Germans, with superior engineering competence, normally kept the lead. With inferior planes and prevailing winds that drove them behind the German lines, British and Canadian pilots suffered heavy losses. Those who survived and shot down five or more enemy aircraft became aces: of the top twenty-seven British aces, ten were Canadians. Among all the aces of the war, Lieutenant Colonel W. A. Bishop ranked third with seventy-two victories; in fifth place, with sixty, was Commander Raymond Collishaw.

Creation of the Overseas Ministry, with its hardening grip on Canadian interests, revived pressures for a separate Canadian air arm. Canadians in British squadrons grumbled at the lack of promotion and the absence of sympathy with their interests. Unless they had transferred from the CEF, they served on British terms. Yet somehow Ottawa never became very interested. What advantages would outweigh the un-doubted costs and complications? The enormous extent of Canadian participation—forty per cent of pilots by 1918—persuaded the Brit-ish that separate Canadian squadrons would tear their own service apart. Not until the very end of the war were two squadrons of a Cana-dian Air Force authorized, and they never saw action.

Conscription Crisis

By early 1917, Perley and his staff had brought some order out of the Canadian mess in England. The Canadian Corps was on the verge of its first great victory. A new British government was ready at last to consult its Dominion allies.

In the wake of the 1916 disasters, a cabinet revolt deposed the de-cent, drunken Herbert Asquith. With substantial subterranean help from Max Aitken, Lloyd George emerged as Britain's new prime minister. Old rules no longer applied. Dominion premiers, self-made men like Lloyd George himself, might as well be involved. "We want more men from them," Lloyd George explained to his officials, "We can hardly ask them to make another great recruiting effort unless it is accompa-nied by an invitation to come over and discuss the situation with us." The invitation was despatched, the Canadian Parliament dutifully ad-journed, and on March 2, 1917, the first meeting of an "Imperial War Cabinet" opened.

Though the colonial politicians by no means shared as much influ-ence or information as they imagined, they soon had enough facts to convince them of the dire state of the war effort. They learned of wide-spread mutinies in the French army, the imminent collapse of the Rus-sian front, and the frightening success of Germany's new submarine offensive. For Borden, the war cabinet was the institutional device he had long sought to co-ordinate imperial policy. He also understood that the price of involvement was an honourable commitment to pro-vide the means. Britain not only wanted more men; she must have them if the war was not to be lost. In spare moments, Borden visited the Corps in France, camps in England, and every military hospital he could reach. He saw what Canadians at home would never see: wound-ed men destined to return again and again to the trenches until they were dead or so terribly mangled that not even the army would ac-cept them for battle. Borden was in England for the victory of Vimy

Ridge and he could count the toll: 10,602 dead and wounded would have to be replaced.

Borden returned from England in a grim mood. It was now unthinkable to cut Canada's contribution. Australia, far smaller in population, maintained five divisions. Yet each Canadian division needed twenty thousand replacements a year. Only Hughes's dismissal had prevented a 5th Division, commanded by his son, from going to France. It waited in England until the reinforcement issue could be settled.

Hughes certainly deserved some of the blame for recruiting failures though few ever acknowledged that his chaotic methods had found almost half a million volunteers. Barely thirteen thousand of them were French-speaking. Thanks to Hughes, the militia's careful tradition of *Canadien* representation was forgotten. The 1st Division had a single French-speaking company. The second contingent had a single battalion, the 22nd. Yet the problem went deeper. Since Confederation, successive ministers and generals had simply ignored the special emotional and linguistic needs of a militia for French Canada. Red tunics and the Union Jack worked in Orillia, not Victoriaville. A few excellent and devoted officers were outweighed by misfits and time-servers in the thirteen CEF battalions that struggled for *Québécois* recruits. A few units were first-rate: the 163rd *"Poil-aux-pattes,"* raised by Bourassa's errant lieutenant, Olivar Asselin, or the 189th, tough *Gaspésiens* who included two future Victoria Cross winners. Both units were broken up to fill the ranks of the 22nd Battalion after Courcelette.

Myths and alibis fail to explain Quebec's recruiting record. There never was a "Methodist recruiting officer" as O.D. Skelton later claimed. Not even the 22nd Battalion could fill its ranks. Laurier's wholehearted recruiting effort consisted of two brilliant speeches. Quebec was the only province in which Ottawa spent money for recruiting—$30,000 to Colonel Arthur Mignault in 1916. He achieved little. Nor did Henri Bourassa transform Quebec attitudes by his campaign against Ontario's suppression of French-language education. The refusal of Ontario politicians, Liberal and Tory, to compromise at a time of national crisis says much about their priorities, but French Quebec showed no burning sympathy for the *blessés de l'Ontario,* for all the eloquence of their leaders. Having a respect *nationaliste,* Colonel Armand Lavergne, tell them not to join "a somewhat interesting adventure in a foreign country" only confirmed a decision made long before.

Across Canada, most men of military age never volunteered. Those who lived on farms, were married, or had jobs or deep ancestral roots in the country were least likely to enlist. By no coincidence, the Maritimes ranked only a little ahead of Quebec in recruiting rates. More industrialized than other provinces, Quebec offered the most well-paying jobs in wartime munitions and textile plants. No wonder recruiting was easier in the Gaspé than in Montreal. Neither France nor England had much emotional appeal to a people that had been abandoned by the Old World eight generations earlier.

Outside Quebec, the search for "slackers" neatly reinforced old racial and religious antagonisms. A few Toronto businessmen launched a *"Bonne Entente"* movement, aimed at ending Quebec's alienation from the national effort. Banquets and oratory changed little. Arguments grew nastier. Patriotic leagues warned that volunteering creamed off the best and bravest. Bourassa himself scolded English Canadians for leaving their country to "racially inferior" immigrants. His enemies wondered whether the French would be the real inheritors.

In imitation of the British, the government finally approved national registration. To allay resistance from labour and Quebec's Catholic hierarchy, Borden declared that registration would be voluntary. A fifth of the cards never came back. Of the 1.5 million replies, only 286,976 appeared to come from eligible men. A canvass of 2,000 in Winnipeg produced not a single volunteer. Next, the government announced a Canadian Defence Force. If men would not fight overseas, perhaps they would help guard Canadian ports, canals, and internment camps. A well-publicized effort to raise 47 battalions found 1,858 men; most of them eventually transferred to the CEF. It was not enough.

On May 18, 1917, two days back from England, Borden made his announcement. "All citizens are liable for the defence of their country," he declared, "and I conceive that the battle for Canadian liberty and autonomy is being fought today on the plains of France and Belgium." At the end of a long speech, he recalled the men he had left behind. "I know from my personal experience that they cannot realize the thought that their country, which summoned them to her service, will be content to desert and humiliate them." Arthur Meighen, the solicitor general, set to work on a Military Service Act, based on the selective service law adopted by the United States when it entered the war on April 6.

Later, generations of Liberal historians insisted that Borden dreamed up conscription to save his party or to distract the public from the imminent collapse of Canada's newest transcontinental railways. This is absurd. Certainly the Tories were in trouble. Liberals had swept every provincial election since the war and Laurier felt confident of a triumphal come-back. But Borden had no illusion that a noisy chorus of pro-conscription editors, politicians, and letter-writers spoke for Canada. In Australia, a far more homogeneous country than Canada, voters had twice rejected conscription. Quebec's opposition was certain. Organized labour seemed politically feeble but who knew what loyalties it claimed? Farmers in Ontario and the West wanted sons and labourers to stay home to harvest increasingly profitable crops. Such opponents were quiet but they had votes and by July it was certain that there would be no conscription before a federal election.

In Quebec, the opposition was no longer quiet. In Montreal, recruiting parties were assaulted. That spring, when Borden's postmaster general, Pierre Blondin, and Major-General Lessard set out on a last attempt to recruit a French-speaking battalion, they met silent crowds and resentful priests: they collected ninety-seven recruits. Archbishop Bruchési of Montreal nervously supported the government; Cardinal Bégin in Quebec was polite; all over Quebec, the parish clergy was frigidly hostile.

Like so many Canadian disputes, the conscription debate was a dialogue of the deaf. Henri Bourassa saw Borden as an imperialist, handing over Canadian money and lives at Britain's command. Borden despised Bourassa as a narrow provincialist, fanning petty grievances. In the war, Canada was now an ally, setting an example. Like many Americans before 1917, Bourassa insisted that the war was not Canada's concern. At best, it was a chance to get rich, but only if men stayed home to produce munitions and food. The prime minister had fought such arguments in the United States. He believed that Bourassa's case was servile and unworthy. Borden defied the stereotype of Canadians as a selfish, materialistic people: behind his dull, colourless personality, burned idealism.

On the principle of full commitment, he was unyielding; on the means he was flexible. To the dismay of some Tories, Borden set out at once to forge a coalition with Laurier. The Liberal leader refused. He was angry that Borden had proclaimed conscription before seeking a coalition. Borden offered to delay conscription until a general election. Again Laurier refused. He was certain that Liberals would stick by him: party meetings in Winnipeg and Toronto repudiated the coalitionists. Above all, Laurier feared a fresh humiliation from Bourassa and the nationalists if he joined Borden.

On one point, Laurier was wrong: conscription shattered Liberal unity. Party militants, united by hope of victory and hatred of Tories, could pass resolutions. Liberal editors and elected politicians had to face the public and its very different perceptions of the war and politics. As ever, Laurier also underestimated Borden. Threading his way past Liberal leaders and his own blind partisans, Borden sought out second-rank Liberals. Finding them nervous and indecisive, the prime minister armed himself with two fresh weapons. A Military Voters' Act extended the franchise to every man and woman in the CEF. To simplify an election conducted across a U-boat-infested ocean, soldiers would vote Government or Opposition. Those without close home links could choose their own constituency. Both parties, the Minister of Justice sweetly suggested, might wish to direct votes where they would do the most good. More serious and questionable was the Wartime Elections Act. Simultaneously it gave the vote to mothers, wives, and sisters of serving soldiers, and took it away from citizens of enemy origin naturalized since 1902. Women's votes, explained Arthur Meighen, would speak for men who had given their lives; the disfranchised would be exempt from conscription. Only closure jammed the law past a furious Liberal opposition.

Both measures had their effect. The new women voters would surely support help for their men; the disfranchised represented a key bloc of Liberal support, especially in western Canada. Prominent Liberals began reconsidering their options. On October 6, Borden dissolved Parliament. Five days later, he announced a Union government committed to conscription, prohibition of liquor, and abolition of party patronage. Every provincial premier save Quebec's Sir Lomer Gouin promised support. An admiring Tory colleague confessed that he would match Borden against Job in a patience contest any day. A coalition Liberal, Major-General Sydney Mewburn, took the militia department; his Conservative predecessor, Sir Edward Kemp, would go to London. Perley, confirmed as High Commissioner, agreed to manage the overseas election.

Borden's coalition seemed certain of victory. In Quebec, Laurier was secure, with a resentful Bourassa compelled to offer support. Elsewhere the Liberal Party was in ruins. Even William Lyon Mackenzie King discreetly offered Borden his services. Rebuffed, he salvaged his

career by running for Laurier in Ontario. There were few such prominent Laurierites save in the Maritimes where party loyalties outweighed
even war fever. Yet, as weeks passed, Unionist confidence faltered.
Squeezing Liberal and Tory ambitions into a single candidacy produced
a flurry of quarrels. At Kitchener, anti-conscription demonstrators
howled Borden off the platform. General Mewburn, touring rural Ontario, had to promise that farmers' sons would not be conscripted. A
nervous message from overseas led to exemption for soldiers' next-of-
kin. The promises worked. By election day, the Unionist campaign
had become a crusade of English-speaking Canada against Bourassa
and the German kaiser. Thanks to election promises, conscription had
been reduced to a punishment for "slackers" and French Canadians.

The results of the December 17 election confirmed the impression:
153 seats for Borden and 82 for Laurier, all but 20 of them in Quebec.
Labour candidates, campaigning against conscription, were utterly
routed. Yet popular opinion was by no means as lopsided as the new
Parliament. Without the service vote, the Unionists had a majority of
barely a hundred thousand. Military voters added two hundred thousand to the margin and switched the outcome in fourteen of Laurier's
ridings but, thanks to W. F. O'Connor, the chief returning officer, many
soldiers who improperly switched ridings had their ballots set aside.

Overseas, Currie and his men grumbled at the interminable delays
in making conscription effective. Only in December did the Military
Service Act come into effect. It was not a brilliant success. Pressed for
compromises and for the full protection of individual rights, Meighen's
law said more about exemptions and appeals than service. Boards of
Selection, in which government and opposition were equally represented, nominated 1,239 local tribunals. Their decisions could be questioned by 195 appeal courts and by a central appeal judge, Lyman
Duff of the Supreme Court of Canada. Potential conscripts and their
lawyers could find grounds for exemption which ranged from family
hardship to conscientious objection. When the first class — single
men from twenty to thirty-four years of age—was notified in October
1917, 280,510 of the 404,395 filed for exemption.

Local tribunals proved unpredictable. Most western Mennonites
gained exemption but not even Duff accepted the arguments of the
Plymouth Brethren or Jehovah's Witnesses. In Quebec, local boards
granted almost blanket exemption to French-speaking applicants but,
according to Duff's recollection, "they applied conscription against

the English-speaking minority in Quebec with a rigor unparalleled." On January 3, when the first conscripts were ordered to report, barely twenty thousand appeared. Many who had failed to win exemptions simply disappeared. The small federal police forces, the Dominion Police in the east and the Royal Northwest Mounted Police in the west, had the thankless job of tracking them down. In Quebec, a clash seemed inevitable.

It came on the Easter week-end in Quebec City. Military police seized a young man with no papers. Furious crowds attacked the military service registry and tossed records into the snow. Then they roamed the streets, smashing windows of English-owned businesses. Police did nothing. Ottawa despatched General Lessard and the only available troops, seven hundred soldiers from Toronto. At night on Easter Monday, a few soldiers, trapped in a square and pelted with ice and snow, opened fire. Four civilians were killed; many were injured. The violence shocked everyone. The riots stopped. Quebec clergy commanded faithful Catholics to obey the law. Ottawa took sweeping powers to conscript anyone who interfered with the Military Service Act. Quebeckers settled down to wait for political vengeance.

Meanwhile, Canada and her allies faced a new, more appalling threat. German armies, enormously reinforced after the October Revolution took Russia out of the war, stood poised to attack. On March 21, they struck. The British Fifth Army, still recovering from Passchendaele, was the target. German tactics, tested in late 1917, were brilliantly innovative. A short, massive artillery bombardment was followed by deep thrusts by tough, specially trained "storm-troops." Smoke, fog, and poison gas blinded defenders. British strongpoints were isolated, bypassed, and destroyed later. In a week, the Fifth Army almost ceased to exist. The disaster was repeated again and again as German attacks drove weakened and demoralized French and British troops from some of the most blood-soaked ground on the Western Front.

In France, allied generals reacted desperately. At Doullens on March 26, Sir Douglas Haig finally accepted the authority of a single allied commander, France's Marshal Ferdinand Foch. In Canada, Borden felt the need for equally drastic action. The farce of the Military Service Act must be ended. On April 12, after bitter cabinet debate, all exemptions were cancelled.

The political risks were real. In Parliament, the Unionist majority fell from seventy-one to forty-three. Robbed of sons and labourers, farmers completed spring seeding as best they could, but on May 15, five thousand of them invaded Ottawa. Borden listened politely but ignored their appeals. Newspaper editors sneered at the "hayseed profiteers." Like Quebec, farmers, too, would want vengeance.

Later, historians claimed that conscription was a failure. Only 24,100 conscripts actually fought in France. The experts are wise after the event. No one in 1914 predicted that the war would last four and a half years. No one in 1917 knew that the war would be over in a year. The Military Service Act was designed to find 100,000 soldiers. At war's end, 99,561 MSA men wore the uniform of the Canadian Expeditionary Force. The chief victim of the long delay was the 5th Division. Despite election promises that its units would remain together, the division was broken up early in 1918. Because the Canadian Corps, by incredible luck, never actually felt the brunt of any of the German offensives, 20,000 men from the 5th Division satisfied its reinforcement needs until August.

By 1918, wartime policy in Canada no longer depended on accidents or enthusiasm. Conscription was only the grimmest and most divisive consequence of Borden's political commitment to allied victory.

War of Attrition

For most Canadians, there was an unbridgeable gulf between their own experience of war and the actual fighting. Even in Britain, ships and leave trains delivered mud-stained, weary troops only hours away from the trenches. Sometimes people along the English coast would hear the rumble of distant guns. Only surplus officers, sick and wounded, and, in 1918, a few "Old Originals" on furlough could tell Canadians of the fighting, and the most honest of them had the least to say.

Yet war transformed every aspect of life, from skirt-lengths to industrial engineering. Every conceivable reform, from the single tax to a patronage-free civil service, found fresh arguments from the war. A nation stripped down for the struggle could no longer afford self-indulgence in alcohol. "To Hell with profits," exclaimed Joseph Flavelle to shocked businessmen when he contrasted their grumbles with the problems of the wounded men he had seen in England. Reports of huge profits in his bacon-exporting business, emerging soon after he became a baronet, destroyed his public reputation and encouraged abolition of aristocratic titles for Canadians.

Early in 1918, the Union government gave the rest of Canadian women the vote. Just as important for women was a growth of employment opportunities. Encouraged by cloying publicity and specially designed costumes, women now worked as "conductorettes" on streetcars, as "farmerettes" in harvesting crews, and in increasingly varied jobs in the munitions industry. Employers provided lunch rooms, extra rest periods, and women supervisors but drew the line at equal pay. Women's influence lay behind the wartime prohibition of the import, sale, and transportation of liquor for the duration of the war — though the government also insisted it wanted to conserve grain.

If, as the clergy had argued, the war was a fiery furnace, from which a finer Canada would emerge, social reformers hastened to define the new society. William Irvine's *Farmers in Politics* gave western rural protest a programme. Salem Bland's *The New Christianity* urged Christian socialism. In New York, Mackenzie King finished *Industry and Humanity*, a turgid volume that, nonetheless, marked the author as a man of modern ideas. More important than books was experience. A host of public servants, thrust into new and exciting responsibilities, suddenly realized that government intervention need no longer be a byword for corruption and inefficiency. Administrators of the Canadian Patriotic Fund showed all who would heed them that poverty was a function of family size, not basic income. The Military Hospitals Commission and its successor, the Department of Soldiers' Civil Reestablishment, created a network of vocational training to supplement its medical and rehabilitation facilities. A new Board of Pension Commissioners offered the radical notion that benefits should be solely linked to disability rather than to rank or previous income. Out of the war came a National Employment Service, a federal Department of Health, and powerful official arguments for health and unemployment insurance.

In 1915, Borden insisted to Parliament that his policy was "not to interfere with the business activities of the country." Four years of war transformed the *laisser-faire* tradition. By 1918, a fuel controller threatened coal merchants with prison if they were caught hoarding. A food controller, a cost-of-living commissioner, a chief censor, and other officials, appointed because of wartime need or a supply crisis, had all the powers they needed under the War Measures Act to investigate, direct, advise, inspect, and control. Of course, most of the new officials were, themselves, businessmen. As food controller, W. J. Hanna of Imperial Oil rejected rationing and employed travelling salesmen as agents to check soaring food prices. His Food Board sponsored a "Keep a Pig" campaign, instructed housewives on cheap recipes, and distributed a thousand Ford tractors to farmers at cost. It was the Food Board that dreamed up the regulation that most delighted Borden: an "anti-loafing law" that threatened punishment for any man or boy not gainfully employed. Appointed when America's entry into the war threatened Canadian coal supplies, the Fuel Controller had to keep industry moving and Canadians from freezing. On "Fuelless Days" they merely shivered.

The war even broke Sir Thomas White's determination not to impose direct taxation. In 1916, his resolution cracked with a tiny business profits' tax. Income tax remained unthinkable until July 25, 1917. White bowed to demands that the government conscript wealth as well as men. In 1918, when Canadians completed their first T-1 forms, only 31,130 people had to pay. Despite pledges that the new Dominion War Income Tax would vanish with the peace, it persisted as one of the hardiest survivors of the Great War.

Such innovations seemed inescapable. By 1917, Britain was financially so exhausted that she could no longer afford Canadian munitions. Facing catastrophe, Flavelle desperately borrowed the over-run on White's war bonds and Victory Loan. American orders saved him. If Canadians tendered for seven per cent under the American price, Washington agreed, they could have the business. Having recovered their capital from early profits, the IMB's contractors found the price cut no hardship. Still, the Board's income fell by a third between 1917 and 1918. By the last year of the war, food and fuel were in acutely short supply. Ontario in 1917 ordered farmers to plant more food, but not even armies of students and soldiers could harvest the crops. In the coal mines of Alberta and Cape Breton, labour trouble was endemic.

The war grew as grim as the economy. At Halifax, on December 6, 1917, a French munitions ship caught fire. The biggest known man-made explosion to that time devastated much of the city and neighbouring Dartmouth, killed 1,630 people, and left many more mutilated and blind. A savage winter blizzard added to the misery of the homeless and rescuers alike. Somehow the city struggled back to life. There was no choice. Men, munitions, and every kind of export passed through Halifax. By the summer of 1918, big new German submarines had crossed the ocean; crowded sea lanes, filled with American troop-ships and cargo vessels, were suddenly at risk. Half-ruined Halifax was again a naval base. Captain Walter Hose, summoned from command of the *Rainbow*, helped improvise a fleet of tiny trawlers and drifters, manned by amateurs, as some kind of answer to the threat.

Overseas, the mood was no brighter. After its 1917 mutinies, the French army could make no serious effort. The British Fifth Army collapsed because its battalions had been bled white in 1917; the War Office forced amputees back into uniform to meet its manpower needs. Only the Americans seemed to have energy and optimism, but they also insisted on helping on their own terms. So, increasingly, did Canadians. Currie refused to imitate the new British organization of nine infantry battalions to a division, though the Canadians could then have formed a small army of six divisions instead of a single corps. To the fury of ambitious surplus officers, Kemp and Borden accepted Currie's argument: the Canadian Corps would fight better as it was. When Currie also insisted that his corps be kept together during the dangerous German offensives, Haig's patience broke. The Canadian general, he complained, had become too conceited. His political superior, the Earl of Derby, could only counsel resignation to Canadian demands: "We must look upon them in the light in which they wish to be looked upon rather than the light in which we would wish to do so."

In London, Kemp made his own uncomfortable demands on the British. As Overseas Minister, he had ended Perley's practice of letting the generals run their own organization. Kemp created his own version of the Militia Council. Next, he insisted on extending his authority through Haig's headquarters to the Corps himself. Over acute reservations from the British—and from Currie who wanted no political meddling with his units—a Canadian Section in France under a politically experienced brigadier allowed Kemp to keep in touch not only with the Corps but with thousands of Canadian troops scattered through France. It was an arrangement appropriate for a junior but sovereign ally.

That status was reaffirmed by Sir Robert Borden when he returned to England in the spring of 1918. He had reason to be angry. For all the apparent openness in 1917, no one had told the Dominion premiers of the planned drive to Passchendaele. When Borden summoned Currie to advise him on the disastrous offensive and the catastrophic March defeats, the Corps commander delivered a long, searching, and possibly self-serving indictment of British sloth, lack of foresight, stunting of talent, and misleading intelligence. Canadians, naturally, stood as brilliant exceptions, laying wire when British generals ordered their men to build tennis courts. Borden was furious. "Mr. Prime Minister," he told Lloyd George, "I want to tell you that if there is a repetition of the battle of Passchendaele, not a Canadian soldier will leave the shores of Canada as long as the Canadian people entrust the government of their country to my hands." Lloyd George was so pleased at the denunciation of British generals that he compelled some of them to hear Borden repeat himself. Then he set up a committee of prime ministers to spend the summer reviewing the conduct of the war, past and future. The committee's importance can be over-estimated. Its draft report, urging intervention in Russia and recommending husbanding the British army in 1919 for a decisive blow in 1920, was unsigned when Borden left London on August 16.

Borden's experience in London came close to confirming Bonar Law's gloomy judgement in 1915 on the problems of creating imperial policy. Only when Borden was in London did Canada have a voice in the Empire's councils. Speeches, banquets, and public acclaim were flattering but power did not derive from social intercourse. More than most British leaders, Lloyd George felt a kinship with colonial politicians as fellow outsiders to Britain's governing class, but even he would not share key decisions with them. In 1914, Sir Robert Borden had been at least a theoretical imperial federationist, seeking for Canada a share in ruling the world's greatest empire. The war had put theory to the test. It did not work.

If anything, the war showed how much easier it could be to deal with Canada's oldest enemy, the United States. Washington remained forever confused about Canada's precise status and certainly the British Embassy was unlikely to admit that Canadians had a voice of their own. However, when diplomats could be side-stepped, Americans talked business and made decisions. Sir Joseph Flavelle had profited from that fact in 1917; a year later, his agent, Lloyd Harris, became the logical person to head a wartime Canadian mission to the United States.

When the Admiralty did nothing about the U-boats active in the western Atlantic in 1918, it was the United States that sent escort ships and flying boats from its naval air service. Young Canadians, recruited for a hurriedly improvised Royal Canadian Naval Air Service, went to the Massachusetts Institute of Technology for their training. The precedent had been set when the Royal Flying Corps switched its Canadian training operation to Texas for the winter of 1917-18. However pro-British Borden and his colleagues considered themselves, they found it almost dangerously easy to work with the Americans.

That alliance would have grown deeper as the United States mobilized its strength. In August, as the Canadian Corps prepared for its first major battle of the year, the Americans had only a handful of divisions in the line. Haig had promised there would be no more big offensives in 1918. Instead, he proposed to shove the Germans back from the vital railway town of Amiens which they had nearly captured in the spring. The Canadians and Australians, 9 divisions in all, would be backed by 2,000 guns and 470 tanks. Instead of the usual leisurely bombardment, the attack would come as a sudden shock. Canadians moved south secretly. Now that wireless was part of an army's communications, special units sent floods of messages to conceal the Corps's movement. Aircraft buzzed overhead to conceal the rumble of tank tracks.

On August 8, at dawn, the battle began. It was the triumph the generals had prayed for: only a single Canadian division, the 4th, was caught by machine-guns. Tanks, better armed and more reliable than in 1916, worked in partnership with infantry. In new tactics, aircraft zoomed in on German targets, blasting them with bombs. Like the Germans in March, platoons and companies went forward as teams, bypassing the toughest resistance. In a single day, the Canadians covered thirteen kilometres at a cost of 1,306 dead and 2,803 wounded. The German frontline divisions almost ceased to exist. General Erich Ludendorff, the German chief of staff, called it "the black day of the German army in the history of this war." The losses could never be replaced and the number of prisoners, two-thirds of German casualties, showed that morale had finally begun to crack.

It had not broken. By August 9, the advance had run out of steam. Currie had learned a lesson: stop when you are winning and shift direction. By August 11, when Haig allowed Currie to change fronts, the Canadians had faced troops from eighteen German divisions. The new objective was no easier: the Hindenburg Line, fortifications the Germans had taken two years to build. There was no easy way. From August 26 to 30, the 2nd and 3rd Divisions battered a way through most of the Fresnes-Rouvroy line at a cost of 6,000 men. Every officer of the 22nd Battalion, including a future Governor General, Major Georges Vanier, was killed or wounded. After a week's rest, the 1st and 4th Divisions pushed on through the even more imposing Drocourt-Quéant line. It took two days but again the cost was 6,000 dead or wounded.

One major obstacle remained, the unfinished Canal du Nord. Again Currie insisted on time to prepare. Battered divisions absorbed their first big drafts of conscripts while Currie devised a risky plan. He would advance on a narrow front, seize a bridgehead, and pour his divisions through the gap. Everything depended on planning, efficiency, toughness—and luck. On September 26, the attack began. It succeeded. Then, for more than a week, Canadians fought their way toward Cambrai. On October 11, the town fell.

For 47 days, the Canadians formed the spearhead of the British army. The price was 30,802 casualties, more than half the fighting strength of the Corps. The gains now seem meagre: 18,585 prisoners, 371 guns, 2,000 machine-guns. Yet the Canadians were ending the war by destroying the German army. The Germans never quite crumbled but they fell back and Canadians led the way in pursuing them. Now war was in the open, as generals had dreamed. Soldiers, trained in trench war, were unprepared for long marches and the real hunger when waggons and camp cookers failed to keep up. The Germans fought tough rearguard actions. The war zone was far behind; artillery barrages would kill more French civilians than German troops. At the industrial city of Valenciennes, the Canadians worked patiently around the outskirts to safeguard the population. It worked. The Germans, trying to break out, lost 2,400 in dead and prisoners; 80 Canadians died.

Drenched by steady November rains, Canadians crossed the Belgian border and headed for Mons, the town where the war had begun for the British army in 1914. Now it was the Germans who fought behind canals and fortified houses. All day on November 10, soldiers of the Royal Canadian Regiment and the 42nd Battalion from Montreal fought their way through the suburbs. By daybreak on November 11, the enemy had fled. At 9 A.M., a message finally reached the front lines: at 11 A.M., all firing could cease. The war was over.

In Canada, the last months of the war, with their terrible casualty lists, were shared with an extra misery. A worldwide influenza epidemic reached the United States in early September. Days later, cases were reported in Ontario and Quebec. Schools closed, factories shut down. Railway, telephone, and postal services were crippled for weeks.

In some small communities, no one was left to nurse the sick and helpless. No death toll could ever be established but by the end of 1918, between thirty and fifty thousand Canadians had died. Perhaps the epidemic helps explain the strange hysteria which sent Canadians into the streets on November 9 to cheer the end of the war. No one yet knows how the rumours began. On November 11, real rejoicing resumed.

The war had cost 60,661 Canadian men and women killed in battle or from wounds, or dead in accidents or from the diseases of war. There is no simple count of those who returned too maimed in mind or body to resume a normal life: certainly it was larger than the toll of dead. The war effort had sought to unite Canadians. Instead it divided them: French and English, patriots and "slackers," Canadians and "aliens." Perhaps the deepest division of all was between those who had spent the war years in Canada and those who could now return from months and years overseas.

War Wounds

November 11 was not armistice day for all Canadians. Near Tulgas, south of Archangel, that was the day six hundred men of the new Red Army almost overran a Canadian field battery. At the other end of Russia at Vladivostok, four thousand Canadians prepared for an interminable winter. At Baku on the Caspian, Canadians helped organize White Russians against Lenin's Bolsheviks.

They, like the two divisions of Canadians who hurried forward to occupy Rhine bridgeheads at Bonn and Cologne, were reminders of Canada's new role in the world. Canadians were in Russia because their prime minister had helped draft a report arguing for revival of the Eastern Front. Sharing in decision-making meant sharing in the consequences. War-weary Canadians were not interested. Not even Borden's cabinet could understand why the prime minister insisted on spending the post-war months in Paris and London nor did they much care whether or where Canada's name appeared on the Treaty of Versailles. They wanted their leader. Civilians wanted normality. Soldiers wanted to go home.

Coping with returned soldiers was Ottawa's biggest post-war concern. Unlike the United States, where President Wilson virtually forbade post-war planning, Ottawa had been preparing since 1915 —

precisely to avoid the "pension evil," an avaricious veterans' lobby, and other unhappy American experiences after the Civil War. By 1919, the Board of Pensions Commissioners had developed the most generous benefit rates in the world—and some of the strictest criteria for granting them. The Department of Soldiers' Civil Re-establishment, heir to the Military Hospitals Commission, not only operated hospitals, nursing homes, and tuberculosis sanatoria, but it also had developed elaborate plans for retraining and placing disabled soldiers in jobs. Productive employment, the government proclaimed, would be a veterans' benefit that would long outlast public generosity. For the able-bodied, the best cure for the army-bred diseases of idleness and dependence was a full dose of self-reliance.

For Canadian demobilization planners, the war could hardly have ended at a worse time. Munition workers were laid off by the hundred thousands at the start of the winter slack season, at a time when morale and creativity still suffered from the influenza epidemic. By the time the three hundred and fifty thousand men of the CEF could come home from overseas, only Halifax and Saint John were available as ports. Railways claimed they could transport only twenty thousand a month from maritime ports. As if ships were not already scarce, noisy complaints about conditions on one vessel compelled overseas officials to accept only the very best. In turn, Currie and his generals insisted that the Corps come home in organized units and that men must have a chance to visit England. In March, seething discontent burst into violent riots at Kinmel in north Wales: five died and twenty-seven were hurt. More riots followed in May. In both cases, the British authorities somehow managed to find extra ships and by July, months ahead of expectations, all but a small remnant of the CEF was back in Canada.

Returning troops faced bunting, bands, speeches, and hidden fears. Would soldiers understand how much civilians had suffered with meatless Fridays and fuelless Mondays? Had army life crushed initiative or ingrained habits of drinking, swearing, gambling, and social license? The long months overseas allowed the army to complete demobilization swiftly. The 20th Battalion was typical. It reached Toronto Union Station on May 24, 1919. The unit formed ranks, marched up Yonge Street, and dispersed, never to parade again. Next day, men lined up at the Exhibition grounds to sign a few last papers, collect back pay, and obtain tickets if they needed to travel farther. Veterans kept their uniforms and steel helmets. Troops of the 27th

Battalion were asked whether they would mind staying in uniform as a government reserve during the Winnipeg General Strike. Yes, they would mind very much! The unit baggage was augmented by some boxes of machine-guns and ammunition but when the battalion reached the troubled city, it broke up as rapidly as any other.

Medical advances meant that more sick and wounded soldiers had survived than in previous wars. The result was a large and continuing responsibility, aggravated because the post-war depression and high levels of unemployment utterly undermined the optimistic hope that a little retraining would produce self-sufficiency. Two full years after the armistice, 6,520 veterans were still in hospital. By 1925, a total of 20,115 widows, children, and destitute parents of dead soldiers qualified for pensions. The number of disability pensioners grew steadily from 42,932 men and women in 1919 to 77,967 by 1933. Though veterans' organizations complained incessantly of government red tape and stinginess, Canadian pension rates matched or even exceeded those of the United States. In the inter-war years, the annual cost of veterans' programmes and pensions ranked second as an expense behind service of the national debt. The total cost by 1935, $1,153 million, exceeded the total revenue from income and business profits' taxes since 1917, $1,133 million.

Though a few small British veterans' organizations had existed in Canada before 1914, the Great War Veterans' Association (GWVA), formed in Winnipeg in 1917, rapidly emerged as the major national voice for ex-CEF members. Its leaders, chosen almost inevitably from those who had returned wounded, gave priority to the disabled in a growing agenda of demands. This fitted Ottawa's priorities and the GWVA enjoyed easy access to government policy-makers. The hundreds of thousands of able-bodied veterans had other priorities. A noisy populist campaign for a $2,000 bonus embarrassed the GWVA's established leaders, split the association, and ultimately foundered on the Borden government's refusal to add a billion dollars to the national debt. That defeat robbed both veterans and a few Tory opportunists like Mayor Tommy Church of Toronto of hope that the returned men could be moulded into a powerful right-wing voting bloc. By 1925, the GWVA, with its strident, populist policies, had been absorbed with a number of smaller organizations, into the Canadian Legion, firmly controlled by senior officers like Sir Richard Turner and Sir Percy Lake. Compared to its American, Australian, and European counterparts, the

Legion was discreet, cautious, and non-partisan. Individual branches of the Legion, as of the GWVA, sometimes attacked "aliens," Communists, and labour organizers; their national organizations were more concerned with preserving solvency and influence.

Discretion seemed a prudent response to Canada's post-war mood. Never, not even with time, would Canadians romanticize the Great War. The extent of the sacrifices was mocked by the pathetic results: a shattered Europe, squabbling allies, a League of Nations whose critics were already legion. Safe behind the Atlantic, protected as much now by a new United States Navy as by the British fleet, Canadians would go crusading no more. In 1922, when Arthur Meighen, as opposition leader, responded to a threatened Anglo-Turkish war with Laurier's ringing phrase, "Ready, aye, ready!", he was utterly disavowed.

Caught between post-war turbulence and a yearning to return to normal, the Union government hurried to restore a peacetime defence organization. Word of radical plots in Vancouver led a nervous Sir Thomas White to ask Borden to arrange for a British cruiser to anchor offshore. Borden refused. The Winnipeg General Strike persuaded Mewburn to raise the maximum permissible strength of the permanent force to ten thousand men. Turbulence passed; normality reasserted itself. In 1914, Hughes had created the CEF; in 1919, the aged Major-General Otter was given the task of integrating the new, battle-worthy organization with the old volunteer militia. His policy, guided by Sir Arthur Currie, was more political than military. More important than a balanced militia army was an organization that allowed any hospitable community a company or even a regiment. If a good CEF battalion like the 3rd Toronto's refused to mix with the two historic regiments that had given it birth in 1914, let it survive on its own. To ease the transition, regimental names replaced the old numbers. There was one exception. At General McNaughton's urging, the CEF's only French-speaking battalion became part of the permanent force as the Royal 22nd Regiment. The west also got its own regular regiment, Princess Patricia's Canadian Light Infantry.

Long tradition and conspicuous wartime service eased the post-war re-establishment of the militia; newer services were less fortunate. Few Canadians knew anything of the Halifax Patrol, and the service hardly inspired legends. The Royal Canadian Navy had almost died in 1913; it almost did so again. Lord Jellicoe, a former British First Sea Lord, urged a variety of peacetime organizations costing from $4 to $20 million a year; Borden's naval minister, C. C. Ballantyne, settled for a frugal plan costing $2.5 million. The cabinet turned him down. A furious minister sent telegrams disbanding the entire navy. "The Navy League spent half its revenue on messages," Sir George Foster wryly noted, "Halifax and Esquimalt were up in arms and the rest of the Ministers were asking who did it." A little navy of three warships, two submarines, and the Royal Canadian Naval College survived—for the moment.

An air force was more popular. Thousands of Canadian flyers came home from the war, their exploits already admired. A nation preoccupied with transportation needed little persuasion about the potential of flying. Even the GWVA demanded a Canadian air force with "the workers sharing in the management." Yet both the infant Canadian air forces at the end of the war were disbanded. In June 1919, a seven-member Air Board was formed to regulate civil aviation and develop policy. Its plan called for a combination government air service and a kind of air militia based on wartime pilots and mechanics. Prodded by a British gift of $5 million in aircraft, parts, and equipment from its war surplus and by an American gift of the flying boats at Halifax, the government approved a Canadian Air Force in April 1920. By the summer, government pilots were making themselves useful spotting forest fires, hunting smugglers, delivering treaty money, and even reporting on geological formations.

By 1921, the Unionists had exhausted themselves and the country. On December 6, 1921, Canadians elected their first minority Liberal government. Mackenzie King's Liberals, largely from Quebec, could hold power only with votes from the Progressives, a wobbly coalition of sixty-four rural members from Ontario and the west. It was a Parliament that could agree on little save the folly of defence spending. "The people of this country do not propose to submit to the god of militarism," warned the *Farmers' Sun*, "We have just fought a five years' war to make wars to cease." Agnes Macphail, Canada's first woman MP, was a devout pacifist. So was J. S. Woodsworth, leader of the tiny labour group and a future founder of the Co-operative Commonwealth Federation. Most Canadians rejected pacifism but they applauded anyone who denounced "merchants of death," general staffs, and preparedness. Liberals themselves were split on a host of issues, from the tariff to freight rates, and Quebec MPs had a special score to settle with the military; anti-militarism united the caucus. In 1922, C. G. Power, a Quebec back-bencher and CEF veteran, demanded a $300,000 cut in spending on militia training. By the time fellow caucus members were finished, $700,000 had been slashed.

The new prime minister was not at all displeased. As James Eayrs has noted, King had "a marked aversion to the military life and the military mind. . . ." In opposition, he had attacked every unionist defence proposal. What enemy, he demanded, was the government arming against? Once in power, King himself was acutely embarrassed when Cape Breton magistrates in 1922 and 1923 requisitioned most of the tiny permanent force to overawe striking coal miners. The Militia Act was at last changed to put both the responsibility and the cost of aid to the civil power squarely on provincial governments. The Liberals wiped out reserve training by the new Canadian Air Force. When the great powers, at Washington in 1922, met to haggle over naval reductions, King announced Canada's grand gesture: an immediate 40 per cent cut. The naval college was closed, ships were sold, and the Royal Canadian Navy emerged with two small destroyers. By a rare stroke of luck, Commodore Walter Hose, who now commanded the service, was allowed to establish companies of a thousand-man Royal Canadian Naval Volunteer Reserve across Canada. For a service whose chief problem was nationwide indifference, the RCNVR was the shrewdest investment it ever made.

Eager for any kind of cheap reform, King's government seized on the notion of unifying the militia and naval service departments. A single department, claimed Major-General James MacBrien, the first Canadian-born Chief of the General Staff, would prevent competition for personnel and resources. Sir Eugène Fiset, retiring as deputy minister to become a Liberal MP, insisted that amalgamation would save millions. George Graham, introducing his National Defence bill in April 1922, summed up the arguments most likely to appeal to his fellow MPs: "What I want to accomplish, if I possibly can, is to have a well-organized, snappy defence force that will be a credit to Canada without being too expensive." Parliament was content; Graham's 1922-23 estimate of $12,242,930 cost each Canadian $1.46, about a fifth of the defence burden Americans carried in that peaceful year.

Liberal defence policy was more cheap than snappy. Among the military, the war had raised expectations and given Canada what she had never had before: real home-grown expertise. MacBrien, Hose, and McNaughton headed an impressive array of experienced, competent professionals. Slowly they realized that their peacetime careers would be limited to a few aging destroyers, obsolete equipment brought home by the Canadian Corps, and reconditioned aircraft for which the Royal Air Force had no further use. Unifying defence headquarters did not help. In the new Defence Council, service heads brought unequal resources to the struggle for a share of them. MacBrien, as Chief of Staff, was supposed to be more than the voice of the army but he remained a soldier, with two allies in the adjutant general and the quartermaster general. Hose, as director of the naval service, never accepted subordination to a general and in the deputy minister, Georges Desbarats, formerly civil head of the naval service, he had a powerful ally. Humblest of all, as a mere associate member, was the director of the Canadian Air Force (CAF).

The CAF's chief weapon was Sir Willoughby Gwatkin; he and allies on the Air Board had wisely insisted that the new service be more than a military air force. J. A. Wilson, secretary of the Air Board, declared that an air force "must be based on a sound economic development for Peace uses." At the same time and rather before the fact, Gwatkin insisted to the British that the new Canadian service was securely established. On February 15, 1923, the British granted the title of "Royal." Only a year later, on April 1, 1924, did King's government formally legislate the existence of a "Royal Canadian Air Force." Most officers and men of the old service transferred to the new, adopting the uniforms, badges, and youthful traditions of the RAF.

In the 1920s, the Canadian services struggled to avoid stultification. Junior and senior officers of the permanent establishment tried to keep up with their professions by reading, writing for a *Canadian Defence Quarterly* launched by MacBrien in 1923, and attending courses in Britain. The RCAF was reminded by its RAF connection and intermittent exposure to Lord Trenchard's doctrines on air power and aerial bombardment that it was more than an organization of bush pilots. Lacking any Canadian training facilities at all, the Canadian navy depended entirely on the Royal Navy. If its officers returned with the Royal Navy's attitudes and accent as well as its expertise, that was the consequence of government policy.

Denied public support or a clear purpose (other than Colonel J. Sutherland Brown's Defence Plan No. 1, a recasting of age-old schemes for war with the United States), peacetime service drifted gently from reality. Instructors, who had survived Vimy Ridge and Amiens, swung gas rattles and pretended to a few recruits that they represented machine-guns. Canada's soldiers saw new tanks, anti-tank guns, and machine-gun carriers — but only in the newsreels. Militia officers did their best to revive their units and complained that a militia commission no longer commanded social status. Canada, after all, had been flooded with generals and colonels. A little of Canada's prosperity trickled into the militia estimates: by 1929, they reached $21 million. Yet, without a palpable threat, who could say Canada was unprepared? Indeed, influential experts insisted that preparing for war made it happen. No one, after the Great War of 1914-19, wanted that.

V The World War

Ending a Truce

Few Canadians in the 1920s realized that the Armistice in 1918 would be no more than a truce. Whether or not the Great War had been the "war to end all wars," they knew that they did not plan to go crusading again. Nothing was more objectionable about the new League of Nations than Article X of its covenant, requiring members to join in mutual security even to the point of war. Critics referred scornfully to the "League of European Victors." The absence of the United States (partly because it had objected to having Canada treated as a sovereign power) made the League all the more embarrassing for Ottawa. King might lecture assembled delegates at Geneva on the virtues of conciliation but he would never allow the League to draw Canada into war. "It is for Parliament to decide whether or not we should participate in wars in different parts of the world," King explained in 1923. While the Liberal leader never denied that Britain might call on Canada in a major war, he did his utmost to ensure that the summons would never be sent.

Deep in the bowels of the Woods Building, home of the new Department of National Defence, Colonel Brown added more secret plans to his mobilization scheme for a war with the United States: Plan No. 2 envisaged war with Japan, with Canada neutral or involved; No. 3 devised a new CEF for a European war; No. 4 considered aid in an imperial war — perhaps a black uprising in South Africa or trouble on India's Northwest frontier. Such documents would doubtless have confirmed all of King's prejudices against soldiers. Instead, his Liberal government preferred to see the services making themselves useful. Militia and naval officers envied the RCAF's civil flying as a lever for public funds and a source of fame. General MacBrien promoted the army's Northwest Territories and Yukon Radio System, a network of stations that began at Mayo and Dawson in 1923 and spread across the southern Arctic. General McNaughton, as Chief of the General Staff, promoted military collaboration with the National Research Council in fields ranging from photogrammetry to his own specialty, a cathode-ray direction finder, a forerunner of radar. The navy, split between two coasts and short of fuel, could only "show the flag" in Canadian and Caribbean ports and lend its meagre support to the forces of order in the El Salvador civil war of 1934.

If the Conservatives had not won in 1930, McNaughton would almost certainly have resigned in frustration at his nit-picking minister, Colonel J. L. Ralston. More serious than picked nits was Ralston's refusal to approve new equipment or to allow the building of a government arsenal. The Liberals would not be "Merchants of Death"! The Tories might well have been more sympathetic. A new minister promptly ordered six tiny Carden-Loyd machine-gun carriers. The Depression intervened. Defeated for ignoring the problem, the Liberals left office in time to let R. B. Bennett's government face the full brunt of collapsing revenues, mass unemployment, and economic ruin. In the Bennett years, governments poured a billion dollars into aid for Depression victims, only to be called stingy. To find the money, politicians and officials ransacked budgets. Defence was an obvious target.

Fearful of riot and disorder, the Tories squeezed the militia and the 3,000-member permanent force only gently. Other services were more vulnerable. Far from finding safety in its civil operations, the RCAF was ordered to fire 78 of its 177 officers and 100 of its 729 airmen when Ottawa cut "luxury flying." The "Big Cut" shattered morale and left a deep bitterness that sister services suffered no such reductions. In 1933, ordered to slice $3.6 million from the budget, McNaughton decided to save $2 million by chopping out the RCN. Coast defence could be handled better by aircraft. Commodore Hose again fought a brilliant rearguard action. For a third time, the navy escaped elimination. Interservice hostility was accentuated.

McNaughton's active mind made him a valued advisor to the Bennett government in many fields. Horrified at the plight of the single unemployed — potential soldiers in any future war — McNaughton argued that the army could put them to work clearing airfields, building barracks, and repairing historic sites, at a total cost of a dollar per man per day. The government nervously approved and, by the summer of 1933, McNaughton reported eight thousand men at work. In the United States, a similar scheme, the Civilian Conservation Corps, was one of the triumphs of Roosevelt's New Deal. The Canadian scheme helped destroy Bennett. Unlike the CCC, McNaughton's organization was as civilian as possible in appearance but a military atmosphere spilled out in regulations banning unions and with ex-CEF sergeants hired as foremen. Left in the camps for years as the Depression dragged on, the relief campers felt forgotten, condemned, and derided by their wage of twenty cents a day. Far from being immunized from radical ideas, as McNaughton hoped, the young men became the easiest recruits for Communist organizers. Hundreds joined the "On-to-Ottawa" trek in 1935 and shared its bloody conclusion on Dominion Day at Regina. When voters went to the polls that September, the army's relief camps helped restore the Liberals.

In 1935, Canadians chose "King," not "Chaos," but the Liberal slogan fitted the entire world as well as Canada alone. In 1931, when Japan found a pretext to invade Manchuria, the world found excuses not to intervene. It would use them again and again. In 1933, Hitler came to power in Germany and promptly set out to restore his country to the status of a great military power. By 1936, he had repudiated the Versailles settlement, restored conscription, and set out to build a powerful navy. In 1935, Mussolini's Italy set out to fulfil an old dream, the conquest of Ethiopia. Left in Geneva amidst the change of government, the Canadian delegate, W. R. Riddell, proposed that oil and steel be added to a League embargo. The world buzzed at the "Canadian initiative." In Ottawa, King was furious. Surely Riddell must realize that Mussolini's admirers were legion among Quebec Catholics and nationalists! At King's command, the "Canadian initiative" vanished from Geneva. An accident had allowed Canada to play a small, public role in appeasing the dictators.

King acted with consistency and widespread approval. Among the prominent, only J. W. Dafoe of the *Free Press* disapproved. There was no will to fight Hitler's occupation of the Rhineland in 1936, the *Anschluss* of 1937, or the 1938 Munich agreement to sacrifice Czechoslovakia to Neville Chamberlain's hope that a satisfied Germany would allow "peace in our time." Even the Jewish and political refugees fleeing Nazi horrors were unwelcome. Such would-be immigrants had no friends in such powerful ministers as Ernest Lapointe or Fernand Rinfret, to say nothing of anti-Semites and most of the unemployed.

A few Canadians, mobilized by the Communist Party, fought fascism in Spain. A cruel civil war between a Soviet-backed republic and a military junta dependent on Italian arms and Nazi airpower became an idealists' crusade. Twelve hundred Canadian volunteers in the International Brigades — proportionately more than from any other country but France — were chiefly alumni from McNaughton's relief camps. In Spain, they found a cause and more than a third found a grave.

After serving with the Lincoln and Washington battalions and a scattering of other units, Canadian volunteers pleaded successfully for a national unit. In July 1937, the Mackenzie-Papineau battalion was formed. From the first futile assault at Fuentes de Ebro on October 12 to the long, miserable retreat back to the Ebro a year later, the "Mac-Paps" were, as they were later ironically termed, "premature anti-Fascists."

Canadians had mixed emotions. Maxime Raymond, a Quebec nationalist, was glad to see them go: "it will rid us of these undesirable people, provided they do not return here." Ernest Lapointe, the minister of justice, pushed through a Foreign Enlistment Act promising two years in prison for any Canadian serving against a friendly power. Both sides, Lapointe explained, were "friendly." Woodsworth's CCF, pacifist and anti-Communist, preferred to finance Dr. Norman Bethune's blood transfusion unit. When the Mac-Paps returned in 1938, Canadian officials first had to assure themselves that private sponsors would pay for transportation and any medical costs.

By then, Canadians realized that they no longer lived in "a fireproof house, far from the sources of conflagration" as their League delegate, Senator Raoul Dandurand, had smugly boasted in 1927. Newsreels of war and military arms had their impact. By 1936, the United States had developed long-range bombers that could reach Europe across the Arctic Circle with a single refuelling stop. Surely Europeans could do the same, perhaps seizing a base in Canada's empty Arctic. In a grim report to the incoming Liberal government, McNaughton warned that Canada had not a single anti-aircraft gun, that armament at Halifax and Esquimalt was defective, and that Canada had only twenty-five obsolete service aircraft and not a single bomb.

Mackenzie King had no more taste for defence spending than he ever had and his defence minister, Ian Mackenzie, was a hard-drinking CEF veteran from British Columbia, unlikely to stir his cabinet colleagues. Convinced that war was impending, senior British officers wondered for the first time whether they could count on Canada. King gave them little encouragement but he did open contacts with Washington. In 1938, the hemispheric commitment became public when President Roosevelt came north to receive an honorary degree at Queen's University. The people of the United States, he declared, "would not stand idly by if domination of Canadian soil is threatened by any other empire." "We too have obligations as a good, friendly neighbour," King replied, "and one of these is to see that, at our own insistence, our country is made as immune from attack or possible invasion as we can reasonably be expected to make it."

King was ingenious. Surely Canadians of all backgrounds could at least unite on home defence. Continental defence imposed unfamiliar priorities for military thinkers whose expectations had rested somewhere between "Buster" Brown's Defence Plan No. 1 and despatch of a new CEF. Now the neglected RCAF and the humiliated RCN would grow; the militia was relegated to third place.

In 1936, after five years of urging by the militia staff, a paper strength of fifteen divisions was cut in half. Scores of regiments were disbanded, amalgamated, or converted to tank, artillery or armoured car units (without, of course, buying the necessary equipment). In 1938-39, only 46,251 militia trained, compared to 55,000 in 1913. There would not have been arms, equipment, or uniforms for more.

The navy, in contrast, prospered. Between 1936 and 1939, permanent force strength doubled to 191 officers and 1,799 ratings. A couple of extra destroyers were purchased each year from 1937 and Canadian shipyards delivered four new minesweepers.

RCAF expansion was more dramatic. Even the Bennett government had approved a five-squadron reserve in 1932 and allowed the purchase of a few military aircraft. Under the Liberals, the air force budget grew from $3.1 million in 1935-36 to $30 million in the 1939-40 estimates. Late in 1936, the RCAF was finally relieved of its civil aviation chores and in 1938 it emerged as the equal of the militia and RCN. A Chief of the Air Staff, Air Vice-Marshal G. M. Croil, controlled the expanding RCAF through Eastern and Western Air Commands and an Air Training Command. To underline the new defensive status of Canada's army, Liberal plans called for little more than modern coast artillery.

As Britain also scrambled to rearm, Canadians found their traditional arms sources hopelessly backlogged. Any Canadian manufacturer who considered entering so risky and innovative a business could reflect on the plight of the John Inglis Co. The Toronto firm's contract to make seven thousand Bren light machine-guns was turned into a *cause célèbre* by Colonel George Drew. Citizens taught to associate arms production with original sin easily believed Drew's claims that a washing machine manufacturer was unfit to make machine-guns. The British, anxious to use rearmament to solve their own unemployment problems, shared very little business with Canada. They did want men. Since 1919, a steady trickle of Canadians had crossed the Atlantic to join the RAF. In 1938, the British proposed a modest aircrew training programme in Canada to increase the flow. Ottawa bluntly refused. If Canada had to go to war, one factor was infinitely more important in the minds of King and his colleagues than pilots or guns: Canada must be united. British training bases in Canada would produce paroxysms of outrage not merely in Quebec but across the country.

Indeed, it still seemed unlikely in 1938 that Canada would go to war at all. Only the Communists professed to uphold democracy against fascism and their frail credibility crumbled with reports of Stalin's purges. In French Canada, influential opinion favoured Mussolini if not necessarily Hitler, and King's Quebec lieutenants were still shaken from the 1936 election of Maurice Duplessis at the head of a coalition of conservatives and nationalists. Quebec was not alone in its isolationism. Two decades were not enough to blur the horrors of the Great War; newsreels and illustrated magazines warned that new horrors would be unimaginable. F. R. Scott, the Montreal poet, lawyer, and son of a well-known CEF chaplain, warned: "Elderly sadists of the last war are emerging from their obscurity to join the war-dance again, their eyes glistening and their mouths watering as they think of the young men whom they will send to the slaughter." Canadians, insisted Frank Underhill, a Great War veteran and the editor of the *Canadian Forum*, should stuff their ears with the tax bills of the previous war and forget European appeals.

In all Mackenzie King's long political career, perhaps no achievement was as remarkable as or improbable as bringing Canada united into the Second World War. His own mind had never been in doubt. "If a great and clear call of duty comes," he said in 1923, "Canada will respond, whether or not the United States responds, as she did in 1914." Like his much-admired counterpart, Neville Chamberlain, King could resent the forces drawing Canada into the maelstrom: "The idea that every twenty yeas this country should automatically and as a matter of course take part in a war overseas for democracy or self-determination of other small nations, that a country that has all it can do to run itself should feel called upon to save, periodically, a continent that cannot run itself. . . seems to many a nightmare and sheer madness." It was a nightmare and madness King steeled himself to face.

Through the winter of 1939, while the armed forces waited for mea-

In war, imitation is often the wisest form of survival. The Canadiens *adopted the buckskin shirt, leggings, and moccasins of their native adversary. Indians needed the white man's firearms. Primitive muskets were heavy, easily damaged and hard to load but the heavy ball did fatal damage at short range.*

A shirt-sleeved Montcalm congratulates his troops after their victory at Carillon. The painting, from the Fort Ticonderoga museum, is meticulous on details of uniform and topography but real battlefields could not be arranged with such artistic decorum.

A *The* Carignan-Salières *regiment was among the first to try out the novel idea of wearing the same uniform: a chestnut-brown coat and breeches, stockings, and a black felt hat. Officers like this one could wear what they chose or a more costly version of the other ranks' clothes. Shoes fitted either foot.*

B *A soldier of the* Compagnies Franche de la Marine *lived up to the nickname of colonial regular by adapting to local conditions. For summer campaign he left behind his heavy white coat and stiff tricorne hat and adopted Indian leggings or* mitasses. *Soldiers had to shave once a week but regular baths would not be common for another century and a half.*

C *An ensign of the* Régiment de Berry *wore the long greyish-white coat and breeches, black gaiters, and a gold-laced tricorne hat common to officers in Montcalm's line battalions. Junior officers carried the colours, symbol of pride in the regiment and the rallying point in battle.*

D *Wolfe formed grenadier companies into a battalion called the* Louisbourg Grenadiers. *In an army of small, undernourished men, grenadiers formed an elite of the tallest and strongest. The mitre-shaped grenadier cap, evolved from the soft cap worn by the soldier of the* troupes de la marine, *was intended to make the grenadier seem even taller and more imposing.*

A

B

C

D

Sir William Pepperell's Boston militia land from Commodore Peter Warren's fleet to capture Louisbourg in 1745. The artist knew nothing of the actual events or the setting but be could be certain that the patriotic British public would be eager to purchase engravings of the event. Accuracy was purely coincidental.

Wolfe's attempted landing at Beauport, depicted by one of his aides-de camp, Captain Hervey Smith, reflects training in topographical drawing. The scene, with its slightly disembodied violence, has a realism that commercial war art would shun.

Vaudreuil believed that the British fleet would never reach Quebec. If it did, fireships would destroy Admiral Saunders's ships at their moorings. While this painting suggests the terror a fireship attack could inspire in a fleet of wooden, tar-soaked ships, alert and competent seamen could usually fend off the hazard.

Wolfe's capture of Quebec, a familiar illustration in Canadian history books, reflects the artist's need to tell the whole story in a single scene. Nothing, however, obliged the artist to be accurate. The market for instant and imaginative war reporting was as great in 1759 as it still is.

Wolfe was not at all amused by Brigadier George Townshend's caricatures, whatever pleasure they may have given the general's other long-suffering subordinates. The general's dismay at the state of the "necessary houses" was not so much sanitary but, as the French text suggests, because the accompanying insects might be French spies.

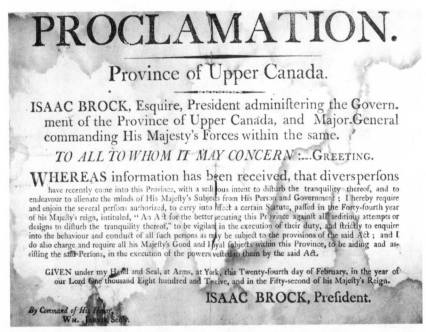

PROCLAMATION.

Province of Upper Canada.

ISAAC BROCK, Esquire, President administering the Government of the Province of Upper Canada, and Major-General
commanding His Majesty's Forces within the same.

*TO ALL TO WHOM IT MAY CONCERN :—*Greeting.

WHEREAS information has been received, that divers persons
have recently come into this Province, with a seditious intent to disturb the tranquility thereof, and to
endeavour to alienate the minds of His Majesty's Subjects from His Person and Government ; I hereby require
and enjoin the several persons authorized, to carry into effect a certain Statute, passed in the Forty-fourth year
of his Majesty's reign, intituled, " An Act for the better securing this Province against all seditious attempts or
designs to disturb the tranquility thereof," to be vigilant in the execution of their duty, and strictly to enquire
into the behaviour and conduct of all such persons as may be subject to the provisions of the said Act ; and I
do also charge and require all his Majesty's Good and loyal subjects within this Province, to be aiding and as-
sisting the said Persons, in the execution of the powers vested in them by the said Act.

GIVEN under my Hand and Seal, at Arms, at York, this Twenty-fourth day of February, in the year of
our Lord One thousand Eight hundred and Twelve, and in the Fifty-second of his Majesty's Reign.

ISAAC BROCK, President.

By Command of His Honor,
Wm. Jarvis, Sec'y.

*"Most of the people have lost all confidence," Brock discovered on the eve of the
War of 1812, "I however speak loud and look big." While some historians
denounce the theory that "great men" make much difference to history, it is
hard to see how Upper Canada would have resisted invasion without Isaac
Brock.*

As a grand, romantic portrayal of Queenston Heights, this painting takes as many liberties with truth as the earlier portrayal of the capture of Quebec. "Push on York volunteers" was said, if ever, on the road from Fort George, not by the dying hero, whose wound appears, in fact, to have killed him almost instantly.

Châteauguay was a confused minor battle in which an ill-led and irresolute American column was held off by French Canadian fencibles, British regulars, and Canadien militia. In national mythology, it formed a convenient pair with Queenston in suggesting that both founding peoples were zealous in Canada's defence.

Lundy's Lane in 1814 was the bloodiest, most dogged struggle of the campaign in Upper Canada. British redcoats and American regulars, fully trained after two years, fought each other to a weary standstill. Because the Americans withdrew, the British could claim victory but illusions of easy superiority were gone.

Henri Julien's drawing of "un vieux de '37," published in 1916, became such a totem of Québécois nationalism that the Front de Libération du Québec used it for communiqués during the October crisis. Since the events took place in early winter, even a devoted patriote *would have been more warmly dressed.*

Lord Charles Beauclerk left a portfolio of sketches of the events of the 1837 rebellion, later published in London in 1840. At St. Eustache, a succession of flamboyant leaders hurriedly abandoned the patriote cause. The brave remnant, under Dr. Jean-Olivier Chénier, held out to the end in the parish church. Chénier and many others died when the church was burned.

From a Drawing by W. R. Callington, Engineer, Boston, from an Actual Survey made in 1837.

Improvements in engraving techniques allowed magazine readers to follow events more closely. British purchasers of this depiction of the Niagara River and the destruction of the Caroline *would be more entertained than informed. Ideas of scale, as of punctuality, were flexible.*

The Montreal Volunteer Cavalry were among the units created by the British after the 1837-38 rising to act as a rural police and to discourage deserters from the garrison. The drawing, by a British officer, reflects a mildly snobbish astonishment that the young colonials would actually have handkerchiefs as well as runny noses.

Canadian militia at Thorold, called out for the Fenian Raid of 1866. Equipped and partially trained by the British, with regular regiments to set an example of discipline and drill, Canada's new volunteer militia probably reached its highest state of efficiency during the Confederation decade.

Resplendent with silver, white linen, and adopted tradition, the officers' mess at Stanley Barracks was an outpost of British military tradition and a firm defiance of the Canadian militia's egalitarian tendencies. Militia officers were "gentlemen," whatever their origins or occupations.

The horse lines at a turn-of-the-century militia summer camp. Often soldiers in cavalry or artillery units brought their own horses to camp. The straw hats, issued for the camp, were generally known as "cows' breakfasts."

*After the 1885 campaign, Sir Fred Middleton posed proudly in the
uniform he had designed for himself. A mildly pompous old gentleman,
Middleton was also a shrewd and experienced veteran who ignored
much bad advice from Canadian superiors and subordinates and
ended the campaign far sooner and with less bloodshed than most
people had expected.*

Among those present with Middleton's column in 1885 was Canada's first war photographer, Captain James Peters of the permanent force artillery. This product of his unwieldy and fragile apparatus shows gunners cleaning a nine-pounder and preparing ammunition under a sergeant's supervision.

A genial and side-whiskered Sir Frederick Borden, accompanied by Colonel William Otter, strides forward to review the troops at Niagara-on-the-Lake. Between them, Borden and Otter probably contributed more than anyone to preparing the Canadian militia for the ordeal of the First World War.

School cadets parade through Guelph, under the supervision of teachers, officers, and a faithful dog. While Canadians might deplore the idea of peacetime conscription for adults, even Canadiens approved of it for school boys. By 1914, most provinces enforced compulsory cadet training in the schools.

Instructors of HMCS Niobe pose for a photograph as part of a discreet and largely unsuccessful attempt to popularize "Laurier's Navy." While the Royal Navy had serious doubts that a colonial squadron could ever become truly efficient, it sacrificed some very able officers and petty officers to make the attempt. The "sennet hats" were a concession to summer heat.

Lieutenant-General Sir Sam Hughes, with suitable cronies, prepares to descend from his private car to inspect thousands of thirsty, sweating CEF recruits at Camp Borden in the summer of 1916. The war transformed Hughes from an eccentric militarist into a seeming national saviour to his ill-informed fellow Canadians.

The Imperial Munitions Board employed 250,000 Canadians, among them 40,000 women. Women had always been part of the labour force but their presence at the heart of the war effort, in non-traditional jobs, was part of a tide of change that swept every Canadian institution.

*Toronto's Mayor Tommy Church congratulates departing Italian reservists.
Many of the young men in Canada's prewar wave of immigration were
summoned home for service on both sides.*

*Canadians set up their Vickers machine-guns during the battle for Vimy Ridge.
The water-cooled Vickers served with Canadians until the Korean War. In the
First World War, machine-guns dominated the battlefield though artillery shells
caused more casualties.*

Sir Arthur Currie, commanding the Canadian Corps, and Field Marshal Sir Douglas Haig. While the pear-shaped ex-school teacher was Haig's choice, he soon found that Currie had a mind of his own and an independent channel of communications. Currie made the Canadians into allies, not subordinates.

At a field kitchen just behind the front lines at Hill 70, a few Canadians drink tea and share some possibly obscene thoughts about the photographer. Canadian soldiers liked to think of themselves as adaptable, with a professional skill as "scroungers."

The battlefield at Passchendaele. In the sea of mud, wounded men drowned but shell explosions did relatively little damage. Currie warned that it would cost 16,000 casualties to win a purely symbolic victory. Haig insisted. Currie's estimate was just about right.

By 1917, Britain was vigorously recruiting and training Canadians for the war in the air. The Imperial Munitions Board helped establish airfields and began manufacturing aircraft. By the war's end, a quarter of the flying personnel in the Royal Air Force were Canadian.

Major-General Sir Archibald MacDonell, "Batty Mac" to his men in the 1st Division, poses in 1924 with sergeants of his old regiment, Lord Strathcona's Horse. The postwar forces inherited the prestige of the Canadian Corps but they were also left with its obsolete equipment and ideas.

A woman ambulance driver changes a tire on her Canadian Red Cross ambulance. More than a manpower shortage brought women into unfamiliar wartime occupations. The prewar feminist movement had encouraged some women to shatter old middle-class stereotypes of women's role and potential.

Some of 5,000 Canadians waiting to return on one of the "monster ships," the Olympic. Canadian social scientists have rarely asked about the impact of years of military service on the wartime generations. How far were attitudes to family, locality, and the State changed by life in the armed forces?

Canadians in the Mackenzie-Papineau Battalion were mobilized by the Communist Party to serve in the Spanish Civil War. Proportionately, Canada contributed more volunteers to the International Brigades than any country except France. More than a third of them never returned.

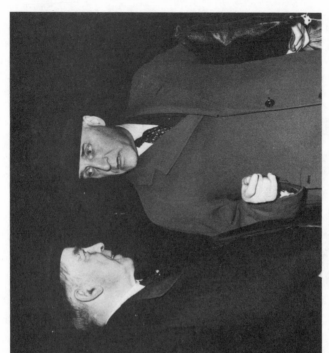

William Lyon Mackenzie King and his Minister of National Defence, Colonel J.L. Ralston. The prime minister set a higher priority on national unity and Liberal party survival than on total commitment to the war effort. Most Canadians approved.

Loyal citizens— do not hoard

RATIONED
SUGAR ½ lb. a week PER PERSON
TEA ½ of the usual PURCHASE
COFFEE ¾ of the USUAL PURCHASE

Early attempts at rationing depended on a lot of voluntary compliance and the fact that most Canadians in the 1940s patronised their local grocer. The German submarine war and the Japanese sweep through South-East Asia cut into supplies of commodities which Canadians had taken for granted.

The internment of 23,000 Japanese Canadians in 1942 had more to do with racial prejudice in British Columbia than with any problem of national security. Though the army, navy and RCMP insisted it was unnecessary, political opportunism prevailed. Internees could take only what they could carry; the rest was left for the Custodian of Enemy Property.

A Canadian pilot in a Hurricane fighter, workhorse of both RAF and RCAF fighter squadrons overseas. Thanks to the BCATP, Canada again provided more than its share of flying personnel to the British services.

Corvettes, it was said, would roll in a heavy dew. In the stormy North Atlantic, life aboard became a frigid, water-soaked struggle for survival. Denied much chance for peacetime preparedness, the Royal Canadian Navy could only do its best.

A Consolidated Liberator of the RCAF over a convoy gave a powerful sense of security for merchant seamen and their escorts. Without air cover, a convoy was hopelessly vulnerable to hovering German wolf packs.

Canadian Typhoons on an improvised airfield in Normandy wait for a tank-killing mission. Though air forces preferred independent roles of strategic bombing, they made some of their most dynamic wartime contributions in close support of armies. Without air support, victory in Normandy might have been impossible.

Lieutenant-General E.L.M. Burns and his predecessor, Lieutenant-General H.D.G. Crerar, stride along an Italian lane in 1944 for the benefit of an official photographer. First World War veterans who had worked doggedly at their profession between wars, neither Crerar nor Burns quite managed to capture the imagination or the devotion of their subordinates.

Major-General Guy Simonds listens to one of his brigadiers. A young prewar artillery officer, Simonds emerged as one of the few Canadian generals with a flair for mobile warfare. More cautious colleagues mistrusted him and one even looked for evidence to prove him insane.

A sergeant of the Governor General's Horse Guards briefs tank crews during the advance to Arnhem in April 1945. These are veterans though some of them are also very young.

Men of the South Saskatchewan Regiment wait the call for their Bren gun section to cross the canal embankment and find out what awaits them on the other side. It was the desperate shortage of trained infantry that led to the conscription crisis of 1944.

A medical officer who survived the Japanese prisoner of war camps meets his son for the first time. One of the unresolved problems of both world wars was setting a fair basis of compensation for physical and mental suffering which went far beyond the strains of conventional civil life.

An English war bride meets her French Canadian inlaws and discovers, for the first time, that they do not have a common language. Canadians returned from overseas in both world wars with wives and even a few husbands who had to make the triple adjustment to marriage, a new country, and a peacetime world.

Canadian chiefs of staff meet with NATO's land forces commander, Field Marshal Viscount Montgomery. From the left, Lieutenant-General Howard Graham, Air Marshal Hugh Campbell, General Charles Foulkes, and Vice-Admiral Harry DeWolf.

The postwar world was dominated by the image of the mushroom cloud and the nuclear explosion which created it. In 1946, when it was tested at Bikini Atoll, few even realized the hazard of radiation which, when added to the unprecedented release of heat, light, and blast, presented humanity with its most terrible threat since creation.

The Korean War, combined with a mild recession, brought recruits flocking. Preference was given to veterans of the previous war who had found difficulty in adjusting. The defence minister guessed that enough volunteers could be found—but he had to cut recruiting standards to meet the target.

Men of Princess Patricia's Canadian Light Infantry on the march in North Korea. While its soldiers were volunteers, enlisted for special service, most Canadians tended to think of them as professionals, enlisted for a remote, necessary, but not very interesting war.

HMCS Athabaskan and her three sister ships were the pride of Canada's navy a decade or more ago. As gas-turbine helicopter-equipped destroyers, they were state-of-the-art in anti-submarine warfare. As time passes, even Canada's most modern ships slide into obsolescence.

As in wartime, Canada's defence needs can no longer ignore the talent and enthusiasm of half the population. The advent of women on a career basis in the peacetime armed forces has only begun to transform the values and institutions of a profoundly male environment.

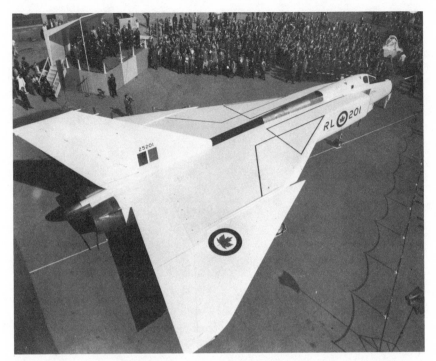

The roll-out of the first CF-105 Arrow in 1958. Pride goeth before a fall. Although the cost and development problems of the Arrow would rapidly become standard in subsequent major weapons systems, the Arrow persuaded both Liberal and Conservative Governments that Canada could not afford to play in the major leagues any longer. Within months, every prototype, part, and drawing had been destroyed and both national pride and technological potential had been dealt savage blows.

Canadian-made Cougars of the 12e Régiment Blindé Canadien at Canadian Forces Base Gagetown. Part of the cautious re-armament of the Canadian Armed Forces in the 1970s, the Cougars represented a gesture to "Priority One" or the protection of domestic sovereignty. They certainly had no place on a European battlefield.

After years of delay, argument, and escalating costs, Canada began acquiring the CF-18 Hornet as a combined answer to both her NATO commitment and to her air-interceptor needs at home.

The Canadian forces were reluctant to abandon separate uniforms in 1967 and showed little more enthusiasm when the Mulroney government restored them in 1985. In the interval, they acquired a distinctly American look, symbolizing Canada's current imperial linkages.

Peacekeeping became a major activity for the Canadian forces, beginning in Kashmir in 1948 and extending to Cyprus in 1964.

Media scrutiny and interpretation is a major factor in modern conflict as rival sides manoeuvre to capture public opinion. At Oka in the summer of 1990, discipline and a little good luck allowed troops of the 5th Mechanized Brigade to emerge from their confrontation with the Mohawk Warriors' society with credit and without bloodshed.

Only Canada's CF-18 fighters, stationed at Qatar, met the high-tech standards of the 1990-91 Gulf War, although Ottawa's concern for domestic public opinion kept them out of the earlier, more dangerous phase of the air attack on Iraq.

gre stocks of new equipment, King prepared the country. If Britain were threatened by air bombardment, he warned, Canada would be at her side. Even clearer was another message: if Canada went to war, there would be no conscription. Deliberately, Lapointe gave the harsh message, King the reassurance. King's new Conservative opponent, Dr. R. J. Manion, echoed the no-conscription pledge; it was the one promise that might reconcile a seemingly conservative Quebec to the Tories. King's own sentimental love of England led him to a master stroke in his pre-war preparations, the Royal Visit of 1939. A soft-spoken, diffident King George VI and his out-going, gracious consort accomplished more than even devout monarchists could have expected. For a few weeks, Canadians were lifted out of themselves and their Depression-era gloom. Communities vied with each other to achieve pageantry and colour. All three armed forces helped supply both. On the west coast, four destroyers escorted the royal couple to Victoria. At Halifax, a flight of Hurricanes showed the RCAF's new though meagre resources. Everywhere guards and escorts from the militia and permanent force buttoned on slightly threadbare scarlet tunics and whitened or polished ceremonial helmets. Montreal's nationalist Mayor Camillien Houde astonished Canadians with the warmth of his welcome to the royal couple.

What mattered was that Canadian isolationism had been anaesthetized. It was asleep when Hitler's troops plunged across the Polish border on September 1, 1939. It had not woken by September 10 when Canada's Parliament decided on war.

Phoney and Total War

Days before the Germans invaded Poland, Canada took war precautions. Militia call-outs from the reserves guarded key points. Two destroyers headed south from Esquimalt to the Panama Canal. Aged RCAF aircraft flew to war stations at Halifax. No one protested. On September 10, when Parliament voted for war, only three MPs (among them the CCF's venerable J. S. Woodsworth) dissented. The unemployed headed to the nearest armoury to enlist. Montreal's French-speaking regiments were among the first to meet their quota of volunteers.

Like most Canadians, King felt no exhilaration. If Hitler did not win, he concluded, Stalin certainly would. His government felt aloof from the outcome. When service chiefs presented a $500 million mobilization plan, the cabinet chopped it in half. The army could send a single division overseas; another would train in Canada. Navy plans for ships and men were slashed. Only RCAF plans for aircrew training survived unscathed. An expanded air force would be justified as a home defence precaution; most of the money would stay in Canada; above all, a big RCAF could never lead to conscription.

King's war policy was simple: avoid the policies that had led Borden into trouble. Conscription was the most obvious trap but so were profiteering, hoarding, and inflation. A Wartime Prices and Trade Board swiftly took shape to deter all three. Instead of looking to posterity, the two frugal Nova Scotians who managed wartime finances, J. L. Ralston and J. L. Ilsley, would insist on a pay-as-you-go policy. Above all, Canada would not fight to the last man and dollar: the war effort presumed limited liability.

Just how limited became apparent when Britain renewed its request for a Canadian role in RAF aircrew training. Memories of 1917-18 and of the steady trickle of RCAF trainees compelled to seek a career in the British service underlined the appeal. King's only regret was that the proposal had not forestalled his offer of an army division. Still, long weeks of haggling ensued. On King's birthday, December 17, a British Commonwealth Air Training Plan could at last be announced. At a cost of $600 million ($350 million from Canada) the BCATP would deliver twenty thousand Canadian, British, Australian, and New Zealand aircrew a year. At King's insistence, the statement described the plan as Canada's "most effective contribution to the war effort." Ottawa seemed untroubled by the fact that Canadian graduates would disappear into the RAF and that even RCAF squadrons overseas would be organized and paid for by British taxpayers. Cheapness outweighed nationalism.

During the rancorous negotiations, King had blurted, "This is not our war," to the astonished British. Widely publicized, the phrase did the Liberals no apparent harm. When Maurice Duplessis sought a fresh mandate as Quebec's saviour from conscription, King's Quebec colleagues criss-crossed the province to defeat him, echoing the no-conscription pledge. On October 25, Adélard Godbout's Liberals swept Duplessis from office. In neighbouring Ontario, King's other great enemy, Premier Mitchell Hepburn, tried another tack. Touring makeshift barracks and the drafty exhibition halls where army recruits huddled, Hepburn had no trouble collecting evidence of a scandalous unpreparedness. A hostile resolution from Hepburn Liberals and opposition Tories in the Ontario legislature was too valuable ammunition for "Fighting Bob" Manion and federal Tories to ignore. King summoned Parliament, delivered a throne speech, and called a snap election before opposition members could reply. Canadians responded by giving King the most one-sided majority in memory: 184 Liberals to only 39 Tories, 10 Social Crediters, 8 CCFers and 4 independents. Manion lost his seat. If King's war effort was as phoney as the war along the Maginot Line in France, Canadians obviously did not mind.

A few weeks later, they might have felt differently. On April 9, Hitler struck at Norway. A month later, the German *blitzkrieg* sliced through the Netherlands and Belgium, out-flanking France's fortifications. British and French armies reeled back. On June 4, the last British soldiers were hauled from Dunkirk; their equipment was abandoned. On June 12, the French commander-in-chief advised his government to give up.

Suddenly Canada was Britain's biggest partner in the war. She did her pathetic best. Four destroyers and the only RCAF squadron with modern aircraft left at once for England. The 1st Canadian Division had been there since December 1939. A brigade was sent to Brest in a fool's errand to help hold Brittany. It returned at once, leaving behind much of its hard-won equipment. In Canada, most of the phoney-war restraints were forgotten. Parliament passed a National Resources Mobilization Act, granting sweeping powers to control manpower — though only for home defence. When Montreal's Mayor Houde denounced national registration, he was swiftly interned. So were hundreds of Nazi, Fascist, and Communist supporters (Moscow's sudden 1939 alliance with Berlin switched most of Canada's Communists into fervent enemies of the war effort).

To maintain the BCATP, the RCAF had to replace British resources with planes, engines, and equipment purchased in the neutral United States or from Canada's primitive air industry. Overnight the RCN would need every escort vessel that could be built to combat a U-boat threat that would emanate from most of the ports of Europe. The militia (renamed in the summer of 1940 the Canadian Army) now readied the 2nd and 3rd Divisions for overseas. A batch of obsolete tanks, dug out of the Texas sand and purchased as scrap iron by Canada's pioneer of armoured warfare, Major-General F. F. Worthington, arrived in Camp Borden. A single army tank brigade grew to become the 4th and 5th

Armoured Divisions and two supporting armoured brigades, filled out the converted cavalry regiments.

At the outset of war, King removed Ian Mackenzie as minister of national defence. Norman Rogers, his able replacement, died a year later in an air crash. On June 10, 1940, Colonel J. L .Ralston returned to the department from the Finance portfolio. A gallant CEF veteran with integrity as shiny as his high-domed forehead, Ralston's appetite for detail was as insatiable as ever. A greater contrast to Sir Sam Hughes could not be imagined. C. G. "Chubby" Power, bibulous but shrewd, joined him as Associate Minister for Air; Angus L. Macdonald, the charismatic Liberal premier of Nova Scotia, dutifully came to Ottawa to take charge of the navy. It was a powerful team for a superhuman task: building fighting forces where none had existed.

In Washington, the task looked impossible. If Britain fell, a defenceless Canada would endanger the United States. On August 16, Roosevelt lifted his phone and invited his good friend "Mackenzie" to meet him next day at Ogdensburg. A scribbled memorandum recorded their meeting: a Permanent Joint Board on Defence would "consider in the broad sense the defense of the northern half of the western hemisphere." An ecstatic King imagined himself as matchmaker for a new Anglo-American alliance. In London, Britain's new prime minister, Winston Churchill, grumbled that there might be "two opinions" about that. When Churchill and Roosevelt met off Argentia, Newfoundland, in 1941 to issue their Atlantic Charter, the matchmaker was not invited. The Ogdensburg agreement simply made Canada a junior and submissive partner in American defence preparations. In this momentous event, needless to say, Parliament was given nothing to decide.

The crisis of 1940 created at least the atmosphere of total war. Its symbol was not King but C. D. Howe, the new Minister of Munitions and Supply. Short, terse, perpetually rumpled, Howe's brilliance lay in his capacity to grasp first principles and to use able men. As an engineer, he had built many of Canada's massive grain elevators; as Minister of Transport, he had put together Trans-Canada Airlines. Business instantly suspected him. Ilsley, as the new Finance Minister, was horrified by his methods. Officials insisted that his department was in chaos. If Howe had not narrowly escaped drowning when his ship was torpedoed, his visit to England in the fall of 1940 might have ended his political career. Instead, he returned as a war hero, with orders for anything Canada could produce, including a great deal the country's industries had never even tackled, from bombers to binoculars.

Tax concessions, credits, and a direct investment of $1.5 billion released the country's industrial potential, dormant since 1929. The ingenious notion of accelerated depreciation, allowing industrialists to reap profits from even a short-run war contract, made patriotism profitable. Iron and steel production doubled. The automotive industry, already well-adapted to military needs, tripled its output. By 1943, Britain and her allies travelled in Canadian military vehicles. Eventually, a total of twenty-eight Crown corporations produced whatever private industry would not touch, from artificial rubber at the Polymer plant in Sarnia to enriched uranium at Eldorado's refinery in Port Hope.

Ilsley had a right to be resentful. Howe and the "dollar-a-year" men he recruited as top officials hardly worried about money. Most of the devices White had reluctantly pioneered in the earlier war, from Victory Bonds to war savings stamps, were dusted off and introduced with patriotic fanfare. When provinces rejected the Rowell-Sirois recommendation that they hand over direct taxing powers to Ottawa, the federal government took them anyway in a series of deals that guaranteed provinces their pre-war revenues or help with their debt burdens. Full employment and regular pay cheques contributed far more than higher tax rates to the government coffers. A booming economy supported the war effort. In five years, federal revenue from income, corporation, and inheritance taxes grew sixfold. The war added $12 billion to the national debt, half of it borrowed from individual Canadians. Howe's massive war production, most of it sold to allies, also helped defray Canada's war costs.

As in the earlier war, there was a catch. Britain's financial reserves, emptied by the earlier war, had never been rebuilt. By the end of 1940, the United States "cash and carry" policy for arms sales had exhausted Britain's dollar holdings. Since Canada needed Britain's dollars for her own American purchases, Canadian munitions output was threatened. For Britain, Roosevelt offered lend-lease terms, with repayment at the end of the war. Canada might eventually have claimed the same arrangement but only when she, too, was bankrupt. At war's end, she would face economic paralysis. The earlier war provided the precedent for a solution. As before, a rearming America needed Canadian munitions and military supplies while Canada needed credit. Able officials, led by the Finance Department's Clifford Clark, worked out a deal. On April 20, 1941, King appeared at the president's Hudson River estate of Hyde Park to sign the agreement. In effect, the two economies were integrated for the duration. Britain's debt to Canada could pile up as unconvertible sterling balances. As his agent in the United States, Howe chose an enterprising young brewing magnate, E. P. Taylor. Within a year, Taylor had far exceeded Canada's quota of war orders. Americans did not seem to mind.

Hyde Park solved one problem. There were many more. A sudden strike at the vast aluminium smelter at Arvida allowed the huge pots to "freeze." Howe's demand for soldiers to crush the strike, stymied by generals who insisted on obeying the law, drove the minister to resign. He returned to office, armed with special powers to use troops against saboteurs. When the giant National Steel Car aircraft plant at Malton, notoriously mismanaged, refused to mend its ways, Howe seized it in a night. It emerged as Victory Aircraft, the major Canadian producer of bombers.

A host of dramatic achievements and Canada's remarkable wartime industrial expansion have cast a warm glow over the war years. Canadians have forgotten the price paid for starting from scratch. It was easier to build industries and reward their owners than to get factories to deliver on time. No one ever has explained why Canadian-made Lancaster bombers were heavier and therefore more dangerous to their crews than British-produced planes. Inland shipyards, accustomed to building vessels for the Great Lakes, adjusted painfully to the complexities of warship construction. Canadians marvelled that they could produce radar; warships compelled to use the Canadian equipment suffered from its inferior quality, as did their convoys.

Howe's real miracle was transforming the Canadian economy, not just helping to win the war. By 1943, 1,239,327 Canadian men and women delivered $8.7 billion in industrial production. New machinery and growing skills gave Canada a chance to be a fully competitive industrial power by the end of the war—if she chose to stay in the race. Howe's production priorities also emphasized American and British markets: Canada's own military leaders, with their shopping lists, were as unwelcome in munitions policy-making as they were in most other aspects of Liberal government. The competing demands of munitions-making and the military brought Howe and Ralston into open conflict. "Our whole war effort," Howe complained to the House of Commons in June 1942, "is being distorted at the present time by the undue emphasis now being placed on men for the army overseas."

The fact was that a country that had too many people in the 1930s now had too few. Eleven million Canadians, eight million of them over age eighteen, could not meet all the military and civilian needs. From June of 1940, the crisis grew. With it, the demands of total war came home to Canadians as they never had in the earlier conflict. Exhortation by government committees and councils gave way, in October 1941, to National Selective Service (NSS). A flutter of resolutions in 1942 brought most Canadian men and then women under NSS control. By September, when young women were ordered to register, no able-bodied man aged seventeen to forty-five could drive a taxi, sell real estate, or help produce beer, toys, sporting goods, or a further list of "non-essentials." From September 1, 1942, no one could be fired or quit a job without giving Selective Service a week's notice.

While Selective Service dictated where and how Canadians would work, the Wartime Prices and Trade Board (WPTB) tackled inflation. Full employment, rocketing public spending (from $553 million in 1939 to $5,322 million in 1944), and scarcity pushed prices up fifteen per cent in the first two years of war. Under a hard-drinking Scot, Donald Gordon, the WPTB stepped in. From December 1, 1941, prices were frozen. Wages, tied to 1926-29 levels, could be notched up only with proven increases in the cost of living. When Japan entered the war and German submarines cut off Caribbean sources, the WPTB stepped in with rationing. Gasoline, meat, butter, and tires and, in most provinces, liquor, were rationed. Canadians learned to get by on half a pound of sugar a week. Tires became unobtainable save for those with high priority — who got wretched substitutes made from synthetic rubber. Most car-owners put their vehicles on blocks. Instead of prohibiting liquor, as in the earlier war, the WPTB simply commanded that whiskey be watered. "Mackenzie King whiskey," as scornful contemporaries called it, survives to the present day.

By British or European standards, Canadians were unbelievably well off. Clothing and most food were not rationed, though some items, such as nylon stockings, virtually disappeared. Most people discovered what officials already knew: complex and voluminous regulations can only be enforced by consent. Patriotic appeals to sacrifice luxuries and engage in busy-work, like other efforts to mobilize the "Home Front," had diminishing effect. Most grocers kept a little extra butter or meat under the counter for faithful or well-heeled customers. The knowledgeable learned where a little gasoline could be purchased without coupons or questions. A favoured few knew where to get silk stockings, a set of good tires, or vintage Scotch. In Montreal, the WPTB's rules had little effect and Montreal's example was contagious.

Still, the war was wearying and, for most Canadians remote. Many resented the endless flow of regulations and the necessity to meet them with at least an appearance of patriotic compliance. Even more worried about the post-war years. Would Canada simply return to a hopeless, demoralizing economic depression? Would the rules of *laisser-faire* demolish the immense productive machine the government had created, leaving most people to fend for themselves in the wreckage?

In *1984*, the English writer George Orwell based his anti-utopia on wartime London as he had known it. Many Canadians had a far more positive view of their wartime society than they had of their past or their likely future. Whatever its fears and frustrations, there were features of their experience of "total war" that many Canadians wanted to preserve, particularly the high level of employment. Governments and opposition parties would ignore that feeling at their peril.

A People's War

By late 1941, most Canadians believed they were involved in total war. To a degree unimagined in the earlier war, men and women as well were directed, regulated, rationed, and exhorted. Victory Bond campaigns covered billboards with their lurid warnings. School children collected bottles, cans, and even milkweed, knitted squares for afghan rugs, and contributed sticky quarters to buy war savings stamps. Comic books, written and printed in Canada, assured young readers that the enemy was cruel, fanatical, and, fortunately, dumb. Adult fiction conveyed a similar message with only a little added sophistication. Radio, unknown in the earlier war, added immediacy to war news and authenticity to propaganda. Lorne Greene, reading the ten o'clock news, became known as the "Voice of Doom." Particularly when they looked south at their neutral neighbours, Canadians felt part of the struggle.

Yet the war effort was not total. When the director of Selective Service, Elliott Little, proposed closing non-essential industries altogether to meet a military call for four hundred thousand men, the WPTB warned that Canadians would not tolerate spartan living and added rationing. The government agreed and Little resigned. His successor, Arthur McNamara, proved a little more malleable. As a war leader, Mackenzie

King safeguarded his objectivity. Unlike Borden, who visited war-wounded constantly and drew from them the courage to introduce conscription in 1917, King stayed away from hospitals. Compelled, for publicity reasons, to visit troops in England, he felt physical revulsion. "I felt what was like a dart pass through my bowels. It made me sick and faint. . . . I cannot talk their jargon of war." The troops, kept waiting in the rain, booed their prime minister. Few ever knew of King's own wartime tragedy when a favourite nephew, a navy surgeon, went down with the destroyer *St. Croix* in 1943.

If total war had a slogan, it was conscription. Was Canada serious about the war if, unlike every other belligerent including Australia, it left the fighting to volunteers? In 1940, the National Resources Mobilization Act had allowed a cautious step. Men called up for thirty-day courses were obvious candidates for army pressure to "go active." Many did. More did not.

All three armed services faced recruiting difficulties, particularly in finding the skilled technicians and tradesmen required for modern war when Howe's factories offered so much more. The army's difficulties were most acute. The reasons were not surprising. The RCAF offered most aircrew a commission and everyone a mixture of glamour and new skills. Particularly for its prairie recruits, the RCN operated in a distant and exotic environment. The army had no mysteries. Talk of a modern, mechanized fighting force fooled no one. Anyone with a father or an uncle in the Great War knew what to expect—or avoid. All three services recruited women—fifty thousand in all—but the Canadian Women's Army Corps had the toughest time finding volunteers.

The army was caught in a paradox. Most people, politicians included, assumed it could be content with men who could not meet the educational or physical qualifications of the rival services. In fact, the earlier war had emphasized the need for high mental and physical standards if fighting troops were to endure the strain of battle. The CEF's inadequate standards had contributed substantially to the post-war burden of disabled veterans. The prime minister had no patience with such arguments. The generals, he insisted, merely wanted conscription. Some undoubtedly did. Others, like General A. G. L. McNaughton, recalled to command the troops in England, distinctly did not. The fact was that the generals had nothing to do with the matter. Politicians, editors, and public opinion made conscription an issue.

The campaign began, inevitably, with the fall of France. "Germany must be defeated," declared *Saturday Night*, "even if we all have to live like the Germans." A year later, when Hitler attacked the Soviet Union, Canadian Communists switched sides again, proclaimed a sudden devotion to Mackenzie King and country, and demanded total war. On the other political flank, the leaderless Tories turned in desperation to the elderly Arthur Meighen. Never quite the ogre Liberals had portrayed him as in Quebec, Meighen now forgot his painful efforts to understand *Canadiens* in the new excitement of battling King. Not only Conservatives but the country could be rallied by conscription. Bored with its many good works, the Canadian Legion busily mobilized five hundred other organizations in its "Call for Total War." A few prominent Liberals, like Hepburn or Premier J. B. McNair of New Brunswick, added a non-partisan look to the conscription campaign. By November 1941, a Gallup poll found sixty-one per cent of Canadians content with the war effort but sixty per cent demanding conscription. King had reason for alarm, and the death of Ernest Lapointe on November 26, 1941, left him with no powerful Quebec lieutenant to share the load.

A month later, on December 7, the Japanese raid on Pearl Harbor brought the United States into the war. Even in peacetime, it had drafted a huge army. Now, both countries watched a seemingly invincible Japan pour into South-East Asia. At Hong Kong, two raw, ill-equipped Canadian battalions shared the fate of the entire garrison when it surrendered on Christmas Day. Of 1,975 Canadians who had sailed from Vancouver in November, only 1,418 survived battle, prison camps, and slave labour. All of them bore the marks of a terrible ordeal.

However, the Pacific War had little direct impact on Canada. Invasion, service commanders patiently explained, was physically impossible. A single Japanese submarine lobbed a few shells at the Estevan Point Lighthouse and fled, after the first and only direct enemy attack on Canadian soil since 1814. It was the indirect impact that mattered. On the shabby pretext that they needed protection from the white majority, 20,886 Japanese Canadians in the coastal region were herded together and then interned in makeshift camps and ghost towns in British Columbia's mountainous interior. Pre-war claims by the RCMP and most service officers that the Japanese Canadians posed no significant threat were ignored. Ottawa understood public opinion.

Mass internment wasted manpower. So did large and unnecessary garrisons. In March, pressure from British Columbia and its cabinet representatives led the government to create a 6th Division and an 8th Division for a new Pacific Command while, for no very good reason, a 7th Division was formed to protect the Atlantic coast. Americans faced a more real threat when the Japanese invaded the remote, fog-bound outer islands of the Aleutian chain and threatened Alaska. In a prodigal deployment of men, machinery, and money, the Americans drove a highway north from Edmonton to Fairbanks and, for good measure, laid a pipeline to bring oil from the Imperial development at Norman Wells. At the height of construction, thirty-three thousand American soldiers and civilians virtually occupied a vast region of Canada with no more evidence of local sovereignty than an occasional post office and ill-enforced liquor laws. Prodded by the British high commissioner, Ottawa appointed a past-president of the Canadian Legion as its "Special Commissioner" and sent him west with an RCAF aircraft to "show the flag."

After a bloody struggle to re-take Attu Island, the American general invited his Canadian counterpart to share in the next assault on Kiska. After a flurry of correspondence which underlined that politicians, and not the local commander, Major-General George Pearkes, would decide where Canadians fought, an Aleutian campaign was approved. The 13th Infantry Brigade, largely composed of NRMA men, trained vigorously with American weapons and tactics and stormed ashore on August 15, 1943, only to find that the Japanese had decamped. Six months of dreary garrison duty were enlivened by correspondence between Canadian tax officials, who insisted that the brigade was within the continental limits and taxable, and Canadian officers who insisted that since they had camped some miles beyond the International Date Line they were exempt. The officials won.

It was perhaps as well. Legally, the NRMA men could not be forced to serve beyond North America. Army stratagems to gain conversions to the General Service category left behind a bitter residue of home service soldiers who had taken all the pressure and abuse their officers could hand out. A Hollywood film on Haitian voodoo provided them with a title: "Zombies." Once the Pacific War began, NRMA men were condemned to serve for the duration. By the summer, thirty-four thousand troops stood guard on the Pacific for an enemy that would almost certainly never come.

Early in 1942, Mackenzie King set out to kill the conscription issue. As Meighen prepared to enter Parliament from the Toronto riding of

York South, backed by Hepburn and a blue-ribbon "Committee of 200," the prime minister suddenly announced a plebiscite to release him from his no-conscription pledge. At a stroke, Meighen was robbed of his key issue and trounced by his CCF opponent. The plebiscite followed. In Quebec *La Ligue pour la défense du Canada* united old *nationalistes* and new in a joint sense of betrayal. A promise made essentially to Quebec would be undone by all Canada. Elsewhere, the plebiscite was little more than a register of patriotism; in Quebec it united a vast spectrum of French-speaking opinion in opposition to conscription. Lawyers and journalists like Jean Drapeau and André Laurendeau, even a youngster named Pierre Elliott Trudeau, shared the campaign and the inevitable sense of defeat. On April 27, 1942, 2,945,514 Canadians voted to release the government from their no-conscription promise; 1,643,006 voted no. English-speaking voters were four to one in favour; *Canadiens* appear to have been four to one against.

As usual in politics, cleverness exacted a belated price. King faced a divided country and a split cabinet. His solution, embodied in a memorable quotation, was "not necessarily conscription, but conscription if necessary." For Lapointe's successor as ranking Quebec minister, Pierre Cardin, such ingenuity could not prevent his resignation. Ralston, too honest for such subterfuge, also chose to resign. Then, reminded of duty, he relented. Ralston's letter remained in the prime minister's desk. Bill 80, removing the limits on the NRMA—but only if Parliament again approved the decision—passed the House of Commons by 158 to 54.

In military terms, the crisis had never been necessary. Indeed, for all the allied disasters of 1942, from Singapore to Tobruk, the war had reached a turning point. At Stalingrad, Soviet troops blunted the *blitzkrieg*. By the end of the year, British soldiers had beaten General Erwin Rommel's Afrika Korps at El Alamein. The United States, with its huge resources, was committed to victory. Canada's own relatively small disasters of the year, at Hong Kong and Dieppe, had cost barely five thousand men.

Indeed, mingled with the government's anxiety about conscription was a fear that Canada might not be seen to have done enough in the war. Nothing annoyed King more than the Canadian predilection for drawing inspiration from Churchill and Roosevelt, rather than from their own fussy, verbose prime minister. Yet, in Canada's brief moment as a senior ally, King had sought no role in grand strategy and Winston Churchill would have been among the last British politicians to have conceded such a role to a mere Dominion. Once the United States and the Soviet Union were in the war, Canada was indeed a junior partner. Twice the British and American war leaders visited Quebec City for conferences at the Château Frontenac. Both meetings settled issues affecting Canadian forces but King was not involved. The reward for his hospitality were some kind words and some useful photographs.

Mackenzie King, claims historian C. P. Stacey, tended to believe the worst of the British and the best of the Americans. On the whole, he was better treated by Whitehall than Washington. To Roosevelt and his advisors, Canada's claim to consideration offered a precedent for Brazil, Costa Rica, or some other humble and opportunistic ally to demand equal time. King, according to Lester Pearson, Canada's wartime ambassador to Washington, "accepted the situation with a mild complaint or none at all." King's vaunted friendship with the imperious Roosevelt was too valuable to be strained by disagreement or even argument.

Canadians were by no means insensitive to their rights. With an eye to future acquisition, Canada carefully kept her forces and senior officers in Newfoundland on a par with their American opposite numbers. Having allowed the Americans to establish themselves in the North, Ottawa grimly paid for the useless permanent facilities rather than risk any United States claim to sovereignty. In the boards and committees through which allied powers co-ordinated their efforts, Canada's assertion of a "functional principle" (devised by the ingenious Norman Robertson of the Department of External Affairs) won a few openings.

Officially, the war carried Canada firmly into the American orbit; unofficially, British influences and examples were rarely more pervasive. Most Canadians found at least some inspiration from Britain's example in the face of defeat. More specific was the influence of economists like John Maynard Keynes and social planners like Lord Beveridge. Massive wartime powers and their result in prosperity and full employment added to the ranks of Keynes's Canadian disciples. Beveridge's promise of comprehensive post-war social security was almost as welcome to Canadians as it was to his British audience. Victory, if certain after 1942, demanded two and a half more years of struggle. Canadians needed argument and hope to sustain their efforts.

As minister of pensions and national health, Ian Mackenzie found himself responsible for post-war reconstruction. A committee under his wing, headed by Principal F. Cyril James of McGill University, found itself in merciless bureaucratic battle with the finance department's Economic Advisory Committee, headed by W. A. Mackintosh of Queen's University. In the struggle, Mackintosh prevailed but James's research director, Leonard Marsh, emerged in mid-January 1943, with a blueprint for comprehensive social security that captured Canadian imaginations. As in 1914–18, the war opened minds to new ideas. Even the Tories had renamed their party Progressive Conservative and endorsed low-cost housing, free collective bargaining for labour, and a commitment to full employment. More dramatic was the startling rise of the CCF in a series of provincial elections and federal by-elections in 1942 and 1943. By September 1943, a Gallup poll reported the CCF slightly ahead of both its venerable rivals. The Marsh Report, claimed the *Canadian Forum*, might be "the price that Liberalism is willing to pay to prevent socialism."

Linked to CCF strength was support from a surging union movement. War industries and full employment once again created opportunities for unionization. Exhortations to employers to pay fair wages and respect unions had no effect. In 1943, Canada experienced its worst year of strikes since 1919. Unionized steelworkers shut down huge mills at Sydney and Sault Ste. Marie. At Windsor, the Ford plant was shut for a month. Militancy caught even union leaders by surprise. Again and again, the issue was not money or wages but the kind of recognition and bargaining rights American workers had won in 1935. A report by a Tory judge, Charles McTague, in the autumn of 1943 emerged, five months later, as P.C. 1003, the National War Labour Order, establishing the basic framework of industrial relations for the next two generations.

More followed. Backed by surveys from the government's War Information Board, Ian Mackenzie argued successfully for more generous and better publicized veterans' programmes, climaxed by creation of a new Department of Veterans' Affairs. The fact that family size determined poverty, argued twenty years earlier by the Patriotic Fund and now underlined by Marsh's report, needed only King's agreement in 1944 to make family allowances possible. Discovery that opponents of the allowances — Howe, Ilsley, Ralston — were also outspoken proponents of conscription helped turn the prime minister's mind. Such men, he persuaded himself, were at odds with the true spirit of Liberalism he himself embodied. Word that his secretary, Jack Pickersgill, had been raised on a war widow's pension reassured King that Canadian moral fibre would survive the largesse.

Out of such reasoning, the foundations of social security were built in wartime Canada. The speech from the throne on January 24, 1944, said little about the war or Canada's role in it. Instead, it promised a Canada in which social programmes for human welfare would be major instruments of government. Family allowances, as a first instalment, would help transform the poor from a majority to a minority in Canadian society.

To keep the Canadians' votes, their government promised a social revolution.

The War From Canada

In the First World War, Canada had played a straightforward role in Allied strategy. Her soldiers had gone overseas to serve the generals' conviction that the war could only be won on the Western Front. Her flyers and her few sailors had been recruited and organized by the British armed services to meet Britain's needs. In the Second World War, Canada's contribution was more complex and dispersed. Units of the Canadian forces served in almost every theatre of war. Canada herself became the base for vast undertakings, from the British Commonwealth Air Training Plan to the vital convoy campaign on the Atlantic. In England, most of Canada's overseas army stood guard for years while Canadian airmen took off for the bomber offensive against Germany. From 1943, Canadian sailors, soldiers, and airmen shared in the reconquest of western Europe.

The war came to at least the margins of Canada. In 1917, Borden had insisted that the front line was in France and Flanders; by 1941 it lapped against the Atlantic shoreline and for a few months of 1942, it even reached up the St. Lawrence when two U-boats penetrated the river. Across the country, at more than a hundred bases, a hundred thousand men and women of the RCAF participated in the operation officially defined as Canada's most important contribution to the war, the BCATP. Instead of the few thousand home defence troops Gwatkin had grudgingly allowed in 1917, a significant field army and a substantial Home War Establishment of RCAF squadrons guarded both Canada's coasts, and extended east and north to the separate Dominion of Newfoundland.

Powerful forces in Canada went far beyond any realistic enemy threat. By keeping a large share of armed forces manpower in Canada, King and his government somehow believed that volunteer recruiting for overseas might somehow suffice. Even when the costs and demands of the BCATP soared with the fall of France and the Battle of Britain, the government cheerfully accepted the expansion because the effort was close to home.

The air training programme absorbed the tiny peacetime cadre of the RCAF. Through their own persistence, private flying clubs managed to become the basis of initial flying training. The Department of Transport scouted the 120 airfields needed in the original plan. Private aviation companies managed the air observer schools and commercial firms provided the bulk of aircraft repair — at no admitted profit. In Air Vice-Marshal R. G. E. Leckie, a former Canadian, the RAF provided a shrewd, firm manager for the BCATP, but the real burden fell on the RCAF.

Despite all the complexities, the RCAF seems to have managed its task with remarkable skill and speed. By October 1941, most of the facilities were in place. Somehow, aircraft were procured from the United States or built in Canada to replace the flow cut off from Britain in the summer of 1940. At the end of 1940, 521 aircrew had graduated —mostly to be turned around as instructors. By the end of May 1942, with its first phase over, the BCATP had graduated 21,824 pilots, observers, navigators, and every other category needed for bomber crews. Advice from Britain and the Plan's own tough experience led to vast improvements in selection, training techniques, and instructor competence. When a second BCATP agreement was negotiated in 1942, the RCAF's new self-confidence was apparent in a crisp deal for fifty-fifty sharing of the $1.4 billion cost and almost none of the bickering of 1939.

One feature of the 1940 crisis was a switch of RAF schools to Canada: eventually there were forty-eight. These were scattered across Canada, welcomed by local communities, and in 1942, integrated wholly in the BCATP administration. The new agreement called for Canada to provide half the trainees, Britain forty per cent, and Australia and New Zealand the rest. Would-be flyers from Norway, France, Czechoslovakia, and other conquered European countries also found their way to the BCATP in growing numbers. By the end of 1943, schools were graduating 3,000 flyers a month. In fact, just as the RCAF became desperate about meeting its quota, cutting its educational and age level, the RAF came to the striking discovery that it had far over-estimated its aircrew needs. As thousands piled up in depots and schools, the BCATP training flow was slashed sharply in 1944 and cut off almost wholly in March 1945 — only to revive somewhat for the Pacific war. In its history, the BCATP generated 131,355 aircrew graduates, including about 50,000 pilots. The price included 856 fatalities. Some mark of the efficiency of the programme and the change in aviation was that in 1918, after two years of experience, the RAF Canada schools lost a student for every 5,800 hours flown; by 1944, the rate was one fatality for every 22,388 hours flown.

Once trained, BCATP graduates became part of the endless train of men and resources that ran the gauntlet of German submarines to reach the only Allied outpost in Europe. For the Royal Canadian Navy, the half-forgotten work of the Halifax Patrol in 1918 became a precedent for its most important task in history. After 1941, Hitler could probably only have won the war by cutting the Atlantic shipping route and ending the flow of goods from North America. If Britain had not been starved into submission, she would have lacked the means to continue the war. Even the more remote Soviet Union might have been crippled for lack of resources brought at enormous cost up the Norwegian coast to Murmansk. Three times threatened with oblivion, some irony of history made the most scorned of services the most decisive Canadian contribution to the war.

The role did not come easily. In 1939, the RCN was still tiny: six destroyers, five minesweepers, and perhaps three thousand men in its regular and volunteer reserve establishments. Its senior officers yearned to be a "real" navy, not an escort service. In the crisis of 1940, four of the RCN's destroyers crossed to aid the Royal Navy, first off the coasts of France and then in the confused, mismanaged struggle to protect merchant shipping off England. U-boat skippers called it their first "Happy Time," so easy were the pickings. For the RCN, there was no such joy: its first loss was HMCS *Fraser*, sunk ignominiously in a collision.

The fall of France transformed the naval war effort as it affected each Canadian service. The leisurely purchase of rich men's yachts and fishing trawlers for escort duty, the rearming of the three elegant Canadian National liners, *Prince David, Prince Henry*, and *Prince Robert*, as armed merchant cruisers, were not enough. Belated recognition that escort vessels would be desperately needed set inexperienced Canadian shipyards to the task of building sixty-five corvettes. Each of the little warships, built like whaling vessels, could carry a four-inch gun and the minimum gear for locating and hitting a submarine. Corvettes "rolled in a heavy dew" and they promised a cramped and sometimes hellish existence for their tiny crews but they were all that was possible in the crisis.

While shipyards struggled to build naval ships and the cargo vessels that would be even more desperately needed, the naval reserve divisions helped recruit and train the thousands of recruits who, by 1945, would become a navy of 93,000 men and women. Canada's merchant marine not only expanded to provide crews for an ultimate 456 ships (compared to 38 ocean-going vessels in 1939); it also provided scores of officers for their navy. Their experience and navigating skill were vital assets for a growing fleet of little ships.

For them and for almost all the RCN in 1939, anti-submarine warfare was a mystery. Few Canadians had seen ASDIC, the Royal Navy's underwater sound-ranging device. Even the British lacked experience in detecting propeller and engine noise from submarines or the infinite tricks that water temperature, fish, and wrecks could play. Using ASDIC and experience (if they had it), commanders of escort vessels could only do their best to keep submarines away from convoys. They were fighting first-class professionals. U-boat skippers had learned from the earlier war and from an aggressive, scientific approach to their work. They were backed by an intelligence system that had cracked the British naval code until late 1940 and which knew convoy codes until the spring of 1943. Having Ultra, Britain's answers to German codes, only helped the navy in 1941 when a captured German submarine gave up the vital key.

Whatever else it might be, submarine warfare was not a business for amateurs. Though escort vessels were sometimes hit, it was the slow, lumbering merchantmen that were the real U-boat targets and their crews paid a terrible price when submarines converged in "wolf packs," outsmarted escort groups, and broke into the lines of vulnerable merchant vessels. The real heroes of the Atlantic war were the civilian seamen. An estimated quarter of them did not survive the war. Among them were Canadians, working for $75 to $100 a month and a war risk bonus of $44.50. In the 68 Canadian ships that went down, 1,148 Canadian seamen died.

By 1941, the RCN's role in the convoy struggle was set. British es-

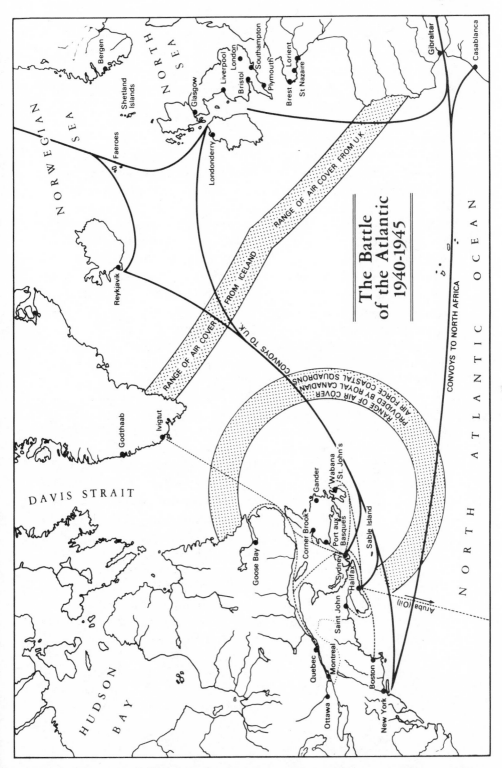

The Battle
of the Atlantic
1940-1945

cort groups took convoys to Iceland and then to Newfoundland; inexperienced and ill-equipped Canadian groups covered the third leg, between St. John's, Newfoundland, and Halifax or New York. On May 31, 1941, Commodore L. W. Murray opened a headquarters at St. John's. A few days later, the first three Canadian corvettes joined his flag and, by July, his force was escorting convoys as far as thirty-five degrees west.

Hardly had the Canadians taken over than they were supplanted. By sinking American ships in 1940, the U-boats had given President Roosevelt a pretext to jerk an isolationist United States deeper into the war. Of course, if the Americans wanted to protect convoys, no Canadians in the summer of 1941 would object. Canadians were hopelessly ill-equipped for the struggle: they lacked ASDIC, efficient radar for sighting surfaced submarines and the long-range aircraft which already had emerged as the real sub-killers. If Canadians had had illusions of proficiency, they had been shattered by the fate of Convoy SC42. Between September 9 and 16, 1941, a German wolf pack sank fifteen of sixty-four ships before RAF aircraft and a British escort force arrived. The Canadian escort group, mostly corvettes, had been outnumbered and badly outclassed.

Given time, amateur crews became proficient. The folly of racing to sea without adequate training and "working up" became obvious, whatever the justification. The RCN's deeper problems included a naval headquarters struggling desperately to improvise new ships and crews, with no time to insist on better tactics or costly new equipment. Ottawa was too close to politicians, too far from the ocean. The British Admiralty had to satisfy its own commanders' pleas for the best possible ASDIC and radar; if the Canadians did not even bother to ask, the British could be excused for not offering. HF-DF, the high-frequency direction-finding equipment sailors called "Huff-Duff," was not fitted on RCN destroyers because Naval Service Headquarters insisted it was "not yet proven." It was, in fact, already a war-winner, pin-pointing U-boats to be avoided or killed. So was radar but Canadian-made sets, proudly displayed by C. D. Howe, were too primitive to be much help. Admirals, trained in peacetime penny-pinching and in dutiful respect to politicians, were ill-fitted to fight for their sea-going subordinates.

The Americans, far behind the Royal Navy in anti-submarine technique, provided little professional assistance when they took over in Newfoundland. After Pearl Harbor, they could no longer even provide escort vessels as the United States Navy rushed its forces to the Pacific to avenge Japan's early victories. American admirals rejected urgent warnings that U-boats were moving towards the Caribbean in large numbers. Convoys, they insisted, were as unnecessary as coastal blackouts. As a result, German submarines devastated half a million tons of American coastal shipping in the spring and summer of 1942, slaughtering helpless tankers outlined by Miami's neon lights. Canadian corvettes finally went south to help, registering a number of U-boat kills. When Germans retaliated by slipping into the St. Lawrence, they had another easy time, sinking nineteen Canadian cargo ships and two small naval vessels. A horrified Mackenzie King ordered troops, aircraft, and ships to the scene and closed the river for the balance of the war, cutting Canada's export capacity by a quarter. Rarely have two submarines and a timid politician produced so cheap and useful a victory!

The winter of 1942–43 was the most desperate of the Atlantic war. Free to operate from the Bay of Biscay, German submarine strength at sea rose from 91 to 212. Canadian ships in 1942 had had four U-boat kills. That winter, they had none. Nothing but terrible weather seemed to cut into the German toll. In November, 119 ships, 729,160 tons, were lost. That was almost twice the rate at which Allied shipyards turned out replacements. Foul mid-winter weather cut losses in December and January but they resumed in February — 63 ships — and in March — 108. Two convoys, HX229 and SC122, whose ordeal was later described by Martin Middlebrook, lost 22 of 88 ships in 3 terrible, hopeless days. Drowned or dead of exposure were 360 people, including 2 women and 2 children.

There were many reasons. For the time being, the Allies had lost the German naval code and frantic efforts to break the new one had yet to pay off. The harshest truth was that the RCN was also part of the problem. Working with the Royal Navy, slipping salt-stained and battered into Londonderry, taught them just how primitive and inadequate their ships and equipment really were. Canadians did not need to find out the value of aircraft as hunters and killers but the RCAF squadrons in Eastern Air Command had no long-range aircraft and no means of getting them. Liberator bombers, from RAF Coastal Command, had saved the remnants of HX229 and SC122 but Canada had none. In the "black pit" beyond aircraft patrol range, U-boats revelled in relative immunity. As a further irksome feature, an American vice-admiral commanded convoy and escort operations in the North-West Atlantic long after most U.S. ships had departed.

British, American, and Canadian concerns coincided in the Atlantic Convoy Conference at Washington in March. For once, discussion was crisp and purposeful. Subcommittees settled overdue questions of tactics, organization, and equipment. With American consent, Britain and Canada would share responsibility for the North Atlantic. From a headquarters at Halifax, Admiral Murray took over a vast, gloomy expanse of the Atlantic from 47 degrees west and south to 29 degrees north. In a world divided into operational sectors, Murray would be the sole Canadian among the Allied commanders. Meanwhile, several Canadian escort groups were transferred to warmer, easier waters, escorting convoys to Gibraltar and into the Mediterranean, acquiring equipment, skill, and confidence in equal measure.

By happy coincidence, the new organization took effect as conditions began to improve. In May, thanks to British pressure, the RCAF began to acquire the long-range Liberators it so desperately needed to close the "black pit." A stream of escort vessels, including the new twin-screw frigates, allowed creation of powerful support groups. Aged Hurricane fighters and Swordfish biplanes, mounted on catapults on merchant ships, gave convoys their first direct air support. Small escort carriers, built on merchant ship hulls, would follow. In June, British naval intelligence finally broke the German code. In Ottawa, Vice-Admiral Percy Nelles, blamed for the RCN's technical deficiencies, was replaced as Chief of Naval Staff and sent to Britain as Senior Canadian Flag Officer.

In May, the tide turned. Of 130 U-boats in the Atlantic, 41 were lost, one of them commanded by the son of Hitler's naval commander, Admiral Karl Doenitz. Codebreakers learned the astonishing news on May 24: German submarines were ordered from the North Atlantic. Losses had been too terrible. Of course they returned, with new weapons. In September, it was the acoustic torpedo, programmed to home in on propeller noise. One victim, HMCS *St. Croix*, lost all but one of her crew as a second and a third rescuing British warship went down. The ingenuity was countered as usual. Canadians contributed CAAT gear, a towed noise-maker that drew off the acoustic weapons. In the fall of 1944, there was fresh danger from U-boats with snorkels or underwater breathing devices and the prospect of hydrogen peroxide as a fuel. No longer would submarines have to surface for air and battery recharging. The balance swung to the U-boats—and returned, with Allied hunter-killer groups of aircraft carriers and destroyers. By March 1945, Doenitz had 463 boats on patrol compared to 27 in 1939. The last Canadian warship lost in the war, HMCS *Esquimalt*, was torpedoed off Halifax on April 16, 1945; a Canadian merchantman, the *Avondale Park*,went down even later as the last German victim of the conflict.

Yet, between them, the RCN and the RCAF had turned the tide. Vast tonnages crossed the ocean unscathed. Training and hard experience in both services paid off as Canadians extended their role closer to British waters. Of the RCN's twenty-seven confirmed U-boat sinkings, twenty occurred east of the thirty-fifth meridian and seventeen took place after November 20, 1944. At its height, in autumn 1943, 229 Canadian ships, 21,000 seamen, and eleven RCAF maritime patrol squadrons with supporting facilities had been committed to the Atlantic struggle. The costs had been high. In the winter of 1943, the British director of anti-submarine warfare noted that eighty per cent of merchantmen sunk in two months had Canadian escorts. Effective fighting navies take more than three years to create. A few tough professionals, like Commander J. S. D. "Chummy" Prentice, who sank three of Canada's U-boat total score, could be multiplied a hundredfold—but only with time and experience. Canada had needed Britain as teacher and supplier; the RCN learned fast in tough times.

Canadians in Britain

In December 1939, a month longer than it took them in 1914, Canadians began reaching England in strength. The 1st Canadian Division, this time carefully based on pre-war mobilization plans, and a single RCAF squadron waited through the first weeks of the *blitzkrieg*. Two more RCAF squadrons arrived that year—all that Canada could offer for the epic Battle of Britain. By the end of 1940, the first thin trickle of BCATP graduates began to arrive though most had been diverted as instructors or, if Canadian, to home-defence squadrons.

Article 15 of the BCATP Agreement guaranteed that RCAF squadrons would be formed overseas and that Canadian aircrew would be identified as such "to the highest extent possible." That was not, in the RAF view, very high. The more Canadians — and Australians, South Africans, New Zealanders, and even Americans—poured into RAF squadrons, the more objection there would be to pulling effective units to pieces to inflate Dominion egos. In May 1941, Ralston and the new British air minister, Sir Archibald Sinclair, agreed that Britain would create and pay for 25 new RCAF squadrons but by the end of the year, only 500 of 8,595 Canadian BCATP graduates flew with the RCAF. Ten more squadrons were formed in 1942, 4 in 1943 and 3 in 1944 when 6 more transferred from Canada's Home War Establishment. By the end of the war, the RCAF had 48 squadrons overseas and 40 more in Canada. From 1943, Canadians assumed the full cost of their own overseas squadrons but by 1944, 60 per cent of Canadian aircrew still flew in RAF squadrons.

In the RCAF, "Canadianization" was a painful issue. Pilots and navigators might be obscenely contemptuous of such issues but even they grumbled at British policies such as the inexplicable rules that made some flying personnel into officers while others remained as sergeants. More senior officers knew they would lose chances for experience and professional advancement without Canadian squadrons, wings, and groups, while the RCAF itself would be hurt if its achievements were buried within RAF publicity. While the air minister, C. G. Power, did his best for Canadian rights, the RCAF overseas wondered whether pompous, penny-pinching politicians ever understood the problem.

From the first, the Canadian Army was determined to preserve its separate identity and, unlike the RCAF, it could appeal to the traditions of two wars in its own defence. General A. G. L. McNaughton, promoted from leading a division and an army corps to command of a full army of 125,000 men in 1941, was determined that his troops would fight shoulder to shoulder as they had in 1918. In Ottawa, where a new Chief of the General Staff fought the army's full expansion programme through the suspicious cabinet, one selling point was the dramatic role such a force could play in a new Second Front. "This is the kind of army a soldier dreams of commanding," Major General Kenneth Stuart assured the influential Grant Dexter of the Winnipeg *Free Press*: "hard-hitting, beautifully-balanced, incredibly powerful."

Stuart's words seemed to have little application to the rather ponderous, ill-officered, and under-equipped force that waited in England while history happened all around. In 1941, the war had moved dramatically south to Yugoslavia and Greece, where British, Australians, and New Zealanders shared another Allied debacle; the war then moved east against the Soviet Union. Stalin's Russia seemed as easy a German victim as France until gradually the distances, the inexhaustible

Red Armies, and, above all, winter slowed and stopped the German forces. In North Africa, Britain reeled back before Rommel's Afrika Korps and somehow stopped. The next year seemed infinitely worse. Singapore fell with a British army and an Australian division; Tobruk, symbol of an earlier valiant North African siege, collapsed in a few days in March. Still, none of McNaughton's men fought. A garrison was needed in England. Canadian forces must not be divided. From Ottawa came word of Mackenzie King's horror that generals would contemplate risking soldiers' lives, not saving them.

Ottawa's reluctance to join in Britain's one real land campaign embarrassed the Canadian generals. They were easy marks for a call for a couple of brigades of the 2nd Division to conduct a quick raid on France in the summer of 1942. In retrospect, it was easy to see what was wrong about the Dieppe operation, especially for an army whose trademark was painstaking planning and systematic preparation. Amphibious rehearsals degenerated into chaos. When the British admiral prudently refused to risk battleships in narrow seas under an untamed Luftwaffe — a lesson from Malaya where two proud capital ships had been overwhelmed by shore-based air power — sea bombardment was forfeited. Air bombardment might have helped but Bomber Command had other interests. Besides, experts blithely insisted, piles of rubble might impede Canadian tanks on the beaches.

In the event, few tanks got anywhere. The landing on August 19 was a succession of accidents, miscalculations, bad luck, and tragedy. Landed in a death trap at Puys, the Royal Regiment of Canada in a few minutes lost 209 killed, the worst toll of any Canadian battalion in the war. Other units almost matched the tragedy of the Toronto unit. Of 4,963 Canadians who set out for Dieppe, 907 died and 1,946 remained as prisoners.

More than most Canadian battles, Dieppe has been clothed in myth and scapegoats' skins. More war-hardened nations would have recognized that amphibious landings are among the most hazardous operations of war. Canadians utterly lacked battle experience; even a few veteran officers or sergeants might have spurred huddled, bewildered soldiers into action. The losses were shocking but they were modest by the standard of the Somme or Vimy Ridge. Nor were they in vain. Common sense might have argued for special assault tanks, improvements in wireless and fire control, and the need for absolute air supremacy, but failure is always a better teacher than success. Dieppe was sadly necessary to persuade politicians and generals that scarce and costly resources would be necessary if the Allies wished to invade Hitler's Fortress Europe.

No one in touch with Canadian army morale ever believed that soldiers demanded a blood-letting at Dieppe as a curb on their frustrations. In fact, Canadian discipline and morale in England were satisfactory by any reasonable standard and they improved remarkably in British eyes with the arrival of the Americans. What did change, after just a brief touch of battle, was the standard of realism in training and the demands on officers. As both improved, so did morale, efficiency, and battle readiness. Still, peace-trained generals, sheltered from operations, never quite realized the brutal demands of actual warfare.

A younger, untried service had long since been in battle. Hundreds, then thousands of young Canadian airmen found themselves in one of the most bloody and controversial campaigns of the war.

Canadian flyers with the RCAF and RAF took part in every kind of air operation, from artillery-spotting to ground-strafing in France. Six squadrons served with Coastal Command, including one posted to the Far East. One of its pilots, Flight-Lieutenant L. J. Birchall, gave the first warning of the Japanese attack on Ceylon. Another squadron included Flight-Lieutenant David Hornell, the RCAF's first Victoria Cross winner. Fourteen RCAF squadrons flew day fighters; three provided fighter reconnaissance and four manned the Beaufighters and Mosquitoes which served as night fighters. Two of Canada's three transport squadrons furnished airlift in the terrible conditions of the Burma campaign. Ottawa suspected that they might somehow be entangled in British imperialism and removed them in 1945; in fact they had been desperately needed for the Fourteenth Army's logistical lifeline across the jungle.

By the time Canadians wanted a say in how their squadrons were deployed, it was really too late. Air Vice-Marshal Harold Edwards, senior RCAF officer overseas, learned only after the event that eight RCAF squadrons had helped provide air cover in the Dieppe landings in August 1942 — and shared the terrible casualties of the day. Even when squadrons were grouped in Canadian wings, they served RAF dispositions. Before the Normandy invasion, 83 Group was built up with a heavy complement of RCAF squadrons to provide backing for the First Canadian Army. When the Second British Army was designated to manage the actual landing, Air Marshal Sir Trafford Leigh-Mallory switched 83 Group to its support. The less-experienced (and all-RAF) 84 Group was assigned to the Canadians.

The biggest and costliest Canadian air commitment was Bomber Command. The original case for an independent Royal Air Force had been the claim that air power would prove to be the decisive weapon of war. Between the wars, enthusiasts like Lord Trenchard, Billy Mitchell of the United States, and Italy's Giulio Douhet insisted that aerial bombardment would shatter fleets, armies, and cities, along with civilian morale. In the 1930s, British voters had been chilled into appeasement by the slogan: "the bomber will always get through." Guernica, Warsaw, and Rotterdam all seemed to prove the air power argument. The Battle of Britain and the blitz of London might have raised questions: they did not. With his back to the wall and no hope of matching German military strength, Winston Churchill was delighted to let Sir Arthur Harris win the war with bombers. Any scruples could be quelled by memories of thirteen thousand British victims of the Luftwaffe.

Critics regarded Harris as a crude barbarian with a few fixed ideas about war. Others, closer to him, believed that Harris felt deep emotional links with the young men he sent to their death in bombers that were underpowered, underarmed, and easy prey for Luftwaffe fighters and anti-aircraft artillery. Such feelings were kept firmly under control. The Bomber Offensive was pursued with a single-mindedness reminiscent of the frontal assaults of the earlier war.

Daylight raids over German cities and industrial targets led to intolerable casualties. Night bombing was a little less costly but hopelessly inaccurate. Allied propaganda insisted that bombers hit pin-point targets on military and industrial objectives. In fact, the incendiary and blockbuster bombs were aimed at civilian populations with much the same purpose of terror that had inspired the Luftwaffe. The Allied bomber attacks cost Germany 560,000 dead and 675,000 injured, most of them women and children, but German war production until the spring of 1945 was cut by as little as 1.2 per cent.

As in the earlier war, Canadians had no chance to debate the strategy or morality of the bomber campaign. If they had, the senior RCAF officers, who learned their air power doctrines at the RAF staff college, would probably have echoed Harris as enthusiastically as most of their British and American colleagues. British, American, and Canadian officers ignored the strategic issue and immersed themselves in the tactical and technological problems of trying to cut aircraft losses and reach targets more accurately. Four-engined bombers, electronic navigation aids, and special Pathfinder aircraft to spot targets all helped a little, but not even the well-armed American B-17 could fend off German fighters. In 1942, when Canadian airmen first became seriously involved in Harris's campaign, only one crew in three survived a thirty-mission tour of duty. In a sample BCATP navigators' course, fifteen out of fifty graduates survived the war, ten of them as prisoners of war. Young Canadians who had joined the RCAF to escape their fathers' memories of hopelessness in the trenches found themselves in no less a hopeless and bloody struggle in which their own survival became improbable and their most likely victims women and children.

By October 1942, four complete RCAF squadrons served in Bomber Command. A fifth, 425 (Alouette) Squadron was formed as a symbolic gesture to French Canada though its working language was English and its ground crews, as in other squadrons, remained largely British. At the outset of 1943, eleven Canadian bomber squadrons were assembled as 6 Group, RCAF under Air Vice-Marshal G. E. Brookes. Six Group was overdue, essential if the RCAF was to develop staff and senior officers, and for most people, unpopular. As if the problems of the bomber offensive were not bad enough, 6 Group seemed to make them worse. Canadians were torn from familiar crews and squadrons to join strangers with nothing more in common than RCAF membership. Canadian squadrons believed themselves—perhaps unfairly— last in line for new aircraft and improved technology. Only in August, 1943, did the first Lancasters appear. Later than other groups in Bomber Command, the Canadian squadrons flew obsolete twin-engined Wellingtons and the tough but ill-armed Halifax. Moreover, the 6 Group stations in the Vale of York were farther from their targets than any in England, more likely to be fogged in when aircraft returned from a night raid, and most prone to the icing conditions which proved fatal to dozens of bombers and crews.

The inevitable result was a grim casualty toll; from March 5 to June 24, 1943, 6 Group lost 100 aircraft, 7 per cent of its strength. A 5 per cent loss was considered crippling. Morale sagged. Symptoms included failure to take off, early returns, and a soaring total of aircraft found unexpectedly unserviceable just before departure. On January 20, 1944, 147 of 6 Group's bombers were ordered out on a Berlin raid: 3 failed to take off, 17 came back early, and 9 were lost. Next day, when 125 were ordered out, 11 never took off, 12 returned early, and 24 were reported missing. Bomber Command was worried.

Changes began with a new commander on February 29, 1944. Air Vice-Marshal C. M. McEwen brought with him a brilliant First World

War flying record, professional experience, and an unwelcome fondness for traditional military discipline. Canadian pilots abandoned their casual "fifty mission" look. More practical was McEwen's insistence on navigational training, faster conversion to the more powerful, better-armed Lancasters, and improved ground crew and administrative efficiency. Best of all, Harris's raids on Germany were interrupted by preparations for the Normandy invasions. Blasting railways and defences in France cost fewer casualties than flights to Berlin or the Ruhr. So did the fact that most targets were close enough to permit a fighter escort. By the time 6 Group was switched back to targets in Germany in October, most of McEwen's crews had been together long enough to acquire experience, skill, self-confidence, and a few of the life-saving tricks that ensure longevity in battle. By the end of 1944, McEwen's command boasted the highest accuracy and the fewest casualties of any group in Bomber Command. Thanks partly to leadership but chiefly due to better aircraft and a critical reprieve, the Canadian bomber group had turned its reputation around.

The value of the bomber offensive against Germany is still hotly debated. Canadians who are willing to pronounce Hong Kong or Dieppe as costly blunders are understandably hesitant to condemn an operation which continued relentlessly through most of the war. It is too painful to admit that 9,980 young Canadians, to say nothing of the many thousands of other airmen from every Allied nation, died to very little purpose. Yet the Canadian toll in Bomber Command was greater than the death roll of the Canadian Army as it fought from Normandy to the Hochwald Forest. Because Bomber Command enjoyed priority, Coastal Command was denied the long-range aircraft needed to combat the German submarines in the Atlantic. Even when the huge strategic bomber force was grudgingly transferred to support General Eisenhower's invasion of Normandy, inexperience, unsuitable equipment, and an astonishing lack of communications led to tragic accidents and heavy losses among American and Canadian ground troops.

Victory denies the victorious the necessity of reflection. Faith in airpower survived the Second World War. German industrial power, its target, survived to the final months of the war, allowing Hitler's armies and navy to retain a remarkable technological advantage. Without heavy bombing of course, they would have been even stronger. German aircraft and rocket production were particularly hard hit.

Canada's own navy felt some of that German lead as her admirals struggled to branch out from their new and begrudged identity as a "corvette navy." Early in the war, Canadian officers and seamen were drafted into British carriers and cruisers to relieve a British manpower shortage and to gain experience in working major warships. In 1944, the RCN took over two escort carriers, the *Nabob* and the *Puncher* and, as part of preparation for the Pacific War, acquired two cruisers in early 1945. When the Allies developed fleets of landing craft, the RCN made its contribution. Two motor torpedo boat flotillas, manned largely by Canadians serving in British coastal forces, became RCN units. Everywhere the RCN found that German skill and materials were not limited to U-boats.

The major fleet units of the RCN were destroyers, many of them serving in Canadian flotillas with the British Home Fleet at Scapa Flow. Two of them, HMCS *Haida* and HMCS *Athabaskan*, gave Canadian admirals the kind of fighting tradition they desperately wanted. On April 25, 1944, the two destroyers off Brittany chased three German destroyers through a minefield and sank one of them. Three days later, the *Athabaskan* fell victim to a torpedo. The *Haida* drove one of the German attackers ashore, returned, despite strict orders, to hunt for survivors, and then abandoned its cutter to make its own way back to England loaded with men from its sunken sister-ship. Three days after D-Day, the *Haida* and *Huron* avenged the *Athabaskan* by sinking another German destroyer.

All three Canadian services sent thousands of men to fight for and from Great Britain. Each of the services numbered many men who were fully integrated in British units. CANLOAN officers, seconded from the army to meet a serious shortage of British junior officers, fought in every theatre from Malaya to Norway, and with the Indian as well as the British army. Thanks to BCATP and the navy's arrangements, most Canadian airmen and many seamen had similar experiences. In each service, some form of the issue of "Canadianization" emerged. Nowhere would it matter more than in the struggle to liberate Europe.

Liberation of Europe

Compared to the navy and air force, Canada's army was the Cinderella service. Canadians considered airmen romantic and sailors exotic; soldiering was a dirty, dangerous, brainless business. In Ottawa, where every military question was examined through a filter marked "conscription," it was clear that the RCN and RCAF would never cause trouble; the generals, on the other hand, were suspect from September 1939. Someone, even in modern mechanized war, had to do the actual hand-to-hand fighting, but Ottawa kept hoping that it would be someone else.

Perhaps only J. L. Ralston, the army's tough, unappreciated champion in the cabinet, could have won approval for the army overseas. By 1943 it had grown to three infantry divisions, two armoured divisions (somewhat smaller than the infantry formations), and two tank brigades. Thousands of soldiers served in ancillary units, from tunnellers working at Gibraltar to companies of the Canadian Forestry Corps, once again in the woods of northern Scotland. Nor did the army lack for staff. Instead of the single corps headquarters of 1918, General McNaughton's army included staff and supporting troops for two army corps headquarters and an army headquarters as well as a large and growing Canadian Military Headquarters in London. The years in Britain and a kindly national characteristic of finding sinecures for failures encouraged a proliferation of special units, staffs, and cadres, all doubtless invaluable. Though 730,625 men and women joined the Canadian Army during the war, the actual number of fighting troops was smaller than in Sir Arthur Currie's Corps in the Great War.

Manpower was a preoccupation. This time, mobilization had depended on actual militia units, not the *ad hoc* battalions of the CEF. The order of battle included French-speaking regiments of infantry, artillery, and armour. It was not much easier to find French-speaking volunteers than in the earlier war but, in its fumbling way, the army did its best, in contrast to the unilingual RCN and RCAF. Senior officers like McNaughton and Stuart (a native of Trois-Rivières) were more sensitive than their counterparts in the earlier war. At the same time, there is no evidence that the army's greater sensitivity in this and other matters greatly improved recruiting. Blandishments would not fool Canadians into doing what they did not wish to do.

By early 1943, victory seemed to be a matter of time. In England, R. B. Bennett scornfully commented that Canadians in 1942 would celebrate their fourth Christmas without firing a shot. The Winnipeg *Free Press*, Liberal oracle in the West, demanded that a division be sent somewhere, anywhere. The Montreal *Gazette*, with great conviction but no evidence, reported widespread mental illness in the

Canadian Army because of inaction. Ottawa became concerned. What would voters say if victory came before Canadian soldiers had done any fighting? After polite preliminaries, the British asked for a Canadian division and tank brigade for the forthcoming invasion of Sicily. McNaughton's alarm at the splitting of his army was soothed by a chance to study the operation plans and an informal assurance that the Canadians would return when Sicily had fallen.

The Sicily invasion on July 3, 1943, was the kind of battle innoculation Canadian troops badly needed. An easy landing slowly built into bitter fighting against a resourceful German rearguard. By the time the Canadians reached the Straits of Messina on August 6, they were aggressive, battle-hardened soldiers. Major-General Guy Simonds, commanding the 1st Canadian Division, had proved himself to a critical General Montgomery as an able field commander. No other Canadian would ever quite meet Monty's standards. At Agira and Regalbuto, Canadians had won costly, difficult battles. Behind the lines, there had been sour moments. The Allied commander, General Dwight Eisenhower, had somehow forgotten to mention the Canadians in his first report of the invasion. When the correction was made, the announcement came from Washington before a proud Mackenzie King could tell Canadians. When McNaughton asked to visit the Canadians during their first days in Sicily, Montgomery bluntly refused: Simonds and his men did not need distraction in their first battle. A furious McNaughton flew back to London.

Yet, even as public relations, the Sicily campaign was a triumph. In Ottawa, ministers now demanded more action. Perhaps, King told himself, fighting in Italy involved fewer casualties than in France. To the dismay of theatre commanders, Canada offered reinforcement: I Canadian Corps headquarters and the 5th Canadian Armoured Division. A raw armoured division would be little use in the hills of Italy and an untried corps headquarters would be no use at all. Politics prevailed: the Canadians came. McNaughton, too, was outraged. "The important thing for Canada at the end of the war," he pleaded with Ralston, "is to have her army together under control of a Canadian." The minister and his colleagues took their advice in Ottawa.

General McNaughton's opposition to the break-up of his army undermined his own position. Politicians want agreement, not arguments, from their officials. The British, too, had found McNaughton a prickly associate and his explosion in Sicily was a warning that he would not

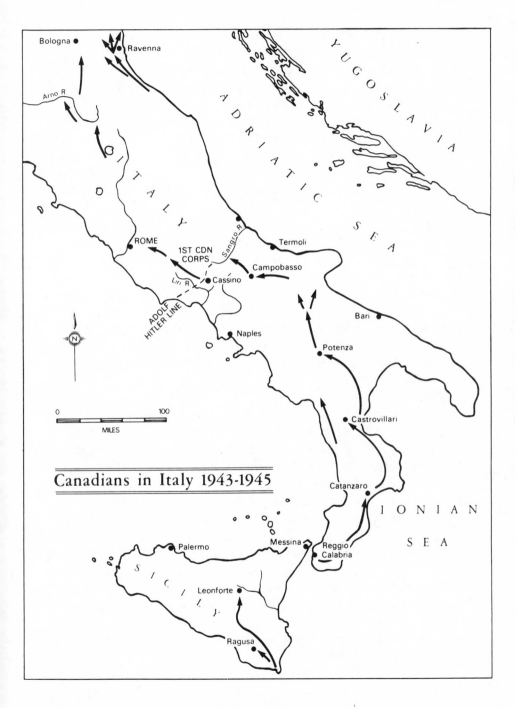

Canadians in Italy 1943-1945

be a good subordinate for Montgomery when the real Second Front came. Yet the key strike against the Canadian general was that he was too old, too set in his ways, perhaps too preoccupied by technology, to keep a firm grip on his army. In Exercise "Spartan," a massive 1943 deployment of troops, Canadians tangled themselves in a monumental traffic jam while McNaughton was absent for hours, watching a complex bridging operation. Ralston took British advice. By the end of December, a fit and lively looking McNaughton returned to Canada, recalled "on grounds of health." His successor, after a brief interlude commanding the Canadian Corps in Italy, was Lieutenant-General Harry Crerar.

King's faith that fighting in Italy would be relatively bloodless was fantasy. In Sicily, the Canadians had suffered 2,310 casualties, 562 of them fatal. Churchill's fond image of the "soft underbelly" of Europe proved ironic to those sent to fight there. When Italy capitulated in August, German divisions poured south, transforming mountains, rivers, vineyards, and towns into obstacles for advancing Allied forces. The Gustav Line, built across Italy's narrow waist, stopped Eisenhower's armies well south of Rome. At Ortona, the little coastal town which Canadians took house by house in December, Canadian medical officers faced their first cases of battle exhaustion. The victory cost the 1st Division 1,372 lives.

Crerar stayed in Italy for only a few weeks before he and Simonds returned to England to prepare for D-Day. Montgomery, unfortunately, was unimpressed by Crerar nor had Simonds welcomed his arrival. The next Canadian commander, Lieutenant-General E. L. M. Burns, was a soldier of formidable intellectual ability but so dour in manner that subordinates nicknamed him "Smilin' Sunray."*

In the spring of 1944, the British Eighth Army (with its Canadian Corps) was switched to Italy's west coast to punch a way north to the hard-pressed Anzio beachhead and to Rome. Canadian tanks helped drive a gap through the Gustav Line and Burns was given the further task of penetrating the Hitler Line. The battle took the corps four days and cost nine hundred Canadians, mostly from the 1st Division. For the pursuit, the army commander, Sir Oliver Leese, launched both I Canadian Corps and a British corps up the narrow Liri Valley. The re-

---

*SUNRAY was the codename for any commander.

sult was a traffic scramble, confusion, and more than enough delay to permit Germans to escape and re-establish themselves. The Eighth Army's dream of taking Rome before the Americans faded and on June 4, the city fell to the Free French and the Americans. The blame, Leese insisted, fell squarely on Burns and his unwanted, untried corps headquarters.

Two days later, Italy was the forgotten front. On June 6, 1944, the Allies had staged the greatest combined operation in history. Under a grey, glowering sky, 5,000 ships had swept into the Baie de la Seine to disembark 107,000 soldiers and 7,000 vehicles in a single day. The night before, thousands of airborne troops had helped seal off the battlefield. Canadians had shared in every aspect of the battle. RCAF squadrons and Canadians with the RAF flew with the Second Allied Tactical Air Force and with Bomber Command. So massive were British and American air resources that the Allies had divided their forces equally between Normandy and the Pas de Calais, maintaining German uncertainty long past the crucial moment. Canadian destroyers, frigates, and minesweepers were part of the huge Allied fleet that kept a wide corridor free of surface or underwater threat. HMCS *Prince Robert* and *Prince David*, rebuilt as headquarters and landing ships, watched over three RCN flotillas of landing craft ferrying assault waves to the beaches. More than 10,000 Canadian seamen in 110 Canadian warships shared in D-Day.

One of five assault beaches, JUNO, had been assigned to the 3rd Canadian Division and 2nd Canadian Armoured Brigade. Beyond the beachhead, men of the 1st Canadian Parachute Battalion had landed with the British 6th Airborne Division east of the British front. The Canadian beach was tougher than most. Air and naval bombardment had scarred the German defences without knocking them out. Surf and beach obstacles kept most of the supporting tanks from crashing ashore with the first waves but the infantry fought as they had been taught in endless rehearsals. By nightfall, they had carried the Canadian front farther inland than any Allied division that day. The cost, 1,074 dead, wounded, and missing, was taken from the best-trained units of the army but it was half what Allied planners had expected.

It was only a beginning. Staff officers had predicted a bitter fight for the beaches; they had not thought as hard about the subsequent battles through dense Norman countryside, where every feature favoured German defenders. In the two days after D-Day, Canadians were bent and bloodied by encountering a nemesis that would dog them to its own ultimate destruction, the 12th SS Panzer Division, formed from the *Hitler Jugend*. Even long training was no substitute for battle experience; Canadians won it the hard way. When weary Canadians failed to take the airport at Carpiquet, near Caen, General Montgomery demanded removal of the divisional commander. Instead, with a little better preparation and time to reorganize, Canadians helped take Caen on July 9. The fighting cost another 1,194 men.

Beyond Caen, British and Canadian divisions faced more open country, deceptively inviting to tanks. The deception was that each village and forest was ready-made as a fortress for German troops, tanks, and the formidable 88 mm anti-tank guns. Absolute Allied air supremacy was the attackers' one asset but it could not help much at night. Through the hot weeks of June, Canadian tanks and infantry kept up the pressure at a bloody cost. At Verrières Ridge, the Black Watch, a Montreal militia regiment, had only 15 survivors from a long, hopeless assault. "I guess," one of them explained, "that that's what they expected from the Black Watch." The whole operation cost 1,965 men, mostly from the 2nd Division. By holding most of the German armour on their front, Montgomery's divisions made it possible for General Omar Bradley's Americans to break through in Operation "Cobra" on July 26-27. No one could then have predicted Hitler's insistence that his generals renew their attack. Their struggle to obey gave Allied airpower fresh targets and created a giant pocket from Mortain to Chambois containing two whole German armies.

Closing that pocket from the north became the first real task of Lieutenant-General Guy Simonds' II Canadian Corps. The air force promised "carpet bombing"; Simonds himself devised "Kangaroos," armoured personnel carriers hurriedly improvised behind the line. On the night of August 7, Operation "Totalize" began. The 2nd and 3rd Divisions, with heavy tank support, rolled over the obstacles that stopped them in July. Then Simonds's two armoured divisions, the 4th Canadian and the 1st Polish, pushed through. At once, inexperience exacted its price. Bewildered crews lost direction. Germans, never more dangerous than in defeat, fought back brilliantly. Colonels and generals lost control. Allied bombers managed to unload part of their destruction on the Canadian rear, causing confusion, demoralization, and casualties. "Totalize" stopped on August 10, far short of its objectives.

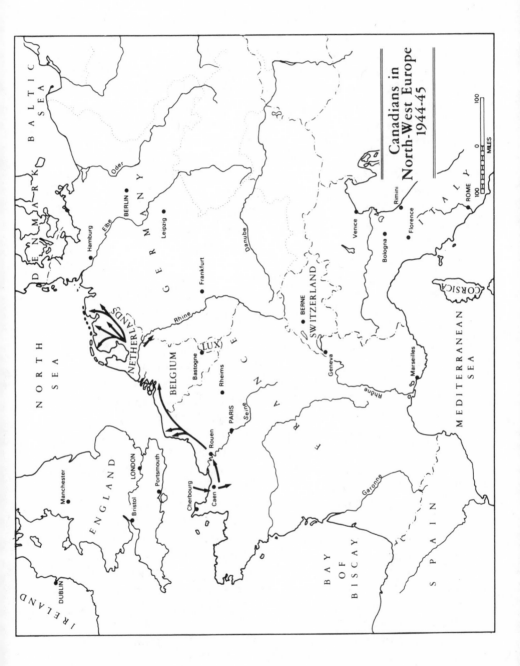

Canadians in
North-West Europe
1944-45

MILES

A frustrated, angry Simonds allowed his men to catch their breath and ordered a daylight version of the attack, this time called "Tractable." It had the makings of a disaster. The night before, Germans had captured a copy of the Canadian plans. They were alerted. Perhaps they simply could not believe it was happening. Tanks and vehicles formed up in dense columns and rolled forward under huge pillars of dust. Guided only by glimpses of dark red sun through the haze, drivers simply plunged ahead. Occasional tanks and carriers raced across the front of columns, utterly lost. At an unforeseen obstacle, a steep-banked creek, infantry swarmed from their perches on tanks and vehicles and stormed across to take the high ground. Two days later, on August 16, Canadians entered Falaise, their objective.

There was more to do. While General George Patton's Americans waited impatiently at Chambois, the exhausted Canadians and Poles were left to cut off the German escape route across the River Dives. Tank and infantry columns forced their way south. The Polish armoured division, effectively plugging the main route to safety, narrowly escaped annihilation as German armour and infantry fought desperately to overwhelm it. At St. Lambert, a handful of Canadian infantry and tanks played their own tiny version of the same epic. Only on August 21 could Simonds send help. The Normandy campaign was over.

The Germans left 400,000 dead, wounded, and prisoners behind, more than twice the Allied losses. Canadians had shared the worst of the campaign and their losses, 18,500 dead, wounded, and missing, showed it. Among Montgomery's divisions, none had lost as heavily as the 3rd Canadian. The 2nd Canadian Division was next. Such losses were testimony to Canadian courage and determination against a skilled, well-equipped enemy. They were also the price of inferior equipment, such as the vulnerable, under-gunned Sherman tank, and of overconfidence and inexperience. For all their years in England, Canadian soldiers and their officers had too many lessons still to learn when they went into battle. Each of the divisions in turn paid a price in heavy losses and frustrating failure for errors it rapidly learned not to make. Too many senior officers, the official historian later observed, had not taken their pre-battle responsibilities seriously enough. They were replaced, but at a cost.

From Normandy, the full Canadian army, strengthened by British divisions, the Poles, and contingents from countries soon to be liberated, moved up the coast on the Allied flank. Crerar's task was to liberate ports vital for Allied re-supply; the Germans were just as determined to defend them with every resource of siege-craft and to yield them, if necessary, as shattered wrecks. As they tackled Le Havre, Dieppe, Boulogne, Calais, and Dunkirk, Canadian battalion commanders reported only a fraction of their proper fighting strength.

From Italy, too, came reports of an acute shortage of infantry reinforcements. The losses on the Gustav and Hitler lines had coincided with the start of the Normandy campaign. Then, after the fall of Rome, Canadians found themselves in reserve as the Allies bickered over strategy. Americans insisted on a landing in the south of France; Churchill persisted in demanding an advance from Italy through the Ljubliana Gap into Austria and the Balkans, forestalling Stalin's victorious armies. Canadians at the Volturno River were not consulted.

At the end of August, Burns finally got his orders. The Canadian Corps was switched north to the Foglia River on the Adriatic; to attack the newest German defence system, the Gothic Line. Meanwhile, the Americans and Churchill would each have their way; the Canadians would carry out the British side of the compromise. For Burns and his headquarters it was a final trial. Only direct intervention by Crerar and General Stuart had stopped Leese from breaking up the Canadians or giving them a British commander. Now they must prove themselves.

The Gothic Line was a murderous test: 479 anti-tank guns, 2,375 machine-gun nests, a score of tank turrets set in concrete. Battle-ready and experienced, the Canadian troops deployed with the hard-driving efficiency that was missing in Normandy. Even the Germans were stunned by the new fighting style. In only four days, the 1st and the 5th Armoured were through. Then, as usual, the Germans came up with fresh surprises. At each of the dozen rivers the pursuing Canadians had to cross, a fierce battle ensued. A month of steady fighting cost the Canadians 4,000 casualties and 1,500 cases of battle exhaustion. Sir Oliver Leese was fed up. At the end of October, the Canadians were withdrawn to rest, Burns was fired, and on November 5, Lieutenant-General Charles Foulkes arrived from North-West Europe to take command. "Though progress was not always as rapid as desirable," Burns later confessed, "nevertheless, during our period of action we went further and faster than any other Corps."

Conscription and Victory

The combined impact of Normandy and the Gothic Line offensive in Italy brought Canada face to face with the crisis Mackenzie King and his government had tried hardest to avoid. The facts were plain and inescapable: there were not enough trained infantry reinforcements to keep the army's fighting battalion even remotely up to strength. Moreover, the fact was public knowledge, proclaimed by Major Conn Smythe, owner of the Toronto Maple Leafs, who had returned wounded from France. Reinforcements reaching Normandy, Smythe insisted, were "green, inexperienced and poorly trained." Cooks and clerks had been forced to masquerade as trained soldiers. Smythe's solution was widely echoed: the NRMA men must be sent overseas at once.

Word of the crisis persuaded Colonel Ralston to see for himself in Italy and France. His investigation was characteristic. Systematically, he tracked down reports of untrained reinforcements and proved most of them to be false. He took no claim at face value, whether from generals, war correspondents, or veteran regimental sergeant-majors. The same conscientious honesty led him to his conclusion: "I regret to say that conditions and prospects of which I have learned," Ralston cabled King on October 13, 1944, "will I fear necessitate reassessment in light of the future particularly regarding infantry involving, I fear, grave responsibilities."

That was a wordy understatement. The prime minister was almost beside himself. The war was virtually over and won. King could not believe that an army of over half a million soldiers, half of them overseas, could not dig out a mere fifteen thousand infantry reinforcements. Why had Ralston, Stuart, Crerar, and other generals insisted that army expansion would not lead to conscription for overseas service? Was there no way out?

The questions were legitimate; the answers complex. The war might well have ended in 1944 if, inexplicably, Montgomery had not halted the British advance at Antwerp without clearing the estuary of the Scheldt, or if rain had not stalled British armoured columns, making Arnhem and its embattled airborne troops "the bridge too far." Canadian casualties might have been lower if Crerar's soldiers had been better trained or if Canadians in Italy had not been hurried into the Gothic Line assault when the Italian theatre had been too drained of troops to provide a diversionary attack. The crisis might never have developed if Mackenzie King had not insisted on splitting the Canadian Army between the two widely separated campaigns, entailing two administrative organizations and a long time in transit. If the Canadian Army used more men than the British and Americans in administrative roles, it was partly because Ottawa had insisted on a two-front war.

In Canada, the manpower crisis might have been alleviated if the RCAF had not hoarded highly qualified volunteers for its over-expanded aircrew training programme. The army's own reinforcement system, as General Burns later pointed out, had its own major flaws. Working from British experience in North Africa where the Luftwaffe caused casualties in the rear areas as well as in the front lines, the army kept too many reinforcements for the artillery, engineers, army service corps, and other supporting arms and services and too few, relatively speaking, for the infantry battalions that now suffered almost all the losses.

General Stuart, now commanding the Canadian Military Headquarters in London, understood politics, suppressed early warnings from his staff, and hoped for the best. Only in August would he admit the problem. One might then rage, condemn, and mourn—King and his colleagues would do all three—but the army needed fifteen thousand trained men. When Canadian voters discovered what being under-strength meant to the men of an infantry company or platoon, they might not be put off with a soft answer. In specific terms, it meant more frequent duty as a sentry or on patrol, more digging, more risk, much less sleep. It was, in short, dangerous and miserable. Certainly a veteran battalion commander like Ralston did not need an explanation.

The earlier conscription crisis of 1942 had been conceived in domestic politics; the 1944 crisis reflected a real, intractable problem. It displayed King at his most agile. The prime minister's sense of outrage was understandable. He had kept his Liberal Party united to the very eve of victory. He had placated pro-conscriptionists and anti-conscriptionists. He had bowed to the right wing of his cabinet in 1943 and to the left in 1944. Now he faced his ultimate test.

His first ploy was to seek official assurance from Churchill that conscription would not be necessary so close to victory. The British leader was dismayingly non-committal: Britain's own manpower crisis, after six years of conscription, was forcing her to break up divisions and battalions to supply other formations. Next, General Stuart was excoriated and his successor, Lieutenant-General J. C. Murchie, was interrogated. There was no escape. Earlier, King had contemplated resignation if conscription was forced on him. Now, in his plot-filled mind, he spied a conspiracy at the heart of his own government. Was it a coincidence that Ralston, Howe, Ilsley, and all the others who now called for conscription had also opposed his social reform measures? Were they scheming to hand over the Liberal Party to reactionaries?

A letter from a right-wing back-bencher, demanding that NRMA men be sent overseas, was proof enough. King would fight back. He had a man. A year before, McNaughton had come home a bitter and unemployed hero. All three parties, even the CCF, had courted him as a candidate. King had considered him a potential Canadian-born Governor General. Now he had another thought; McNaughton certainly opposed conscription and he also detested Ralston.

On November 13, with only his French Canadian lieutenant, Louis St. Laurent, briefed, King readied his trap. McNaughton, he told the cabinet, was the man to make the voluntary system work. Ralston, he recalled, had never withdrawn his 1942 letter of resignation. Ministers sat stunned as Ralston rose, shook hands around the table, and left. Not one of his allies followed him. McNaughton was the new minister. Surely, he believed, his personality and prestige would sway the NRMA men. Next day, McNaughton met his generals, listened to their misgivings, and promptly issued a press statement that his discussions had only convinced him that "continuation of the voluntary system will produce the reinforcements."

McNaughton had no magic. The NRMA men were unimpressed. At Vancouver, General Pearkes assembled his senior officers to explain the problems to the press. King was outraged: "These men in uniform," he raged, "have no right to speak in ways that will turn the people against the civil power." On November 22, Murchie and other senior officers reported formally to the new minister: volunteering was not working. It was, McNaughton confessed, "like a blow in the stomach." The entire military machine, he warned King, would run down.

This was absurd. Officers who resigned could be replaced. Murchie had given a judgement which, on the facts available then and since, was irrefutable. It is no act of mutiny to tell the truth. Yet, to King, the notion of a "general's revolt" was too useful to ignore. It fitted his view of the military. It superseded the mutiny that really mattered—the imminent resignation of pro-conscription ministers. It would frighten the anti-conscriptionists. On November 22 McNaughton had to go to the bar of the House of Commons (he was and remained unelected) to announce that 16,000 NRMA men would go overseas if Parliament approved. It did, by 143 votes to 70, with 34 Quebec Liberals among the dissenters. Among them, C. G. Power had resigned his post as minister of national defence for air.

In Montreal and Quebec, there were demonstrations. More terrifying by far, at Terrace, remote in the mountains behind Prince Rupert, a brigade of NRMA soldiers mounted guns on the single rail line and declared they had gone on strike. Senior officers, summoned by Pearkes to the conference at Vancouver, returned and quietly restored discipline. Most of the men boarded trains for Halifax. Some deserted but claims of "Zombies" throwing rifles overboard or fleeing into the woods are largely fabrications. Almost 13,000 conscripts went overseas, 2,463 served in battalions, and 69 were killed.

That was an anti-climax. As in 1918, wholly unpredictable coincidences eased the reinforcement crisis. Certainly during the month of debate and manoeuvering in Ottawa, men were needed. At Boulogne, Calais, and Le Havre, Canadians staged bloody, destructive sieges, but far worse fighting faced them after Montgomery's fatal decision to let his advance guard rest at Antwerp. Its magnificent harbour facilities were useless until the Scheldt estuary was cleared. Until then, the Allies were at the utter limit of a supply line stretching back to Cherbourg.

The Scheldt battlefield was as unpleasant as any that could be imagined and the Germans had exploited its potential with all their usual skill. The polder land was flooded. Narrow dykes, sprayed by machine-guns and registered for accurate artillery fire, provided the only access. Crerar, sick with dysentery, handed over his army to Simonds, and Foulkes was promoted and sent to Italy to take over I Corps. Two Canadian divisions, the 3rd and 4th Armoured, were sent to squeeze out the Breskens pocket south of the Scheldt; the 2nd Division pushed across the Beveland Isthmus. It took three miserable weeks. Casualties were high. For the second time, the Black Watch was virtually wiped out — on Friday, October 13. When Beveland was finally cut off, Simonds ordered his infantry to storm across the long narrow causeway to Walcheren. After dreadful losses, the deed was done by the Régiment de Maisonneuve, only to find that the bridgehead was a hopeless base for further attacks. The flooded island finally fell to a bloody amphibious assault by British troops and Royal Marines. The price for the Scheldt was 3,550 Canadians, 2,000 of them from the 3rd Division.

The Scheldt battle was the grim counterpoint to the 1944 conscription crisis. Any weary, sodden Canadian, transferred from South Beveland, might have given justification enough for a genuine generals' revolt yet no sooner had the government acted than the need evaporated. When Canadians went into winter quarters along the Waal and the Maas rivers, casualties were chiefly due to trench foot and pneumonia. In Italy, too, the Canadians settled down north-west of Ravenna to wait for a spring offensive into the Lombardy Plain. In January 1945, when British and American chiefs of staff met at Malta, they agreed that Eisenhower needed more troops in North-West Europe. The Canadian request that their army be reunited, made half a year before McNaughton became minister, was now opportune. From mid-February to mid-April two divisions of Canadians were on the move and out of harm's way.

The same could not be said of Canadians already in the Netherlands. In early March, the 2nd and 3rd Canadian Divisions began a tough, slugging advance into the Hochwald Forest. German paratroopers, the élite of Hitler's army (actually of his airforce, since German airborne troops belonged to the Luftwaffe), contested every metre of the advance. There were still no easy victories. The 9th Canadian Highland Brigade, invited as a ceremonial honour to cross the Rhine with the famous British 51st Highland Division, found itself in a furious, costly battle at Speldoorp. Yet, all too plainly, the war was winding down. On the eastern front, where the vast bulk of the Wehrmacht had passed through the meatgrinder of the Red Army, resistance was cracking. Canadian divisions, fresh from Italy, attacked the 25th German Army in western Holland, and on April 11, American troops finally met the Soviet army on the Elbe. On April 21, 1945, British troops entered a devastated Hamburg. The first sickening encounter with the German death camps gave a sudden, chilling significance to claims most Canadian soldiers had dismissed as mere propaganda. Only gradually did the hideous evil of Hitler's regime sink in. Prisoners of war, released in their thousands, had shared more than a little of it.

For a reunited Canadian army, the last weeks of the war were spent liberating the northern Netherlands, meeting occasional resistance, particularly from units of the Dutch ss. To the south, units of the 1st Polish and 4th Canadian Armoured Divisions fought their way into Germany. The caution of soldiers anxious not to be the last casualties in a victorious war was balanced by the urgent need to save a starving, flooded Dutch population and by the fear that, somehow, the Nazis would launch some fearful reprisal before their defeat. 1 Canadian Corps pushed into western Holland, avoided the destruction of Apeldoorn by prudently waiting for it to be surrounded, and halted its advance on April 19. There was really no point in going farther and it made more sense to use military transport to stockpile food for a starving population than to blast a few miles deeper into the flooded landscape. Besides, the Canadian divisions had suffered 6,300 casualties, 1,482 of them fatal. At Wageningen on May 5, General Foulkes accepted the surrender of the German armies in the Netherlands. Next day, the war against Hitler was over.

For most Canadians, that was the real war. They met VE Day with wild rejoicing—in Halifax and some other cities, too wild. Anxious to protect businesses that had been hugely profitable during the war, Halifax merchants closed down the city and assumed that thousands of sailors, soldiers, and airmen would find somewhere else to do their celebrating. The outcome on May 8, fuelled by sixty-five thousand bottles of looted liquor and one hundred thousand quarts of stolen beer, was an orgy of vengeful destruction. A government investigation found a convenient scapegoat in Admiral Murray: he was accused of failing to provide adequate security or alternative entertainment. Canada's military leaders had fair notice of the treatment they could expect from a grateful nation.

Canadians celebrated victory more than the return of peace. Opinion surveys still found that many Canadians looked anxiously forward to unemployment and a renewed depression. For Mackenzie King, prudence dictated an appearance of radicalism: Canadians could count on him for a "New Social Order" and more of the wartime standard of economic management, not a return to old ways. The federal election of June 11, 1945, caught the Tories split between those who cried "me too" and others who complained that King was bribing Quebec with family allowances. As for the over-confident CCF, Canadians preferred social policies without socialism. King won his party a narrow majority of five seats. The armed forces vote, Conservative in 1940, switched to the Liberals, with the CCF, at thirty-three per cent, a strong second. Overseas, the vote was strongly CCF though turn-out was low. In Prince Albert, service voters had their vengeance: Mackenzie King was personally defeated by their votes.

Of course, for Canadians starving in Hong Kong prison camps or dying in Japanese mines—or for Japanese Canadians facing their fourth spring of internment, the Pacific War remained a terrible reality. Canadians would share in defeating Japan but a weary, aged prime minister could not decide how. Would Canadian contingents serve with the suspiciously imperialist British or the dangerously possessive Americans? Whatever was done would be limited: John Bracken, the latest Tory leader, had hurt his cause badly by promising conscription for the Pacific.

As usual, Ottawa's solution was a compromise. A new division, the 6th, would be formed from overseas veterans. Since volunteering guaranteed early return to Canada, men were easily found. For the first time, a Canadian division would be organized and equipped on American lines. A special RCAF contingent, christened "Tiger Force," chiefly composed of Lancaster squadrons, would join the American General Curtis LeMay's efforts to pulverize Japan's cities. Only the RCN would work with the British, using the opportunity to fulfil the admirals' dream of a big-ship fleet.

The dream promptly became a nightmare. The RCN's first cruiser, HMCS *Uganda*, was already off Okinawa when crew members announced that it was their right to go home. They had never enlisted to fight Japan and Ottawa had proclaimed only volunteers would serve. To the embarrassment of their officers and of Naval Headquarters, crew members would not budge and the warship turned for home. On the way, the crew learned that on August 6, a new and horrifying weapon of war had destroyed the Japanese city of Hiroshima. Three days later, it was the turn of Nagasaki. The atomic bomb only precipitated a peace movement discreetly working in Tokyo. On August 14, the world war was finally over. Every Canadian who survived could go home.

VI   The Long Cold War

Reconstruction

At least a few Canadians were aware of the atomic bombs that had precipitated Japan's surrender. In 1942, the British had transferred their nuclear research to laboratories at McGill University in Montreal. Uranium from Great Bear Lake, refined at Port Hope, provided physicists with their research material, though higher-quality African uranium fuelled the bombs. When Americans insisted on taking full control of weapons research, enough nuclear expertise and activity still remained in Canada to give her a special insight into the potential and terrors of the most terrible force humanity had yet unleashed. Insiders, as yet, had no full understanding that radiation might be as terrible a by-product as heat, blast, and flash, but Canadians were early and knowledgeable critics of nuclear arms.

Of course, that knowledge was tightly restricted to insiders (and Soviet agents). For the most part, Canadians could rejoice in victory, and congratulate themselves on escaping almost wholly unscathed. At war's end, Canada stood third among the nations in the number of fighting ships, fourth in airpower, and high in the list of armies. All three services had finally achieved impressive efficiency. More significant still was Canada's post-war wealth. The war cost Canadians $18 billion, $10.5 billion of which was added to the national debt, yet the gross national product reached $11.8 billion in 1945 and would continue to climb. While Britain had gone irreversibly into debt, the Hyde Parke agreement kept Canadian-American trade and settlements in balance. In the name of post-war trade, Ottawa wrote off some of the principal and much of the interest on Britain's $1.2 billion war debt. The country could well afford it, though Quebec backbenchers put up a furious resistance.

After the First World War, Canadians and their governments had struggled with limited success to return to the more normal world they remembered from 1914. In 1945, the effort was far less determined. "Orderly decontrol" was the official slogan for the dismantling of the WPTB empire and its counterparts, but this time, Ottawa was infinitely more careful about tearing down social benefits Canadians had come to accept during the war years. Rent controls faded despite tenant protests; P.C. 1003, did not. Diluted whiskey continued, to the benefit of national revenues, distillers, and probably even the drinkers. Women dropped out of the workforce, as they had not after 1918 — proving that their participation was due to economic as well as social pressures. The memory of their wartime role — and such adjustments as day-care and maternity leave — survived as arguments for a later generation which wished a fuller role in the labour force.

The great lesson of the Second World War was best summarized by Lorne Morgan, a University of Toronto political economist, whose pamphlet, *Homo the Sap*, contrasted the energy, creativity, and prosperity of wartime Canada with the timid misery of the Depression years. Did Canada, he asked sadly, need a state of permanent war to make full use of her people and resources? If so, *homo canadiensis* was indeed a sap. It was a threatened indictment Canada's post-war leaders would remember for a full decade.

Unlike the despairing mood of 1918, Canadians were buoyant if nervous. After sixteen years of war and depression, families now had money to spend. Business grumbled at bureaucrats and regulations but the habit of looking to Ottawa for leadership was not easily forgotten. Having created war industries, C. D. Howe set out just as aggressively to convert the economy for peacetime purposes. Double depreciation was tax incentive enough for most industrialists. If foreign investors were first in line to buy old war plants, Howe had no complaints. The goal was fast conversion, satisfied consumers, and fulfilment for the key Liberal promise of 1945: "a high and stable level of employment."

Returning service personnel, male and female, shared the benefits. Unlike their fathers in 1919, able-bodied veterans received generous incentives to establish themselves in farming or fishing. Employers, private as well as public, were compelled to offer veterans their old jobs. War Service Gratuities distributed $752 million in purchasing power. Training benefits sent 150,000 veterans to university and 130,000 to vocational training programmes. Those who did not qualify for training or the Veteran's Land Act got rehabilitation grants to help buy homes or furniture.

A post-war depression never had a chance to start. Unemployment insurance, established in 1940 partly as a way to sop up spending power, had a reserve of a quarter of a billion dollars by 1945. Post-war training not only gave universities some of the best and most serious students they had ever seen; it kept many veterans off the job market until the economy had re-adjusted to peacetime.

Post-war Canada was no paradise. Returning veterans faced families and communities that could never understand their problems. War brides, far more numerous than in 1914-19 because of the time Canadians had spent in England, encountered cruelty and prejudice as well as kindness, and cultural poverty as well as relative material abundance. Almost everyone faced shortages. Rationing lasted to 1947 and, for a few items, to 1948. Through their unions, workers struggled to hang on to wartime gains. In 1946, Canada experienced its worst year of strikes since 1919. By winning, unions helped ensure working Canadians a share in the post-war boom and a more mature collective bargaining relationship during the ensuing thirty years. By 1947, Canada's GNP had climbed far beyond its wartime peak to reach $15.5 billion. Canadians had done well out of the war.

With such prospects, few Canadians had any intention of staying in uniform. The government had promised the Allies 25,000 troops and 11 RCAF squadrons for the occupation of Germany. If Ottawa had any intention of extending its commitment past March 1946, a storm of domestic criticism, backed by sit-down strikes by homesick servicemen, changed its mind. Over strenuous British objections, Canada's occupying force came home in the spring of 1946.

In Ottawa, the service chiefs had already learned the fate of their post-war plans. The navy asked for a task force with 2 aircraft carriers, 4 cruisers, and 20,000 men. The army's Plan G called for 55,788 regulars, 155,396 in the reserves, and a "training force" of 48,500 based on compulsory service. The RCAF proposals for 30,000 in a permanent force, 15,000 in auxiliary squadrons, and 50,000 in reserve sounded almost modest. Government response was frosty. The army's yearning for conscription, declared Mackenzie King, was "perfectly outrageous." The RCN's plan was cut in half; the army was lucky to be allowed 25,000 regulars and the RCAF would have to be content with 16,000. In choosing the army's peacetime chief of staff, the government bypassed Simonds in favour of the junior but more diplomatic Lieutenant-General Charles Foulkes.

Painful readjustment continued when Brooke Claxton became minister of national defence at the end of 1946. A Montreal lawyer who enjoyed reminding generals that his highest CEF rank was sergeant, Claxton was best known as a liberal Liberal who had steered family allowances into operation in time for the 1945 election. He was also a minister with ideas. The rambling wartime temporary buildings which housed the three service headquarters were promptly juggled into an integrated system: operations staff in one building, personnel and pay staff in another, supply and equipment directorates in a third. Despite vigorous RCAF opposition, Claxton created a Defence Research Board, a research arm that functioned virtually as a fourth service.

Wartime experience suggested that Canadian senior officers were political illiterates. The services proposed a Canadian Joint Services Staff College for middle-rank officers while the higher ranks broadened their minds at the Imperial Defence College in Britain or at the National War College in the United States. A British officer, Major-General J. F. M. Whiteley, backed by Dr. O. M. Solandt, first chairman of the Defence Research Board, and Lester Pearson from External Affairs, urged that Canada act on her own. On January 5, 1948, Claxton opened the National Defence College at Kingston. Students from the Canadian, British, and American forces, senior civil servants, and an occasional defence-minded civilian would spend the year ranging over the strategic problems of Canada and the world. Claxton's choice of commandant, Lieutenant-General Simonds, proved a success. The army and RCAF created separate staff colleges. The minister's fondness for tri-service integration became the lever for re-opening the Royal Military College, closed for officer training since 1942. General Foulkes, who wanted officers to pass through civil universities, was outmanoeuvred by the influential RMC ex-cadet club and overruled by Claxton. The remodelled RMC would educate officers to a high academic standard and prepare them for all three services.

Post-war adjustments were just as hard for men in the ranks as they were for admirals and generals. Lagging pay scales, a lack of quarters for families, and competition for jobs in a booming economy left only a few attractions to service life. The RCAF's new jet aircraft at least offered pilots and ground crew a fresh challenge. In a new role as a Mobile Strike Force, the army's three regular infantry regiments received parachute training and new air-portable equipment. Soldiers also won public recognition when they fought floods in the Fraser Valley in 1948 and virtually took charge of an inundated Winnipeg in 1950.

The navy's problems were most acute: there was a need for high technical competence, but this was superimposed on shipboard conditions and attitudes which provoked minor mutinies by 1949. An investigation headed by Rear-Admiral Rollo Mainguy into events on two destroyers and on the new aircraft carrier *Magnificent* condemned the failure of officers to respond to legitimate grievances, especially about leave and pay. Royal Navy accents and snobbery were too prevalent. The peacetime navy was compelled to think through new and wiser approaches to discipline and routine.

Canada's breakneck demobilization of wartime forces was by no means unique: proportionate to its enormous strength, the United States moved even faster. Yet, even as the two neighbours disbanded their forces, their diplomats and service officers wrestled with an ugly postwar reality.

It took the Communist coup in Czechoslovakia in February 1948, or perhaps the Berlin blockade a month later, to force European and North American democracies to recognize the Cold War. Until then, discretion, wishful thinking, and war-engendered sympathy helped people overlook the fact that, alone among the major powers, the Soviet Union had maintained large armies after 1945, had retained its conquered territory, and was managing the nations of eastern Europe as virtual colonies. Canada's attitude was illustrated by the plight of Igor Gouzenko, the Soviet cypher clerk who fled the Russian embassy on September 6, 1945, with evidence of widespread Soviet spying. Mackenzie King was deeply upset: by his embarrassing revelations, Gouzenko forced the government to act against her pro-Soviet traitors. Would Canada then be held responsible for breaking up the great wartime alliance?

Most insiders were more cold-blooded. As early as 1944, British planners had identified the Soviet Union as a great potential enemy—though it was not expected to be a threat before 1955-60. American planners agreed. Guilt-ridden by their failure to stop Japanese surprise attacks in 1941, they were convinced that a future war would start in the same unexpected way. Routes built to supply the USSR could be reversed for a Soviet attack on North America. Like it or not, Canada would be involved. The old age of imperial defence was over: in 1948, a satisfied Foulkes returned from London to announce its death: the British, he reported, "are taking a much broader and more realistic view of defence matters." Now the imperial capital was Washington.

The war had taught Ottawa how fast Americans moved when their interests were concerned and how little weight Canadian appeals carried in the United States. Canadians might have sat back and allowed Americans to enjoy both the authority and the burden of defending the continent. Alternatively, they might have assumed the incredible cost and responsibility of keeping Canada secure against both the Americans and the Russians. Instead, Canadians compromised, continuing with the Permanent Joint Board of Defence (PJBD), doing as much or as little as sovereignty dictated. "If we do enough to assure the United States," one of King's advisors assured his peace-loving master, "we shall have done a good deal more than a cold assessment of the risk would indicate to be necessary." The armed forces were pleased. King's desire to stand well with the White House might make him more susceptible than Congress to U.S. military calls for preparedness.

The government also yearned for alternatives. For all King's scorn for the League of Nations, his growing fear of the American nexus made him a cautious supporter of the United Nations. Its charter became Canada's excuse for not joining a Washington-inspired hemispheric defence agreement signed at Chapultepec late in 1945. In urging their post-war organizations, Canadian service chiefs used the United Nations, not continental defence, as their justification. Yet the American pressure continued. The airborne role of Mobile Support Force suggested that Canada could tackle small Soviet lodgements in the Arctic. An Arctic research centre at Fort Churchill gave all three services a northern foothold.

Canadian service commanders were not entirely enthusiastic about the PJBD or continental defence. Like their U.S. counterparts, they suspected that any Soviet attack on North America would be a diversion, holding back U.S. and Canadian forces from the real war in Europe. However, one PJBD proposal was accepted in its entirety virtually without public discussion. On February 12, 1947, a bilateral agreement cautiously committed Canada to American weapons, equipment, training methods, and communications. The British pattern, established since 1907, would be allowed slowly to fade. "As an underlying principle," King sternly insisted, "all cooperative arrangements will be without impairment of the control of either country over all activities in its territory." American equipment might or might not be superior to British patterns; it seemed more likely to be available in a crisis. As a legal counterpart, a Visiting Forces Bill in 1947 gave American as well as British officers command of their own forces on Canadian soil. Mild protests were stilled when members of Parliament were reminded that similar legislation for British Commonwealth forces had been adopted in 1933. More than Ogdensburg, the 1947 agreement marked Canadian military integration with its historic enemy.

Such activities were pursued at minimal cost. If Canadian defence spending was a barometer of world tensions, Ottawa looked on the world of 1947-48 with profound optimism: Claxton's department sought only $195,561,641, its lowest post-war budget. Yet the world was visibly in crisis. In 1946, Winston Churchill had given democracies a new phrase: the Iron Curtain. Greece and Italy were saved from it only by massive American aid. In February 1948, Czechoslovakia was whisked behind it. On the other side of the world, Chiang Kai-shek's Kuomintang regime crumbled before the Communist advance. As HMCS *Crescent* stood by to rescue eight hundred Canadians, their puzzled fellow citizens cheered the fall of corruption but worried about its ruthless successor. In western Europe, democratic and often socialist governments wrestled desperately with reconstruction, but they had neither inherited defence forces nor did they have the means to create them. Only exhausted, bankrupt Britain had substantial, efficient armed forces. France, which had also attempted to rearm, had sent the best of its men and equipment to a hopeless colonial struggle in Indochina.

In a darkening world, Canada's response was cautious. Personally, Mackenzie King was appalled by news that the Czech foreign minister, Jan Masaryk, had jumped or been shoved to his death on February 10, 1948, but there was nothing Canada could do or even say about the matter. Nor would the elderly prime minister, in his final months in office, allow the RCAF to join the cargo airlift that sustained West Berlin through much of 1948. Defence estimates for 1948-49 rose significantly — and included the RCN's first Arctic patrol ship — but King was appalled by news that President Harry Truman had restored the draft in the United States. Canadians would join the Communist Party, King warned, if he followed suit. "They will say if we are to risk our lives fighting Communism, we better save our heads by joining them."

That August, King took his fears into retirement. His successor needed no instruction in conscription. Louis St. Laurent, the new Liberal leader, had not survived the 1944 crisis for nothing. Yet far more than King and most Canadians, St. Laurent had a positive view of the world and Canada's place in it. In routine matters, he was content to be chairman of the board, leaving Howe, Claxton, and other powerful ministers to manage their domains; in external policy, St. Laurent was a force.

The first French-speaking prime minister since Laurier, St. Laurent felt little of Quebec's traditional isolationism. Indeed, in a world where the Communist threat had replaced British imperialism as a threat to traditional, clerical Quebec, French Canada's nationalism was shifting from right to left, to become the faith of the province's labour and intellectual leaders; men like Jean Marchand, Pierre Elliott Trudeau, and a chain-smoking journalist named René Lévesque. St. Laurent, who identified with neither the Quebec left nor with Premier Maurice Duplessis, had inherited a suspicion of the British from his French and Irish ancestors. His unexpected empathy for the emerging Commonwealth nations and their spokesman, Jawaharlal Nehru, persuaded St. Laurent and his successor at External Affairs, Lester Pearson, that Canada must seek links to post-colonial nations. Peacekeeping, a military means for Canada to play a more idealistic role in the world, began in 1948 with Canadian officers sent to Kashmir to supervise a shaky truce between Nehru's India and Pakistan.

After 1945, Canadians had not turned their backs on the world, in part because they believed that isolation had caused a second world war and in larger part because they yearned for a higher role than the PJBD assigned them in North America. There was idealism and self-confidence in the notion of Canada as a "middle power," popularized by Pearson and his able lieutenants. In so dangerous a world, there must also be realism. Two world wars had begun in Europe; it was there that a third war would start—or be stopped. Realism and ambition both drew Canada to Paris in 1949.

NATO and Korea

By September 1948, a number of nervous nations had banded together in a European Defence Union with Britain's Viscount Montgomery as chairman. The union was meaningless without acquiring American support. Ottawa joined in the diplomatic offensive; Canada's interests in Western European security were obvious. Experience of the United Nations left no illusions about its potential as a peacemaker. A few years of bilateral defence arrangements with the United States made Ottawa yearn for additional partners. "Twelve in the bed means no rape" became an Ottawa slogan. Canada, of course, was not alone. Even American isolationists grimly conceded that the United States could no longer remain a baleful hermit. At Paris, in April 1949, delegates of ten European states, the United States, and Canada met, argued, and produced the North Atlantic Treaty Organization. As a concession to Canada, Article II of the agreement proclaimed the common political and moral values of the alliance partners.

Whatever Lester Pearson and Canadians might pretend, NATO was a military alliance even if one member, Iceland, had no military forces. It was based, St. Laurent told the Canadian Parliament, "on the common belief of the North Atlantic union in the values and virtues of Christian civilization." Out of deference to Antonio Salazar's fascist dictatorship in Portugal, democracy was not mentioned. If NATO was never the social and cultural agency suggested by Article II, neither was it the military adventure depicted by Soviet propagandists and their Canadian echoes. NATO talk of raising ninety divisions to match Soviet strength was talk. Western Europe was pathetically weak: American strength in Germany amounted to a single under-strength division and a paramilitary constabulary. NATO's real appeal for its members was that by pooling military resources, each partner could do less.

Canada was typical in seeking cut-rate rearmament. Its 1949 defence budget was only $360 million. Her highly publicized contribution to the alliance was a stockpile of obsolescent British-pattern equipment stored since 1945. Handing over a division's worth of equipment to the Netherlands and equal amounts later to Belgium and Italy, plus a regiment of field guns for Luxembourg, emptied inventories and pressured the St. Laurent government to buy replacements from American or Canadian manufacturers. To their surprise, Canadian negotiators found that the United States could be as balky a partner to deal with as Britain. Congress first restricted arms exports and then imposed a "Buy American" policy which kept Canadian suppliers out of a reviving U.S. arms market. Only in October 1949 did a Mutual Defence Assistance Act include Canada as a country where the United States could buy arms for sale offshore. On May 5, 1950, the United States defence secretary formally agreed that Canada could sell $15-20 million in defence supplies to American forces to offset her own much larger purchases.

The NATO countries' leisurely rearmament was suddenly shaken out of phase. On June 25, 1950, without warning, tanks and troops of North Korea struck across the 38th Parallel to push deep into the Republic of Korea. With Soviet delegates boycotting the UN Security Council, there was no veto when Americans demanded action to meet aggression. Already, American planes and ships from the occupation forces in Japan were in action. On July 5, American troops met the

Communist forces and fell back. By mid-July, the remnants of the South Koreans, the Americans, and a British brigade were hemmed in around the port of Pusan. Then with characteristic flair and good fortune, the UN commander, General Douglas MacArthur, unleashed a successful amphibious assault on Inchon, the port of the Korean capital of Seoul, and another on the opposite coast. Caught on both flanks, the North Koreans reeled back. MacArthur sent his army in pursuit, hesitated only briefly at the 38th Parallel, and then raced northward. The troops, he boasted, would be home for Christmas.

For St. Laurent and Pearson, Korea was a test of the United Nations and collective security. In Parliament, all three parties welcomed news that three RCN destroyers would sail at once from Esquimalt. Then they went home for the summer. In August, with UN forces pinned down in a narrow beachhead around Pusan, the cabinet ordered the RCAF's only long-range transport squadron to join the American air bridge to the Far East. More reluctantly, the government agreed to send an infantry brigade group. Parliament, assembled to end a rail strike, was told that the soldiers might be used for any UN operation, not merely Korea.

That summer, NATO (and Canadian) defence planners contemplated the meaning of Korea. MacArthur's campaign had absorbed every mobilized infantry division in the United States. If the Soviet Union had really planned to distract its major enemy, it had certainly succeeded. Canada's contribution of destroyers and an RCAF squadron merely redeployed regular forces. Ground troops might have been found from the Mobile Strike Force but not only would that leave Canada defenceless, the MSF was hundreds of men understrength. Instead, men for Korea would be recruited as a "Canadian Army Special Force." Put on the spot by colleagues, Claxton took a deep breath and promised that the men would be found without conscription. He was right—though barely. A mild recession since 1949 helped; so did the fact that thousands of veterans had not adjusted easily to civilian life. Some might not be ideal soldiers, either, but Claxton curtly insisted that recruiting standards be adjusted to find ten thousand men. The result—after releasing large numbers of unfit men who had been too hastily signed up — was an all-volunteer force with plenty of rough diamonds and battle experience. Though a mere 21 per cent of Quebeckers approved of the adventure, the province contributed 3,134 of the 10,587 men.

By November, the Canadian Brigade was at Fort Lewis, Washington, squeezing weapons out of depleted American stocks. In Korea, the war took a dramatic turn. As MacArthur's men approached the Yalu River, Chinese troops poured across. In bitter winter weather, the UN front collapsed. A Marine division barely fought its way out to the sea. Another U.S. army division was almost annihilated. By the end of February, the UN forces held a line forty miles south of Seoul. A fresh offensive drove the Chinese and North Koreans virtually to the 38th Parallel. When MacArthur hinted that he would extend the war to achieve his promised victory, President Truman finally intervened. MacArthur was fired, returned to a hero's welcome, and duly faded away.

In late 1950, when MacArthur's victory seemed imminent, a single Canadian battalion, the 2nd Princess Patricia's Canadian Light Infantry, left for Korea. By late February, when it entered the line with a mixed British-Australian brigade, disaster had followed disaster. The Patricia's were part of the counter-offensive to the 38th Parallel. On April 22, a Chinese attack shattered a South Korean division north of Kapyong. The Canadian battalion moved into a blocking position on the left of the Kapyong Valley. Beginning at dusk, Chinese assaults poured in on the Canadians. They were driven off, in part by calling artillery fire down on the PPCLI's own positions. Next day, the Chinese withdrew and the battalion had earned a U.S. presidential citation at the comparatively modest cost of ten dead.

The rest of the brigade arrived in the front line on May 25, 1951, eleven months after the war began. That summer, the Canadians seemed to fit naturally into a Commonwealth Division of British, Australian, and New Zealand troops. A mixture of British and American weapons and vehicles would have caused problems in mobile war but the cease-fire negotiations which began on July 10, 1951, tied the fighting to a narrow, unmoving front reminiscent of 1914-18. The war dragged on, marked by patrols, sporadic violent Chinese assaults, and, despite total American command of the air, an increasing volume of enemy artillery and mortar fire. After six months, the original Special Force was replaced by the first battalions of their regiments and, a year later, by the third battalions. In all, some 20,000 Canadians served in Korea, suffering 1,557 casualties, 312 of them fatal. Most losses were suffered by the later battalions of the brigade.

For most participants, Korea was a frustrating war. The country and its people attracted little affection from its alien defenders. Seventeen

United Nations members sent contingents but the Americans were in charge. Never before had the United States fought a major war without hope of a decisive conclusion and her allies feared that American frustration would push Washington to use the atomic bomb. When Truman admitted to a press conference, shortly after the Chinese entered the war, that such a use was "under active consideration," a shocked British prime minister rushed to see him. The Americans huffily insisted that, since the UN had given them responsibility for the war, the president could not be expected to consult his allies!

MacArthur's replacement by the less flamboyant General Matthew B. Ridgeway calmed fears that the septuagenarian general would launch a crusade into Asia. It did not make Americans conscientious about consulting allies. Late in the war, when Canadian troops were sent to quell a messy prison camp riot at Koje-do, Ottawa was distinctly annoyed. Not only had Canadians been trapped in a Communist propaganda victory, their government had not been consulted. On the whole, Canadians preferred to forget about Korea. The interminable ceasefire negotiations, punctuated by outbursts of fighting, served some inscrutable Communist purpose no one else could discern. A war waged far away by regular soldiers aroused little emotional response at home. If taxes rose and consumer spending was curbed, very few Canadians gave any evidence of suffering. Indeed the war and the accompanying United States rearmament banished the 1949-50 recession and ushered in renewed prosperity.

Not everyone was preoccupied with the Far East in 1950. Those who believed that Moscow orchestrated the entire Communist world insisted that Korea was merely foreplay in a clever global strategy. Soviet nuclear tests in 1949 showed that the American monopoly of the atomic bomb was over. The Chinese intervention in Korea, NATO planners now claimed, was a warning that the West had as little as eighteen months to prepare for a major war. General Dwight D. Eisenhower was summoned from the presidency of Columbia University to become Supreme Allied Commander. To give him tactical resources, NATO members promised an "Integrated Force," to be moved at his dictate. When Eisenhower landed in Ottawa on January 16, 1951, his message was blunt: help now would do more than help in a year's time. NATO's worried, defeatist European partners needed reassurance.

Ottawa responded. Remaining stocks of obsolete British equipment poured overseas. Mindful of the BCATP, the RCAF promised to train NATO jet pilots and navigators; soon its schools turned out 1,400 a year. Already it was taking delivery of the F-86 Sabre, built by Canadair in Montreal; it now asked for 350 more. The navy asked for ships and men to resume its escort and convoy role. On February 5, Claxton announced rearmament on a dramatic scale: 100 ships for the RCN, 40 squadrons for the RCAF, an infantry division for the army. The total cost, spread over three years, would be $5 billion. Immediately the army would recruit a brigade group, 10,000 men, for Europe and the RCAF would send 12 squadrons of F-86 fighters to form an air division.

Eisenhower could not complain of the speed of Canada's promise; fulfilment took a little longer. The army's 27th Brigade Group, recruited from reserve regiments, was in Europe by the end of 1951 but the full twelve RCAF squadrons were not ready until the summer of 1953. Canada promised one infantry division three months after fighting began and a second infantry division three months later. General Simonds, now the army's chief of staff, observed that, since no shipping was available, any Canadians planning to fight in Europe had better be there when the war began. He and Foulkes, now chairman of the Chiefs of Staff Committee, had other differences. Foulkes, who solemnly believed in the U.S. defence connection, wanted Canadians to be attached to the American forces in Europe. Simonds fervently disagreed: soldiers at least had more faith in the British. With a little help from External Affairs, still shocked by the American performance in Korea, Simonds won a compromise. The RCAF air division went to Europe under American auspices; the 27th Brigade joined the British Army of the Rhine.

Canadian rearmament involved more than the armed forces. The St. Laurent government, over CCF protests, equipped itself with an Emergency Powers Act. C. D. Howe regained much of his wartime authority over the economy through a Department of Defence Production with full power to "control and regulate the production, processing, distribution, acquisition, disposition or use of materials or the supply and use of services deemed essential for war purposes." The Conservatives, caught between fervour as Cold Warriors and hostility to sweeping government authority, could do little more than tease the all-powerful minister. To their delight and future profit, they discovered that an embattled Howe easily embarrassed his own party by his indignation.

Expansion revived Canada's most durable military problem, manpower. From 1950 to 1953, armed forces strength rose from 47,000 to 104,000. The RCN, desperate for skilled technicians, did not reach its recruiting target until the end of the 1950s. All three services had disbanded their women's components in 1945; the RCAF broke ground in peacetime by reviving its Women's Division. It also had to invest heavily in training its own technical personnel. As ever, the army faced the most acute problems. General Simonds spoke openly of compulsion; Claxton cut him off. Opinion polls showed that 37 per cent of Quebeckers favoured NATO but 83 per cent opposed any form of conscription. Unemployment, not anti-communism, brought *Canadiens* to the 25th Brigade in Korea; by 1952, with better times, the brigade was short 374 infantry, mostly from the Royal 22e Régiment. Simonds's belief that armies are built on *esprit de corps* led to revival of the historic red patch insignia of the 1st Canadian Division, transfer of historic regiments like the Queen's Own Rifles, the Black Watch, and the Fort Garry Horse from the militia, and creation of a Regiment of Canadian Guards, complete with scarlet tunics and bearskins. A more practical aid to morale, opposed by Simonds, was a decision to allow families to join Canadian service personnel in Europe. It was also evidence that the NATO commitment had become a continuing burden.

By 1953, the defence budget had reached $1,907 million, ten times the 1947 level. That year, well-publicized scandals, including allegations of "horses on the payroll," led to the appointment of an associate minister. True to Claxton's dream of service integration, his associate was merely assigned a list of interservice chores. Foulkes's appointment as chairman of the Chiefs of Staff Committee was another step toward integration. A new National Defence Act, passed on June 30, 1953, established a common code of discipline for the three services. Other legislation provided a single system of pay and benefits. When a weary Claxton retired in 1954, his goals of a single defence budget, tri-service personnel policies, a single system of military law, and a single Defence Research Board had been achieved. Not since Sir Frederick Borden had a peacetime defence minister accomplished so much.

Neither rearmament nor Claxton could end interservice rivalries. Over RCAF objections, the navy insisted on developing its own Fleet Air Arm. A bitter contest over research and development funds was not really resolved when the chairman of the Defence Research Board, as arbitrator, merely restored the previous share to each service. When Claxton's concern over the lack of French-speaking officers led to opening of the Collège Militaire Royal de Saint Jean in 1952, the RCAF balked at taking it over. The last thing it wanted was a bilingual institution. Both the air force and the navy remained resolutely English-speaking. Even the army could boast of little more than its acknowledgement of the French fact, the French-speaking Royal 22ᵉ Régiment and a squadron of the newly formed 8th Canadian Hussars.

Such disputes were hidden from the public. On the whole, Canadians accepted rearmament. Times were prosperous. In the universities and the CCF, the old liberal traditions of pacifism and isolationism survived but some of the scholarly heroes of an earlier and isolationist age, like Frank Underhill and Arthur Lower, had enlisted in the Cold War. Canada's few defence analysts were rarely critics. Defence, for those who accept its carnivorous assumptions, usually justifies its ends, whatever the arguments about the means. Canada, in the 1950s, could apparently afford both guns and butter and, indeed, there were influential economists who insisted that spending on guns helped put butter on Canadian tables.

Nuclear War and NORAD

Canadian officials had favoured NATO as an alternative to an unequal continental partnership and because Europe seemed the obvious place where a third world war would begin. Technology and politics altered both assumptions.

In 1952, Americans chose Dwight Eisenhower as president and elected the first Republican administration in a generation. True to its promise, the new regime secured an armistice in Korea on July 27, 1953, exchanged prisoners, and, within a year, had wound down the UN effort. More significant in the long run was a shift in emphasis from costly, unpopular conventional forces to more frightening but cheaper forms of nuclear deterrence. American taxpayers could welcome "a bigger bang for a buck"; draft-age youth and their parents certainly welcomed easier deferral.

Canada felt the consequences. When Soviet testing of a hydrogen bomb in 1953 and the annual May Day displays of air power demonstrated that nuclear deterrence was a two-power game, Canadians realized that they were in the direct line of fire. Instead of being relegated to the week-end flyers of its auxiliary squadrons, air defence became the RCAF's major priority. Certainly Canadians would not be allowed to take it less seriously than their American neighbours. In any case, expanding air defence had much the same appeal as the BCATP in 1939: it would be visible to Americans, popular with Canadians, easy on manpower, and, for those who saw warmongers behind every gun, explicitly defensive.

In 1947, with its eye on the future and with C. D. Howe's warm blessing, the RCAF had sponsored development of an air interceptor for Canada's special circumstances — long distances and sparse navigational aids. The CF-100, with the benefit of two Canadian-designed Orenda engines and a second crew member, would be built by A. V. Roe at Malton. In 1951, Brooke Claxton announced nine new air defence squadrons equipped with the new planes, nine radar stations, and a civilian ground observer corps to spot incoming aircraft. By 1954, Canada's few radar installations had become a Pinetree Line of thirty stations, straggling along the 49th Parallel at a price of $450 million. Canada paid a third of the cost and split personnel and operation expenses with the United States. To gain more warning from faster Soviet bombers, a Mid-Canada Line of electronic scanning devices was begun along the 55th Parallel early in 1955. Already American scientists had persuaded Washington of the need for an Arctic line of radar posts. Since Claxton had accepted full Canadian responsibility for the Mid-Canada Line, American taxpayers bore the enormous cost of a Distant Early Warning Line. A further Canadian reward for the DEW line was belated official American acceptance of Canada's Arctic claims.

Three radar lines plus offshore ships and aircraft might detect invading bombers; only other aircraft could identify and, if necessary, destroy them. By 1956, the CF-100 was too slow to catch Soviet jet bombers; at best a radar controller could vector the fighter on the bomber flight path, giving the pilot a single chance to sight and destroy the target. The real answer would be the CF-105 Arrow, a supersonic successor to the CF-100, with a phenomenal fire-control system. RCAF officers grew rapturous about its potential. Others did not. The aircraft industry, grumbled General Simonds, seemed to have great difficulty in estimating its costs. The admirals kept quiet: the navy's own building programme also proved costly and troublesome before the seventh Canadian-built destroyer escort was delivered in 1957. The army, as Cinderella service, could afford to be jealous of billions poured into aircraft, radar, and warships.

The CF-105 surpassed any aircraft Canada had ever built in both its potential and its cost. In fact, the projected plane represented a changing mixture of American and Canadian engines, weapons, and guidance systems. Each cancelled missile or abandoned fire-control system demanded a costly redesign of the airframe. By 1955, even C. D. Howe was worried: "I can say now," he bluntly warned the House of Commons, "that we have started a programme of development that gives me the shudders." The RCAF cut its orders from four hundred to one hundred aircraft. Frantic sales efforts produced no foreign buyers. Price estimates fluctuated according to the case anyone wanted to make but, by 1957 values, they were enormous. A single Arrow would cost $2.5 to $6 million or even as much as $12.5 million if each plane bore its full share of all aborted development costs.

The CF-105 was only one part of an up-to-date air defence. A supersonic battle would require complex, continent-wide communications and a computer-like mechanism to absorb data and spit out directions to fighters, anti-aircraft missiles, and civil defence authorities. After France wrecked NATO's air defence arrangements by insisting on air sovereignty, Washington insisted bluntly that U.S. security would depend on a separate, bilateral North American Air Defence Command. In February 1957, the Liberal government debated the arrangement, sensed trouble from ardent nationalists, and deferred a decision until after a June election.

Air defence hardly seemed a political issue; another military excursion certainly was. By 1956, Canadians had acquired considerable military experience as truce supervisors in Kashmir, in Vietnam, Laos, and Cambodia with the International Control Commission, and in the UN Truce Supervisory Organization which kept a shaky peace between Israel and her Arab neighbours. On October 29, 1956, a much-provoked Israel abandoned the truce and sent her forces deep into Egyptian territory. By pre-arrangement, France and Britain joined the war. When the Egyptian government failed to collapse, as the British had confidently expected, the U.S.S.R. threatened to flatten London and Paris. As president of the UN Security Council, Lester Pearson's moment came. A UN force, he suggested, would separate the warring parties. Canada's contribution, the Queen's Own Rifles, left Calgary for Halifax. Then there was a hitch. General E. L. M. Burns, the Canadian who served as the UN's chief of staff, was bluntly informed that Egyptians would not welcome soldiers of the Queen. Burns discreetly informed Ottawa that his real need was for competent administrative troops. In

due course HMCS *Magnificent* left for Egypt laden with vehicles, equipment, supplies, and most of a thousand-man contingent from the supporting arms and services. The Queen's Own went back to Calgary.

Pearson's initiative won him a Nobel peace prize. The armed forces
had found a new role as peacekeepers. Many Canadians were pleased
to be useful. Others were furious that Britain's cause had not only
been ignored but disparaged. Surely that was only a small grievance,
and few doubted that Liberals would go on running the country after
the election of June 10, 1957. Instead, Canadians awoke to the prospect of a Progressive Conservative government, a new prime minister
in John George Diefenbaker, and the mild exhilaration of the unexpected. The Liberals chose Pearson as their new leader, defied the new
government and, on March 31, 1958, suffered ignominious defeat. After a second election, Diefenbaker's 208 seats gave him the largest majority in Canadian history.

The new prime minister's military career in the CEF had been respectable but very brief. He had expertise enough in the Tory defence critic
and new minister of national defence, Major-General George Pearkes,
Victoria Cross winner and participant in the 1944 conscription crisis.
Without bothering officials or colleagues, the pair of them had promptly
signed the NORAD agreement. General Foulkes, for one, would have
liked to explain the details to the new government. The responsible
official from External Affairs, Jules Léger, let the matter pass. By his
unwitting consent, Diefenbaker had approved a tightly centralized
defence system. At Colorado Springs, the NORAD commander (or his
Canadian deputy) could order Canadian and American forces into action. Air warfare technology hardly allowed for prolonged reflection
but only when he faced Liberal critics in Parliament did Diefenbaker
realize the full implications. If politicians such as Robert Borden and
Mackenzie King had struggled for Canada's right to control its destiny,
Diefenbaker had unwittingly signed away his country's control of when
it would declare war.

The CF-105 was another problem the Liberals had gratefully deferred.
On October 4, 1958, the day the first Arrow prototype rolled from its
Malton hanger, a Soviet missile carried Sputnik I into orbit. Suddenly
the U.S.S.R. had registered a commanding lead in the new technology
of intercontinental ballistic missiles. Would manned bombers and fighters like the Arrow become obsolete? Bewildered by competing advice, complex technology, soaring costs, and endless imponderables,

the Diefenbaker cabinet simply gave itself a six-month delay. The Arrow programme wandered on while defence officials spoke vaguely of new missile threats and equipment to meet them. On February 20, 1959, it was all over. In minutes, Avro, builder of the Arrows, fired fourteen thousand employees. For reasons as yet unfathomed, the three prototypes and all pre-production models of the aircraft were systematically demolished. As though fatally condemned to prevaricate, Diefenbaker and Pearkes insisted that the Arrow was obsolete in the missile age, that it would be replaced by the Bomarc missile (a weapon designed for use exclusively against manned bombers!). The truth, as Pearkes later confessed, was that Canada simply could not afford an $8 million fighter. Even with a hundred Arrows in service, most of Canada's air would be defended by the U.S. Air Force. The Arrow's passionate defenders seldom deal with the whole problem. Even if the airframe was a marvel, embodying features no one else has ever adopted, its Iroquois engine was far from tested and its avionics and weapons system were still dreams. The Arrow did not exist as a fighter without them and both would have added to the cost and delays.

The Arrow cancellation was the right choice made the wrong way. The Arrow was born in strategic confusion, conceived by service commanders preoccupied with narrow interests, fostered by politicians who felt no need to penetrate the hard core of defence issues. Excluded from serious information while in opposition, Diefenbaker and Pearkes had neither the time nor the will to become fully informed once in power. Concerned about deficits and unemployment, the new government concluded that the CF-105 was too costly for a country in trouble. What was wrong was the savage suddenness with which the project was ended, the result, it would seem, of the personality of the prime minister and of AVRO's president, Crawford Gordon. Later, George Grant would celebrate Diefenbaker as the last hope for Canada's independence. In power, he had taken one hard look at the costs of technological independence, quailed, and fled.

Canada and his government began to pay the price. Eager to help a troubled ally, the United States approved a formal Defence Production Sharing Program. The initial advantages flowed north. Between 1959 and 1969, Canada's favourable balance of defence trade reached over half a billion dollars. Defence industries, developed by Howe, became branch plants for advanced American technology, doing an average business of $600 million a year in the 1960s. In return, Canada would import its major defence items from the United States.

One of those systems was the Bomarc. Conceived by scientists at the University of Michigan and fostered by the powerful Boeing Corporation, the Bomarc owed its survival in large measure to Canadian support. Like most experiments, it was a failure. Only Canadian interest and Boeing's powerful political lobbying allowed a second try — a Bomarc-B with solid fuel and a nuclear warhead. To the end, Diefenbaker kept insisting that the Bomarc had non-nuclear warheads. Canada also needed manned fighters. Whatever the prime minister might tell Parliament, only a human pilot could determine whether a radar blip meant World War III and not a tight formation of geese or an errant airliner. The Americans kindly offered sixty-six aging F-101 Voodoos, already relegated to their Air National Guard. After complicated arrangements to swap Canadian-made cargo planes for the fighters broke down, Canada paid for the Voodoos by taking over American-manned stations on the Pinetree Line.

Between them, the Voodoo and the Bomarc represented a humiliation not even Diefenbaker's talent for bluster could hide. In return for the Arrow, Canada had sixty-six second-rank fighters and a collection of dubious anti-bomber missiles. The much trumpeted missile threat remained unanswered and perhaps unanswerable.

Diefenbaker's confusion was widely shared. In the 1950s, defence had become both terrifyingly simple in its stark potential and incredibly complex in its strategic permutations. Mathematicians and social scientists joined admirals and generals in designing strategy. Americans christened their strategic approach the "New Look" and the chairman of the U.S. Joint Chiefs of Staff, Admiral Charles Radford, boasted that his wartime motto had been "kill the bastards scientifically." Canada's only major contribution to the strategic debate came, typically, from the Defence Research Board. Dr. R. J. Sutherland's "first strike, second strike" concept, claimed an admirer, was as vital for nuclear warfare as Newton's laws were for physics. Victory, the scientist argued, was no longer a matter of who made the first strike but how much retaliatory strength survived for the victim to strike back.

Sutherland's principle gave a new dimension to air defence and to saving the civilian population. If the bombers and missiles of the U.S. counterforce were going to survive a Soviet first strike, would that first strike ever be launched? When intelligence experts noted the enormous Soviet resources devoted to civil defence, pressure built rapidly to match the effort. Millions would certainly die in a nuclear exchange, but millions more could be saved if food, water, and medical supplies were stockpiled and if people were sheltered from radiation. All at once it was governments, not Communist sympathisers or the small community of pacifists, who were bent on making people's flesh creep at potential nuclear horrors — all in the name of justifying costly and inconvenient precautions.

In Canada, civil defence had long bordered on the absurd. After 1948 the coordinator, Major-General Frank Worthington, did his crusading best but few cared. For years, the burden rested lightly on the Department of Health and Welfare. Now it returned to National Defence, to be dumped firmly on the militia. By the early 1950s, the proud role of the reserve army had evaporated. In the Third World War, experts insisted, only forces-in-being would matter. In 1953, units of the Reserve Army mustered a mere fifth of their authorized strength; only fifteen thousand men and women went to camp. Renamed the Canadian Army (Militia) with brave talk of operational roles and modern equipment, the new nuclear reality intervened. Over protests from General Simonds and other senior army officers, Claxton's successor, Ralph Campney, decided in 1956 that the militia would be retrained for civil defence. The generals succeeded in burying the news for a year. It was General Pearkes who served as a reluctant messenger. After 1957, summer camps ended. On May 28, 1959, militia and regular units across Canada began organizing as mobile support columns assigned to target areas. As the generals had foreseen, members abandoned the militia in droves.

As their share in North American air defence, citizens were urged to build and stock fall-out shelters. Newspaper articles explained the significance of heat, light, and blast in a nuclear explosion; radiation was slightly neglected. Teachers trained their students to crawl under desks and to look away from windows at the moment of detonation. The CBC began broadcasting around the clock to be available as anchor of a National Survival network. In theory, a prepared population would not only be more likely to survive but would also face the prospect of war with greater fortitude. Reality was different. Soviet propagandists could hardly have devised a more ingenious way to alarm and divide a population. The absurdity and amateurism of the precautions played counterpoint to the horror of the threat. In Britain, the United States, and Canada, peace movements and demands for unilateral nuclear disarmament were not new but the National Survival programme helped give the Canadian movement new life and a pile of officially approved evidence. In 1960, the Liberal Party proclaimed its uncompromising opposition to Canada's acquisition of any nuclear weapons. The CCF, now becoming the New Democratic Party, fervently endorsed nuclear disarmament. Cards, letters, and petitions poured in on the prime minister.

John Diefenbaker had been no faint-hearted Cold Warrior. In an election speech to an audience of Canadians of East-European origins, he had even pledged to roll back the Iron Curtain. In power, his stridency was muted. Defence spending fell from $1.8 billion in 1957 to $1.5 billion in 1960. During a world tour, Diefenbaker sought to retain the Third World friendships established by his Liberal predecessors. By June 1959, his old friend and ally, Howard Green, had acquired the External Affairs portfolio. A CEF veteran better known as a crusader against oriental immigration, Green gradually emerged in an unexpected guise as an idealist, fervently opposed to nuclear weapons and suspicious of their fiercest wielder, the United States. They were emotions shared, in some measure, by his able deputy and fellow British Columbian, Norman Robertson.

On October 10, 1960, Pearkes withdrew gracefully to be lieutenant governor of British Columbia. His successor, a former Calgary teacher and artillery officer, Douglas Harkness, set out to fight his department's battles in cabinet. His task was almost impossible. Green's influence was in the ascendant. After his one tough decision over the Arrow, Diefenbaker seemed to have retreated into chronic indecision, camouflaged by strident denunciations of enemies, public and conspiratorial. Only one policy line was clear: Canada would not acquire nuclear weapons.

The problem was that, since 1957, she had acquired little else. The sole alternative to a nuclear warhead for the Bomarc was a load of sand. Voodoo fighters could fly but to hit the enemy they needed nuclear-tipped rockets. So did the F-104 Starfighter, a light tactical bomber built by licence in Montreal for RCAF squadrons in Europe. So did Honest John missiles purchased for the army. Nuclear opponents in the cabinet had a further argument: at Congressional insistence, Americans must guard and control any nuclear devices. Their presence, critics claimed, would infringe on Canadian sovereignty. The fact that such contingents could already be found at most Canadian bases made no difference. Politicians reading their mail or glimpsing knots of nuclear protesters did not need rational arguments.

As the Cold War edged into its greatest crisis, Canada's newest weapons sat helpless on the ground.

Integration and Unification

On October 25, 1962, American networks broke into programming to switch audiences to the White House. John Kennedy had decided to confront the Kremlin. Barely a hundred miles from the American mainland, the Soviet Union had established missile bases in Cuba. Until the bases were removed, Kennedy warned in his hard New England accent, Cuba would be blockaded. At once NORAD's commander ordered DEFCON 3, a state of alert just prior to actual war. Americans, their allies, the whole world waited breathlessly. Then, melodramatically, the Soviet ships carrying missiles to the Caribbean altered course. Aerial reconnaissance showed missile sites being dismantled. The other fellow had blinked. President Kennedy, for many, became the last American hero.

For Canadians, the Cuban missile crisis gave no pleasure. Like other major allies, Canada had received a sudden emissary, bearing a package of fuzzy air photos, but from a northern neighbour much more was expected: instant readiness. Her Bomarcs and Voodoos covered not just Montreal and Toronto but the heavily populated northeastern United States. In the crisis, Diefenbaker and his cabinet had spent two days debating the alert, furious that Canadian life and death should be determined by a foreign president, still seeking vengeance for his humiliation at the Bay of Pigs a year before.

Unofficially, Canada had been a more dependable ally than the prime minister knew. Without authority, Douglas Harkness ordered an alert, though leaves were not cancelled. Within thirty-six hours, RCN destroyers had relieved American warships needed for the Cuba blockade. Yet Diefenbaker was confident that Canadians shared his views. For two years his daily mail had run heavily in favour of nuclear disarmament. In 1961, James M. Minifie, widely known as the CBC's Washington correspondent, published *Peacemaker or Powdermonkey*, an eloquent argument for Canadian neutralism. When the NDP was formed in 1961, its convention was awash in nuclear disarmament buttons. In the 1962 election, defence could hardly be an issue because Tories, Liberals, and the NDP were indistinguishable.

The Cuban missile crisis changed everything. Nationalists might rejoice that Diefenbaker asserted Canada's independence; nuclear disarmers argued that the confrontation proved their fears. Far more Canadians, indifferent to the complexities of defence and foreign policy, felt deep disquiet. Even before the crisis, polls found a surprising shift in favour of arming the nuclear weapons Canada had acquired. After the crisis, a torrent of media criticism made more Canadians aware of the government's confusion and evasions. On January 4, 1963, NATO's retiring supreme commander, General Lauris Norstad, stopped in Ottawa and made it undiplomatically clear that, whatever the prime minister might say, Canada had indeed committed itself to a nuclear role in the alliance. Six days later, after a visit to Washington, the Liberal leader exploded his own bomb. At a nomination meeting in Scarborough, Lester Pearson proclaimed that a Liberal government would honour Canada's nuclear commitments but would then negotiate a non-nuclear role. Despite stinging abuse from peace activists, Pearson now knew that he commanded public opinion. The Tories would be split.

John Diefenbaker knew his danger. In a virtuoso performance on January 25, he denied the nuclear commitment, insisted it would be settled at a forthcoming NATO meeting, and excoriated his opponents. Five days later, in a move without precedent, the United States government delivered itself of a "clarification." The Bomarc-B had never had a non-nuclear warhead; the Voodoo could not perform its role without nuclear missiles; Canada's choice of weapon systems confirmed her nuclear role in NATO. Twice in a month Americans had called Diefenbaker a liar. It was tactless, insensitive, and absolutely true. No one knew it better than Douglas Harkness. On Sunday, February 3, he resigned. Two days later, even New Democrats and Quebec *Créditistes*, who might well have favoured Diefenbaker's defence position, joined the rush to defeat him.

The election of April 8, 1963, should have been about defence. The NDP insisted a decision about nuclear weapons was at stake. Diefenbaker promised an unequivocal statement on arms policy. It never appeared. Instead, the prime minister set out to prove that a politician is rarely more free from tough questions than in the give and take of an election. Wattles quivering, forefinger shaking, Diefenbaker rallied his party. Some saw him as a regional messiah; others as a deceitful windbag.

The latter were fewer than they imagined. The Liberals, certain of victory, emerged only narrowly on top, with a minority of seats. Bleary-eyed on the morrow of a flawed victory, Pearson and his associates could not have believed that they would run Canada for a full generation.

Whatever the national outcome, service voters had shown a decided preference. Pro-Liberal in every election since 1945, in 1963 they voted seventy per cent Liberal, twenty per cent Tory, and a mere four per cent for the NDP. They expected much. They forgot that Liberals would also have scrapped the Arrow, joined NORAD, and trimmed defence spending during the 1957-60 recession. Canada's military wanted Liberal stability because so much else had changed. In 1951, Canada's commitment to NATO's "integrated Force" gave confidence to a demoralized Europe; by 1963, NATO's European partners appeared to be thriving economically and well able to defend themselves. Canada, herself, faced increasing commercial rivalry from once-shattered former enemies. NORAD, designed for bomber threats, would have to change out of recognition to face intercontinental ballistic missiles — if that was even feasible.

Liberals cheerfully blamed Tories for confused defence policy but when ministers look bad, departments share the responsibility.

Certainly there was much wrong in the defence department. A report on government organization, headed by J. Grant Glassco, was unflattering. In the Department of National Defence, more than two hundred interservice committees had become bottlenecks. Administrative confusion had added waste and delays to development programmes ranging from the CF-105 to the army's modest effort to develop its own armoured personnel carrier. Triplication of pay, recruiting, public relations, and intelligence systems added to costs, not to efficiency. Each of the three service chiefs had independent access to the minister but neither he nor the chairman of the Chiefs of Staff Committee had any way of evaluating each service's demands. One result, Glassco noted, was a shift in defence spending from new equipment to wages. In 1954, capital spending took 42.4 per cent of the budget; by 1962, the share was 18.9 per cent and falling.

The Liberals had promised a searching review of Canadian defence policy, usually a political code-word for wait and see. That was not the intention of Pearson's choice to head national defence. Paul Hellyer was a forty-year-old Toronto contractor, an MP since 1949, an aggressive man with few of the gentler political graces. In opposition, Hellyer had done more than anyone to switch Pearson from his anti-nuclear stand by his gloomy report on armed forces morale. For most politicians, National Defence was a graveyard. Even Brooke Claxton, ablest of the post-war ministers, had retired exhausted and besmirched. The 1960s would be tough, with the Liberals pledged to spend no more on defence and opposition parties clamouring for less. Yet Hellyer was ambitious. Somehow, his time at National Defence must help him be an obvious choice to succeed Lester Pearson. His achievements must become a byword not just in Canada but the world.

The idea of integration of the armed forces was as old as 1922. Liberal ministers favoured it as the one military reform that appealed to their anti-military colleagues. By 1963, medical, dental, legal, and chaplains' services had been integrated though the reforms produced more senior officers than visible economies. The Glassco Report was a ready-made blueprint for more. Hellyer was not satisfied. Integration from the bottom had failed; he would impose it from the top, with a single Chief of Defence Staff and four functional branches, instead of three powerful services. Nor could Hellyer stop there. As his diary shows, service resistance propelled him further. Even without their heads, the tiresome service rivalries and inefficiencies would persist. Few Canadians outside the small military community would acclaim a head-quarters reshuffling. Even Hellyer may have considered a single-uniform armed force an ultimate step; it soon became an integral part of his personal programme.

The promised Liberal defence review appeared as a white paper in March 1964. Since the previous June, a special parliamentary committee had been thrashing about in defence matters. The white paper was Hellyer's alone. It was long, sometimes vague, and rarely original. Canada's defence problems had not altered with a new government nor would they change much in the ensuing generation. With a respectful nod to the new prime minister, peacekeeping was given top priority in service roles, but Canada would remain in NATO and NORAD and continental defence would rank lowest in importance. The navy would hunt submarines; Bomarcs, Voodoos, Starfighters, and Honest Johns would all have their nuclear tips. Adjectives like "flexible," "mobile," and "imaginative" could not make dreary and frightening realities sparkle. Outside commentators barely noticed Hellyer's promise of a "single unified defence force."

Senior officers, of course, did notice and they were dismayed. This was not what they had expected from Liberals. Each service had its shopping list: tanks and armoured personnel carriers for the army; replacements for the RCN's aging destroyers; a new long-range patrol plane to replace the RCAF's venerable Argus. Hellyer agreed — but the services themselves must meet equipment costs by drastic reorganization. At the special parliamentary committee, General Simonds had suggested that Canada needed a tri-service force like the United States Marines. The image was clever but misleading: marines were in fact highly specialized. To Hellyer, the concept remained persuasive. In a modern world, technology had wiped out distinctions between land, sea, and air war. Three separate services also created practical problems. In 1960, when qualified signallers were needed for UN peacekeeping in the Congo, RCN and RCAF technicians could not be switched to an army task. Making trades and specialties interchangeable would produce more varied careers and more promotion opportunities.

Hellyer moved fast. A month after his white paper appeared, legislation to reorganize National Defence Headquarters was introduced to Parliament. Three months later, while the media focused on flag debates and Liberal scandals, Hellyer's first reform became law on July 7, 1964. Next, the minister turned to regional command structures. The army insisted on geographic commands but Hellyer accepted the RCAF arguments for a functional structure: Maritime Command for the navy and the RCAF's anti-submarine squadrons; Mobile Command for the army's brigade groups and RCAF ground support squadrons; Training Command; Material Command; and Air Transport Command. Communications Command was added later while Canadian forces in Europe would report directly to Ottawa. The new commands were announced on June 7, 1965, and on May 1, 1966, the former camps, stations, and land-based "ships" of the navy became thirty-nine Canadian Forces Bases.

Senior officers expected breathing space to establish jurisdictions and adjust to the most drastic organizational changes in their experience. Hellyer had no such intention. Years before, as an aircrew trainee, he had been dumped into the army as part of the RCAF solution to the 1944 manpower crisis. The memory rankled. So did opposition from senior officers. Hellyer's self-esteem rose. "He has earned the nation's gratitude and its continued support," intoned the Winnipeg *Free Press* in a New Year's Day salute for 1966. The Vancouver *Sun* had even more useful words for a future leadership contender: "young Mr. Hellyer seems to be quietly pulling off what may in time be recorded as this government's greatest achievement." Experts from abroad demanded details of his reforms. The prime minister was delighted. Unification would proceed in the teeth of opposition from the high command.

Whatever their view of integration, few senior officers accepted Hellyer's major premises for unification. In peace and war, Canada's armed forces had been fated to work separately save when the RCN and RCAF co-operated in anti-submarine warfare. The 1964 white paper suggested no new integrated roles. Unification would certainly "Canadianize" the forces by eliminating British-style service uniforms. Instead, the new green uniforms resembled those of the U.S. Air Force while the rank badges would be recognizable to Canada's new imperial protector. The only serious issue was whether a single service could meet the challenges of three different fighting environments of sea, land, and air. The Glassco Commission had concluded that unification would not work. In his own argument, General Simonds illustrated how each environment influenced a junior officer's fundamental decision to fight or flee. An air force pilot decided for himself whether to attack. For a junior naval officer, the decision was made by his captain. An infantry lieutenant had to persuade not only himself but a couple of dozen others to share the hazards. There was a logical reason for some services to stress technical or professional skill while others emphasized personal leadership. Common uniforms and ranks might be neat but they blurred real differences of role.*

To Hellyer and perhaps most Canadians, such arguments were vague or nostalgic. Opposition struck the minister and his chief advisor, Bill Lee, as tantamount to mutiny. Service tradition dictated that those who opposed a policy should resign. Two generals did so in 1964; they were followed in the summer of 1966 by seven admirals. They were joined by Hellyer's first Chief of Defence Staff, Air Chief Marshal Frank Miller. As a protest movement, resignations utterly failed. Ambitious subordinates quickly filled the vacancies. Hellyer's staff reminded jour-

---

*A key factor in imposing a common uniform was insistence by branches like Communications and Logistics, which really would be unified, that they wear the same colours as members of the combatant branches. Such men and women composed half of armed forces personnel.

nalists that the critics enjoyed generous service pensions. Admirals, generals, and air marshals inspired more cartoons than editorials. Canadians had been accused of indifference to military affairs; they now proved the point. Nor did all senior officers agree with the critics. Miller's successor, General Jean-Victor Allard, was shrewdly chosen. A fighting soldier in Italy and Korea, Allard treated unification as an order and an opportunity. A chronic optimist, he found virtues other officers may have overlooked; as a *Canadien*, he respected the fading British traditions, but unification was a unique opportunity to promote the French fact.

In Centennial Year, all Canadians were urged to achieve a special project; Hellyer's task for 1967 was predetermined. Whatever else fell apart that year, a commentator noted, it would not be the armed forces. Yet the Conservatives had finally found an issue. The ambitious Hellyer was treated to delays, criticism, and a filibuster on third reading. The minister's temper visibly frayed. Pearson's resignation could not be long delayed and Hellyer wanted a less controversial department before the succession. Finally, with the help of closure of Parliament, on April 25, 1967, a weary House of Commons passed the Canadian Forces Reorganization Bill. That summer, the three services celebrated their vanishing traditions in a giant Centennial tattoo. Even many unmilitary Canadians found it the most exciting spectacle of the year.

Throughout, Hellyer insisted, with good reason, that armed forces morale depended on equipment, not the colour of their uniforms. By the time he left the department in 1967, Hellyer could feel proud of his achievements. He had out-wrestled generals and admirals, devised a defence organization the rest of the world would surely copy, and stayed close to his budget ceiling of $1.5 billion a year. If the army still drove obsolete Centurion tanks, it had acquired armoured personnel carriers. Instead of the costly F-4 Phantom, Hellyer had insisted that a "global and mobile" armed force with peacekeeping chores could settle for the F-5 Freedom Fighter, a cheaper aircraft designed for Third World air forces which the Canadair plant at Montreal could build. Hellyer had abruptly cancelled navy plans for eight general-purpose frigates but he won approval to buy three submarines from Britain and to build four big "Tribal" class helicopter destroyers. He would have done more without inflation. A destroyer worth $20 million in 1960 cost $50 million by 1968.

Critics complained that the cost of two such destroyers would have paid for Canada's annual aid to India. Hellyer had annoyed the military without placating an anti-military and increasingly isolationist Canadian electorate. Only attrition in manpower, from 120,781 in 1963 to 110,000 in 1967, kept defence within budget. In NATO, Canada's air contribution dropped to six squadrons. Far from adding to equipment budgets, capital spending fell from $251 million in 1963-64 to only $212 million in 1966-67. Instead of cutting roles, as his ablest critic, the NDP's Andrew Brewin, had suggested in 1964, Hellyer had been compelled to add several hundred peacekeepers in Cyprus and assume a role in NATO's northern flank in Norway. As for the CF-5, it was militarily valueless before it left the assembly line.

In any case, for all Hellyer's efforts, Canadians were not deeply interested. In 1967, Walter Gordon, a cabinet colleague, wondered whether Canada even had any business belonging to NATO and NORAD. A welcoming echo came not only from the NDP but from Dalton Camp, president of the Progressive Conservative party. Canadians felt very safe.

The Trudeau Détente

On February 1, 1968, unification of the armed forces formally took effect. Few Canadians cared. The country wore a post-Centennial hangover. A mild recession and rising inflation underlined the vulnerability of a branch-plant economy. Civic moralists pondered the consequences of easy contraception and the drug culture. Those who thought of war looked to the distant, dirty struggle in Vietnam. The sight of American technology blasting a seemingly helpless Third World nation furnished texts in abundance to anti-Americans and the peace movement. Above all, Canadians worried about Quebec. The Centennial mood had been lifted by the glittering triumph of Expo 67; it had been shattered when Montrealers cheered Charles de Gaulle's cry of "*Vive le Québec libre.*"

Suddenly the resolution of every Canadian problem seemed bound up in the enigmatic personality of Pierre Elliott Trudeau. On April 6, 1968, Liberals had chosen a successor to Pearson. Hellyer, who had campaigned so tirelessly for the job, lasted to the third ballot. Trudeau, an MP only since 1965, was ahead from the start. By April 20, he was prime minister. On June 26, he headed the first majority Liberal government since 1957. The enigma remained. As a prank in wartime

Montreal, he had allegedly dressed in a "Nazi" uniform. In 1963 he had voted NDP in protest at Pearson's nuclear change of heart. Trudeau admired such military virtues as courage and fitness but he had Mackenzie King's distaste for military minds. He promised new leadership but tolerated cabinet mediocrities. He devised elaborate machinery for decision-making but remained endlessly indecisive.

Defence was a logical place for the new rational decision-making to start. Analysts like John Gellner had long complained that Ottawa made defence policy backwards, choosing weapons and then finding roles for them. The Trudeau system made no such elementary error. On April 3, 1969, underlining the new importance of his office, the prime minister issued Canada's defence priorities:

(a) the surveillance of our territory and coastline — i.e., the protection of our sovereignty;
(b) the defence of North America in co-operation with United States forces;
(c) the fulfilment of such NATO commitments as may be agreed upon;
(d) the performance of such international peacekeeping roles as we may from time to time assume.

Trudeau had turned the Hellyer priorities of 1964 upside down. Hellyer's lowest concern had been "providing for certain aspects of security and protection within Canada"; as "surveillance," it surged to the top. Peacekeeping dropped to the bottom while NATO and NORAD traded places. In May, Léo Cadieux, Hellyer's successor, went to Brussels to warn NATO leaders that Canada might be cutting its contribution. On June 23, he told Parliament that Canada would soon need only eighty to eighty-five thousand personnel for her defence roles. Three months later, NATO allies learned the meaning of Cadieux's visit. Canada's contingent of ten thousand men would be cut in half, leaving a weak combat group of twenty-eight hundred troops and three squadrons of obsolete Starfighters. The entire contingent would move to Lahr in south Germany, under American auspices. The last British link was broken. The navy's aircraft carrier, *Bonaventure*, fresh from a $12 million refit, would be scrapped. Five of the regular regiments added in the 1950s vanished from the active list. Reserve strength was cut from twenty-three thousand to nineteen thousand. Bases would close.

Once convinced that both shoes had fallen, the forces surveyed the damage and concluded that, without Cadieux, it would have been worse. By arguing that defence was its second biggest industry, Prince Edward Island saved its foggy airbase at Summerside. Other complaints were brushed aside. Defence cuts, the prime minister's office concluded, might even be popular. They did not add up to a policy. With a fifth less personnel, the Canadian forces had lost no role and gained a new one, surveillance. In 1970, Cadieux's successor, Donald Macdonald, explained that the forces' new priority would be guarding Canadian sovereignty and contributing to "the social and economic development of Canada." In that year, the forces opened their first northern headquarters at Yellowknife—with an establishment of thirty-five. While over-fishing and oil and gas exploration made Canadians conscious of their ocean frontiers, Maritime Command dwindled to ten thousand men, and its aging ships and aircraft were increasingly tied up by fuel restrictions and maintenance problems.

Macdonald's 1970 white paper, *Defence in the Seventies*, cautiously included internal security in the task of defending sovereignty. Memories of aid to the civil power had faded but Canadian television viewers were familiar with American soldiers, helmeted and armed, playing their role in the "long hot summers" of the 1960s. British troops had been dragged into the communal violence of Northern Ireland while French soldiers and paramilitary police had recaptured Paris's Left Bank in the violent May Days of 1968. Violence in the United States, Trudeau warned a Queen's University audience in 1969, could easily spill into Canada.

In fact, violence was quite indigenous. Mailbox bombings earlier in the decade had left one military explosives expert crippled for life. In 1969, after Montreal police went on strike, youths chanted revolutionary slogans as they attacked an English-owned bus company. As crowds looted downtown Montreal stores, troops rushed from Valcartier. A year later, on October 5, 1970, a group calling itself the Quebec Liberation Front kidnapped the British trade commissioner in Montreal. Five days later, another FLQ cell kidnapped the Quebec labour minister, Pierre Laporte. Artists, students, and connoisseurs of radical chic promptly lionized the kidnappers. Prominent critics of Robert Bourassa's provincial government met, debated the crisis, and offered themselves as a more competent and conciliatory administration.

Pierre Elliott Trudeau was not amused. On October 14, two days after Laporte was seized, he ordered troops to Ottawa to guard public buildings and prominent politicians. On October 15, at Trudeau's urging, Bourassa formally requisitioned aid to the civil power: battalions of the Royal 22e Régiment, posted just north of Montreal, responded at once. Next morning, at 4 A.M., "after consideration of all the facts and particularly letters received from the Prime Minister of Quebec and the authorities of the city of Montreal, reporting a state of apprehended insurrection," Trudeau invoked the War Measures Act.

It was unprecedented. On the basis of facts then and revealed later, it was unjustified. It was also a brilliant success. Shock was the best safeguard against bloodshed. Trudeau's target was not two frightened little bands of terrorists, one of which soon strangled its helpless victim: it was the affluent dilettantes of revolutionary violence, cheering on the anonymous heroes of the FLQ. The proclamation of the War Measures Act and the thousands of grim troops pouring into Montreal froze the cheers, dispersed the coffee-table revolutionaries, and left them frightened and isolated while the police rounded up suspects whose offence, if any, was dreaming of blood in the streets.

For the Canadian armed forces, the October crisis was an ambiguous experience. It was an exciting test of staff procedures, communications systems, and troops. Few had ever shared in operations of such magnitude. It was also fortunate that the troops could withdraw by November 12 without suffering or inflicting casualties. (One soldier died in an accidental shooting when he stumbled with his loaded weapon.) Thoughtful officers also knew that Trudeau's "Priority One," surveillance of our territory, now posed a greater danger than any other potential role. By proclaiming emergency powers, the prime minister had staked not only his own prestige but that of the armed forces on a satisfactory outcome. In 1972, when the government claimed that it would use the forces again, the Conservative defence critic, Michael Forrestal, offered a prudent warning: "the deliberate use of the military to enforce the will of one group of Canadians over the will of another group of Canadians is detrimental to the credibility of the armed forces." No party was willing to suggest an alternative.

The 1970 crisis had sent the predominantly English-speaking armed forces into a tense French-speaking milieu. Unification had not altered the fact that the working language of Canada's defenders was English. Indeed, the situation had hardly changed in a century. The dominance of English, consciously affirmed in the navy and air force and guaranteed by weight of numbers in the army, had been powerfully reinforced by professional links with the British and then the American armed services. By the 1960s, it seemed clear that *Québécois* would either share fully in the federal state or establish their own sovereign power. In 1965, Trudeau had come to Ottawa to prove that French Canadians could achieve equality; in 1968 he was in a powerful position to make his expectation come true. All-party support for an Official Languages Act marked a splendid theoretical beginning; the armed forces were a logical place to make a practical start.

The forces illustrated most of the problems French Canadians experienced with federal institutions. Few enlisted; even fewer reached high rank. There were obvious reasons. An armed forces career led inevitably to service in unfamiliar and sometimes inhospitable surroundings outside Quebec. Technical training and experience, obtained in the armed forces, commanded a high premium in civil life, but outside the Royal 22e Régiment and some other units and bases in Quebec, French-speaking personnel faced a career of working in English.

There were other ways to make the Canadian forces bilingual but it was almost inevitable that the Royal 22e Régiment provided the model. In 1968, in the wake of the Trudeau victory, Léo Cadieux announced new French language units: HMCS *Ottawa*, a destroyer-escort at Halifax, was the first; a CF-5 squadron at Bagotville was another. At Valcartier, the *5e Groupement de combat* was formed. To provide it with armour and artillery, the *12e Régiment blindé* and a light artillery regiment were created while smaller units guaranteed representation for every branch of the unified armed forces. A "Francotrain" programme created a French-language school for recruits and for many of the three hundred specialist skills. When the final report of the Royal Commission of Bilingualism and Biculturalism demanded more, fresh policies helped establish French-speaking units outside Quebec, enforced bilingualism as a qualification for high command, and imposed a twenty-eight per cent proportional representation in recruiting and promotion.

From being a virtual anglophone monopoly, the Canadian armed forces came, for a time, to resemble the country they served: two mutually resentful solitudes. Despite Cadieux's hopeful promise that he would not "divide the force on a unilingual or geographical basis," he had done so. A defence budget too frail to provide new aircraft or even trucks bore the heavy costs of duplicate training facilities and translated technical manuals. Members of disbanded units grumbled when French-speaking regiments took their place. English-speaking officers, passed over for promotion, grumbled about favouritism. Yet the resentments faded with time. A century of experience had proved that bilingualism by evolution did not happen. In two world wars, unilingualism in the forces had weakened the country they served. Enforced bilingualism was necessary. It was also a success. A generation later, as Jocelyn Coulon would report, Canada's armed forces were a better reflection of Canada's linguistic duality than almost any other federal institution. Few any longer claimed that discipline or efficiency had been sacrificed. If there were victims, they were English-speaking Canadians from regions where knowledge of French was a rare accomplishment.

Of course bilingualism, "Priority One," and, for that matter, unification were political policies that had very little to do with the fighting capacity of the armed forces. Thirty years after 1945, war had faded from experience, even among senior officers. *Defence in the Seventies* had hinted at a conflict between the military and civil functions of the forces. In fact, the conflict went deeper. In the new, rational decision-making structure which Trudeau and the all-powerful Privy Council Office introduced, generals and admirals were anachronisms, easily blamed for decisions they had often opposed. If most of the CF-5 fighters had to be put in storage, it was easier to blame generals than Hellyer for insisting on an unsuitable aircraft. Scrapping the *Bonaventure* after its costly refit, journalists were led to believe, was the admirals' fault. So were costly overruns on the navy's new gas turbine-powered destroyers. The answer, for the prime minister's staff, was "civilianization": in 1972, service heads of branches at National Defence Headquarters were re-titled assistant deputy ministers and, in some cases, replaced by civil servants. Management, insisted the graduates of the Havard Business School who now floated through the Ottawa firmament, was a universal skill. In the prevailing mood, military leadership and perhaps even war itself, were obsolete.

Certainly the 1969 defence priorities reflected the traditions of Laurier and Mackenzie King, not the active internationalism of Lester Pearson. Even peacekeeping had been overcome by national disillusionment, beginning with the Congo in 1960, when Canadians in UN service had been beaten and threatened. In Cyprus, Canadians remained because they had become part of the island economy, not because they kept peace or could deter a Turkish invasion. In 1967, Egypt offended national *amour propre* by expelling Canadian peacekeepers only days before its own catastrophic defeat by Israel. Only reluctantly did Canadians go again six years later. In 1973, American pressure persuaded Ottawa to send two hundred and fifty officers to help oversee U.S. withdrawal from the Vietnam War. Canadians had enough experience to know the circumstances were hopeless; a hundred and twenty days and one death later, they came home.

Canada was no longer a helpful fixer. Under Pierre Elliott Trudeau, she pursued her logical self-interest. In 1969, the prime minister's picked team of policy analysts had unilaterally halved Canada's NATO contingent at the same time that they proclaimed that the country needed closer commercial relations with western Europe. Belatedly, the experts discovered that defence, diplomacy, and commerce might be linked. In 1976, after years of embarrassing indecision, Ottawa finally purchased 128 German-made Leopard tanks for the NATO combat group. The order sweetened European trade negotiations and helped secure Canada a seat at the European Security Conference at Helsinki. It hardly seemed to matter that the tanks themselves were already outdated by German, British, and Soviet standards.

The embarrassing weakness of Maritime Command, compelled to call on reservists and even sea cadets to man some of its warships, worried Ottawa only years after Canada had registered its claim to 5,800,000 square miles of ocean bed. The government's response was a woefully belated building programme of six patrol frigates, to be delivered late in the 1980s, and the purchase of eighteen Lockheed Aurora patrol planes for $1,042 million. The biggest defence contract of the decade, $4 billion for 137 fighters, followed years of political and commercial struggle for the aircraft to replace the worn-out Voodoos and Starfighters. After four of the original six contractors were eliminated because their aircraft cost too much, the winner was the best of two dubious choices, the McDonnell-Douglas F-18D Hornet. The loser, General Dynamics, enlivened the 1980 Quebec referendum campaign by claiming Ottawa had favoured an Ontario branch plant. (An early loser, the Panavia Toronado, had initially involved Canada with Britain, Germany, and Italy, and its specifications were closest to Canadian needs. The Trudeau decision to downplay NATO ended Canadian participation, leaving only American choices.)

Paul Hellyer had promised that integration of National Defence Headquarters would introduce an age of efficiency, co-operation, and economy. Experience had done little to prove him right. In 1972, Lockheed offered twenty-three long-range patrol aircraft for $300 million: by 1978 the price had tripled for five fewer planes. Other equipment purchases were as contorted by political and business pressures. Civilianization, two conflicting white papers, and a grandly titled

"Defence Structure Review" in 1974 had not helped. Perhaps the real problem lay less with the Department of National Defence and its constant procession of ministers than with the concentration of power under a man more brilliant in debate than in decision-making. Ministers could extract promises of seven and even twelve per cent additions to defence budgets but "freezes," "squeezes," and "cutbacks" regularly delayed purchasing decisions and added to their costs.

The world was not as comfortable for Canadians in the 1970s as it had been in the 1960s, but their government did not choose to relieve (or augment) their anxieties by defence spending. In a decade, national defence drew seven ministers, three of them in a single year. Some awaited retirement; others had no prospects. Left to themselves, the services stagnated, focused on the trivia of uniforms, and cautiously rebuilt the old service identities. By 1975, it was again officially permissible to refer to "navy," "army," and "air force." An inflated rank structure became a costly solace for professional sterility: generals and colonels proliferated and privates became scarce. "Civilianization" became a state of mind.

For fifteen years the priorities and resources established in 1969–70 prevailed in the Canadian Armed Forces. A casual observer would have noted few changes. Canada, despite Trudeau's suspicion of alliances, remained a member of NATO and NORAD. Less than eighty thousand men and women in the regular forces, and nineteen thousand more in the reserves, pursued careers and activities of little apparent interest to their fellow Canadians. Very few service members now wore medals earned on active service. Few who joined after 1968 cared much about the old battles over unification and uniforms. The old services had re-emerged in three of the commands established by Paul Hellyer: Maritime for the navy, Mobile for the army, and (seven years later when two commands were merged) Air Command for the air force. Though commanders at Halifax, Montreal, and Winnipeg were remote from policy and equipment decisions, separate service perspectives again had spokesmen. A logistics branch and a Communications Command might be considered as fourth and fifth services.

After 1976, NORAD's focus on missile warning systems left Canada to patrol her own airspace against the fading risk of manned bombers. By the early 1980s, the worst inadequacies in air force equipment were repaired as the CF-18 Hornets made their appearance. Unemployment gave an added argument for a slight acceleration in the six-ship patrol frigate program. As a reminder of Priority One and as substitutes for tanks and tracked armoured personnel carriers, four hundred Swiss-designed wheeled armoured vehicles sat outside militia armouries or in rows at Mobile Command bases, ready for purposes described as "peacekeeping." A variety of acronymic purchases, from ADLIPS (Automated Date-Line Plotting Systems) to TARP (Terminal Aids Replacement Programme) reminded alert taxpayers that modern armed forces needed more than tanks, ships, and planes. Critics claimed that $15 billion committed to defence capital projects should have been spent on more than a million recession-bred unemployed. Defence department officials responded that the purchases created a hundred thousand person-years of work.

In the 1970s, Canada had by no means been unique in the neglect and "civilianization" of its forces. To varying degrees all the NATO partners had shared in the linked afflictions of unemployment and inflation. Since electronic sophistication combined with inflation added exponentially to the cost of new weapons systems, governments had sought any excuse to slow down a ruinous arms race. In the wake of Vietnam, the United States abolished the draft and accepted that its "All-Volunteer Force" would be recruited, on the whole, from the least fortunate of its citizens. If conscription was too much a tradition for other NATO partners to abandon, terms of service were shortened and lightened. While no partner imitated Canada's drastic 1969 force reduction, most quietly allowed combat strength and efficiency to dwindle. Democratic socialist government in Britain and West Germany yearned to contribute to detente and no one could pretend, in an increasingly affluent Europe, that the old tradition of patriotic service burned very brightly.

At NATO's creation in 1949, the likely shape of war had seemed reasonably clear; even in 1960, the majors and colonels of one war would have been the generals of the next. By 1980, two generations had passed without experience of a major war. "War-fighting strategies" for a major European conflict had become a matter of legitimate conjecture. Exercises in a densely populated territory could only hint at the destructive potential of so-called tactical nuclear weapons, deep penetration tactics, or political subversion among combatants and the civil population. Certainly the means existed for a doomsday of universal annihilation though it remained difficult and, for most military thinkers, almost impossible to conceive. In two widely read books, a British general, Sir John Hackett, argued that a world war would come in a combination of conventional and nuclear exchanges, barely winnable by whichever side had prepared most earnestly. Some insisted that the Third World War had already begun with terrorist attacks, guerilla struggles in the Third World, often backed by great powers, and even with the economic rivalry of East and West. Finally, there were those who argued that, through strenuous deterrence or by risk-taking disarmament, war might be prevented altogether.

The End of the Cold War

By the end of the 1970s, the spirit of détente was as out of fashion as social democracy in both America and Britain. The United States had emerged from the Vietnam trauma. In 1980, Americans resented their helplessness when Iranian revolutionaries held the U.S. embassy staff hostage. U.S. voters rejected the amiable, fumbling Jimmy Carter in favour of a right-wing Republican who promised military power, tax cuts, and an end to any wars on poverty. Ronald Reagan was the oldest and, for a time, the most bellicose U.S. president of the century, with the possible exception of Teddy Roosevelt. In Britain and West Germany, right-wing politicians also replaced left-wing believers in détente.

On the whole, Reagan and his allies had little trouble persuading supporters that the Soviet Union had gained in the arms race while the West had sought defence cuts. Modernized Soviet tank armies now faced NATO's depleted divisions. Batteries of the new SS-20 missiles had turned western Europe's major cities into nuclear targets. Most dramatic was the emergence of the Soviet fleet as a world-wide force, challenging American naval dominance from the North Atlantic to the Indian Ocean. During the 1970s, Soviet submarines had discovered routes under the polar ice cap to reach undersea locations off North America. The Reagan administration responded with a wholesale resumption of the arms race. The United States would spend what was needed to retain nuclear parity and to create, in a "Strategic Defence Initiative," an effective anti-missile defence system for its key centres. It would help NATO allies revive the possibility of a non-nuclear defence for western Europe.

Under Reagan, the post-Vietnam flight from fighting was over. The British example in recapturing the Falklands from Argentina in 1982 was a spur. With the world watching and sometimes interfering, a British amphibious force sailed halfway round the world, chanced its fortunes against modern missiles and aircraft and, by the narrowest margin, won a decisive victory. The campaign offered experts technical lessons of missile warfare, warship design, and air tactics, but the political lesson was clear. The peace movement might protest but cheap military victories were as popular as ever. Britain's prime minister, Margaret Thatcher, took an unpopular government to the polls and won a landslide victory. Thatcher's experience was shared by President Reagan when he sent troops to Grenada in 1983 to overthrow an unlovely, Cuban-backed government. The operation was ill-managed and the distribution of medals was absurdly generous, but American voters loved it.

Remote from great power ambitions, problems, or illusions, Canada clung longer to détente. At the very end of his prime ministerial career, Pierre Elliott Trudeau created a modestly funded Canadian Centre for International Peace and Security in Ottawa and toured the world to offer himself as an international peacemaker. Yet Canadians were not wholly immune from world fashion. Before the 1979 election, both Liberals and Progressive Conservatives promised to add 4700 men and women to armed forces strength and to raise capital spending to a fifth of the defence budget. Joe Clark's short-lived Conservative government sought to please its supporters by appointing a task force to consider how unification of the Canadian forces might be unscrambled. The group reported, somewhat inconclusively, to a restored Trudeau régime.

While voters generally supported rearmament, governments could not ignore the voice of peace activists. Cynics might ponder the discreet silence of peace activists when the Soviet Union modernised its tanks, deployed its SS-20 missiles, ignored its commitments to the 1975 Helsinki accords, or invaded Afghanistan in 1979, but the peace movement was not deeply self-critical. Indeed it had been quiescent in the late 1970s, when the Carter administration and NATO agreed to match the SS-20 threat by posting a new generation of Pershing and Cruise missiles in Europe. Nothing less could assure European leaders that their countries would not be abandoned in a crisis. By the 1980s, the peace movement had revived. Demonstrations in Denmark, West Germany, and the Netherlands attracted hundreds of thousands of young people. Many in a rejuvenated movement rejected traditional politics in favour of "Green" parties committed to life and the environment and opposed to bureaucracy, materialism, and the deadly tradition of war.

Peace had a Canadian echo in protests against testing American Cruise missiles over northern Canada. The Trudeau government, happy to do something cheap for NATO and its American ally, was caught unawares. The Cruise represented a new, if not terribly sophisticated, development in the arms race. A small, sub-sonic missile, it was easy to hide and to launch. It was programmed to skim the earth's surface on the way to its target, passing under most radars. Since Canada's north resembled much of the Soviet terrain Cruise missiles would have to cross, the tests made sense to NATO. Large processions in Canadian cities and smaller pilgrimages to the airbase and rocket range at Cold Lake in northern Alberta marked the revival of Canada's peace coalitions. Their numbers grew when Innu protested use of traditional hunting grounds in Labrador as a training range for low-level flying by NATO fighters. On the whole the Liberal government ignored the protesters, though the Prime Minister's last year in office, with its peace-making mission, public disparagement of NATO and the appointment of Geoffrey Pearson, son of the former prime minister, to head the new peace research institute, reflected Trudeau's old faith.

In fact the evidence of the 1984 election hinted that Canadians were not in a pacifist frame of mind. While all party leaders supported world order and disarmament, even Ed Broadbent of the New Democrats deplored the neglected state of Canada's fleet and did nothing to publicize his party's determination to get out of NATO. The Conservatives under a new leader, Montreal lawyer Brian Mulroney, promised voters to uphold the alliance system, enlarge the overcommitted forces, and restore tri-service traditions and uniforms. A Tory landslide left an untried prime minister and 211 eager colleagues free to keep their promises.

The armed forces were caught between the prime minister's desire to be "a good ally" in the opinion of the Reagan White House, the finance department's determination to cut public spending, and the government's eagerness to reward political supporters with contracts and benefits. A tradition of handing the defence portfolio to weak or worn-out ministers did not help. Robert Coates, Mulroney's first choice as defence minister, was a traditionalist whose sole achievement was to introduce three different uniforms. Since members would retain their choice throughout their careers, ships' companies, battalions, and squadrons would parade as motley collections of green, dark blue, and light blue. The new uniforms led to anything but uniformity—as befitted an age of individualism.

Coates left soon after voters learned of his indiscreet visit to a West German bar. His successor was an improvement. Erik Neilson brought the memories of a wartime bomber pilot and postwar military lawyer. He was also a tough political insider with plenty of experience, who ranked as deputy prime minister. The forces gained from Neilsen's influence. Fifteen hundred additional personnel were transferred to Canada's NATO brigade, hitherto an understrength cadre filled out by teenage reservists and cadets for summer manoeuvres. After technical troubles, HMCS *Halifax* was launched at Saint John in May 1988, Canada's first new warship since 1971. The government had already announced that half a dozen more frigates would be built at Saint John. The northern radar lines, so obsolete that some spare parts could only be ordered from Czechoslovakia, were rebuilt, with substantial American help, as a North Warning System, with an array of manned and unmanned stations. Critics complained that Canadians had been made accomplices of Ronald Reagan's Strategic Defense Initiative. Others noted that Canada could do no less to safeguard its Arctic sovereignty.

Patronage and regional favours were nothing new in Canadian defence policy, but the new government was a crude practitioner of an old evil. Prince Edward Island's hopes for a Litton Systems plant faded when provincial voters ousted the Conservatives. Oerlikon's successful $1.1 billion bid to build an anti-aircraft defence system was complicated by the need to locate the plant at St-Jean, Québec, in a cabinet minister's constituency. An ensuing scandal over land sales left the government sliding on its "sleaze factor." The contract to build six additional frigates at the Saint John shipyard was confirmed only after New Brunswick's Liberal government endorsed the Mulroney Free Trade Agreement with the United States. Contracts for minesweepers, in contrast, were distributed two by two, to smaller shipyards. A $1.2 billion contract to maintain the CF-18 fighters was switched from Winnipeg's Bristol Aircraft to Montreal's Canadair when Quebec's Conservative MPs showed their muscle. Bristol had to be content with a $350 million contract to fix the CF-5—which Canadair had manufactured. Contracts for trucks, jeeps, and all-terrain vehicles were handed out as political favours, with "public affairs" specialists—some of them retired generals—smoothing the way. The responsibility for scandals, waste and favours belonged to the government but it was easy to blame "the military."

The Progressive Conservatives had promised a new white paper on defence policy, the first since Donald Macdonald's in 1971. There was plenty to discuss. Were Canada's forces over-committed? Had Canada ignored Pentagon claims of a growing Soviet threat? The American decision to send an icebreaker through the Northwest Passage in 1985 without Ottawa's approval awoke a slumbering concern about Canada's Arctic sovereignty. Could the armed forces help? A costly exercise in 1986 showed what insiders had long suspected: despite a long-standing commitment Canada could not deliver its CAST (Combined Air-Sea Transport) brigade group and supporting aircraft to Norway with adequate speed or security.

Appointed as Neilsen's replacement in the summer of 1986, Perrin Beatty could see the CAST failure for himself. It took him months to get his colleagues to accept the rearmament program the Tories had promised before 1984. Young, ambitious, and successful in two earlier cabinet posts, Beatty resembled Paul Hellyer in seeing National Defence as a stepping stone. He was a reformer, directing admirals and generals to take defence issues to the public, overruling objections to the integration of women in combat units, and improving conditions for armed forces families.

Beatty's real challenge was delivering a defence policy. The long promised white paper, *Challenge and Commitment*, appeared in June, 1987, backed by all the fanfare of his new "communications strategy." Despite a dutiful emphasis on peace and peacekeeping, pictures of Soviet tanks and diagrams of the Soviet threat set the tone. Under Trudeau, the Tories insisted, Canada had shirked her role as a NATO partner. Since the CAST commitment was unrealistic, Beatty proposed that Canada offer NATO a full mechanized division for the central front, backed by a second fully equipped back-up division stationed in Canada. A third army division would provide any necessary home defence. Expanding the reserves to 40000 and integrating them with the regulars, would provide manpower at varying levels of readiness. Additional Auroras, CF-18s, six extra frigates, and new EH-101 anti-submarine helicopters, as well as a rebuilt North Warning system, would strengthen Canada's home defences. So far, the white paper was predictable. Beatty's most imaginative proposal promised the navy a dozen nuclear-powered submarines, capable of operating against attack submarines in all three of Canada's oceans.

The newest idea got the fiercest reaction. The word "nuclear" stirred peace and environmental groups. The prospect of giving Canada a presence under the Arctic ice floes left nationalists silent; some of them insisted that they wanted the Arctic demilitarised. The U.S. Navy bluntly warned that Canadians had no business meddling in nuclear technology nor were they welcome under the polar icecap. The price tag—$8 billions or more— shocked editors, business, and Beatty's cabinet colleagues, particularly since little of the money would stay in Canada. While rival French and British shipbuilders battled for the business, the Mulroney government dithered past the contract deadlines. By the time Canadians went to the polls on November 21, 1988, the nuclear submarine proposal was moribund. Free trade, noisily backed by business lobbies, gave Mulroney his winning issue.

Afterwards, Beatty was shuffled to another portfolio. His Saskatchewan-bred successor, Bill McKnight, brought the defence department into line with a post-election priority, deficit-cutting. In the 1989 post-election budget, the Conservatives offered the nuclear submarine program as a popular cut. The budget also cancelled new tanks and aircraft, cut manpower, and closed bases, chiefly in regions where the Tories had fared badly. Defence, in Ottawa's jargon, was "descoped."

There was a more powerful reason than deficits and domestic politics for scrapping the Beatty blueprint: far from lasting into the next millennium, the Cold War was suddenly over. The advent of Mikhail Gorbachev in 1985 began a transformation first of the Soviet Union and then, in stunning succession, of its Warsaw Pact satellites. Working with the slogans of *glasnost* (enlightenment) and *perestroika* (restructuring), the new Soviet leader sought to invigorate a Soviet society brought close to paralysis. In practice, Gorbachev's reforms helped shake the Soviet system to pieces, producing political upheaval, economic chaos, and ethnic ferment. When he ended the Soviet military role in Afghanistan, troops returned with some of the disillusion Americans experienced after Vietnam. Neither generals nor privates showed much stomach for upholding Soviet authority or ending ethnic conflict in the Baltic and Moslem republics.

In turn the Communist regimes in satellite countries struggled and, almost unexpectedly, collapsed. In Poland, Hungary, and Czechoslovakia, dissidents moved in months from prison to power. On November 9, 1989, East Germany announced that its frontier with the West was open. Excited crowds surged across the Berlin Wall, ugliest symbol of the Cold War, daubed it with graffiti, and then demolished it. Chunks of rubble became souvenirs. After a brief but bloody struggle, Romania joined the tide. As the Warsaw Pact collapsed, the Soviet tank armies had to abandon familiar barracks and training grounds, retreating to the overcrowded squalor of their home bases. In 1990, Soviet leaders swallowed their greatest postwar fear, a reunified Germany. They had little choice: economic aid from prosperous postwar West Germany was the USSR's best hope of avoiding economic collapse, perhaps even mass starvation.

VII   The Awkward Peace

A Change of Era

The 1990s were tough years for many Canadians. They began with a brutal recession, easily the worst since the Great Depression, and continued with a slow recovery that left more than a million Canadians out of work, and the great majority of Canadians with less money to spend. Huge government deficits, accumulated since the 1970s, created a mountain of debt, absorbing more and more public revenue merely to pay the interest. Governments at all levels scrambled to cut their spending, slashing payrolls, closing schools and hospitals, shrinking unemployment benefits even as they and private employers laid off hundreds of thousands of workers.

For many in Canada's Armed Forces, it was a harsh decade too, with national and international commitments that ignored dwindling resources and strength, promises of suitable weapons and equipment repeatedly broken, leaders who could not deliver and who sometimes lost touch with those they led, and the long, humiliating trauma that grew out of a shameful March night in Somalia.

Yet throughout the decade, there were constant reminders, from Oka and the Persian Gulf in 1990 to the skies over Yugoslavia in 1999, that Canada's defenders had not dishonoured their legacy of courage, self-sacrifice, and skill. More than most institutions, military organizations must learn quickly from defeats and failures, recognize their strengths, and keep their goals firmly in mind. That is why a decade many might prefer to forget needs analysis and fresh understanding.

For two generations, the Cold War and its ramifications had justified every major feature of Canadian defence policy, from warning systems in the north, to the men and women stationed in Germany. Even peacekeeping had usually been linked to some new area of East-West rivalry. For forty years, the world had experienced a sometimes terrifying, but often reassuring, stasis. Entire military careers, from recruit entry to pension, had been spent preparing for World War III. Huge corporations, supporting hundreds of thousands of workers and entire cities, had generated weapons and equipment for Cold War armies, navies, and air forces, and profits for their shareholders.

Then, in a matter of a few months of 1989, the Cold War was over. There was no formal armistice, no triumphant parade for the victors, no war-crimes trial for the defeated, but without a doubt the Soviet Union and its ideological system had been vanquished. Since all outcomes in history seem inevitable, it was suddenly hard to believe that the Communists could ever have won. Not only had the arms race ravaged the economies of the Soviet Union and its satellites, feeding corruption and undermining morale, but even the resulting war machine looked shoddy and defective. Repatriating Soviet army garrisons in Germany was a problem, since there were no barracks in Russia for the troops or homes for their families. As for safeguarding Soviet stockpiles of nuclear weapons, poison gas, and biological contaminants, the prospect was almost as nightmarish as war itself.

These problems seemed remote to most Canadians, preoccupied with their own concerns — the rift between Quebec and the rest of the country, a national debt that had reached $709 billion by 1995 (or $25,223 per Canadian), and federal deficits that relentlessly increased the load by $30 billion or more a year. With every major assumption behind the 1987 defence white paper now groundless, what was the justification for spending over $12 billion a year to keep 83,000 men and women clothed, paid, and equipped with ships, aircraft, and tanks?

There were arguments to support the expense. A strong case could be made that Canada had a deep stake in European stability (though, as diplomatic historian Norman Hillmer has noted, few Canadians any longer made the point). Without two superpowers to keep their dependents in line, stability was very much in question. People felt free to rediscover a host of half-forgotten quarrels. Stalin's old empire seethed with national and ethnic rivalries, brutally repressed under Soviet rule. By 1991, the old Soviet Union had dissolved into most of its constituent republics. Some of them — Moldavia, Georgia, Armenia, Azerbaijan — were soon enmeshed in internal or frontier battles. Within the core Russian Federation, ethnically based republics asserted their autonomy, and one of them, Chechnya, under a former Soviet air force general, launched a violent civil war. What would be the role of the former Soviet forces, with their massive stores of weapons? When Ukrainian nationalists re-established the short-lived republic of the early 1920s, they challenged Moscow for the Crimea, including control of the mighty Soviet Black Sea fleet and its base at Sevastopol.

Freed of its own fears of a Warsaw Pact invasion, Yugoslavia's increasingly quarrelsome federation began to dissolve. Its postwar leader, Marshal Josip Broz Tito, had imposed a myth of valiant partisan resistance to the Nazis on a reality of savage civil war between 1941 and 1944, with 1.5 million dead, mostly at the hands of other Yugoslavs. Nationalism was banned, but Tito could not live forever. His death in 1980 left his successors free to rebuild crumbling bases on the old hatreds. In background and outlook, there was not much to distinguish the Serbian Slobodan Milosevic, from the Croatian Franjo Tudjman. Both exploited national myths. Few Serbs still lived in Kosovo, but memories of a terrible battle in 1389 were deeply embedded in Serbian memory. In 1989, in the name of his fellow Serbs, Milosevic crushed Kosovo's autonomy and the rights of close to two million Moslems. Other Yugoslav republics edged toward independence.

Did any of those problems touch a country that seemed, once again, to be Senator Raoul Dandurand's "fireproof house, far from the sources of conflagration"? They might not have if Canada had still been overwhelmingly British or French, but in the multicultural 1990s, citizens pressed Ottawa to support a score of endangered ancestral homelands from the Baltic states to Armenia. Ukrainians in prairie cities guaranteed that the Mulroney government was among the first to recognize a sovereign Ukraine. Canadian diplomats were more cautious about extending NATO's umbrella eastward to protect the fragile democracies emerging from the Warsaw Pact. Russia's even more fragile experiment in democracy would be undermined by a renewed fear of encirclement. NATO took a decade to extend its protection to Poland, Hungary, and the Czech Republic. Its economy in chaos and its armed forces enfeebled, Russia could only wait for better times.

Divided Country, Unstable World

At Meech Lake in 1987, Ottawa and all the provinces had honoured Mulroney's election pledge "to bring Quebec into the Constitution with honour and enthusiasm." Not everyone approved. To Pierre Elliott Trudeau, the Meech Lake Accord undermined his grand design for a Canada of equal citizens. Many English Canadians complained that the Accord gave more rights to Quebec than to the other provinces; Quebec separatists found it equally unacceptable. Native people felt left out. The 1981 amending formula gave Canada and its provinces three years to ratify the Accord. Opposition grew steadily. On June 28, 1990, Newfoundland premier Clyde Wells and Elijah Harper, a Cree politician in Manitoba, independently killed the Accord in their respective legislatures. Having been assured that Canadians respected their claims, Quebeckers felt humiliated. Support for sovereignty soared to 60 per cent, and Canada seemed on the brink of dissolution. Ottawa would need more than Washington's neutrality to help control the damage. And Washington could demand a price.

Just two weeks after the failure of the Accord, on July 11, a clash between Quebec's provincial police and armed Mohawks, claiming treaty lands near Oka, left one officer dead. The Mohawks added several battered patrol cars to the road blockades they had erected. At Kahnewake, sympathetic Mohawks blocked the Mercier Bridge, a major commuter route into Montreal. News media spread rumours of vast caches of automatic weapons and land mines. On August 17, Quebec's premier, Robert Bourassa, requisitioned the army for "public security." As the chief of the defence staff, General John de Chastelain, explained on national television, the army had to prevail. Units of the *5e brigade mécanisée* rolled out of Valcartier towards Montreal. On the principle that overwhelming force would minimize the risk of bloodshed, several thousand troops from Valcartier and Gagetown concentrated outside the two Native communities. On August 26, soldiers patiently pushed Native demonstrators back from the Mercier Bridge, checked for mines and, with help from masked Warriors, dismantled the barriers. Then they encircled the most militant Warriors and their media allies near Oka and stoically endured a barrage of largely verbal abuse. Finally, on September 26, the Natives decided that they had made their point. A final melee as Warriors tried to get away led to an angry and violent demonstration at Kahnewake. Troops held their ground and prepared to shoot. Mohawk leaders barely managed to regain control.

Across Canada, opinions were deeply divided about the merits of Mohawk demands. Warriors nicknamed "Lasagna" or "Spudwrench" became media heroes. But so were Canada's soldiers. The army's restraint, or the discipline that made it possible, was reassuring when bloodshed had seemed the only possible outcome. Quebeckers, in particular, took unusual satisfaction in troops who spoke their language, performed effectively, and avoided further loss of life. It had been rare in the twentieth century that soldiers were popular heroes in French Canada, and the pleasure, however short-lived, was savoured. Thanks to a barely noticed 1987 amendment to the Nations Defence Act, the $83-million bill for the Oka operation was absorbed by the defence budget.

In July 1990, an American political scientist, John Mearsheimer, argued in *The Atlantic Monthly* that a multi-polar world would be more unstable and dangerous than a globe dominated by two cautious superpowers. Within days, his warning came true. On August 2, Iraq invaded Kuwait. No longer a client of the United States or the Soviet Union, Saddam Hussein sent the Arab world's most powerful army to conquer a small oil-rich neighbour Iraq had claimed as a former province.

In Washington, President George Bush responded, rallying allies against naked aggression and the threat to world oil supplies. For once, the Soviet Union was silent, even supportive. Although Canadian opinion was split on active involvement, a brief meeting between Brian Mulroney and Bush sufficed to ensure Canadian backing. At Halifax, dockyard technicians installed anti-aircraft and missile protection on the destroyers HMCS *Athabaskan* and *Terra Nova* and the supply ship HMCS *Protecteur*. On August 24, they left for the Persian Gulf. A month later, a squadron of CF-18s was authorized to move from their base at Baden-Soellingen. By October 9, the fighters were operational at a base in the Gulf state of Qatar appropriately named "Canada Dry." Soldiers in company-strength accompanied the expedition to provide ground defence for the base.

After months of negotiation, preparation, delay, and uncertainty, a final Allied ultimatum expired on January 15, 1991. After a massive aerial bombardment, Allied troops swept through the Iraqi defences. A Canadian field hospital, despatched after the war began, had barely pitched its tents when Iraqi resistance collapsed. On January 27, as huge columns of smoke rose from Kuwait's sabotaged oil fields, fighting ceased. A detachment of Canadian field engineers remained in Kuwait to lift land mines strewn by the invaders.

Peace activists and opposition politicians found plenty to criticize about Canada's presence in the Gulf War. An imam in Edmonton preached holy war against the United Nations. Other Canadian Moslems complained that they had suffered from prejudice and had been interviewed by members of CSIS, Canada's new civilian security service. The complaints did not extend to the armed forces; professional expertise made even Canada's outdated warships highly effective in their blockade role. The "Desert Cats" squadron flew 2,700 sorties without losing an aircraft. The 2,400 Canadians who served in the war came home without a significant casualty. Most of the cost of the Canadian role in the Gulf War, $690 million, was absorbed, like the cost of Oka, by the defence budget; most of an extra $350 million voted by Parliament was used, later that year, to help prairie farmers hit by falling world prices.

Far from being irrelevant in a post–Cold War world, Canada's forces had experienced an unusually busy 1990. Did that alter their prospects? Did Canadians want forces that could uphold President George Bush's "New World Order" or provide heavily armed back-up to the police? Or would Canada follow the post–Gulf War example of Britain and the United States and sharply reduce its victorious forces? Through much of 1991, the Mulroney government struggled to define a defence policy for an unfamiliar world. In April, General de Chastelain found himself pitted publicly against his former deputy, Vice-Admiral Charles Thomas. Since cuts were inevitable, Thomas argued, they must be selective. An obvious economy would be to close most of the thirty-four ramshackle, costly Canadian Forces bases, but Thomas suspected that politics made most of them inviolable. The air force and navy had essential roles in protecting Canada's frontiers; the army, for most purposes, did not, and should suffer the major cuts. De Chastelain had a different view. In a wholly unpredictable world, Canada needed balanced forces and an array of otherwise irreplaceable military skills.

Rank and the 1990 experience, when all three services had been useful, helped de Chastelain prevail, but not wholly. In a major cabinet shuffle on April 21, 1991, Mulroney switched defence ministers. Bill McKnight, a Saskatchewan wheat farmer who had run the department for twenty-six months, was needed in Agriculture. His successor, Marcel Masse, was a long-time Quebec nationalist. As a veteran politician in a very unpopular government, Masse knew that spending made friends; cuts did not. Corporations with a big stake in defence production wanted the government to continue procurement programs, particularly for made-in-Canada products such as ships, vehicles, and communications equipment. The reserves, given a new significance in the 1987 "Total Force" concept of integrating their manpower with the regulars, used their considerable political clout to ensure that future cuts did not come at their expense. Provinces and neighbouring communities fought base closures.

On June 14, 1991, the prime minister foreshadowed his government's policy when he announced to a European audience that Canada would cut its forces in Germany. When Masse delivered his version of defence policy on September 17, media pundits expected the cuts would hit with the impact of a heavy boot. He made it seem more like a slipper. Echoing defence lobbyists, Masse insisted that a country that had spent only 2 per cent of its gross national product on defence could expect no peace dividend. Instead, the defence budget would go on rising faster than inflation. Canadian bases at Lahr and Baden-Soellingen would close by 1995, and regular force strength would fall by 10 per cent, from 82,000 to 76,000, slightly less than in the Trudeau years, but reserves could still grow to 30,000. If NATO wanted, Canada would keep 1,100 personnel in Europe. In Canada, ordnance and supply depots in Ontario and New Brunswick would close, but their contents would be concentrated at Longue-Point in east-end Montreal. Other bases in Canada would be closed, but only after a review process so leisurely that decisions would be deferred past the next federal election.

For the armed forces and for industry, the dividend would be new equipment. With money saved on full-time manpower, the defence department would be in the market for light armoured vehicles and communications hardware useful for peacekeeping. The navy could only count on "up to twelve" of the big *Halifax* class frigates, but it would also get three conventional submarines to replace existing boats, and a new class of "corvettes," too small to carry helicopters. The naval reserve would get its promised minesweepers plus a new headquarters complex in Quebec City. Retiring the two fighter squadrons in Germany and putting their planes in storage would preserve the operating life of the highly stressed CF-18s. In April 1992, Masse announced a billion-dollar contract for a hundred Bell helicopters, to be built near Montreal's Mirabel airport, and an $800-million contract with General Motors for 228 armoured vehicles, to be built at London, Ontario. In July, the department offered $4.4 billion for fifty EH-101 helicopters, of joint Italian-British design, to replace the aged and obsolete Sea Kings and Labradors. A single design would cut the cost of training, spare parts, and the obligatory stack of bilingual manuals.

Canada's allies showed no interest in retaining a small, largely symbolic Canadian contingent in Europe. The Canadian flag came down at Baden-Soellingen and at Lahr on July 30, 1993. After thirty years, Canadian Forces Europe ceased to exist. Canada's role would be played by units based in Canada; while warships from Halifax manoeuvred in NATO exercises, German and British jet fighters swooped low over the Labrador tundra, and their tanks and artillery practised field-firing at western Canadian bases. However, Canadian army and air force units would lose the opportunity to maintain their skills in technologically advanced forms of warfare. Nor would they be able to argue that their aircraft, weapons, and equipment had to be good enough to compete with the very best.

Peacekeeping and Peacemaking

There was one military role almost all Canadians applauded. Since 1948, Canadians had participated in virtually every United Nations peacekeeping operation, and for years it maintained several hundred personnel in the Sinai and later the Golan Heights and on the island of Cyprus. Canadians had taken special pride in the 1988 award of a Nobel Peace Prize to the UN's peacekeepers, and a $2.8-million monument to their memory was unveiled in Ottawa in October 1992.

If there was a criticism of peacekeeping, it was that the UN presence tended to become permanent, and even profitable, for the host region, removing any incentive to seek a lasting solution, and saddling the UN with costs many of its members, including the United States, refused to pay. To Canadians, that criticism applied particularly to Cyprus: at the end of 1992, the prime minister announced that the commitment of a small battalion would end. On June 15, 1993, the last of 20,000 Canadians handed his watch to a British soldier, and an undertaking that had cost twenty-four Canadian lives was over. The UN presence survived without the Canadians; so did Greek and Turkish antipathy.

Meanwhile, Canada accepted new, larger, and more dangerous commitments. In 1991, northern Yugoslavia exploded in ethnic violence. The northern republic of Slovenia seceded, and Franjo Tudjman's Croatia followed, to be met by units of the Serb-dominated Yugoslav army. Murderous fighting and "ethnic cleansing" followed as the Serbs prevailed. Under UN auspices, a large force was authorized to separate the warring sides and end the carnage. The composition was carefully balanced between units from NATO and former Warsaw Pact countries, and Third World contingents. On February 21, 1992, Canada contributed a battalion-sized unit to the United Nations Protection Force (UNPROFOR). Troops and equipment hurried into the region from Lahr.

The UN ordered UNPROFOR headquarters to be located at Sarajevo, better known to the world as home of the 1984 Olympics, or as the site of Archduke Franz Ferdinand's assassination in 1914. Locals knew it better as the capital of the mixed Moslem-Serb-Croat region of Bosnia-Herzegovina and the centre of a strong, Moslem-led secession movement. Indeed, as the UNPROFOR headquarters took shape, a wholly predictable civil war exploded around it. Instead of managing UN forces, UNPROFOR's Canadian deputy commander, Major-General Lewis MacKenzie, a veteran of peacekeeping in Egypt and Central America, found himself dodging shells and machine-gun bullets while he tried to broker peace between Moslems and Serbs and keep the local airport open. To aggravate the problem, the United States and the UN immediately recognized the new Bosnian regime, though its capacity to enforce its claim to sovereignty against resentful and well-armed local Serbs was highly questionable. "Peacekeeping" in Bosnia became a hopeless struggle between mortal enemies, each prepared to use the UN's troops to acquire weapons or exploit world media interest. Criticisms of the UN Headquarters' inability to manage its military forces led to the appointment in June, 1992, of Brigadier-General Maurice Baril from the Combat Training Centre at Gagetown as military advisor to the Secretary-General.

Canada sent a second battalion to serve in Bosnia at Sarajevo and agreed to maintain two large battalion groups, the fourth-largest UN contingent among thirty countries operating in the region. By 1994, two years of operations had cost the defence budget $150 million. Once again, Canadian forces earned a reputation for courage, patience, and self-discipline in harrowing conditions. Many soldiers were reservists, wearing their own badges, but otherwise hardly distinguishable from regulars. Canadian soldiers and airmen endured harsh winters, savage hatreds, injuries, and death. There was little peace to keep. Negotiating with local warlords, surviving challenges by drunken sentries, and threading a way through encounters where the real target was the world media and the first casualty was truth, tested the professionalism of all peacekeepers. For a week in September 1993, troops of the 2nd Princess Patricia's Canadian Light Infantry battled Croatian troops to save Serbs in the Medak Pocket, the biggest Canadian battle since Korea. Like other violence, the battle was downplayed in Ottawa by officials anxious to make peacekeeping look peaceful, and positively denied by Zagreb since the genocidal actions of Croatian troops undermined Croatia's image of righteousness.

Bound by Rules of Engagement that made more sense in New York than in the field, UN soldiers could seldom curb "ethnic cleansing" or even massacres. Observing a civil war fought with utter contempt for human lives left soldiers with lasting psychological scars. At Srebrenica, Dutch troops stood helplessly by as Serb irregulars invaded a UN-declared safe haven and slaughtered thousands of Moslems. Srebrenica shocked the world, and no one interfered when American-trained Croatian troops drove a quarter-million Serbs from the Krajina region, while NATO bombers punished Serb forces in Bosnia. U.S. President Bill Clinton summoned the parties to an air-force base near Dayton, Ohio, and imposed a settlement. To enforce the agreement, NATO troops replaced the UN. Canada promptly substituted a smaller force in the region.

As Yugoslavia exploded in murderous violence, Somalia, on the strategic Horn of Africa, dissolved into savage anarchy. The overthrow of General Siad Barre's Marxist dictatorship left the desert country open to murderous clan warfare. Struggling to relieve starvation, international relief agencies became victims of rival warlords. A small UN contingent sent to protect them was outnumbered and helpless. Humanitarian compassion, strategic interest, and a sneaking desire to repeat the success of the Gulf War persuaded Washington to intervene. Moved by pressure from a powerful ally and by pride in never missing a major humanitarian operation, the Mulroney government decided in August 1992 to send an infantry battalion.

It was an act of hubris. With regular forces shrinking and already over-committed, General de Chastelain had to offer the Canadian Airborne Regiment, a supposedly elite unit in the throes of acute discipline problems. Rather than admit that one of their regular battalions was unfit for service, the army's generals found it easier to replace the commanding officer and hope for the best. As the unit had been training for a possible UN role in the Sahara, it seemed suitable for desert conditions on the other side of Africa. Denied a major role in the Gulf War, some in the army saw the Somalia operation as their chance to perform. Obliged to finance the operation out of the current defence budget, DND officials ordered administrative resources to be trimmed.

No one doubted that the Airborne was tough, aggressive, and even eager to fight. And fighting seemed likely. Initial expectations were for casualties as high as 16 per cent a month. Like the Korean War, the Somalia operation would be "peacemaking" under Chapter 7 of the UN Charter, not another Cyprus. The prime minister put the Canadians under the U.S.-sponsored UNITAF (Unified Task Force — Somalia), not the discredited UNOSOM (United Nations Operation in Somalia). However, when Canadians landed at Belet Huen in northern Somalia, armed gangs evaporated and the Airborne settled in for months of hardship, boredom, and heat in a region where all civil authority had vanished. By day, soldiers rebuilt schools and distributed relief; by night they prowled their camp to catch thieves. Violent encounters led to Somali deaths.

After dark on March 16, 1993 a young Somali intruder was captured. That night, some soldiers tortured and killed him. At least sixteen officers and other ranks, and probably more, heard Shidane Abukar Arone's screams. When military police investigated, the prime suspect hanged himself, and suffered severe brain damage. At home, Canadians learned of the crime largely from an air force doctor, Major Barry Armstrong, who claimed that other Somalis had been murdered by Canadians. The Airborne commander assigned him bodyguards and ordered him home for fear that his soldiers would carry out their death threats. Shidane Arone's death fouled the long, proud tradition of Canadian soldiers as peacekeepers.

An inquiry board, composed of three officers and two civilians, reported on August 31, chiefly on the Airborne's discipline problems. Other issues were left to the processes of military justice. The army's reputation was harmed when the only soldier who suffered severe punishment was a twenty-five-year-old private who had photographed the episode. Some sentences were increased on appeal, but courts martial composed of fellow officers acquitted or merely reprimanded those who had been responsible for the troops involved. The search for scapegoats would not end easily or soon.

Somalia was not alone. On March 2, 1992, Canada agreed to contribute one hundred service personnel to a 22,000-member UN Transitional Authority in Cambodia, to protect free elections, scheduled for May 1993, from attacks by the brutal Khmer Rouge. And in 1993, Major-General Roméo Dallaire took command of a 2,400-member UN force sent to Rwanda to oversee a shaky peace between the murderously antagonistic Hutus and Tutsis. When President Juvenal Habyarimana died in a mysterious plane crash on April 6, his Hutu-dominated army immediately exploded in a nationwide slaughter of Tutsis and moderate Hutus. On April 7, as Dallaire hunted vainly for any army commander willing to restore order, ten Belgian soldiers assigned to guard Habyarimana's successor were seized by Rwandan mutineers and tortured to death. The surviving Belgians and several other contingents pulled out.

Dallaire, ten Canadian officers, and a small battalion of Ghanaians stayed on in Kigali, the capital of Rwanda, doing what they could to protect terrified Rwandans. Reluctantly, France and the United States intervened in force to stop the killings and rescue more than two million starving refugees. By the time Dallaire's successor, Major-General Guy Tousignant, arrived in August, the Rwanda force was 5,500 strong, including 600 Canadians. The UN had belatedly intervened to stop the killings and aid the two million refugees who had fled for their lives. Meanwhile, critics denounced Dallaire for not personally rescuing the Belgians or the half-million Rwandans who had perished in the bloodbath.

Canada's commitment to peacekeeping would continue, from Namibia to Bosnia. After U.S. forces finally intervened in the chaos of Haiti in 1996, for almost two years successive battalions of the French-speaking Royal 22e Régiment formed part of the force that replaced them. A third of a three-hundred-member international police contingent came from Canada.

Cuts and Conflicts

On January 4, 1993, the defence department found itself with a new minister. Kim Campbell had once studied Russian and headed the Vancouver School Board. Brian Mulroney had made her the first female minister of justice, and then, to help prepare her ultimately to succeed him as prime minister, he switched her to National Defence for experience in handling a nuts-and-bolts department. Two days later, General John de Chastelain left to be Canada's ambassador in Washington. His successor, Admiral John Anderson, was a fifty-one-year-old former destroyer captain whose chief experience in Ottawa had been as head of the ill-fated nuclear submarine acquisition team. Both minister and admiral faced a growing political storm over the EH-101 helicopters. Critics demanded to know how a government with an uncontrolled deficit, falling revenues, and record unemployment could afford Cadillac-class weapons. Armed with data from anonymous sources within the department, opposition politicians denounced the $47-million price per helicopter, declared that anti-submarine warfare was old-fashioned, and echoed complaints by rival bidders in the U.S. aerospace industry.

Determined to show ministerial toughness, Campbell backed her department's brief in cabinet and caucus. Recognizing their opponent as a potential prime minister, opposition politicians and media critics were ruthless. Department officials struggled to protect their minister and themselves from political fallout from Shidane Arone's death. Even if Campbell and Admiral Anderson had nothing to do with the state of the Airborne Regiment or its selection for duty in Somalia, the rules of parliamentary accountability held incumbents responsible for all that happened.

On the whole, Campbell did well. Soon after Mulroney announced his departure on February 23, 1993, she launched her campaign for the Progressive Conservative leadership. On June 25, she became Canada's nineteenth prime minister. Tom Siddon became the third minister of national defence in six months. In the summer of 1993, it seemed that Conservative fortunes were recovering. Then Campbell announced a federal election. Among a host of deadly issues was the decision to buy expensive helicopters. Critics had no alternative to the obsolete Sea Kings; it was enough to complain that the new helicopters were expensive and foreign-built. According to taste, the money would be better spent on daycare or deficit cuts.

On election day, October 25, Kim Campbell's government was annihilated. The Liberals took 177 seats. Jean Chrétien, who had denounced the Gulf War involvement, the EH-101s, and almost everything else the Tories had done, became prime minister.

Quebec's continuing fury at the fate of the Meech Lake Accord gave Lucien Bouchard 54 Bloc Québécois seats and leadership of Her Majesty's Official Opposition. Close behind, with 52 seats, was Preston Manning's western-based Reform Party.

While some Reformers had served as officers, and a former admiral joined Chrétien's cabinet, defence had even fewer supporters than in the Mulroney government. David Collenette, a lawyer and party veteran from Toronto, took on the role of minister of national defence. In mid-campaign, Kim Campbell had reduced the anti-submarine helicopter order to 43; Chrétien cancelled it altogether — with a penalty cost of $500 million. On December 15, after less than a year abroad, General de Chastelain came back as Chief of the Defence Staff. The prime minister's nephew, Raymond Chrétien, a veteran diplomat, replaced him in Washington. Too closely identified with Somalia and helicopters, Admiral Anderson left for a NATO staff post in Brussels.

Some Liberals had a dramatic new vision for defence. The Council of 21, headed by former Trudeau chief of staff Tom Axworthy, inspired by Toronto academic Janice Stein, and endorsed by a score of active Liberals as well as former Tory leader Robert Stanfield, urged that the Canadian Forces be restructured as a lightly armed, short-service army, effective chiefly for the more bloodless forms of peacekeeping. The navy and air force, with their costly equipment, would have little place. The Council's proposals were tempting to ministers eager to control the deficit, reduce youth unemployment, avoid costly modern weapons, and exploit the Pearson peacekeeping legacy. Both de Chastelain and his minister fought back. The Council of 21 force would resemble the armies of most other countries in the hemisphere, mainly designed to fight fellow citizens. How would that look to the First Nations or Québécois? Besides, the big-ticket items for the navy and air force, the patrol frigates and CF-18s, had been bought. Should they be mothballed or scrapped?

Still, cuts were due. Defence was the biggest item in the federal account, after interest on the national debt. Chrétien had pledged to slash the federal deficit, and, as an old ally, Collenette conformed to the government's agenda. General de Chastelain insisted on his old plan of a balanced combat-capable armed force able to serve with the armed forces of its old allies. Could savings be found from the department's political spending: from militia regiments with a full slate of officers and few soldiers, or a National Defence Headquarters that absorbed ten per cent of Canadian Forces strength? Much of the defence budget was devoted to the upkeep of buildings, streets, and sewers on more than thirty bases. As personnel strength fell, from 82,000 in 1989 to 75,000 by 1993, the rank structure grew top-heavy, with one officer to 4.3 other ranks. Meanwhile, in Bosnia, Canadian soldiers used obsolete, vulnerable vehicles and shared their limited stock of Kevlar helmets and body armour.

In a white paper released on December 1, 1993, Collenette promised that Canada would have armed forces capable of "fighting alongside the best against the best." Potential enemies were not spelled out. Collenette set a target of 60,000 regulars and 23,000 reserves, hardly more than in 1948. The department's 33,000 civilian workers would shrink to 20,000. Moving service commands to Ottawa would cut three bases and help reduce ninety generals to only seventy. Bases were abandoned in major cities like Montreal, Toronto, and Calgary, where living costs were high and land might be sold for a profit, but also in Chatham on New Brunswick's north shore, Chilliwack in British Columbia, and Cornwallis in Nova Scotia's Annapolis Valley, where the navy and later the Canadian Forces had trained recruits. Buy-out packages were offered to middle-rank personnel. Even some new graduates of the service colleges returned to civilian life, with severance pay as well as a $240,000 education. Their services would not be needed.

Inevitably, politics shaped the cuts. Local protests helped turn Cornwallis into the peacekeeping-training centre long sought by peace activists. Royal Roads, a beautifully sited military college in Esquimalt, was a sacrifice. When the minister grasped the implications of cutting a western Canadian institution, le Collège Militaire Royal de Saint Jean joined the list. Cadets from Quebec would have to accept the hot-house bilingualism of Kingston's RMC. So would Atlantic-region cadets who lacked a year of high school. Another high-profile victim was the National Defence College at Kingston, where senior officers, civil servants, and influential civilians had studied the problems of society and war since 1947.

Reshaping the reserves was the toughest political problem. A three-member commission, headed by Second World War veteran and former chief justice Brian Dickson, examined the reserves to see how they could be trimmed. The report, issued on November 7,

1995, praised the navy, air force and communications reserves, and urged that members get more training, better careers, and job protection if called out to serve. The militia was a harder problem. Its 201 units, ranging from 27 to 264 members, were embedded in history and local communities. The report recommended that units be trimmed and reorganized in seven armour-infantry brigades, but Dickson prudently recommended that the reserves themselves manage the process. Faced with the disappearance or merger of scores of proud but tiny units, honorary colonels checked their Rolodexes and mobilized their defences.

Through the mid-1990s, the department struggled to absorb Collenette's cuts. Thousands of members contemplated an early end to what had seemed secure careers. Meanwhile, the Canadian Forces played a major role in the fiftieth anniversaries of D-Day and the end of the Second World War the following year. On June 3, 1995, dignitaries and veterans stood as the Queen unveiled a monument to Canadians in London's Green Park largely financed by Canadian millionaires Conrad Black and Galen Weston. The Airborne Regiment commemorated its wartime predecessor, the Canadian Parachute Battalion, by staging a drop in Normandy on June 5, 1994. Jostling by former allies for a greater share of past glories was less evident in 1995, when Canadian veterans renewed the long love affair with a liberated Netherlands, and those at home could be reminded of how much Canada had been changed and enriched by the victory of fifty years before.

The Somalia Inquiry

Closer, uglier memories would not fade. Suddenly, the Airborne Regiment was in trouble again. In March 1995, videotapes of the regiment's initiation rites were leaked to the media and displayed to international audiences. They showed men daubed with racist slogans and eating feces, and a black soldier led on a leash. No matter that the events had occurred before the Somalia mission, or that new officers had taken over the regiment. On March 5, Collenette ordered the Airborne Regiment disbanded. When Major-General Brian Vernon, commanding the land forces in Ontario, described the contents of videotapes he had screened as "innocuous," he was removed.

Many damning revelations came through *Esprit de Corps*, a magazine edited by a former infantry corporal, Scott Taylor, and designed especially for the lower ranks of the Canadian Forces. A monthly delight to soldiers seething over low pay and insensitive leaders, the magazine pilloried "the brass" with revelations of extravagance, folly, and "cover-ups." As a propaganda weapon against Canada's regular forces and their generals, the magazine had a powerful influence. When the *Globe and Mail*, a beneficiary of its revelations, almost put the magazine out of business for failing to pay advertising bills, wealthy supporters, including honorary colonels, restored the magazine's finances.

Esprit de Corps was symptomatic of a military organization in disarray. The Somalia affair, and the attempt to make a lowly private the major scapegoat, had dragged the Canadian Forces into contempt, even among its own junior members. Earlier, Canadian soldiers in Croatia had been celebrated for caring for inmates of an abandoned mental hospital at Bakovici. In 1995, the magazine alleged that other Canadian soldiers had co-habited with nurses, beaten up patients, refused to rescue a wounded Serb, and sold a machine gun on the black market. Mostly, they were drunk. Summoned from the UN to command the army, Lieutenant-General Maurice Baril was ordered to investigate. A retired RCMP officer looked into why the investigation had been delayed for two years.

The magazine and other media also helped Major Barry Anderson publicize charges that Airborne Regiment soldiers had murdered Somalis other than Shidane Arone, and that the defence department had organized a cover-up. On March 21, 1996, Collenette announced a no-holds-barred civilian inquiry into the whole Somalia affair, with federal court judge Gilles Létourneau and journalism professor Peter Desbarats. A third member was removed when she turned out to be a good friend of former deputy minister Robert Fowler. Her replacement was Mr. Justice Robert Rutherford, an armoured-corps veteran. The inquiry summoned data, commissioned reports, and interviewed experts on how the Airborne was prepared for Somalia, how the Arone murder was investigated, and why senior officers seemed immune from responsibility. Six months later, when most related courts martial were complete, the inquiry opened, on October 11. The parade of witnesses and revelations delighted the media. Included in the spectacle was a photo of Somali teenagers roped together under a sign reading "I am a thief." A smiling Canadian chaplain stood benignly behind them.

At the end of 1995, de Chastelain retired for a second time, this time to wrestle with the problem of disarming Northern Ireland. His unexpected successor as Chief of the Defence Staff was General Jean Boyle, an ambitious forty-eight-year-old former fighter pilot, who promptly announced that Canada's forces lacked the equipment, training, and reserves to play the role claimed for them in the government's own white paper. Supported by reports that lower ranks were lining up at food bank to feed their families, Boyle pledged a pay raise. Despite a 1990 freeze on federal salaries, on April 1, 1996, Collenette announced a 2.2 per cent increase for non-commissioned members. Boyle also gave subordinate commanders the job of managing their own budgets, with freedom to find non-traditional ways of getting their jobs done at lower cost. Solutions ranged from privatizing messes to buying tools and parts at a nearby hardware store.

When Collenette chose him over the heads of several superiors, he supposed Boyle's chief virtue was that he could not possibly be tainted by the Somalia inquiry. Collenette was wrong. As a former assistant deputy minister for policy and communications, Boyle had been in charge when staff had altered briefing notes given to a CBC reporter. Frustrated in their own search for incriminating documents, Létourneau and his colleagues already had Boyle in their sights. Charged with document tampering, Colonel Geoffrey Haswell insisted that Boyle had been involved. Boyle denied it. At the time, he explained, he had been commandant of RMC, as well as a newly appointed assistant deputy minister. When the Létourneau Commission alleged a "Wall of Silence" at the Department of National Defence, Boyle ordered everyone to stop work on April 9, 1996, and hunt for Somalia-related documents. Among the finds were documents linking Boyle to cover-ups.

In late August, the Chief of the Defence Staff appeared before the Somalia Commission. Darting eyes, verbose answers, memory lapses made Boyle a bad witness. Was he responsible for his subordinates? Of course. Was he responsible for tampering with documents? No. He had, he insisted, been betrayed by subordinates. Military veterans professed shock. Major-Generals Vernon and MacKenzie denounced Boyle personally. Collenette stood by his general, but on October 4, the minister resigned over a minor breach of conflict-of-interest rules. Two days later, Boyle was gone too, six years short of full pension. The government made up the difference and an aerospace firm gave him a job.

Collenette's successor, Doug Young, was a lawyer and cable-company owner from Bathurst, New Brunswick, with a deserved reputation for ruthlessness in two previous departments. The Vice Chief of the Defence Staff, Vice-Admiral Larry Murray, filled Boyle's chair. Young froze promotions, announced a medal for service in Somalia, and invited tenders for fifteen new search-and-rescue helicopters. He also wound up the Somalia Commission. It had run for over two years, sullied dozens of reputations, and despite two extensions, had come no closer to telling anyone how to improve the forces. It would wind up hearings by March 31, 1997, and report at the end of June.

Mr. Justice Létourneau was outraged. Stone-walling by the department, he alleged, had cost a year's delay; so had directives to investigate cover-ups. Opposition politicians and media agreed. When Vice-Admiral Murray appeared in February, his aggressive answers provoked Létourneau to threaten contempt charges. Both sides cooled down, but Murray ended his testimony with a blunt appeal to consider the good Canadians had done in Somalia. Most service members cheered, but media representatives found the testimony of Major Anderson, a month later, more heroic. Unfortunately, explained the commissioners, they would have no time to investigate murders or the role of Robert Fowler, General de Chastelain, or other top brass, or to discover whether Kim Campbell had been involved in the cover-up.

It would have been easier to wind up the Somalia Commission if the scandals had become just a memory. But they kept coming. Lieutenant-General Armand Roy, Deputy Chief of the Defence Staff and commander at Oka in 1990, had to repay $80,000 and resign after evidence emerged that he had padded expense accounts. Newspapers published a photograph of Captain Sandra Perron, a rare woman officer in the combat arms, tied to a tree at Gagetown. She had accepted that treatment because other soldiers had also been tied up, but constant harassment by brother officers had driven her to resign. She was far from alone in her allegations of gender-based abuse. Then a former submarine commander, Dean Marsaw, convicted by court martial of abusing his crew, used a well-publicized hunger strike to regain his rank and speed up his appeal. The appeal court discounted subordinates' testimony and reversed the finding. General Baril denounced the soldiers involved in the Bakovici affair, but, critics noted, too much time had passed for any of them to face a court martial.

For Young, the trickle of shameful stories was the death of a thousand cuts. In January 1997, he announced that the promotion freeze would continue. Since the inquiry had offered no practical advice, he gave four professors who had studied Canada's military six weeks to come up with ideas to enhance morale, efficiency, and ethical sensitivity in the Canadian Forces. Former chief justice Dickson and two others produced an equally hurried report on improving military police and justice. On March 25, Young announced his policy: 60,000 regulars, 30,000 reserves, and "stable and predictable funding levels" were essential for morale. If a quarter of all Canadians now had university degrees, so should all commissioned officers. Everyone associated with military justice and policing needed better training. Since pay was a continuing "dissatisfier," on April 1, non-commissioned ranks got a second small pay increase of 1.5 per cent; officers below the rank of colonel almost caught up with a 2.4 per cent increase.

On July 2, slightly late, the Somalia Commission presented its findings. Whatever its premature deadline, it distributed a ton of blame. Entitled *Dishonoured Legacy*, the report denounced almost everyone in authority at National Defence Headquarters and on the long chain of command to the Airborne Regiment. Except for Young, politicians, including Brian Mulroney and Kim Campbell, were exempt. If the Airborne was undisciplined, ill-trained, and badly equipped, it was the fault of each layer of commander, starting just under the minister. A hundred and sixty recommendations included a new civilian inspector-general with a direct channel to Parliament, a civilian ombudsman to hear grievances, a civilian committee to control the military police, plus scores of proposals for rules, regulations, and controls on military authority. Young was roasted. So was Admiral Murray, whose attitude made him "unfit to be Chief of the Defence Staff."

In a general election on June 2, 1997, Chrétien's Liberals had retained power, but Doug Young was defeated by constituents furious at cuts to unemployment insurance. His successor, former

Toronto mayor Art Eggleton, was as eager as Young to bury the Somalia Commission. "We gave those guys $25 million and twenty-seven months and it isn't enough for them," he told journalists. "How much is enough?" That was dumb. On September 17, General Baril, whose outrage at the Bakovici offenders had pleased politicians and media alike, became Chief of the Defence Staff; Admiral Murray retired to an assistant deputy minister post at the Department of Fisheries and Oceans.

In a formal response to *Dishonoured Legacy* on October 14, Eggleton balked at the inspector-general but adopted 134 of the 160 recommendations, including a long list of orders and regulations, an ombudsman, and a toll-free anonymous snitch-line direct to superior officers and the minister. Commanders would do well to show enthusiasm for accountability, ethics, and gender awareness. Whatever the difficulties of finding recruits, male or female, for the combat arms, women were to fill a quarter of the so-called "kill trades" by the year 2000. And the Canadian Forces was to have more of Canada's visible minorities in their ranks. And, if General Baril's directions were a guide, the Forces would not become "a refuge or a training ground for thugs and bullies."

Soft Power?

In the 1990s, Canadians were urged by leaders of their Liberal government to believe that they could apply "soft power" to human crises. During a score of low-intensity wars in Africa, Asia, and Latin America, land mines had been a source of cruel civilian casualties. Canada's foreign affairs minister, Lloyd Axworthy, took a lead in having them banned. No major producer or user of land mines initialled the treaty, but the effort made many Canadians feel better about themselves. So did efforts to eliminate the use of children as soldiers in Third World conflicts. Axworthy campaigned to win Canada a seat on the UN Security Council to bring greater influence to bear on behalf of human rights, regardless of the underlying UN principle that national sovereignty was inviolable. Sadly, the dilemmas of exercising power, soft or hard, would emerge in Kosovo.

By 1997, Yugoslavia had been reduced to Serbia, the tiny republic of Montenegro, and a deeply resentful Kosovo. When peaceful protests failed to restore Kosovo's former autonomy, a civil war broke out in 1998. Kosovar guerillas murdered Serbs; Serb police retaliated with village massacres. The Milosevic government in Belgrade allowed an unarmed observer force sponsored by the Organization for Security and Co-operation in Europe (OSCE). The observers, including Canadians under Brigadier-General Pierre Maisonneuve, supported Kosovar claims that the Serbs were bent on eliminating the Moslem population. By early 1999, thousands of Albanians had fled and a tragedy was in progress. European foreign ministers, including Russians, urged Slobodan Milosevic to withdraw Serb forces. To back diplomatic pressures, NATO assembled ships and aircraft. Negotiations at Rambouillet, a palace outside Paris, spun out for weeks. Kosovar representatives agreed to reduced autonomy; Serbs insisted on full control. As Yugoslav police and troops poured into Kosovo, OSCE observers retreated to Macedonia. Hundreds of thousands of Kosovo Albanians followed them, spurred by reports of rape, mass murder, and burning homes and villages. During ten days of diplomatic visits, negotiations, and deadlines, three hundred thousand Kosovars were dispossessed.

Would the Russians back their fellow Slavs in Belgrade? With modern Russian equipment, NATO air power could suffer serious losses. On March 24, 1999, NATO decided that the risk was acceptable with careful targeting. Fighter-bombers took off from NATO bases in Italy and Britain. Among them were four Canadian CF-18s, based at Aviano north of Venice, and equipped with infra-red radar. Military lawyers checked targets and gave their approval. General Wesley Clark, the NATO commander, operated distinct tactical plans for his NATO and his high-tech U.S. stealth bombers. Untroubled by the raids since his key installations were safely underground, Milosevic accelerated the "ethnic cleansing" of Kosovo, leaving UN and NATO officials to cope with a million refugees in Macedonia, Albania, and Montenegro. Almost everywhere, Serbs rallied to a national cause; in Toronto, they gathered to hurl firebombs and paint at the U.S. consulate. In some NATO countries, conservatives denounced the intervention as a futile idealism; in others, peace movements denounced military violence. All depended on Russia and on China, whose embassy in Belgrade was bombed in error. Their vetoes might have paralyzed the UN. Indeed, both countries denounced NATO, but offered the Serbs no practical help.

Perhaps they did not need it. General Clark's heavily politicized and high-tech bombing campaign left life in Serbia almost intact. Hundreds of additional aircraft joined his campaign. Canada's Aviano-based force grew to a dozen CF-18s and flew a tenth of the NATO sorties. When the public wearied of the long campaign, experts argued that only a ground war could defeat Serb forces and restore the refugees. Prime Minister Jean Chrétien was one of the first NATO leaders to express the demand. In April, Canada offered a reconnaissance squadron of radar-equipped Coyotes, military engineers, and a squadron of Griffon helicopters. At the end of May, they left for Macedonia to join a British armoured brigade. Late in the bombing campaign, Clark targeted Belgrade's electrical grid. A few raids left the area without lights and Milosevic without an audible voice or presence. That, more than the plight of hospitals, changed his mind. After sixty-four days, he ordered his troops and police to withdraw. Members of the Kosovo Liberation Army and Moslem refugees poured homeward, intent on vengeance. NATO troops, fearful of land mines, followed them. Too late to prevent new atrocities, their leaders grimly concluded that they and their soldiers would be stuck preserving order in Kosovo far longer than any of them wanted.

Buy-Up or Rust-Out?

Grumbling is traditionally a soldier's only right. The Canadian Forces and their supporters exercised that right to the full in the 1990s and the early 2000s. So did the members of most armed forces in the post–Cold War years. And so did their civilian rivals for public spending, from doctors to farmers to prison guards. If the Third World War was not going to happen, surely it was possible to reduce military strength and readiness. In Canada, where business and economic experts insisted that a huge national debt, fed annually by deficits up to $40 billion, threatened national ruin, the top priority for the Chrétien government was a balanced budget and debt reduction. The Liberals' top claim to re-election in 1997, 2000, and 2004 was achieving a surplus, which was achieved in part by cutting defence spending from $12 billion to $9 billion and armed forces strength to only fifty-eight thousand men and women. Opinion polls made it clear that most Canadians sympathized with hard-working, poorly paid service members, but they had no interest in lavishing money on defence. In 1998, reports of service members patronizing food banks and delivering pizza persuaded a House of Commons committee to demand $740 million to improve service pay and living conditions. People in uniform got increases, but financing them depended on further defence cuts.

In some respects, the Canadian Forces were better than defence lobbyists would admit. Faced with rust-out in the 1970s, Canada's navy had proved once again to be the politically shrewdest branch of the Canadian Forces. By the end of the century, its twelve Halifax-class patrol frigates were some of the best and most flexible warships anywhere, even if Mr. Chrétien's vote-winning gambit in 1993 had deprived them of a modern sea-going helicopter, the EH-101. Twelve new Kingston-class maritime coastal defence vessels (MCDVs) gave the navy's reserves a realistic and valuable role in peace or a crisis. The Conservatives had abandoned their own plan to acquire a dozen nuclear-powered submarines, capable of operating in all three of the oceans bordering Canada. After years of delay, the Liberals agreed in 1996 that acquiring four of Britain's best remaining non-nuclear-powered submarines was the most cost-conscious way to maintain Canada's expertise in submarine and anti-submarine warfare, and to provide vast covert surveillance of Canada's sea frontiers. Sadly, more years of delay and half-hearted bargaining added to the cost and time needed to bring the Victoria-class submarines into Canadian service. Opposition politicians jeered at buying second-hand goods. When a fire aboard HMCS *Chicoutimi* during its transfer to Canada cost a young officer's life, a fresh storm of negative publicity exploded.

In comparison to the navy, the air force did badly. Canada's most favoured service in the 1950s and 1960s, with 40 per cent of defence spending, the air forces lost their influence as the Soviet threat faded and they failed to identify a beguiling new role. Selling off Paul Hellyer's never-needed C-5 fighters allowed the air force to modernize sixty of its CF-18s, but the twenty-one fighter squadrons of 1960 shrunk to only four. After exploring privatization of search and rescue — would the rescued pay to be saved? — the cabinet reluctantly agreed to buy fifteen Cormorant helicopters for the role, virtually the same aircraft as the EH-101s Jean Chrétien had cancelled six years earlier. As an economy, the air force sacrificed its over-aged Boeing 707s, but the Mulroney government had insisted that it buy five

Airbus A-310s to help out a struggling Canadian Airlines International. Officials preferred flying by Airbus rather than the smaller, Canadian-built Challenger. Unfortunately, the government refused funds to convert the A-310s for air-to-air refuelling, eliminating part of the equipment needed for a global reach. The only new air force acquisitions in the 1990s were a hundred lightweight CH-146 Griffons, built near Montreal for use in support of the army. To cut costs and speed replacement of fast-vanishing air crew, the air force privatized pilot training and handed over its base at Moose Jaw, claiming that NATO members would be happy to pay for their trainees. Buying suitable training aircraft took years, and pilot training dragged to a halt.

The army was no better off. In Yugoslavia, Serb and Croat bullets riddled Canadian-built Cougars, vehicles designed solely as trainers. Worse still, to save money, training above the company level ceased. Officers lost any chance to manoeuvre battalions or brigades. Reduced to three mechanized brigades at Valcartier, Petawawa, and Edmonton, with a divisional headquarters at Kingston, a 1994 defence white paper promised that the army would provide and sustain indefinitely a single six-thousand-member brigade in support of alliance commitments anywhere. Writing in 1999, American military expert Joseph Jockel found no possibility that an understrength, undertrained Canadian army could keep its main promise.

The Liberals' white paper had pledged that Canada's soldiers could fight the best alongside the best. Instead, essential but unglamorous equipment needs were usually ignored. Politicians boasted of the global reach of Canada's peacekeepers, but missions did not travel by bus. A fleet of C-130 Hercules transports had been ideal replacements for the worn-out C-119 Flying Boxcars in the 1960s. By 1999, most Canadian "Hercs" were older than their pilots. Repairs and maintenance took weeks, not hours; the manufacturer no longer stocked essential but obsolete parts. The Iltis, a cheap, undersized replacement for the Jeep, was also long overdue for replacement. Action was delayed by bickering over specifications and haggling over regional benefits. When Canadian soldiers patrolled Kabul in 2004, they still faced roadside bombs, rockets, and land mines behind the canvas sides of their Iltis trucks. By the 2000s, virtually every significant item of Canadian military equipment was worn out, even by conventional rules of depreciation, not to mention a decade of constant deployments.

Even legitimate procedures turned procurement into a multi-year process. Getting new equipment was further delayed when cabinet ministers held up approvals to extract benefits for their constituents. The price of a pair of boots doubled when boot production was shared between a Montreal factory and a plant in Cornerbrook that promised to employ disabled fishermen. Defence dollars fostered a truck industry for Kelowna, in the British Columbia interior. Replacement costs soared when aircraft manufacturers had to find ways to distribute production jobs to every region represented in the Canadian cabinet.

Any quick fix was complicated. The end of the Cold War in 1990 had collapsed production and competition in the world's vast arms industry, but it did not stop arms development. On the contrary, the massive potential of information management in the computer age promised what enthusiasts called "a Revolution in Military Affairs," or RMA. Unmanned aerial vehicles, or UAVs, carrying radar and television cameras, could reveal the mystery that generals throughout the ages had always yearned to solve: what was happening on the other side of the hill? Digital systems could amass and update billions of bytes of information and convey it instantly to generals, captains, and corporals anywhere. If global positioning systems (GPS) could guide a driver through a strange city, they could lead a lost patrol through mountains or jungle to its objective, or back home to its base.

Huge technological advances were not necessarily the key to victory. They had certainly not saved the U.S. Army in Vietnam, but, without a suitable war to test them, eloquent sales promoters were spurred on by the urgent need of the arms industry for fresh orders. In a culture where newest is portrayed as best, working with obsolete and worn-out weapons and equipment became deeply demoralizing.

Canada's neighbour and military model, the United States, had always been a glutton for expensive but seemingly painless technological solutions to the brutal business of war. If Canadians wanted to remain faithful allies and interoperative partners with the world's most modern army, navy, and air force, Ottawa faced massive spending. Even under President Clinton, the vastly richer U.S. spent 5 per cent of its gross domestic product on defence; Canada spent 1 per cent. Alternatively, and for most Canadians unthinkably, Canada would have to plan its military future in isolation. Amidst all the glories and nightmares of pre-millennial thinking, it seemed both prudent and convenient to defer difficult choices. The re-election of the Chrétien Liberals in 2000 suggested that most Canadians agreed.

Replacing military equipment was a problem aggravated by a couple of decades of cuts, patches, and higher priorities. All three Canadian Forces had been re-equipped for the Cold War in the 1950s. Afterward, expensive defence requirements only occasionally climbed to the top of any cabinet agenda, Liberal or Conservative. The basic problem was as obvious as the federal deficit had been. Much as debts rise if you spend more than you earn, all equipment wears out over time. It wears even faster if you use it in operations. Most Canadian families own some kind of motor vehicle. An accountant might claim that it has twenty years of use, but few families keep a car that long. If, for example, they also drive it over logging trails to bring home the winter firewood, they expect extra wear and tear. So must soldiers who drove their trucks or armoured vehicles over the back roads of Bosnia or Kosovo for a few years, or pilots who flew their CF-18s through the sandstorms of the Persian Gulf or dodged Serb anti-aircraft rockets over Belgrade. One or more of Canada's patrol frigates has been on constant duty in the Arabian Gulf from 1990 to the present.

Why were equipment problems seldom publicized? Any civil servant or serving officer who shared their worries with the public would have been dismissed for political meddling. Who knew whether Canadians even cared. Peacetime military promotions seldom rewarded eloquence, audacity, or even courage. On the eve of the twenty-first millennium, some defence scholars began warning Canadians to get ready to get along without armed forces. Even if sclerotic procurement procedures allowed new equipment to be ordered, it was unlikely to be delivered by the shrunken post–Cold War arms industry before the original item had been hauled to a scrap yard.

Commitments and Capabilities

And why, Canadians asked, should they spend money on weapons? Many no longer believed that Canada's armed forces were intended for fighting wars. Surveys regularly proclaimed that Canadians identified their armed forces with international peacekeeping, though some recalled their domestic role at Oka in 1990.

In 1999 alone, Canadians shared in twenty-three international operations, from the ex-Soviet Georgia to Guatemala, not to mention a post–Cold War series of arms verification over-flights in Europe and North America. Citizens recognized the value of the Canadian Forces during floods, forest fires, and other natural disasters, and wondered only why they were not deployed faster and in larger numbers. When floods struck Quebec's Saguenay region on June 10, 1996, Canadian Forces members based at Bagotville, near Chicoutimi, were promptly on hand to give aid to homeless, disoriented, frightened people. When the Red River flooded southern Manitoba in the spring of 1997, more than eight thousand men and women in green combat uniforms rescued stranded residents, guarded abandoned homes, and devoted back-breaking hours to filling sandbags and building the dikes that saved most of Winnipeg's homes and businesses. In early January 1998, a four-day ice storm toppled trees and hydro pylons across southern Quebec, eastern Ontario, and much of New Brunswick. Fourteen thousand regulars and reservists, the largest-ever civil aid force, mobilized to help millions of people left without heat, light, and often the means to maintain life in a Canadian winter. As the crisis ended, pollsters invited Quebeckers to pass judgment on their experiences. An amazing 89 per cent reported an undiluted admiration for the Canadian Forces. Few Canadians even realized that about seven hundred Canadian Forces personnel, mostly in the air force, worked a 24/7 week in Search and Rescue (SAR) to save an average of six thousand Canadian lives annually.

In January 1999, Toronto's mayor summoned the Royal Canadian Dragoons and its vehicles from Petawawa to help his city cope with a heavy snowfall. Some citizens condemned the mayor for overreacting, but no one criticized the troops. That week, Ottawa announced that a quarter of the Canadian Forces would be on duty over the New Year's 2000 holiday in case the so-called Y2K problem crippled the country's computers. Perhaps because of widespread precautions, almost nothing happened. Only the Canadian Forces, however undersized and poorly equipped, could muster the personnel, skills, resources, and communications to meet the emergency needs of 30 million fellow citizens. That part of a long history continues.

If overseas commitments wore out equipment, uniformed personnel suffered too. Ottawa's Peacekeeping Monument portrays bronze peacekeepers surveying the landscape with binoculars but makes no reference to terrifying patrols across mine-strewn fields or hair-raising encounters with armed and angry partisans. There is no hint of months of family separation, and festering anxieties about whether a dad or mom would return intact. The obvious solution for a stressed-out family was a prompt transfer to civilian life, whatever the cost to the forces in training and experience. After his Rwanda experience, Lieutenant-General Roméo Dallaire became a poster image for hundreds of Canadians transformed by their peacekeeping experiences into victims of post-traumatic stress disorder (PTSD). A hundred more had been crippled by the mysterious symptoms defined as Gulf War Syndrome and originally denied by both American and Canadian authorities. Another hundred reported pain, fatigue, and blindness after filling sandbags with chemically polluted dirt in Croatia. It took years and a special inquiry by Colonel Joe Sharpe before victims could get redress. "It's obvious that we sent people into that theatre healthy," Sharpe concluded, "and we brought them back sick." In a period that fostered higher educational qualifications and military professionalism for Canadian Forces officers, blunt common sense was sometimes sadly scarce.

Faced with dwindling trained manpower, Canadian Forces commanders had to promise no more than one six-month tour in two years. In 1999, General Maurice Baril, Chief of the Defence Staff, combined thanks for a modest budget increase with a plea to Ottawa to reduce commitments and to accept no new ones. Despite his appeal, the prime minister felt compelled that year to order five hundred more troops to help enforce peace in postwar Kosovo. After a disastrous August earthquake in Turkey, the Canadian Forces' Disaster Assistance and Rescue Team (DART) was dispatched to the scene. In September, the government sent a ship, aircraft, and six hundred personnel to join an Australian-led peacemaking force in East Timor. Other Canadian soldiers left to enforce peace in East Africa and Haiti. Henceforth, the government promised, Canada's commitments would respect strict deadlines, whether or not the mission was accomplished.

Hidden in the new century were answers to insoluble arguments about the most appropriate equipment, organization, training, and incentives for Canada's armed forces. As the new millennium dawned, most Canadians had felt almost no imminent threat to their territory for a century and a half, even during two world wars. War itself had receded to the memories not just of fathers but of grandfathers. Only militarists could complain. Immunity from the horror of war is a blessing few other countries in the world can boast. Had Canadians merely been lucky, or had they actually mastered some lessons after the almost endless wars before 1815?

The new millennium would not keep its secrets for long.

VIII   A New Kind of War?

9/12, 2001

On Tuesday morning, September 11, 2001, Captain Mike Jellinek of the Canadian navy took command of the watch at the subterranean headquarters of NORAD, the North American Aerospace Defense Command, near Colorado Springs. By American law, NORAD still looked outward, not inward, chiefly at former Cold War enemies, evidence to its critics of military preoccupations outdated more than a decade after the collapse of the Berlin Wall. An airliner hijacking was reported near Boston, in NORAD's northeastern sector. Local jet fighters had been scrambled. Jellinek phoned NORAD's commander. Could he react? Yes. Before the first hijacked airliner tore into the World Trade Center in New York, Jellinek had fighters vectored on its heading. If passengers on the fourth airliner had not fought their captors and crashed into a Pennsylvania field, NORAD interceptors would have met them over Washington. A Canadian had launched Operation Noble Eagle. Could anyone have saved the three thousand who would die? It was not a question NORAD had to answer.

It ordered every civilian aircraft out of North American skies. Combat air patrols swept over every major city. Non-conforming aircraft would be destroyed. Canadian airports filled with diverted international flights; communities took in marooned strangers without a second thought. Rallying his shocked and frightened country, President George W. Bush declared an unlimited war on terror. Any nation that did not wholeheartedly back the United States in this war would be treated as an enemy. Meeting in an emergency session on Wednesday, September 12, NATO representatives dealt for the first time in their sixty-two-year history with the proposition that had originally created the organization: an attack on one member was an attack on all.

That same morning, September 12, Canadians awoke to learn that the United States had slammed its borders shut, stopping four-fifths of Canada's foreign trade, eliminating 43 per cent of its gross domestic product. This was an economic disaster on the scale of two simultaneous Great Depressions. Huge columns of trucks snaked back from major border crossings. Border cities, economies built on just-in-time deliveries, ground to a halt. By noon, cities farther away felt the crunch. Much that followed in Canada reflected the 9/12 crisis.

Canada had gone to war in 1914 because the British Empire had declared war. British Canadians, at least, responded as British patriots. That experience persuaded W. L. Mackenzie King and most other Canadians that next time "Parliament would decide." In 1939 and 1950, Canada's Parliament had decided on war. It would do so again in 2001, but this time most Canadians understood that the price for neutrality was unacceptable. Canada's 1988 decision to link its trade as well as its defences to its hugely powerful neighbour left the Chrétien government no choice but to reassure President Bush that Canada would do all it could to back the American war. Many countries echoed that pledge; few had Canada's practical obligation to respect it.

Having emerged by 1997 from a crippling federal deficit, Ottawa could pledge billions of dollars to expand and equip its new Border Services Agency and create a new agency to screen all airline passengers for weapons as imaginative as nail scissors or face cream. Less imaginatively named than the U.S. Patriot Act, Canada's Anti-terrorism Act allowed police to arrest and hold indefinitely anyone suspected of terrorism, with few of the protections spelled out in Canada's Charter of Rights and Freedoms. In some respects, Canada's government was better fitted to address security issues than its neighbour. Fifty American states controlled the U.S. National Guard; rival federal intelligence and police agencies guarded their secrets from each other. In Ottawa, the federal government controlled intelligence and the RCMP, and concentrated data flowed through the Prime Minister's Office and the Privy Council Office. An Office of Critical Infrastructure and Emergency Preparedness (OCIPEP) coordinated protection for vital installations such as the Ambassador Bridge between Windsor and Detroit. Structures cannot guarantee wisdom. Critics might protest that terrorists were a predictable response to American imperialism or warn that President Bush was promoting a war on terror as a trick to win a second term in 2004. Such voices were ignored in an epidemic of panic, scapegoating, and political patriotism. The televised collapse of the World Trade

Center sent a wave of emotional solidarity sweeping over Canada. Eighty thousand people felt summoned to Parliament Hill to mourn 9/11's three thousand victims — among them, five Canadians.

Most Americans were too preoccupied with their own crisis to notice. Some in the Bush administration were scornful. In 2000, an alert U.S. border guard caught a Montreal-based Moslem smuggling explosives to blow up the Los Angeles airport. Had the 9/11 terrorists also come from Canada? Canadians might be NATO allies, but President Bush and even President Clinton had complained that Canada's defence expenditures were among the lowest in the alliance, less than 2 per cent of its gross domestic product, compared to 5.9 per cent for the United States, or $476 for each Canadian but $1,465 for each American. In April 2001, when President Bush dispatched Paul Cellucci, a former governor of Massachusetts, as his new ambassador to Ottawa, Cellucci's prime mission was to boost Canada's defence spending. He soon got busy. If Ottawa wanted to lecture Washington on international morality, Cellucci warned a business audience in British Columbia on July 26, 2001, it should "put up or shut up!" The prime minister responded mildly enough to a neighbour's meddling: "We are not having wars of the same nature," he assured the press. Slamming the Canadian border shut on 9/12 would remind Canadians that new kinds of wars demanded big spending too.

Operation Apollo

Ottawa's sudden concern for border security tackled some obvious American concerns, but National Defence was a very minor beneficiary of post-9/12 spending. How could Canada help with Bush's war on terror? Thanks to close American linkages, Canada's navy had a prompt and persuasive answer. The U.S. Navy had been the first American service to offer an original post–Cold War strategy. What use was a navy after the Soviet threat disintegrated? Never could it be more useful, insisted U.S. admirals. With guns, carriers, aircraft, and Marines, the U.S. Navy could project American power over any littoral region (defined as a thousand kilometres inland from the coast). Over 80 per cent of the world's land surface was within navy range. Since the 1950s, making Canadian warships as interoperable with the U.S. fleet as the Americans would allow had been the top priority of Canadian admirals. Too small and poorly funded to have aircraft carriers or nuclear-powered submarines, Canada's fleet included the escort ships any major navy desperately lacks in wartime. Despite budget cuts, Canada's fleet managed to keep a single high-readiness task group in being — a guided missile destroyer, a replenishment ship, and two patrol frigates, alternating between Halifax and Esquimalt. The admirals even had a strategy paper entitled *Leadmark*, plus reminders of how Canada had responded to earlier crises such as the 1990 Gulf War. As U.S. carrier task forces moved to the Persian Gulf to target the Afghan refuge of al Qaeda, the navy reminded Ottawa that a Canadian frigate had been on duty there since 1991. Indeed, the Gulf had almost replaced the North Atlantic as Canada's naval "home from home."

Within hours of the collapse of the World Trade Center, George Bush's war on terror had a battleground. Osama bin Laden's al Qaeda had been such a persistent enemy it was hard to see why Bush had to wait for the 9/11 attacks to declare war. Bin Laden's terrorists had trained under the protection of Afghanistan's radical Islamic Taliban regime. Its leader, a one-eyed veteran of war with the Soviets, the Mullah Omar, refused to hand over Osama bin Laden for American punishment. With no American bases or dependable allies next to Afghanistan, the U.S. Navy offered its littoral strategy to punish al Qaeda and Taliban alike. By early October, the United Nations Security Council was close to echoing NATO's indignation at Afghanistan-based terrorism. For once, Russia and China agreed: if Washington wanted to attack the Taliban regime that the Americans had created and armed to defeat a pro-Soviet regime a decade earlier, the irony was not lost on them. What sweeter vengeance than to let the Americans wrestle with their own ferocious creation!

On October 7, 2001, Prime Minister Chrétien visited President Bush in Washington; that evening, General Ray Henault, General Baril's successor as Chief of the Defence Staff, issued a ten-day warning order for Operation Apollo. On October 17, Commodore Drew Robertson and three of his four ships cleared Halifax for the Arabian Sea. Diverted from a NATO exercise, HMCS *Halifax* joined later. On arrival in the Persian Gulf on November 26, after an eight-thousand-mile passage, the Canadians were assigned to escort ships of a U.S. Marine Expeditionary Unit off the coast of Pakistan. Once the marines were established in Afghanistan, Robertson's force moved to the sensitive Straits of Hormuz, cruising under the sights of Iranian Silkworm rockets. Next, the Canadians oversaw the "Parking Lot," where up to 150 of the world's tankers and freighters had dropped anchor. On dark nights, a few bolted for Iraq to capture rich profits in contraband for their owners. Using HMCS *Halifax*'s helicopter, the Canadians made precise digital photographs of the waiting ships, making it easier for allied warships to identify and seize suspected blockade runners. Ultimately, Robertson's force spent most of its time conducting and directing allied warships in "leadership identification operations" — or LIO — boarding ships, dhows, and open motorboats or "go-fasts" in the Gulf to identify al Qaeda agents amidst swarms of Pakistani migrant labourers heading to jobs in oil-rich Arab countries. Meanwhile, HMCS *Preserver* distributed 17 million litres of fuel oil and a host of other needs to a hundred and twenty U.S. and allied ships in the Gulf. With a commodore aboard and a record of professionalism and dependable collaboration, American commanders cheerfully delegated responsibility for allied warships to the Canadians, as they had in the earlier Gulf War.

When Commodore Robertson's six months were up, Esquimalt's battle-ready task force took its place and a third rotation, at Halifax, made ready. Sadly, two complete task forces was the limit for the Canadian fleet. It could easily yield two of its twelve patrol frigates to the Gulf, but Canada had only two replenishment ships, *Preserver* and *Protecteur*, and nine detachments of worn-out Sea Kings. It even had four destroyers, each fitted with the communications and space needed for a headquarters, but personnel shortages dictated that only three of them were in commission. One of those just happened to be undergoing a major refit. After only two rotations, Canada mustered only two frigates at a time for Operation Apollo, and the task force commander had to squeeze himself and a reduced staff into narrow spaces carved out of a frigate's crew quarters. Given his important role with allied navies, the Canadian commodore might have transferred his pennant to an American destroyer, but, as the navy's official historian curtly noted: "That would be unacceptable politically to Canadian sensitivities." The lack of a replenishment ship compelled Canadian ships to rely on the U.S. fleet train or on allies. The two Sea Kings, the large hangar, and extra maintenance staff in

Preserver and *Protecteur* were even more badly missed since there was nowhere for frigate-sized helicopter detachments to turn for major overhauls, complex repairs, or a replacement Sea King.

Ships and helicopters were not Canada's only contribution to the American-led war on Afghanistan's Taliban leadership. In a land war fought largely by the U.S. Air Force's bombers and by army special forces, Canada had sent its own tiny Joint Task Force II, created for anti-terrorist emergencies after the Canadian Airborne Regiment was disbanded. A force clouded in secrecy, JTF2's presence in Afghanistan was unveiled to Canadians only when the *Globe and Mail* ran a front-page photograph of soldiers in green camouflage uniforms shoving Afghan prisoners out of an aircraft. Americans wore sandy-brown. A more substantial contribution was the 3rd Battalion of the Princess Patricia's Canadian Light Infantry (3 PPCLI), sent from Edmonton to help defend the U.S. base at Kandahar. To link Canada and Afghanistan, Canada needed a staging base in the Arabian peninsula, so a suitably named Camp Mirage was established in a hospitable but discreetly unnamed Arab emirate. In addition to a detachment of C-130 Hercules from 8 Wing in Trenton, a couple of Lockheed Aurora long-range patrol aircraft were established at Camp Mirage to make up for the lack of Sea King helicopters on later rotations of Canadian warships. Aged radars and a lack of infrared sensors restricted the over-aged Auroras to daytime operations, but dedicated ground crews kept them flying with impressive dependability.

Sadly, Canada's involvement in the American invasion of Afghanistan ended in tragedy. On April 18, 2003, members of 3 PPCLI staged a night exercise at Tarnak Farm, south of Kandahar. U.S. air controllers were warned, but two American F-16 pilots paid no heed. Flying overhead, Major Harry Schmidt saw flashes on the ground and asked permission to attack. "Hold fire," replied his controller. Schmidt rolled his plane and dived. Flying his last mission before retirement, he released a laser-controlled 150-kilogram bomb on what he hoped were Taliban fighters. Instead, he killed four Canadian soldiers and wounded eight more, Canada's gravest losses since the Korean War. The "friendly fire" losses shocked Canadians and fed an anti-American mood.

Other Commitments

If the navy played the lead for Canada in President Bush's war on terror, the other Canadian services had ample competing worldwide commitments. Throughout the 1990s, governments had financed the Canadian Forces as though a shrunken peacetime force could return to barracks and wait for the next war. Then Canada had responded to virtually every crisis the mass media chose to cover, from Guatemala to East Timor. Trusting that being useful would win both public esteem and a reprieve from budget cuts, generals and admirals had been "ready, aye ready" for almost any challenge. Finally, after becoming Chief of the Defence Staff in 2000, air force General Ray Henault had had to plead for a year of relative reprieve for his troops. Ottawa's concern for a crisis-plagued world did not rest. In 2004, a typical year, five hundred Canadian members of Task Force Haiti struggled for six months to bring order out of political chaos as a vital prerequisite to alleviating suffering in the world's most impoverished country. When they came home, RCMP and civilian police officers continued their work. Hundreds of other Canadians shared both UN and non-UN truce supervision on the borders of Israel. As a veteran UN peacekeeper, Canada had subscribed early to a Danish initiative for SHIRBRIG, a Multinational Standby High-Readiness Brigade. Consequently, in 1999 it had to share in SHIRBRIG's first deployment to the war-ravaged frontiers of Eritrea and Ethiopia. Again in 2004, elements of SHIRBRIG deployed to Liberia, where a devastating civil war had raged for years.

As a twelve-year involvement with the former Yugoslavia slowly faded, the Middle East remained the major Canadian preoccupation, but the focus had shifted from the Mediterranean to the Persian Gulf with the American assault on the Taliban regime. Historically, Afghanistan has usually proved easy to conquer. Invaders, from Alexander the Great to Leonid Brezhnev, could exploit desperate poverty, corrupt rulers, and bitter tribal conflicts, and 2001 proved to be no exception. Reinforcing an anti-Taliban Northern Alliance with airpower, well-equipped special forces, funds, and reinforcements from across the former Soviet border defeated a regime that had made enemies among the country's warlords by zealous suppression of opium production. By the spring of 2002, Mullah Omar and Osama bin Laden had fled south to the turbulent tribal regions of northwestern Pakistan. Three months earlier than they had expected, Americans and their allies faced what had always been the failure of any invasion of Afghanistan: creating stability.

Neither civil nor military leaders in the United States had any enthusiasm for this task. Delighted by the political and legislative leverage a popular war had given him, President Bush was persuaded by his chosen advisors to complete a task his father had seemingly left unfinished in 1991: crushing another former U.S. ally, Iraq's Saddam Hussein, and bringing democracy to his oil-rich country. Pretexts ranged from Saddam's ruthless oppression of Kurds and Shiites, who had taken the earlier war as an opportunity to rebel, to a vaguer allegation that Iraq was building nuclear, biological, or chemical weapons of mass destruction (WMD). Far from being implicated in al Qaeda, Saddam represented a secularism that Osama bin Laden despised. Reasons hardly mattered. Flushed with victory in Afghanistan, Bush's advisors, led by Defense Secretary Donald Rumsfeld, cut back the forces their generals wanted for an Iraq invasion. How much more glorious would be a victory on a shoestring. As for warnings from former general Colin Powell that without Saddam, Kurds, Shiites, and Sunnis would battle each other, advisors assured Bush that Iraqis would greet invading Americans with the same enthusiasm Europeans had shown their liberators in 1944. A dose of democracy would then sort out ethnic conflict.

As Operation Iraqi Freedom took shape, Canada's military leaders wondered what role they would play. At the United Nations, Canadian delegates tried to cool opposition to the American plan. They failed. This time, Russia and China had no sympathy whatever with overthrowing a former regional ally and client. Neither did France, which depended on Iraq for its oil. When Tony Blair, Britain's prime minister, supported Bush's plan to remove a murderous tyrant, his own Labour supporters jeered, and moved to unseat their most popular leader in decades. In Ottawa, Jean Chrétien remembered that Canada had committed itself to the United Nations and multilateralism since San Francisco in 1945, took a deep breath, and made Canada's reluctance discreetly evident. The Bush administration was annoyed, contemptuous, and utterly undeterred.

Operation Athena

Canadians in the Middle East were also annoyed, a little contemptuous of Ottawa, and worried. In Afghanistan, they noted that the Americans cancelled most of their costly development promises designed to underpin the newly elected regime of Hamid Karzai. Iraq was the new priority. Some U.S. forces remained, but most were extracted for Operation Iraqi Freedom. When Canada claimed that it lacked the troops to replace 3 PPCLI after its six-month term, critics attributed the claim to sour grapes for the friendly fire incident at Tarnak Farm, as well as the Chrétien government's refusal to be an ally in Iraq. The incident was largely ignored in the United States. After victory in 2001, American news media had almost forgotten about Afghanistan. At least partly on Canada's suggestion, Washington transferred its Afghan command responsibilities to its NATO allies in Brussels. The Europeans might be slow, litigious, and timid, as Americans in Bosnia had complained, but who cared if they took over a dangerous and even impossible task?

In the Persian Gulf and at Camp Mirage, the new war in Iraq made less difference than might be imagined. Canadian warships already had a UN mandate to block the passage of oil and other strategic supplies to and from Iraq, but by 2003, most of their attention was focused on the hunt for al Qaeda agents crossing the Gulf. In June 2003, Canada's two Aurora maritime patrol aircraft came home from Camp Mirage; in October, Operation Apollo became Operation Athena. As its contribution to the NATO-led International Security Assistance Force (ISAF), Canada promised a force of two thousand soldiers as part of a multinational brigade at Kabul, the Afghan capital. A Canadian, Major-General Andrew Leslie, took command of Task Force Kabul. In February 2004, Lieutenant-General Rick Hillier, a bluff Newfoundlander and former officer of the Royal Canadian Dragoons, left his post as Chief of the Land Staff in Ottawa to become ISAF commander for the next six months. Hillier had won the most senior international appointment of any Canadian since Lieutenant-General E. L. M. Burns took over the United Nations Emergency Force in 1956. Following an American "privatization" model, Ottawa assigned construction of a billion-dollar defended camp at Kabul to ATCO, a well-known Alberta-based contractor. Soldiers were now too scarce and costly to work as cooks, carpenters, and electricians; civilians now accompanied armies to war, as they had hundreds of years earlier.

Mullah Omar and the Taliban had not accepted their fate quietly. As early as March 2002, the Taliban leader had addressed followers by radio; in April, his agents were distributing AK-47 rifles in northern Kandahar province. In August, Taliban raiders attacked U.S. and Afghan posts along the Pakistan border. High technology, from night vision to constant aerial surveillance from unmanned aerial vehicles, gave the Americans a commanding advantage. Invaders were repeatedly spotted and apparently destroyed. Fighting back with suicide bombers and improvised explosive devices (IEDs) was less a copy of similar tactics in Iraq, NATO commanders insisted, than a symptom of desperation.

Outsiders offered an alternative analysis. If media coverage of the death of eighteen American soldiers in Mogadishu back in 1993 had unnerved Washington enough to pull U.S. peacemakers out of Somalia, a similar killing of troops in Afghanistan or Iraq might also convince the U.S. and its rubber-spined allies to go home. After twenty years of non-stop war, fanatical opponents were as plentiful in Afghanistan and the Moslem world as hidden stockpiles of bombs, rockets, and explosives, and the population was suspicious of infidel invaders who spoke no local language and who readily used their firepower to kill youngsters and old people.

"Heavy Lifting"

International commanders tend to be diplomats as much as military leaders. An officer with international experience in NATO, as deputy commander of a U.S. army corps based at Fort Hood, Texas, and commanding a multinational division in Bosnia, General Hillier was blunt. In a command structure devoted to pompous polysyllabic pronouncement, he preferred to be clear and explicit. Hillier saw at once that the problems of ISAF were many and serious. It was underfunded and severely undermanned. Most NATO members, and especially their voters, regarded Afghanistan as hopeless and none of their business. Nor was the Afghan government an easy ally. Whatever its promises of democracy and consultation, old realities prevailed. Twenty years of war had shattered even a primitive infrastructure.

There was no civil service, police, or court system. Like previous Afghan governments, the Karzai regime had little influence over its people beyond the shadow of Kabul. Germany had pledged to train an Afghan police force; Italy agreed to develop a judiciary. Neither NATO partner gave their task much priority. The police commander was Rashid Dostum. As a leader of the Northern Alliance, he had locked his Taliban prisoners in containers, dragged the steel boxes into the desert, and left them. After eight years of drought across Afghanistan, farmers found little to grow beyond opium poppies. Once again, the raw material for heroin was Afghanistan's chief agricultural export. Impoverished farmers might work the fields, but most of the proceeds of the drug trade clung to the fingers of war-lords or even found their way to finance the Taliban. Opium eradication, a priority for both the U.S. and NATO, turned farmers into bitter enemies. Without revenue from poppies, how could they feed their families? Orthodox Islam might condemn narcotic drugs, but the Taliban had no scruples about making rural friends if that gave them safe passage through the hills and valleys of Afghanistan.

Afghanistan had seldom been more than a patchwork of tribal alliances. Even the biggest tribe, the powerful, warlike, and pro-Taliban Pashtun had understood its limits. Its members lived on both sides of the Afghan-Pakistani border. By 2003, they had won large areas of southwestern Afghanistan away from the Karzai government. Pakistan's General Perez Musharraf claimed to have lost four thousand soldiers in an unpopular struggle to assert his sovereignty on his side of the Northwest Frontier. U.S. and NATO leaders suspected that Pakistani military intelligence was closely allied to the Taliban forces Pakistan had helped create for the U.S.-financed war against Soviet forces in Afghanistan in the 1980s. Unfortunately, if the U.S. or NATO weakened Musharraf, and Taliban sympathizers overthrew his regime, as seemed all too possible, Islamic radicals would henceforth control about fifty Pakistani nuclear warheads.

What was needed, Hillier believed, was some "heavy lifting." Specific NATO members needed to take responsibility for Kandahar, Helmand, Khost, and other border provinces. Otherwise, the U.S. victory of 2001 might easily be reversed. When Hillier returned to Ottawa in 2004 as a new Chief of the Defence Staff, he ignored his predecessors' colourless prudence and set out to make himself both a public figure and, if he could, a political force. The Taliban, he announced, were "scumbags" and "a bag of snakes." Critics deplored such a vulgar abandonment of neutrality; sympathizers already realized that Canada was not keeping peace in Afghanistan but fighting a war against an enemy who killed nurses, doctors, teachers, and Canadian soldiers.

The Taliban, they agreed, were not slightly misguided patriots but tyrants and killers, and Canadians had a stake in their defeat. If that meant claiming one of the posts of danger, Canadians had done so before, in two world wars and Korea. Since the Americans had been fighting almost alone on Afghanistan's vulnerable frontier, there was also credit to be reaped in Washington for a much bolder commitment of Canadian "boots on the ground." Canada's Liberal government, now headed by Paul Martin, agreed late in 2005 to abandon the relative security of Camp Julian and return a two-thousand-member reinforced battalion group to the former base in Kandahar, with a commitment to stay until 2009. The British took responsibility for the adjoining and equally embattled Helmand province.

In Kandahar, Canadian soldiers faced an intensification of the Kabul experience with bomb and rocket attacks and suicide bombers. After two soldiers died in Kabul in their fragile Iltis, Major-General Leslie had explained, as their commander, that soldiers needed to see and be seen by Afghan civilians if ISAF was to win their trust. Instead, Ottawa commanded that all patrols be conducted in armoured vehicles. Finally, the fragile Iltis was replaced by a partially armoured Mercedes-Benz G-Wagen, backed by turreted LAV-3s, and other wheeled armoured vehicles.

Patrolling could still be fatal. Indistinguishable from Afghan civilians, safe behind the thick mud walls of Afghan villages and farmhouses, and armed with rocket-propelled grenades and light, durable, accurate AK-47s, the Taliban were disciplined and cunning fighters, with all the fervour of men fighting for what they believed in. Canadians were fighters too, professional soldiers reinforced with members of historic militia units. However, they were strangers in a strange and uncongenial land, bereft of the appreciation their grandfathers remembered from liberated France or Holland. How could they win hearts and minds if safety compelled their convoys to race down the centre of a highway, as far away as possible from any IEDs buried on either shoulder of the road? Was that old man on a bicycle a bone-weary farmer pedalling homeward, or a malevolent

Members of the First Regiment, Royal Canadian Horse Artillery (from left to right): Bombardier Gauthier, Master Bombardier Fehr, Gunner Gingrich, Sargeant Redford, and Captain Nicola Goddard, the first female Canadian soldier to die as a combatant.

suicide bomber? Who could tell them apart without a humiliating strip search? Canadians could meet their hosts in a village *shura* or conference. Did anyone notice that women and children had discreetly withdrawn as a preliminary to a massacre? When Canadian diplomat Glyn Berry's escorts failed to notice, he paid with his life.

Panjwaye, thirty kilometres west of Kandahar, was a Taliban stronghold and a challenge to the Canadians. The district was home base for suicide bombers and ambushes, and evidence to nervous Afghans that the Taliban would soon be back. During a patrol through the district on May 19, an artillery officer, Captain Nicola Goddard, became the first Canadian woman soldier ever to die as a combatant. In another conflict that day, Sergeant Michael Denine became the first winner of Canada's Medal of Military Valour (MMV). Seizing a damaged machine gun and disdaining cover, he opened such rapid, accurate fire that Taliban attackers were silenced.

In July 2006, Canadian and Afghan troops launched Operation Mountain Thrust, another campaign to expel the Taliban from Panjwaye. When the guerillas chose to stand their ground, they were pinned down under a merciless barrage. Suddenly, the troops were urgently needed in neighbouring Helmand. British paratroopers, dropped to rescue supplies from the Taliban, had been cut off and trapped. After several days and a single death, the Canadians rescued their allies and returned to Panjwaye to finish their job. Major Charles Wright won his MMV by leading his badly outnumbered company to the heart of the Taliban position. The enemy scattered.

With their limited numbers, what the Canadians could not do was occupy captured ground. Once they returned to Kandahar, the Taliban returned to Panjwaye, boasting of their "victory" and killing "traitors." Operation Medusa was a third, even more comprehensive bid to retain control of Panjwaye. Backed by American and British air support, Dutch artillery, and Danish infantry, members of the 2nd Battalion of the Royal Canadian Regiment surrounded the Taliban on September 2. On the 3rd, they attacked, at a cost of four soldiers' lives. For September 4, officers called in air support. A pair of American A-20 Thunderbolts mistook the target, killing a Canadian soldier and wounding thirty more. The battle continued, with growing allied firepower, ground and air. On the night of September 13, radio intercepts suggested that Taliban was clustering in the village of Pashmul for a last stand. ISAF forces closed in. Instead, before dawn, the survivors burst out of their positions and headed for Gulistan in the west side of neighbouring Farah province. There they burned a hospital and administrative building, dispersed the local Afghan police, and waited for winter. ISAF proclaimed a victory, though at a cost of five Canadians and one American dead and forty-four Canadians wounded, plus fourteen British airmen killed when their Nimrod surveillance aircraft crashed.

The announcement was premature. Within a day of victory, four Canadians, four British, and four American soldiers had been killed by rockets, bombs, and roadside explosives. In October, Canadian troops launched a fresh battle in Panjwaye, and again in December, this time joined by fifteen elderly Leopard tanks, specially flown from Wainwright, Alberta, to provide added firepower and protection. On December 3, 2006, the tanks pounded Taliban trenches at Ma'sum Ghar in Panjwaye, the first Canadian tanks in action since the Korean

War. ISAF also launched bombing sorties, though the casualties seem to have been chiefly civilians who had returned to their homes.

In Vietnam, American troops had sortied into the jungle to kill enemies, returning with inflated body counts and leaving the ground to the Viet Cong. When NATO headquarters in Brussels boasted of five hundred dead enemy at Panjwaye, the Taliban denied it. Could a mere two thousand Canadians based at Kandahar protect a civilian population scattered across hundreds of square kilometres of mountains and valleys? Could it ever corner an enemy that, when defeated, could flee to safety across a Pakistan border Canadians were forbidden to cross? In 2007, Canadians could only keep faith with their commitments to both American and NATO allies, learn more of their hosts' languages and customs, and become even more familiar with the tactics, strengths, and limitations of the Taliban.

A New Government

The election of Stephen Harper's minority Conservative government on January 23, 2006, reinforced the earlier Liberal commitment to Afghanistan and NATO. General Hillier gained a seemingly more congenial minister in Gordon O'Connor, a former fellow officer in the Royal Canadian Dragoons. The wisdom of shipping fifteen obsolete Leopard tanks to Afghanistan was as obvious to the minister as it was to the general. Newer, air-conditioned Leopards would be leased from the Dutch in 2007, plus a hundred new German-built tanks to put armour back in the Canadian land force inventory by 2010. The importance of linking defence to development and even to diplomacy was also obvious. Once Operation Medusa was complete, Canadian engineers began driving a road, code-named "Summit," from Panjwaye to Kandahar. Casualties continued, but Afghans needed to see that their lives might be improved. Nature helped. The winter of 2006–7 brought the rains back after a near decade of drought. Canadians had stalled poppy eradication in their district in hope of making local friends, but rain brought the hope of healthier and more legitimate crops, if they could ever be harvested and marketed. Well aware that the Afghan national police were poorly paid, frequently corrupt, and resented by the civilian population, Canada funded the recruiting of a Pashtun-based auxiliary police, answerable to village rather than provincial authorities. While they might well identify with the Taliban rather than the Karzai government, risks had to be taken to win. Even enemies had to be cautiously brought into negotiations about a future that Afghans would ultimately have to manage for themselves.

By the end of March 2007, fifty-one Canadians had died in Afghanistan, and five times as many had been wounded, a ratio that reflected the protective quality of tactical vehicles and body armour, not to mention improved battlefield first aid. Most wounded returned to duty, but almost a hundred returned to Canada with life-changing injuries. Far more would suffer the symptoms of post-traumatic stress disorder, aggravated by the strain of constant risk in a harsh, dust-blown land, by turns insufferably hot and bitterly cold. No Canadian ever conceived of Afghanistan as a holiday or retirement haven. Yet few Canadians served there without wishing a better life for Afghan men and women and children too, and often helping to make it happen.

Transformation

In Ottawa, the Canadian Forces began warily and then with almost indecorous enthusiasm to welcome the new Conservative government. On paper, Conservative defence policies were cautious and certainly uncomfortable for senior officers accustomed to moulding policies to comply with those of their American counterparts. Conservatives had put their emphasis on a vote-getting and Canada-first defence policy, with Canadian Forces growing by twenty thousand more regulars and an extra ten thousand members of the reserves, with financial resources to protect the Arctic and maintain front-line units in major cities to protect residents from terrorist threats and natural disasters.

However, Stephen Harper echoed Brian Mulroney's desire for "good relations, excellent relations" with Washington. He had retracted his earlier enthusiasm for Operation Iraqi Freedom, but was eager to accept credit for the Liberals' more aggressive Afghan policy. Most significantly, the Conservative prime minister accepted the warnings that rust-out could leave Canada without any effective armed forces. Paul Martin's Liberals had promised a rather vague five-year program of spending. At the end of June 2006, Harper crossed Canada and, during a single week, announced a total of $19 billion in new equipment purchases, including four new C-17 Boeing Globemasters and seventeen C-130J Hercules for $11.5 billion; fourteen heavy-lift CH-47 Chinook helicopters, also from Boeing; $1.2 billion for 2,000 medium transport trucks for the army; and $2.9 billion for three brand new joint support ships for sea support and amphibious operations. As the regional and bureaucratic clamour for shared benefits arose, Harper defied the Opposition and even the Auditor General in order to get fast delivery of the specific equipment his military commanders had selected. A military procurement process that had accepted a decade of delays as full speed was largely set aside.

If the Canadian Forces leadership got much of what it had sought, it offered the new government the buzzword made popular in Donald Rumsfeld's Pentagon: *Transformation*. General Henault had used the word late in the 1990s to encapsulate his vision of an armed force adapted to the high-tech marvels of the Revolution in Military Affairs (RMA). It was a vision that did not captivate most of Henault's Liberal Party bosses. If the RMA's potential had been evident in lightning victories over the Taliban and Saddam Hussein, its limits had been made even more evident in the sad aftermath in both Iraq and Afghanistan. Slogans about "three-block war" or "fourth-generational warfare" offered few practical insights into the identification of fanatical enemies in a culturally unfamiliar population.

General Hillier had a different and more substantial vision of Transformation, based on abandoning the structures and priorities of the Cold War and embracing the world revealed by President Bush's global war on terror. Eliminating the single, oversized operational planning staff at National Defence Headquarters, Hillier reorganized its members into a command system that fit the corresponding global structure of Rumsfeld's Pentagon and challenged the growing autonomy of three theoretically unified but increasingly independent armed services. A Canada Command (CANCOM), divided into Regional Joint Task Forces (RJTF), would respond to home-front events and mesh, if it could, with a new American Northern Command (NORTHCOM). CANCOM would focus on the Conservative's domestic priorities. A Canada Expeditionary Force Command (CEFCOM) would integrate Canada's global operations, whether for UN, NATO, or national purposes, and seek a "strategic, focused and decisive effect." A Canadian Special Operations Forces Command (CANSOFCOM) would train and command the kind of special forces that had overthrown the Taliban in 2001. A Canada Operational Support Command (CANOSCOM) would provide logistical support, organizing equipment, food, and maintenance for the three operational commands.

To give resources to CANSOFCOM, a new 750-member Canadian Special Operations Regiment (CSOR), modeled on the U.S. Rangers, emerged before the end of 2006 as the first truly new Canadian regiment since the Second World War. The CSOR would perform unconventional operations in Canada and overseas, and would specialize in counterinsurgency, counterterrorism, and intelligence roles. It would leave the JTF for smaller, more "surgical" operations. As a Special Operations Task Force (SOTF), the Special Operations Regiment would be part of a Special Contingency Force (SCF), composed of navy, army, air force, and special operations units capable of land and sea operations. To deliver it, Hillier argued a case for what he called "BHS" — Big Honking Ships — armed, protected, and large enough to carry and deliver the Special Contingency Force wherever it was needed in Canada or around the world.

Like the Afghan commitment, General Hillier's version of Transformation had an obvious place for the navy and air force, but they would essentially act as auxiliaries of soldiers who would be putting their "boots on the ground." Prime Minister Harper's 2006 equipment announcements reinforced his general's plan. New transport planes and helicopters could deliver soldiers and their equipment to battle stations. So too might the navy's three promised support vessels, unless they were joined or supplanted by Hillier's "Big Honking Ships." Well-trained, aggressive Canadian soldiers might well be welcomed by influential allies. Effective combat troops were in painfully short supply in NATO, as Afghanistan had revealed.

They could also suffer casualties, as Canadians had painfully come to recognize. Were soldiers, alive and dead, the contribution their fellow citizens really wanted to make to imposing peace on a dangerous world? Did they have a choice? As a proud and able warrior, General Hillier's priorities were understandable. His political masters after 2006 shared many of his instincts. So had Brian Mulroney's government in the first half of its mandate. It had forgotten its commitments in its years of declining electoral support.

Accustomed to the comforting feel of exercising "soft power," many Canadians might not agree with the hard stand of General

Hillier and the Harper government. Few of their leaders bothered to link the image of soft power with the tragic weakness that allowed the Srebrenica massacre of thousands of Bosnian Serbs sheltering behind a battalion of UN peacekeepers. Thanks to Lieutenant-General Roméo Dallaire, Canadians knew how soft power had forced him to abandon hundreds of thousands of Rwandan Tutsis to be victims of genocide. Even in Afghanistan, NATO members' reluctance to provide enough soldiers had allowed the Taliban repeatedly to infiltrate Panjwaye, murdering those who had welcomed and assisted Canadians, and forcing ISAF to launch fresh counterattacks and to suffer fresh casualties.

Most Canadians have treated issues of peace and conflict with an energy-saving indifference. Many worry about their new military dependency on the United States. Some cling to their faith in Senator Dandurand's "fireproof house"; others hold to the self-indulgent morality of the 1960s; still others insist that any sense of insecurity in the post–Cold War is a militaristic fantasy. Others see 1914 being replayed in the Middle East or Africa.

Throughout history, a few Canadians have felt entitled to use the armed forces to pursue satisfying careers or to acquire distinctions for themselves. Nothing has been as destructive of the Canadian Forces' reputation or influence as the selfish rivalry of services, branches, components, regiments, and ambitious individuals. Integration, unification, and "civilianization" were all primarily due to the failure of professional advisors to provide successive civilian ministers of defence with transparent, persuasive, and prioritized advice. Canadians have often been better served by conscientious politicians than by uninspired professional careerists. Fortunately, we have also been saved by honest and heroic exceptions.

Good fortune does not last forever. Canada's claims to oceans and Arctic sovereignty are no longer a matter of indifference in an overcrowded world. Canada's retreat from the industrial and technological competence she created for herself by 1945 has left her militarily and economically dependent on a single, increasingly isolated neigbour, a relationship tightened by the Free Trade Agreement of 1989. Late in the twentieth century, Canadians learned that their own vast country, along with the oceans around it, has ecological limits. In a shrinking world, there are no fireproof houses anywhere.

A Reading List

Abbreviations

CHR	*Canadian Historical Review*
CMH	*Canadian Military History*
CMJRmc	*Canadian Military Journal/Revue militaire canadienne*
DCB	*Dictionary of Canadian Biography*
HP	*Annual Report of the Canadian Historical Association*
HS-SH	*Histoire Sociale/Social History*
IJ	*International Journal*
JCS	*Journal of Canadian Studies*
RIHM	*Revue internationale d'histoire militaire*

In General

Canadians blame each other for ignoring their warlike past, but like most people, they have written more on military history than on other subjects. Veteran warriors write about the most exciting episodes of their lives and most readers find war more fascinating than the timber trade. Canadian military historians also benefited from early official sponsorship and finding, in Colonel Charles Stacey, a superb professional mentor. The history of much of Canadian military history has been ably summarized by Tim Cook in *Clio's Warriors: Canadian Historians and the Writing of the World Wars* (Vancouver, 2006).

Among the general introductions to Canadian military history, the Stacey influence is apparent. The Hon. G.F.G. Stanley was Stacey's deputy before he wrote *Canada's Soldiers: The Military History of an Unmilitary People* (Toronto, 1974). Two other members of Stacey's directorate, J.L. Granatstein and J.M. Hitsman, dealt in a well-informed way with a central issue in Canada's military experience in *Broken Promise: A History of Conscription in Canada* (Toronto, 1977). Another Stacey appointee, D.J. Goodspeed, wrote *The Armed Forces of Canada, 1867-1967: A Century of Achievement* (Ottawa, 1967), a dependable and well-illustrated history of the three services. Norman Hillmer and J.L. Granatstein, both alumni of the Defence

Department's Directorate of History, contributed an accessible linking of Canada's foreign and defence policies in *Empire to Umpire: Canada and the World to the 1990s* (Mississauga, 1994). A continuing Canadian undercurrent in war and peace is presented by Thomas Socknat, *Witness Against War: Pacifism in Canada, 1900-1945* (Toronto, 1987). Though suffused with preaching, Jack Granatstein gave the army a centennial overview in *Canada's Army: Waging War and Keeping the Peace* (Toronto, 2002).

Canadian naval history was overshadowed by the energy and productivity of the army's historians. G.N. Tucker, *The Naval Service of Canada: Its Official History* (Ottawa, 1952) is more solid than entertaining, and it says little about operations. The gap has been filled by Tony German's readable history, *The Sea Is at Our Gates: The History of the Canadian Navy* (Toronto, 1990), by Roger Sarty, *The Maritime Defence of Canada* (Toronto, 1996), and by several sets of academic papers, notably James A. Boutillier (ed.) *The RCN in Retrospect, 1910-1968* (Vancouver, 1982), W.A.B. Douglas (ed.) *RCN in Transition: Challenge and Response, 1910-1985*, (Vancouver, 1988), and by Michael Hadley, Rob Huebert, and Fred W. Crickard, (eds.) *A Nation's Navy: In Quest of Canadian Naval Identity* (Montreal & Kingston, 1996). At the end of the century, Marc Milner and the University of Toronto Press gave the navy its first full-length history in *Canada's Navy: The First Century* (Toronto, 1999).

While the air force has attracted much popular history, memoirs, and journalism, the official history of the Canadian air force only began to appear in 1980 with S.F. Wise's *Canadian Airmen and the First World War* (Toronto, 1980). Two more volumes have since appeared: W.A.B. Douglas, *The Creation of a National Air Force* (Toronto, 1986), and Brereton Greenhous et al., *The Crucible of War, 1939-1945* (Toronto, 1994). Stan Kostenuk and John Griffin provided a useful but dated reference work, *RCAF Squadrons and Aircraft* (Toronto, 1977), and Larry Milberry's *Sixty Years: The RCAF and Canadian Forces Air Command, 1924-1984* (Trenton, 1984) will satisfy most enthusiasts.

Two essay collections designed for classes are currently available, both from the same publisher: B.D. Hunt and R.G. Haycock, *Canada's Defences: Perspectives on Policy in the Twentieth Century* (Toronto, 1993) and Marc Milner (ed.), *Canadian Military History: Selected Readings* (Toronto, 1993).

I. The Ancien Régime

Though the Royal Commission on Aboriginal People urged Canadians to incorporate First Nations history, the necessary research is only beginning, particularly on pre-contact aboriginal conflict. Bruce Trigger's magnificent *The Children of Aataensic: A History of the Huron People to 1660* (Montreal, 1976, 2 vols.) discussed native attitudes to war. On the Iroquois wars with the Ancien Régime, see R.A. Goldstein, *French-Iroquois Diplomatic and Military Relations, 1609-1701* (The Hague, 1969).

It is hard to find a thoroughly satisfactory synthesis for the French-Indian-Aboriginal struggle for North America before 1760. One side is ably presented in Jack Verney's *The Good Regiment: The Carignan-Salières Regiment in Canada, 1663-1668* (Montreal & Kingston, 1991). For English-speaking readers, a sympathetic synthesis of New France's defence problems is in W.J. Eccles, *France in America* (Toronto, 1972), and in two of his articles, "The Social, Economic and Political Significance of the Military Establishment in New France" (*CHR*, 1971) and "The French Forces in North America During the Seven Years War" (*DCB*, vol. III). Gerald Graham, *The Empire of the North Atlantic: The Maritime Struggle for North America* (Toronto, 2nd ed., 1958) remains a classic of naval strategy, and Christopher Moore's *Louisbourg Portraits: Life in an Eighteenth Century Garrison Town* (Toronto, 1982) is a master work of social history. George Rawlyk, *Yankees at Louisbourg* (Orono, 1967), is an account of the extraordinary 1745 siege.

G.F.G. Stanley's *New France: The Last Phase, 1744-1760* (Toronto, 1968) explains the colony's fall with careful symmetry; for more passion, read Guy Frégault, *Canada: The War of the Conquest* (Toronto, 1969). John Shy, *Toward Lexington: The Role of the British Army in the Coming of the American Revolution* (Princeton, 1965), was a realistic look at the British forces in the Seven Years War, while Lee Kennett, *The French Armies in the Seven Years War: A Study in Military Organization and Administration* (Durham, 1967), explains why New France had to be a side-show. More modern French research is evident in Colonel Jean Delmas, *Conflits de sociétés au Canada français pendant la Guerre des sept ans* (Vincennes, 1978). The 1759 siege of Quebec, so decisive in Canadian and Quebec history, has inspired some good books, but one of the best is C.P. Stacey, *Quebec, 1759: The Siege and the Battle* (Toronto, 1959).

II. The British Empire

Both the British army in Canada and the pre-Confederation militia still await comprehensive books, though many of the specialized studies have been done. Among them is J.M. Hitsman's *Safeguarding Canada, 1763-1871* (Toronto, 1968). Also valuable for the earlier period are John Shy's *Toward Lexington* and Piers Mackesy's *The War for America, 1773-1783* (London, 1964). G.F.G. Stanley's *Canada Invaded, 1775-1776* (Toronto, 1973) and Robert M. Hatch, *Thrust for Canada: The American Attempt on Quebec in 1775-1776* (Boston, 1979), treat a near-run campaign. Barbara Graymount's *The Iroquois in the American Revolution* (Syracuse, 1972) and S.F. Wise's "The American Revolution and Indian History" in John S. Moir (ed.), *Character and Circumstance: Essays in Honour of D.G. Creighton* (Toronto, 1970), deal with aspects of the conflict that should be better known.

A number of books have dealt with the Loyalists, among them Robert S. Allen, *The Loyal Americans: The Military Role of the Loyalist Provincial Corps and their Settlement in British North America, 1775-1784* (Ottawa, 1983), and Christopher Moore's *The Loyalists* (Toronto, 1984). Rather more books have dealt with the War of 1812, among them two popular volumes by Pierre Berton, *The Invasion of Canada* and *Flames Across the Border* (Toronto, 1981, 1982). Berton did not supersede J.M. Hitsman's *The Incredible War of 1812* (Toronto, 1965), a work of lively scholarship and, considering Hitsman's acute physical handicaps, of remarkable courage as well. G.F.G. Stanley's *The War of 1812: Land Operations* (Toronto, 1983) reflects scholarship and good sense — and the difficulty of abstracting this particular war from the movement of fleets and ships. And, since all history would die without posthumous wisdom, see Wesley B. Turner, *British Generals in the War of 1812: High Command in the Canadas* (Montreal & Kingston, 1999).

As 1914 approached, the British and Americans made elaborate plans to celebrate a century of peace. Someone even invited the Canadians. The legend of peaceful coexistence was challenged half a century later by C.P. Stacey's pamphlet, *The Undefended Border: The Myth and the Reality* (Ottawa, 1962). The diplomatic and military details were provided by Kenneth Bourne, *Britain and the Balance of Power in North America, 1815-1908* (London, 1967).

Engineers like Colonel John By, despatched to prepare Canada's defences, faced problems described by George Raudzens, *The British Ordnance Department and Canada's Canals, 1815-1855* (Waterloo, 1979). How far did other British soldiers shape Canada? Elinor Kyte Senior, *British Regulars in Montreal: An Imperial Garrison, 1832-1854* (Montreal and Kingston, 1981), attempted to provide some detailed answers. Military records should have been a rich source for social historians. An example of their potential is Jacalyn Duffin's "Soldiers' Work, Soldiers' Health: Morbidity, Mortality and Their Causes in an 1840s British Garrison in Canada" (*Labour/le Travail*, 37, Spring 1996).

An episode in which British troops played a necessary but tragic role was the rebellions of 1837 and 1838. See Joseph Schull, *Rebellion: The Rising in French Canada, 1837* (Toronto, 1971). C.P. Stacey's *Canada and the British Army, 1846-1871: A Study in the Practice of Responsible Government* (London, 1936) has been only partly bypassed by Hitsman and Bourne. Robin Winks, *Canada and the United States: The Civil War Years* (Montreal, 1960), flattened some old beliefs about a troubled time. A specific border issue was dealt with by Hereward Senior, *The Last Invasion of Canada: The Fenian Raiders, 1866-1870* (Toronto, 1991).

American preoccupations tended to crowd out other problems on the Pacific coast. See Barry Gough's *Gunboat Frontier: British Maritime Authority and Northwest Coast Indians, 1846-1890* (Vancouver, 1983) and Glynn Barratt, *Russian Shadows on the British Northwest Coast of North America, 1810-1890: A Study of Rejection of Defence Responsibilities* (Vancouver, 1985).

III. The Young Dominion

With Confederation, Canadians had to learn to live at peace with the United States. Some on both sides continued to think of war. One was George T. Denison, whose *Soldiering in Canada* (Toronto, 1900) expressed the views of an outspoken Toronto militia colonel. Two books by Desmond Morton, *Ministers and Generals: Politics and the Canadian Militia, 1868-1904* (Toronto, 1970) and *The Canadian General: Sir William Otter* (Toronto, 1974), describe the nature and limits of Canada's defence forces before the First World War. Jean-Yves Gravel, *L'Armée au Québec (1868-1900)* (Montreal,

1974), reflects the *Canadien* experience in a single battalion, the 9e Voltigeurs, while the 26th Oxford Rifles feature in Chris J. Amstead's "Patriotism and Camaraderie: Workingmen in a Peacetime Militia Regiment, 1907-1954" (*HS-SH*, 1995). Richard A. Preston's *The Defence of the Undefended Border: Planning for War in North America, 1867-1939* (Montreal, 1977) revealed that both sides made plans for a cross-border war, and the Americans made them longer.

If winning the west was the greatest collective goal of Confederation, C.P. Stacey argued that the military played an essential role. See "The Military Aspect of Canada's Winning of the West" (*CHR*, 1960). Desmond Morton wrote a strictly military history of the 1885 campaign, *The Last War Drum* (Toronto, 1972). A later account of events is R.C. MacLeod and Bob Beal, *Prairie Fire: The 1885 Northwest Rebellion* (Edmonton, 1984). MacLeod also established both the military and the police role of the NWMP in *The North-West Mounted Police and Law Enforcement* (Toronto, 1976).

The most comprehensive book on Canada's involvement in British defence concerns is Richard A. Preston's *Canada and "Imperial Defense": A Study of the Origins of the British Commonwealth Defence Organization, 1869-1919* (Toronto and Durham, 1967), supplemented by Bourne and, for a short, significant period, by Norman Penlington's *Canada and Imperialism, 1896-1899* (Toronto, 1965). Roy MacLaren's *Canadians on the Nile, 1882-1898* (Vancouver, 1978) is a sensible account of Canadian involvement in the Sudan. The need for a comprehensive history of Canadian contingents in the Boer War was finally met by Carman Miller, *Painting the Map Red: Canada and the South African War, 1899-1902* (Montreal and Kingston, 1993), and, shortly after, by Brian Reid, *Our Little Army in the Field: The Canadians in South Africa, 1899-1902* (St. Catharines, 1996).

The period of military expansion and reform between 1900 and 1914 is described by Morton, *The Canadian General,* and by Carman Miller, "Sir Frederick William Borden and Military Reform, 1896-1911" (*CHR*, 1969). As an aspect of Canada's imperial ideology, militarism is discussed in Carl Berger's *The Sense of Power: Studies in the Ideas of Canadian Imperialism, 1867-1914* (Toronto, 1970), and its application to the young is described by Desmond Morton in "The Cadet Movement in the Moment of Canadian Militarism" (*JCS*, 1978). A major event for the pre-war militia is described in Mark Reid, "The Quebec Tercentenary, 1908: Canada's First National Military Pageant"

(*CMH*, 1999). The hero of Canadian militarism, Sam Hughes, has benefited from a largely laudatory biography by R.G. Haycock: *Sam Hughes: The Public Career of a Controversial Canadian, 1885-1916* (Waterloo, 1986).

The origins and early problems of the Canadian navy are described in Tucker's first volume of *The Naval Service of Canada*, by German, *The Sea Is at Our Gates*, and by essays in the Boutilier, Douglas, Sarty, and Hadley collections.

IV. The Great War

Much has been published about Canada during the First World War, and probably much more will appear to recall an event that left little unchanged. G.W.L. Nicholson's *Canadian Expeditionary Force, 1914-1919: The Official History of the Canadian Army in the First World War* (Ottawa, 1962) remains the basic source for strictly military history, though readers may be attracted to some of the fascinating appendices in A.F. Duguid's unfinished *Official History of the Canadian Forces in the Great War, 1914-1919*, vol. I (Ottawa, 1928). Another official history, Sir Andrew Macphail's *Medical Services, 1914-1919* (Ottawa, 1925), is thin and obsolete, though it rebuts H.A. Bruce's polemic, *Politics and the C.A.M.C.* (Toronto, 1919). S.F. Wise's *Canadian Airmen and the First World War: The Official History of the Royal Canadian Air Force*, vol. I (Toronto, 1980) demonstrates an approach to social history by listing every Canadian pilot.

There are, of course, many academic studies of the war. In *When Your Number's Up: The Canadian Soldier in the Great War* (Toronto, 1993), Desmond Morton explains how soldiers were recruited and trained, how they fought and why, and what became of them when they were wounded, captured, or repatriated. He depends heavily on a book by William Rawling, *Surviving Trench Warfare: Technology and the Canadian Corps, 1914-1918* (Toronto, 1992). Morton's *Fight or Pay: Soldiers' Families in the Great War* (Vancouver, 2004) tells what happened to the women they left behind. A new book, published in April 2007, challenged conventional patriotic history in ways that invite more such analytical work: Geoffrey Hayes, Andrew Iarocci and Mike Bechtold (eds.), *Vimy Ridge: A Canadian Reassessment* (Waterloo, 2007).

Lacking a new official history for this period, interest in the navy might begin with Michael Hadley and Roger Sarty, *Tin-Pots and Pirate Ships: Canadian Naval Forces and German Sea Raiders, 1880-1918* (Montreal and Kingston, 1991). Two books dealt with Canadian involvement in Russia's revolution, J.A. Swettenham, *Allied Intervention in Russia, 1918-1919, and the Part Played by Canada* (Toronto, 1967) and Roy MacLaren, *Canadians in Russia, 1918-1919* (Toronto, 1976).

Participants left their own experiences in family diaries and published memoirs. Among the best are R.H. Roy (ed.), *The Journal of Private Fraser, 1914-1918, Canadian Expeditionary Force* (Victoria, 1985), and W.R. Bird's *As We Go On* (Toronto, 1930), republished as *Ghosts Have Warm Hands* (Toronto, 1960). Half a century after the war, more memories appeared. Among the better collections were Daphne Read (ed.), *The Great War and Canadian Society* (Toronto, 1978), and William B. Mathieson, *My Grandfather's War: Canadians Remember the First World War, 1914-1918* (Toronto, 1981). Two remarkable books about the war are David Macfarlane's *The Danger Tree: Memory, War and the Search for a Family's Past* (Toronto, c. 1991) and Sandra Gwyn, *Tapestry of War: Politics and Passion: Canada's Coming of Age in the Great War* (Scarborough, 1992).

Many national figures have formal biographies, among them Robert Craig Brown, *Robert Laird Borden*, vol. II (Toronto, 1980); Michael Bliss, *A Canadian Millionaire: The Life and Business Times of Sir Joseph Flavelle Bart* (Toronto, 1978). The Canadian Corps commanders have a number of biographies, notably Jeffery Williams, *Byng of Vimy: General and Governor-General* (London, 1983), and A.M.J. Hyatt, *General Sir Arthur Currie: A Military Biography* (Toronto, 1987). Among biographies and memoirs of officers with a future are E.L.M. Burns, *General Mud* (Toronto, 1970), J.A. Swettenham, *McNaughton*, 3 vols. (Toronto, 1968-1969), and R.H. Roy, *For Most Conspicuous Bravery: A Biography of Major-General George R. Pearkes, V.C., through Two World Wars* (Vancouver, 1977).

As an issue, conscription was dissected by Granatstein and Hitsman in *Broken Promises* and, for Quebec, by Elizabeth Armstrong, *The Crisis of Quebec, 1914-1918* (Toronto, rev. ed. 1974). Jean-Pierre Gagnon's *Le 22e bataillon (canadien-français), 1914-1919, Une étude socio-militaire* (Quebec, 1986), which also grew out of the

Directorate of History, provides monumental detail on French-Canadian participation in the war. Thomas Tremblay, the colonel of the 22nd, left a very revealing diary: *Journal de Guerre, 1915-1918* (Montreal, 2006). Three regionally focussed histories show the rich potential of thinking locally: Barbara Wilson's *Ontario and the First World War* (Toronto, 1970), John H. Thompson, *The Harvests of War: The Prairie West, 1914-1918* (Toronto, 1979), and Claude E. Léger, *Le bataillon acadien de la Première Guerre mondiale* (Moncton, 2001). Dozens of articles could have grown out of J.A. Corry's seminal "The Growth of Government Activities in Canada, 1914-1921" (*HP*, 1940). One that did is David Smith, "Emergency Government in Canada" (*CHR*, 1969). Another unfamiliar wartime activity is explored by Jeff Keshen in *Propaganda and Censorship during Canada's Great War* (Edmonton, 1996). Wartime politics were explored by John English, *The Decline of Politics* (Toronto, 1977), and the unconscious evolution of Ottawa's authority over its troops is the theme of Desmond Morton, *A Peculiar Kind of Politics: Canada's Overseas Minister in the First World War* (Toronto, 1982).

A number of historians have tried to explain the war to a very different generation. Desmond Morton and J.L. Granatstein, *Marching to Armageddon: Canadians and the Great War, 1914-1919* (Toronto, 1990), is clear, well-illustrated, but brief. More popular was Pierre Berton's *Vimy* (Toronto, 1986). Daniel Dancocks, a military historian in Calgary, wrote books that got better and better until his untimely death. Two of the best are *Spearhead to Victory: Canada and the Great War* (Edmonton, 1987), which deals in fact with the "last hundred days," and *Welcome to Flanders Fields: The First Canadian Battle of the Great War: Ypres, 1915* (Toronto, 1988). Another useful modern commentary on the last days of the war is Shane B. Schreiber's *Shock Army of the British Empire: The Canadian Corps in the Last 100 Days of the Great War* (Westport, 1997).

Between the wars, most Canadians tried to forget a dangerous world while others struggled to memorialize their wartime experiences in a mountain of poetry, novels, and regimental histories. The defence consequences were described by James Eayrs in two volumes of his *In Defence of Canada*, vol. I, *From the Great War to the Great Depression* (Toronto, 1964) and vol. II, *Appeasement and Rearmament* (Toronto, 1965). Norman Hillmer and William McAndrew, "The Cunning of Restraint: General J.H. MacBrien and the Problems of Peacetime Soldiering" (*CDQ*, 1978), gives an account of inter-war civil-military relations that later generals might recognize. And Alex Morrison outlines the emergence of the militia as a political pressure group in *The Voice of Defence: The History of the Conference of Defence Associations: The First Fifty Years, 1932-1982* (Ottawa, 1982).Yet, as Jonathan Vance reported in *Death So Noble: Memory, Meaning and the First World War* (Vancouver, 1997), the response to the tragedy was quite conservative and many veterans resented their treatment; see Desmond Morton and Glenn Wright, *Winning the Second Battle: Canadian Veterans and the Return to Civilian Life, 1915-1930* (Toronto, 1987). And some Canadians became "premature" anti-fascists in Spain. See Mark Zuehlke, *The Gallant Cause: Canadians in the Spanish Civil War, 1936-1939* (Vancouver, 1996). To understand Canada at the outset of another world war, see Norman Hillmer, Robert Bothwell, and Roger Sarty (eds.), *A Country of Limitations: Canada and the World in 1939* (Ottawa, 1996).

V. The World War

The problems of creating official military history in both world wars are described by C.P. Stacey in his memoirs, *A Date with History* (Ottawa, 1982). His single-volume history of the Canadian army in the Second World War was soon supplanted by two sturdy red volumes, *The Official History of the Canadian Army in the Second World War*, vol. I, *Six Years of War* (Ottawa, 1955), and vol. III, *The Victory Campaign* (Ottawa, 1960). The set was completed by G.W.L. Nicholson's vol. II, *The Canadians in Italy* (Ottawa, 1956). Stacey returned to a unified National Defence Headquarters to produce his magisterial *Arms, Men and Governments: The War Policies of Canada, 1939-1945* (Ottawa, 1970), clad in an appropriate tri-service green. The RCN had to be content with Tucker's *Naval Service of Canada*, vol. II, and a popular history, Joseph Schull's *The Far Distant Ships* (Ottawa, 1950), published before many of the RCN's problems in the Battle of the Atlantic could be acknowledged. During its existence, the RCAF failed to publish any official history, a task left for a unified Directorate of History.

Two official historians, W.A.B. Douglas and Brereton Greenhous, found time to produce an unofficial history, *Out of the Shadows:*

Canada in the Second World War (Toronto, rev. ed., 1995), which anticipated the harsher judgements of a postwar generation of historians. Other general histories of the war have been published by J.L. Granatstein and Desmond Morton, *A Nation Forged in Fire: Canadians and the Second World War, 1939-1945* (Toronto, 1989) and, for the war's final year, *Victory 1945: Canadians from War to Peace* (Toronto, 1995). Granatstein and Peter Neary also wrote *The Good Fight: Canadians and World War II* (Mississauga, 1995). In *Maple Leaf Against the Axis: Canada's Second World War* (Toronto, 1995), David Bercuson deals only with Canadians in combat. Barry Broadfoot's *Six Years of War, 1939-1945: Memoirs of Canadians at Home and Abroad* (Toronto, 1977) offended purists since the author felt free to "improve" as well as select memories, but the book is readable, moving, and probably defensible.

The pre-war and wartime politics of the King government are dealt with sympathetically by J.L. Granatstein, *Canada's War: The Politics of the Mackenzie King Government, 1939-1945* (Toronto, 1975), and, from an opposing perspective, in D.G. Creighton's *The Forked Road: Canada, 1939-1957* (Toronto, 1976). No one knew more in wartime Ottawa than Grant Dexter; see Frederick W. Gibson and Barbara Robertson (eds.), *Ottawa at War: The Grant Dexter Memoranda, 1939-1945* (Winnipeg, 1994). A painfully controversial wartime policy is viewed from both sides of the Pacific by Patricia Roy, J.L. Granatstein, Masako Iino, and Hiroku Takamura (eds.), *Mutual Hostages: Canadians and Japanese During the Second World War* (Toronto, 1990). See also Jonathan Vance, *Objects of Concern: Canadian Prisoners of War Through the Twentieth Century* (Vancouver, 1994).

Conscription in the Second World War is described by Granatstein and Hitsman in *Broken Promises* and by André Laurendeau, *La Crise de la conscription* (Montreal, 1962) and translated in Philip Stratford (ed.), *Witness for Quebec* (Toronto, 1973). See also W.R. Graham, *Arthur Meighen*, vol. III, *No Surrender* (Toronto, 1965); E.L.M. Burns, *Manpower in the Canadian Army* (Toronto, 1956), a critique of generals as well as politicians. Stacey's *Arms, Men and Governments* and Roy's *For Most Conspicuous Bravery* offer other perspectives. Women were crucial to the government's manpower policies even if they had no part in their formation; see Ruth Roach Pierson, *Canadian Women and the Second World War* (Ottawa, 1983).

Canada is the theme of a volume in the U.S. Army's official history series: Colonel Stanley Dzuiban, *Military Relations between the United States and Canada, 1939-1945* (Washington, 1959). See also R.D. Cuff and J.L. Granatstein, *Ties That Bind: Canadian-American Relations in Wartime from the Great War to the Cold War* (Toronto, 1977), and Ken Coates and W.R. Morrison, *The Alaska Highway in World War II: The U.S. Army of Occupation in Canada's Northwest* (Toronto, 1992).

A number of Canadian wartime politicians have memoirs or biographies, notably in Robert Bothwell and William Kilbourn, *C.D. Howe: A Biography* (Toronto, 1979), Norman Ward (ed.), *Memoirs of Chubby Power: A Party Politician* (Toronto, 1966), and Dale C. Thomson, *Louis St. Laurent, Canadian* (Toronto, 1967). Military commanders are much scarcer, particularly if they had no political involvement, as might be said of E.L.M. Burns, *General Mud*, J.A. Swettenham's *McNaughton*, vol. II, or Lieutenant-General M.A. Pope, *Soldiers and Politicians* (Toronto, 1962). An exception is Dominick Graham's *The Price of Command: A Biography of General Guy Simonds* (Don Mills, 1993). One of the best biographies of the most admired citizen-soldier of the Second World War is Douglas Delaney's *The Soldiers' General: Bert Hoffmeister At War* (Vancouver, 2005). A carefully researched collective biography by J.L. Granatstein, *The Generals: The Canadian Army's Senior Commanders in the Second World War* (Don Mills, 1993), answers many questions about the army's leadership, as does Harris's *Canadian Brass*, but Canada's wartime admirals and air marshals remain shadowy figures.

As in the earlier war, lower-ranking soldiers have left moving accounts, often focussed on their own unit. See, for example, Farley Mowat's *The Regiment* (Toronto, 1973) or *And No Birds Sang* (Toronto, 1979), Jean-Charles Forbes, *Fantassin pour mon pays, la gloire et . . . des prunes* (Quebec, 1994), or George Blackburn, *The Guns of Normandy: A Soldier's Eye View, France, 1944* (Toronto, 1995), and its two sequels. Earle Birney's superb novel, *Turvey: A Military Picaresque* (Toronto, 1949), revives memories for anyone who wore battledress.

With time, the nuanced judgements of Stacey's histories have been challenged by younger contemporaries and later generations. Colonel John A. English's *The Canadian Army and the Normandy Campaign: A Study of Failure* (New York, 1991) reflected a critical view of Canadian generalship. So did Dennis and Shelagh Whittaker's *Tug of War: The Canadian Victory that Opened Antwerp* (Don Mills, 1987), *Rhineland: The Battle to End the War* (Toronto, 1989), and *Dieppe: A Firsthand and Revealing Account of the Most Controversial Battle of World War II* (Whitby, 1992). Other accounts designed for a later generation include Daniel Dancocks, *The D-Day Dodgers: The Canadians in Italy, 1943-1945* (Toronto, 1991), R.H. Roy, *1944: Canadians and the Normandy Campaign* (Toronto, 1984), J.L. Granatstein and Desmond Morton, *Bloody Victory: Canadians and the D-Day Campaign* (Toronto, rev. ed., 1994), and Jeffrey Williams, *The Long Left Flank* (Toronto, 1989), an account of the Canadians' struggle up the coast of Europe.

Terry Copp offers a knowledgeable and less critical perspective of the Normandy campaign in *Fields of Fire: The Canadians in Normandy* (Toronto, 2003) and, with the late Robert Vogel, a sympathetic account of what ensued: "No Lack of Rational Speed: First Canadian Army Operations, September, 1944" (*JCS*, XVI, 3-4, Autumn-Winter, 1981-2.) Copp and Vogel's series *Maple Leaf Route* (Alma, Ontario, 1983-1985) features excellent maps and illustrations for anyone retracing the Canadian campaigns in north-west Europe, and their message is renewed in *Cinderella Army: The Canadians in Northwest Europe, 1944-1945* (Toronto, 2006). Copp and Bill McAndrew collaborated on an important monograph, *Battle Exhaustion: Soldiers and Psychiatrists in the Canadian Army, 1939-1945* (Montreal and Kingston, 1990).

As controversial as Dieppe was Canada's involvement with Hong Kong. See Brereton Greenhous, *C Force to Hong Kong: A Canadian Catastrophe, 1941-1945* (Toronto, 1996) and, more recently, Tony Banham, *Not the Slightest Chance: The Defence of Hong Kong, 1941* (Vancouver, 2003). Profound personal accounts of their experiences have come from many veterans, notably George S. Macdonell, *One Soldier's Story: From the Fall of Hong Kong to the Defeat of the Japanese* (Toronto, 2002).

The appearance of Marc Milner's *North Atlantic Run: The Royal Canadian Navy and the Battle for the Convoys* (Toronto, 1985) and its sequel, *The U-Boat Hunters: The Royal Canadian Navy and the Offensive Against Germany's Submarines* (Toronto, 1994), went far to make up for the absence of the RCN's official history, as did David Zimmerman's *The Great Naval Battle of Ottawa* (Toronto, 1988), a revelation of the complex needs of managing a fleet a thousand miles away. Canada's closest brush with the war is described by Michael Hadley, *U-Boats Against Canada: German Submarines in Canadian Waters* (Montreal and Kingston, 1985). Such books finally gave personal memoirs a context, notably Alan Easton's *50 North: An Atlantic Battleground* (Toronto, 1969), James B. Lamb's *The Corvette Navy* (Toronto, 1977), and Hal Lawrence's *A Bloody War: One Man's Memories of the Canadian Navy, 1939-45* (Toronto, 1978). Hugh Garner's novel, *Storm Below* (Toronto, 1971), reflects his own experience on the lower deck of a wartime corvette. More justifiably than most others, the merchant marine has felt neglected in wartime histories; see Frederick Watt, *In All Respects Ready: The Merchant Navy and the Battle of the Atlantic, 1940-1945* (Scarborough, 1985).

Two volumes of the RCAF's official histories, W.A.B. Douglas, *The Creation of a National Air Force*, vol. II (Toronto, 1986), and Brereton Greenhous and Norman Hillmer, *The Crucible of War, 1939-1945*, vol. III, *Air Policy and Operations Overseas* (Toronto, 1994), cover the war years. Former RCAF members have used their retirement to write memoirs. Among the most interesting are Murray Peden's *A Thousand Shall Fall* (Stittsville, 1979), J. Douglas Harvey, *Boys, Bombers and Brussels Sprouts* (Toronto, 1981), and Bill Olmstead, *Blue Skies: The Autobiography of a Canadian Spitfire Pilot in World War II* (Don Mills, 1987). A rare perspective from the ranks of the RCAF is Robert Collins, *The Long and the Short and the Tall: An Ordinary Airman's War* (Saskatoon, 1986).

VI. The Long Cold War

Second World War veterans came home to a very different Canada; see Peter Neary and J.L. Granatstein, *The Veterans' Charter and Post World War II Canada* (Montreal, 1997), and Barry Broadfoot, *The Veterans' Years: Coming Home from the War* (Vancouver, c. 1985). Canadians shared unusual affluence and an inextricable involvement with a dangerous world. In further volumes of *In Defence of Canada*, James Eayrs describes Canada's Cold War defence policies: vol. III, *Peacemaking and Deterrence* (Toronto, 1972), and vol. IV, *Growing Up Allied* (Toronto, 1980). See also John Holmes, *The Shaping of Peace: Canada and the Search for World Order* (Toronto, 1979), and John English, *The Worldly Years: The Life of Lester Pear-*

son, vol. II, *1949-1972* (Toronto, 1992). A cost-cutting defence minister presided over Canada's rearmament; see David Bercuson, *True Patriot: The Life of Brooke Claxton, 1989-1960* (Toronto, 1993). For an account of one of Canada's major cold-war commitments, see Sean Mahoney, *War Without Battles: Canada's NATO Brigade in Germany, 1951-1993* (Toronto, 1997), and on command in the 1950s, Howard Graham, *Citizen and Soldier: The Memoirs of Lieutenant-General Howard Graham* (Toronto, 1987).

A Canadian version of "revisionist" history was John Warnock's *Partner to Behemoth: The Military Policy of a Satellite Canada* (Toronto, 1970). Others have insisted that fear of Soviet power was state paranoia; see Reginald Whitaker and Gary Marcuse, *Cold War Canada: The Making of a National Insecurity State* (Toronto, 1995) and Merrily Weisbord, *The Strangest Dream: Canadian Communists, Spy Trials and the Cold War* (Montreal, 1994). Indeed, Canadians were involved in trying to restrain the Cold War and the arms race; see Albert Legault and Michel Fortmann, *A Diplomacy of Hope: Canada and Disarmament, 1945-1988* (Montreal and Kingston, 1992).

Korea may have been, as John Melady claimed, *Canada's Forgotten War* (Toronto, 1983), despite about two books a decade and two official histories, H.F. Wood's *Strange Battleground: Official History of the Canadian Army in Korea* (Ottawa, 1964) and Thor Thorgrimmson and E.C. Russell's *Canadian Naval Operations in Korean Waters, 1950-1955* (Ottawa, 1965). Personal memories were recorded by John Gardam, *Korea Volunteer: An Oral History from Those Who Were There* (Burnstown, 1994). The latest volumes are Ted Barris, *Deadlock in Korea: Canadians at War, 1950-1953* (Toronto, 1999), David Bercuson, *Blood on the Hills: The Canadian Army in the Korean War* (Montreal and Kingston, 1999), and William Johnston's important *A War of Patrols: Canadian Army Operations in Korea* (Vancouver, 2003).

Canada's goal was to keep the war from becoming too exciting, as Denis Stairs argues in *The Diplomacy of Constraint: Canada, the Korean War and the United States* (Toronto, 1974). One way to do so was as a peacemaking intermediary, a role adopted before the 1956 Suez Crisis, as James Eayrs points out in *Vietnam: The Roots of Complicity* (Toronto, 1983), the fifth volume of his series. As a leading participant, General E.L.M. Burns recorded his experience in *Between Arab and Israeli* (Toronto, 1962). Alastair Taylor, David Cox, J.L.

Granatstein, *Peacekeeping: International Challenge and Canadian Response* (Toronto, 1968), recalls the heyday of peacekeeping optimism. Fred Gaffen's *In the Eye of the Storm: A History of Canadian Peacekeeping* (Toronto, 1987) provides a more sober overview of the most popular role of Canada's armed forces.

The Cold War made home defence an issue, at least for the air force. An American, Joseph T. Jockel, has written one of the best accounts of Canadian-American alliance dilemmas in *No Boundaries Upstairs: Canada, the United States and the Origins of North American Air Defence, 1945-1958* (Vancouver, 1987). Canada's savage defence debate in the early 1960s is backgrounded by Jon B. McLin, *Canada's Changing Defence Policy, 1957-1963* (Baltimore, 1967), and described in J.L. Granatstein's *Canada, 1957-1967: The Years of Uncertainty and Innovation* (Toronto, 1986). Typical tracts for the time were by CBC Washington correspondent James M. Minifie, *Peacemaker or Powdermonkey: Canada's Role in a Revolutionary World* (Toronto, 1960), Lewis Hertzman, John Warnock, and Tom Hocken, *Alliances or Illusions: Canada and the NATO-NORAD Question* (Edmonton, 1969), and Peyton V. Lyon, *The Policy Question: A Critical Appraisal of Canada's Role in World Affairs* (Toronto, 1963). A number of authors have bemoaned the fate of the Avro Arrow, among them E. Kay Shaw, *The Avro Arrow* (Toronto, 1978), and James Dow, *The Arrow* (Toronto, 1979). Amidst such fervour, NDP defence critic Andrew Brewin's *Stand on Guard: The Search for a Canadian Defence Policy* (Toronto, 1964) sounds surprisingly moderate, while James Eayrs mustered arguments for the abolition of Canada's defences in "The Military Policies of Contemporary Canada: Principles, Problems, Precepts, Practices," reprinted several times but notably in Richard Leach (ed.), *Contemporary Canada* (Durham, 1967).

The saga of unification is described by W.J. Kronenberg, *All Together Now: The Organization of National Defence in Canada, 1964-1972* (Toronto, 1973), defended by its two chief proponents, Paul Hellyer, *Damn the Torpedoes: My Fight to Unify the Canadian Armed Forces* (Toronto, 1990), and Jean-Victor Allard and Serge Bernier, *The Memoirs of General Jean V. Allard* (Vancouver, 1988), and denounced by many, among them Rear-Admiral Jeffrey V. Brock in the second volume of his elegantly written memoirs, *The Dark Broad Seas: Memoirs of a Sailor* (Toronto, 1981). Other views may be found in Keith Cameron's article "The Royal Canadian Navy and the Unification Crisis" in Boutilier, *RCN in Retrospect*, and David P. Burke, "The Unification of the Armed Forces" (*RIHM*, 1982). The background and consequences are described by Colonel Douglas Bland in *The Administration of Defence Policy in Canada, 1947 to 1985* (Kingston, 1987) and *Chiefs of Defence: Government and the Unified Command of the Canadian Armed Forces* (Toronto, 1995).

The Trudeau years began with a crisis and continued with increasing constraint on the size and effectiveness of the unified forces. The crisis inspired a number of books, among them Gérard Pelletier, *The October Crisis* (Toronto, 1971), and Dan G. Loomis, *Not Much Glory: Quelling the FLQ* (Ottawa, 1984). Use of troops inspired John Gellner's *Bayonets in the Streets: Urban Guerillas at Home and Abroad* (Toronto, 1974). The history and practice of aid of the civil power is described by Desmond Morton in "No More Disagreeable or Onerous Duty: Canadians and Military Aid of the Civil Power, Past, Present and Future" in David DeWitt and David Leighton Brown (eds.), *Canada's International Security Policy* (Scarborough, 1995).

The Trudeau era inspired several books, both descriptive and critical. Hector Massey (ed.), *The Canadian Military: A Profile* (Toronto, 1972), includes some useful essays. Colin Gray's *Canadian Defence Priorities: A Question of Relevance* (Toronto, 1972) anticipated the Macdonald white paper. Brian Cuthbertson, *Canadian Military Independence in the Age of the Superpowers* (Toronto, 1977), reflected contemporary nationalism. Gerald Porter, *In Retreat: The Canadian Forces in the Trudeau Years* (Ottawa, 1978), and Peter Newman, *True North: Not Strong and Free* (Toronto, 1983), were forceful grumbles, as was Jack Granatstein's later *Who Killed the Canadian Military?* (Toronto, 2004). A much more positive view of the Canadian Forces at the end of the 1980s was provided by Jocelyn Coulon, *En Premiere Ligne: Grandeurs et misères du système militaire canadien* (Montreal, 1991).

VII. The Awkward Peace

The undeclared end of the Cold War brought major reductions in spending on the Canadian Forces and increased demands on its members. Scandals also promoted higher education and even scholarly professionalism among serving officers, reflected in a number of serious service-sponsored periodicals. The official history of Canada's military role in the first post–Cold War crisis, the Gulf War, appeared within five years: Richard Gimblett and Jean Morin, *Operation Friction: Canadian Forces in the Gulf War* (Toronto, 1996). See also Jocelyn Coulon, *La dernière croisade: la guerre du golfe, et le rôle caché du Canada* (Montreal, 1992). Almost immediately Canadians found themselves in a major decade-long commitment in a dissolving Yugoslavia, chronicled by Major General Lewis MacKenzie, *Peacekeeper: The Road to Sarajevo* (Vancouver, 1993), and a mission to Somalia that ended in shame, frustration, and scandals, recorded by a problem-plagued commission of enquiry; see Gilles Létourneau et al., *Dishonoured Legacy: The Lessons of the Somalia Affair*, 7 vols. (Ottawa, 1997), and Peter Desbarats, *Somalia Cover-up: A Commissioner's Journal* (Toronto, 1997). For another view of Somalia and the Airborne Regiment, see David Bercuson, *Significant Incident: Canada's Army, The Airborne, and the Murder in Somalia* (Toronto, 1996), Sherene Razack, *Dark Threats and White Knights: The Somalia Affair, Peacekeeping and the New Imperialism* (Toronto, 2004), and Donna Winslow's fascinating *The Canadian Airborne Regiment in Somalia: A Socio-Cultural Inquiry* (Ottawa, 1997). For a broader view of Canada's peacekeeping commitments, see Jocelyn Coulon, *Soldiers of Diplomacy: The United Nations, Peacekeeping and the New World Order* (Toronto, 1998). A more critical view of Canadian performance came from Carol Off, *The Lion, the Fox and the Eagle: A Study of Canada and Justice in Yugoslavia and Rwanda* (Toronto, 2000).

Members of the Canadian Forces and their dependents made their voices heard. The magazine *Esprit de Corps* assailed the military hierarchy, and its editor, Scott Taylor, and Brian Nolan collected their charges in *Tarnished Brass: Greed and Corruption in the Canadian Military* (Toronto, 1996). A more balanced but critical account by a sergeant in the former Airborne Regiment is James Davis, *The Sharp End: A Canadian Soldier's Story* (Vancouver, 1997). See also Claude Savard, *Journal intime d'un béret bleu canadien en ex-Yougoslavie* (Montreal, 1994). Service families suffered from low pay, high stress, and long separations. See Deborah Harrison, *No Life Like It: Canada's Military Wives* (Toronto, 1994); see also John A. English, *Lament for an Army: The Decline of Canadian Military Professionalism* (Toronto, 1998).

Analyses of Canada's defence problems and ideas for reform proliferated. Some of the most provocative came from University of
Toronto political scientist Janice Stein. See "Ideas, Even Good Ideas,
Are Not Enough: Changing Canada's Foreign and Defence Policies"
(*IJ*, 1994-95). A variety of problems, issues, and views may be found
in David B. DeWitt and David Leighton Brown, *Canada's International Security Policy* (Scarborough, 1995).

VIII. A New Kind of War?

One source of celebration for Canada's defenders was the arrival of
women among the ranks of respected military analysts. In *The Revolution in Military Affairs* (Montreal and Kingston, 2001), Elinor Sloan
introduced a description and analysis of a seemingly decisive version of war, and followed it with a more sober critique, *Security and
Defence in the Terrorism Era: Canada and North America* (Montreal
and Kingston, 2005).

In the century that began militarily with a terrorist attack on
Canada's neighbour, the United States, the Canadian Forces seemed
to lack everything but fervent opinions on its problems. As in the
First Gulf War, the navy was the first to produce a history of its role:
Richard Gimblett's shrewdly political *Operation Apollo: The Golden
Age of the Canadian Navy in the War Against Terrorism* (Ottawa,
2004). Rival services had to wait until their performances could be
assessed.

Meanwhile, a host of books and articles, often by officers who had
transferred their careers to universities or think tanks, summarized
the end-of-century deficiencies. Among these works were Douglas
Bland's explanation of equipment and personnel deficiencies in
Canada Without Armed Forces (Kingston, 2004), John English's
*Lament for an Army: The Decline of Canadian Military Professional-
ism* (Toronto, 1998), Jack Granatstein's *Whose War Is It? How Canada
Can Survive in the Post-9/11 World* (Toronto, 2007), and Hugh Segal's
collection of familiar experts for the IRPP, *Geopolitical Integrity*
(Montreal, 2004). Perhaps the briefest and best summary of Canada's
military condition in 1999 came from a sympathetic but perceptive
American in Joseph Jockel's pamphlet, *The Canadian Forces: Hard
Choices, Soft Power* (Toronto, 2004), published by the Canadian
Institute for Strategic Studies. One beneficial outcome of the Soma-

lia Inquiry was the creation of a Canadian Defence Academy to foster professional study and reflection. Given the small size of
Canada's professional armed forces, its *Canadian Military Review* is
an impressive source of both history and contemporary military
thought.

Issues of procurement and budgeting were not simple, however
inviting they might seem to political and service partisans. A very
useful article for anyone who wants to understand Canadian Forces
equipment problems is by a former inspector-general, Howard Marsh,
though it bears an unnerving title and is published by the leading
defence lobbyists: "Sensitivity Analysis of Canadian Defence Spending; Value for Money Cost of the Canadian Forces" in Brian S.
MacDonald, *Understanding the Crisis in Canadian Security and
Defence* (Ottawa, 2005). To help politicians, the media, and the
public to understand its complexities, Alan Williams published
Reinventing Canadian Defence Procurement: A View from Inside
(Montreal and Kingston, 2006).

Appendix I

Canadian Military Organization

Canadian military organizational terms have been fairly constant since 1900, although specific organizations have changed frequently and significantly. The following diagram gives a very rough guide to organizational terms in the British and Canadian armies in the two world wars.

Formations

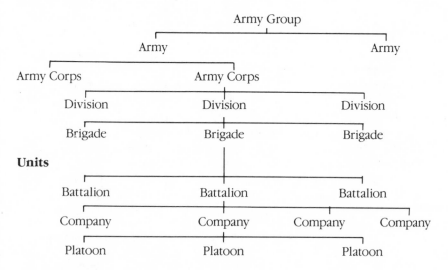

(The diagram ignores artillery, signals and other vital arms and services, each with its own organizational terms.)

How Many Personnel?

Formations:	**Commanded by**	**Approximate Size**
Army	General	200,000 to 400,000
Corps	Lieutenant-General	60,000 to 100,000
Division	Major-General	15,000 to 25,000
Brigade	Brigadier	3,000 to 6,000

Units		
Battalion/Regiment	Lieutenant Colonel	600 to 1,000
Company/Squadron/Battery	Major/Captain	80 to 200
Platoon/Troop	Lieutenant	20 to 40

Appendix II

Canadian Military Terminology

The study of any field of history depends on some familiarity with the terminology, ideas and doctrine of those involved. This is true of political, economic, labour, and business history; military history is no exception. A number of terms that may be unfamiliar are explained in C. P. Stacey's little booklet, **An Introduction to Military History for Canadian Students** (Ottawa, Queen's Printer, 1959). Others can be found in a dictionary. What follows is a superficial introduction to a few basic ideas.

Ranks

Military organizations are hierarchical. In the following chart, the ranks customarily used in the army and militia are listed in the lefthand column. Corresponding titles for the naval and air forces are in the centre and righthand columns.

Commissioned Officers

General	Admiral	Air Chief Marshal
Lieutenant General	Vice-Admiral	Air Marshal
Major General	Rear Admiral	Air Vice Marshal
Brigadier (General)	Commodore	Air Commodore
Colonel	Captain	Group Captain
Lieutenant Colonel	Commander	Wing Commander
Major	Lieutenant Commander	Squadron Leader
Captain	Lieutenant	Flight Lieutenant
Lieutenant	Sub-Lieutenant	Flying Officer
Second Lieutenant	Midshipman	Pilot Officer

Non-Commissioned Officers

Regimental Sergeant-Major	Chief Petty Officer I	Warrant Officer I
Company Sergeant-Major	Chief Petty Officer II	Warrant Officer II
Staff Sergeant	Petty Officer I	Flight Sergeant
Sergeant	Petty Officer	Sergeant

Other Ranks

Corporal	Leading Seaman	Corporal
Lance Corporal	Able Seaman	Leading Aircraftsman
Private	Ordinary Seaman	Aircraftsman II

Particular variants of these ranks (e.g. Bombardier for Corporal in the artillery) will be found. Note that there is a difference between a rank (e.g. Lieutenant General) and an appointment or position (Corps Commander).

Index

358

284, 294, 295, 302; and 1837 Rebellion, 74–75; defences, 51, 83; conscription, 154; October crisis, 256–257; ice storm (1998), 293
Montreal Fire Brigade, 86
Moose Jaw, 294
Moraviantown, Battle of, 62
Morgan, Daniel, 44
Morgan, Lorne, 226
Morrison, Lt. Col. John, 64
Mortain, 214
Moscow, 181, 206, 271
Moskito, 77, 85
Moslems, 278, 279, 291; refugees, 292
Mosquito bomber, 204
"Mountain Thrust," Operation, 313
mounted infantry school, 110
Mulroney, Brian, 265, 268, 315, 317; government, 268, 274–275, 289; and Somalia, 279
multiculturalism, 272
multinational brigade, Kabul, 308
multinational Standby High Readiness Brigade (SHIRBRIG), 306
Munich agreement, 175
munitions, production, 146, 153, 160, 177–178, 183
Munitions, Ministry of (British), 133
Munitions and Supply, Dept. of, 182
Murchie, Lt. Gen. J. C., 219, 220
Murray, General James, 35, 36, 38, 41, 42, 51
Murray, Rear Admiral L. W., 198, 200, 223, 290
Murray, Vice-Admiral Larry, 288, 289
Mushareff, General Pervez, 310
Mussolini, Benito, 175
Mustang fighters, 207
mutinies, naval, 228–229
Mutual Defence Assistance Act, 233

Nabob, HMCS, 208
Nagasaki, 224
Namibia, 271
Nancy, HMCS, 69
Napanee, 128
Napierville, 75
Napoleon Bonaparte, 53, 63, 66, 70
Natal, 113
national debt, 166, 225, 271
National Defence Act, 170, 238, 274
National Defence College, 228, 284
National Defence, Dept. of, 170, 173, 182, 231, 245, 249–250, 260, 262, 267
National Defence Headquarters, 251, 259, 260; reorganization of, 316

National Employment Service, 158
"national factories," 134
National Guard, U.S., 301
national identity, ix, x
National Policy, 99
national registration, 153, 181
National Research Council, 173
National Resources Mobilization Act (NRMA), 181, 190; men, 189, 218, 220
National Selective Service, 185, 186
National Steel Car Co., 184
National Survival, 245, 246
National War College (U.S.), 228
National War Labour Order (P.C. 1003), 192
nationalists and defence, 268
nationalistes, 126, 152–153, 232
nationality, Canadian, 39–40, 107–117, 118, 119, 144, 145, 180
natural disasters, 293; and Canadian Forces, 297, 316
naval building race, 77
Naval Headquarters, 198, 224
naval policy, Canadian, 124–126, 169
Naval Service Act, 125
Navy, Canadian. *See* Canadian Navy
Navy, French, 12, 17, 22–25, 31, 32, 35, 46, 47, 80
Navy Island, 74
Navy League, 169
Navy, Royal Canadian. *See* Royal Canadian Navy
Nazis, 175, 181, 222
Nehru, Jawaharlal, 232
Neilson, Erik, 266, 267
Nelles, Vice-Admiral Percy, 200
Nelson, Admiral Lord, 66, 108
Nelson, Robert, 75
Nelson, Wolfred, 74
Netherlands, 25, 181, 222, 223, 233, 264, 279, 285; troops, 279
New Amsterdam, 10
New Brunswick, 18, 50, 51, 53, 75, 79, 81, 86, 125, 288; and War of 1812, 55–56; militia, 85, 86, 90; and ice storm (1998), 297
New Deal, 174
New Democratic Party, 246, 247–248, 249, 254, 265
New England, 4–5, 12, 18, 22, 39–40, 43, 44, 55, 69, 122, 247
New France, xi, 5, 6, 8, 9, 12, 13, 14, 18, 21–22, 25, 28–30, 39, 41, 43; and trade, 13; and Indian war, 13, 14, 15; Seven Years War, 38–39; defences, 2, 18–21, population, 21–22; military influences, 21–23; defeat, 33–36, 38, 41

unilateral disarmament, 245
Union of Soviet Socialist Republics (USSR).
  See Soviet Union
Unionist government, 155–156, 157,
  167–169, 170
United Kingdom. *See* Britain
United Nations, 230, 233–234, 239, 277–281,
  286; and Korea, 235–236; Charter, 280,
  293; Declaration of Human Rights, 293;
  and Somalia, 279–280; and Cambodia,
  281; and Rwanda, 281; and Second Gulf
  War, 307–308
United Nations Emergency Force (UNEF),
  241–242, 308
United Nations Operation in Somalia
  (UNOSOM), 280
United Nations Protection Force
  (UNPROFOR), 278
United Nations Task Force (UNITAF),
  Somalia, 280
United Nations Truce Supervisory
  Organization (UNTSO), 241
United Provinces of Canada, 82, 87, 90;
  defence, 82–83
United States, xi, 47, 50, 54, 63, 70, 71, 80,
  93, 106, 107, 132, 164, 165, 166, 167, 173,
  205, 229, 232, 233, 245, 263, 274–275,
  281, 308; War of 1812, 55–70; Civil War,
  80–83; and Canada, 54, 71–72, 88–89, 93,
  122, 162, 176, 182–184, 191, 229–230,
  233, 243, 248, 259, 302, 315, 318; and
  defence of North America, 182, 189, 229,
  241, 265, 302; government, 267; and war,
  xii, 178, 180, 190–191, 259, 263; selective
  service, 231, 239, 262; forces in
  Afghanistan, 306, 308; as peacemaker,
  Somalia, 309; and Afghanistan, 307; and
  opium eradication, 310
United States Air Force, 242–243, 252; and
  Afghanistan, 308
United States Army, 55–56, 58–69, 71, 80,
  82–84, 98, 100, 102, 163, 212, 214, 216,
  234, 295
United States Marine Corps, 302, 303
United States Navy, 50, 59, 62–63, 65, 68,
  111, 168, 198, 199, 200, 268; and war on
  terror, 302, 303
United States State Department, 71
United Steelworkers (USWA), 192
universal military training, 122
universal degrees for officers, 289
University Quarterly, 125
universities, 226, 239
Unmanned Aerial Vehicles (UAVs), 295, 309
Upholder class submarines, 92

Upper Canada, 50, 53, 58, 59, 70–71;
  defence, 52, 81; War of 1812, 55–56,
  58–69; Rebellion, 1837, 73–75, 76
Utrecht, Treaty of, 18, 21

Valcartier camp, 127, 130, 132; Canadian
  Forces Base, 256, 294
Valenciennes, 164
Vale of York, 206
Van Buren, Martin, 76
Van Rensselaer, General Steven, 58
Van Rensselaer, Rensselaer, 74
Vancouver School Board, 281
Vanier, Maj.-Gen. Georges, 163
Vauban, Sébastien Le Prestre, marquis de, 22
Vaudreil family, 28, 29, 30
Vaudreuil, Philippe de Rigaud, 18, 21, 22
Vaudreuil, Pierre de Rigaud, 21, 27–30,
  33–34, 35, 37, 39, 40, 41
Vauquelin, Robert, 32, 34
VE Day, 223
Venezuela, 110; crisis, 110–112, 113
Venice, 291
Verchères, Madeleine de, 16
Verchères, Marie de, 16
Verdun, 143
Vernon, Maj.-Gen. Brian, 285, 287
Verrières Ridge, 214
Versailles, xi, 31, 34; Treaty of, 165, 175
Verville, Jean-François de, 22
veterans, 10, 70–71, 166–167, 169, 224,
  226–227, 285
Veterans Affairs, Dept. of, 192
veterans' battalion, 54
Veterans' Land Act, 226
veterinary service, 147
Vicksburg, 83, 88
Victoria (British Columbia), 99, 115, 147,
  179
Victoria Cross, 117, 204, 242
Victoria, Queen, 75, 81–82, 86, 106, 117
Victoriaville (Quebec), 152
Victory, HMS, 66
Victory Aircraft Co., 184
Victory Bonds, 134, 183, 186
Victory Loan, 160
Vietnam, 241, 254; war, 259, 262, 270, 295
"Vieux Brûlot," 74. *See also* Sir John
  Colborne
Vikings, 1
Vimy Ridge, Battle of, 144, 151–152, 171,
  203
Vincent, Brig. Gen. Henry, 60, 61
Virginia, 44; militia, 26–27
Visiting Forces Act, 230